PUBLIC-PRIVATE PARTNERSHIP

PUBLIC–PRIVATE PARTNERSHIP

New Opportunities for Meeting Social Needs

Edited by
HARVEY BROOKS
LANCE LIEBMAN
CORINNE S. SCHELLING

Published for the
American Academy of Arts and Sciences

BALLINGER PUBLISHING COMPANY
Cambridge, Massachusetts
A Subsidiary of Harper & Row, Publishers, Inc.

82943

International Standard Book Number: 0-88410-482-6

Library of Congress Catalog Card Number: 83-27564

Printed in the United States of America

Library of Congress Cataloging in Publication Data

Main entry under title:

Public/private partnership.

   Includes bibliographical references and index.
1. Industry—Social aspects—Addresses, essays, lectures.
2. Social policy—Addresses, essays, lectures. 3. Social problems—Addresses, essays, lectures. I. Brooks, Harvey. II. Liebman, Lance. III. Schelling, Corinne Saposs.
HD60.P82 1984   361.8   83-27564
ISBN 0-88410-482-6

Contents

PART I THE PUBLIC AND PRIVATE SECTORS

PART II PATTERNS OF PUBLIC-PRIVATE RELATIONS

List of Figures

List of Tables

Preface

American public opinion about large public and private institutions is not consistent. On the one hand, there has finally come to be wide recognition that the interrelated circumstances of modern urban life require collective enterprises. As recently as twenty-five years ago there were still arguments about the legitimacy of zoning, Social Security, and fluoridation. Fifteen years ago, it was still argued that our system of medical care was and should be both individual and private. Now, most people take for granted the need for collaborative interventions of various kinds and the inevitability of large public and private institutions. At the same time, U.S. ideology has retained its traditional skepticism toward such institutions. Since the 1880s, and still in the 1980s, attacks on big companies will draw a crowd. One can also attract respectful attention by denouncing the evils of local, state, and national government.

There are contradictions aplenty in this collection of popular views. Somehow we will either have to accept big government or big business or adopt more modest goals. Indeed, we probably have to accept big government *and* big companies *and* limits to our grandest hopes. Certainly, we need a more refined and more accurate understanding of the benefits and costs of using particular institutional arrangements as means of pursuing particular ends. In fact in recent years the United States has not limited itself to the traditional repertoire of institutional arrangements when attempting new tasks. Rather, innovative structures have been employed: Comsats and Conrails and UDAGs and OICs and CETAs. We have developed new forms of public and private participation to gain the advantages that different institutions seem to offer.

The management of Control Data Corporation have long recognized the possible advantages to the nation from imaginative partnership between business and government. In 1981 representatives of Control Data approached the American Academy of Arts and Sciences to consider how the Academy might play a role in connection with the commemoration of the twenty-fifth anniversary of the company's founding. The idea was that the Academy might help explore the philosophy of CDC and its founder and chairman, William C. Norris, of seeking to turn social needs—jobs, job training, education, corrections—into profitable markets, usually by arrangements that included government participation. The Academy realized that the CDC approach raised broad and serious questions about American institutions. John Voss, the Academy's Executive Officer, called together a group of academic and business people to think about the design of an Academy study of the potential for and the limits to an expanded role for private corporations in meeting social needs, and of the possibilities for new modes of public-private collaboration. This book is the product of that study.

The American Academy's traditional approach is to seek reasoned expressions of divergent perspectives. The Academy does not devise policy guidelines, nor does it take an advocacy role. Instead Academy studies present contrasting viewpoints in an effort to illuminate complicated, controversial problems. CDC endorsed this approach and offered to support the study.

Late in 1981 a steering group prepared a study outline and commissioned papers. A meeting to discuss drafts of the papers was held in June 1982 with the authors and an equal number of invited commentators from universities and business. Additional chapters were commissioned to fill gaps uncovered during the discussions. Drafts were then revised and edited for publication in this volume.

Just as the environments for public and private institutions are intertwined in the United States, and just as separate social problems cannot be discussed in isolation from one another, so the topics considered in this book overlap and interconnect in many ways. Harvey Brooks and Thomas McCraw describe the problems and the possibilities and put goals and opportunities in perspective, making clear that many simple assumptions and generalizations are not true now and were not true in the American past. In the next part of the book, the authors contribute various "cuts"—various interpretations—of aspects of recent history, emphasizing both complexity and possibility. For Charles Haar, the stimulating and coordinating role of the federal government is an essential component. For Ted Kolderie, local urban communities differ, and solutions must and can be tailored properly. For Jordan Baruch, significant private, as well as public, entrepreneurship is both essential and possible. For Orlando Patterson, reviewing Jamaican experience, even all three—national commitment, local tailoring, and private efforts—were insufficient. And for Marc Bendick, Jr., measurable consequences of experiments at contracting public services to the private sector demonstrate no quick and easy efficiencies. Altogether, these analyses of experience are promising, as well as cautionary.

The third part of the book is more theoretical. William Baumol applies economic theory to the question of evaluating the appropriateness of specific interactions between the private and public sectors. Robert Clark analyzes the competing legal theories that seek to explain the authority of corporate directors and managers. One of Clark's questions is whether legal ideas offer a justification for actions by corporations that do not have as their goal the maximization of profits. James Worthy develops management theory for the nontraditional tasks recently undertaken by large companies. As with the lessons from experience, theoretical discussion provides bases for expectation and for hesitation.

In the final part, authors look to the future. William C. Norris offers his vision and his experience. Robert Reich connects corporate opportunity to intelligent government policies of leadership and reward. Peter Drucker sees the underlying initiative as resting with business. James Sundquist shows the relevance of some fundamental facts about the U.S. system of government. Franklin Long looks at the opportunities for interactions between multinational business firms and underdeveloped countries. Finally, Lance Liebman concludes with a discussion of the competing legitimacies of the public, private, and not-for-profit sectors.

These authors have studied different aspects of a single story. Since they talk about different things, their insights and conclusions vary greatly. All seem to accept, however, that American arrangements are evolving and must continue to evolve; that shibboleths about government and business obscure; that new public-private arrangements promise real benefit to the public; and that for cultural and institutional reasons, absent economic or social crisis, realization of those benefits will be difficult and slow. The messages from these authors seem to be partnership, imagination, flexibility, and entrepreneurship.

ACKNOWLEDGMENTS

This book has benefited from the ideas of many people in addition to the editors and authors. Unfortunately we cannot mention all who assisted us in defining the topic and formulating a coherent study. We do, however, want to express appreciation to several who throughout the project were particularly helpful.

Special thanks are due to Robert D. Schmidt, former Vice-Chairman of Control Data Corporation, and Jerr Boschée, General Manager, Public Relations, Control Data Corporation. While helping us understand, and then extend our outlook beyond, the philosophy and experience of one innovative company, they constantly reminded us of the need to be concrete and grounded in reality. In many different ways they made possible a book that will assist business people, academics, policymakers, and others in thinking more clearly about a major national issue of the 1980s.

James C. Worthy of Northwestern University—with feet planted firmly both in the business and academic communities—continually gave us the benefit of his wisdom and experience. Among Academy Fellows, we are particularly grateful to John R. Meyer, Kennedy School of Government, Harvard, and Austin Ranney, American Enterprise Institute, for advice and guidance.

And as many of us know, without the initiative of John Voss, Executive Officer of the Academy, this book would never have been started, much less completed.

Harvey Brooks
Lance Liebman
Corinne S. Schelling

✳ *PART I*

THE PUBLIC AND PRIVATE SECTORS

 *Chapter 1*

Seeking Equity and Efficiency:
Public and Private Roles

Harvey Brooks

INTRODUCTION: THE REACTION
AGAINST THE PUBLIC SECTOR

The Great Depression of the 1930s was seen largely as a failure of the private sector. The remedies proposed and implemented over the next half century were federal interventions to correct both the inequities and the inefficiencies perceived to be the result of market failure. By contrast the economic crisis of the late 1970s and early 1980s tends to be viewed as a failure of the public sector, indeed as a product of the inefficient preemption of too large a fraction of the productive resources of the major industrial countries by their public sectors.[1] A typical expression of this view is summarized in the following quotation:

> [A] pattern has become established of initiating new government programs, broadening the coverage of existing programs, and increasing benefits per recipient. . . . [This] pattern has been accommodated by the willingness of the American people to cut defense outlays as a share of GNP and to live with higher taxes and the adverse effects of large federal deficits . . . [which] would use up a very large portion of the available pool of savings and would sorely limit capital formation and dampen productivity growth.
>
> (Meyer 1982: 12)

The views of the causes of both private failure in the 1930s and public failure in the 1980s are certainly debatable, but there is little question that they are representative of widely held political perceptions. In fact the depth and duration of the Great Depression were exacerbated by deflationary monetary and fiscal policies, as well as by competitive protectionism and retaliation among the industrial countries, which added to the deflationary forces. Conversely the current crisis has been fed by a loss of dynamism in the private sector and, especially in the United States, by managerial and investment policies inappropriate to a radically altered international competitive environment (Vernon 1982). Furthermore, Thomas McCraw in Chapter 2 of this book points to large variations in the size of the public sector among the industrialized countries, and the weak correlation between the fraction of gross domestic product (GDP) claimed by the public sector and the economic performance of the country. Thus the evidence that public sector spending is the source of the current malaise is at best inconclusive. On the other hand, it is true that the dynamic economies of East Asia, including Japan, have generally smaller public sectors than Western countries and have maintained public policies that favor private saving and discourage consumption, especially of housing and consumer durables (Scott 1982).

The conventional wisdom in the United States has been that it is the explosion of welfare costs that has driven the growth of the public sector since the 1960s, but in fact the "surge in social spending over the past two decades occurred despite little if any growth since 1972 in programs targeted primarily to lower income groups" (Meyer 1982:15). Indeed, "despite all the rhetoric about welfare costs, outlays for AFDC [Aid for Dependent Children] will constitute no more than 1 percent of the federal budget in the early 1980s" (Meyer 1982:18). The big increases in social spending have been for Social Security and Medicare, which are not income related. It is these "middle class entitlements" that have driven the growth of the public sector throughout the Western industrialized world (Peterson 1982). There is little question that the expansion of these entitlement programs has been an important source of the overemphasis on consumption at the expense of saving, but they have not until very recently been the focus of criticism of government social programs. Rather, criticism has focused on the programs targeted at low-income groups and on the work disincentives that these programs are believed to create.[2] Middle class entitlements are also important disincentives to private saving.

When all transfer payments, both in cash and in kind, are taken into account, the federal social programs of the 1960s and 1970s have indubitably reduced the incidence of poverty as officially defined, although the rate of reduction flattened out at the end of the

1970s. However, when one considers latent poverty—income exclusive of government transfers of all kinds—the favorable trends existing since the end of World War II actually reversed after 1975. That is to say, the fraction of families with *earned* income below the official poverty line began to increase (Murray 1982:5; Pear 1982). There are several possible interpretations of this phenomenon, but one that has been put forward by the critics of the welfare state is that the explosive growth of transfer payments after the end of the 1960s generated sufficient work and savings disincentives to decrease the proportion of families able or willing to "make it" through their own efforts alone, without the supplementary benefit of government entitlements.

One might argue equally well, however, that the growth of latent poverty was due to the malperformance of the market economy, and it was merely fortuitous that the growth of social spending came along in time to offset the failures of the private market. It is difficult to find definitive evidence to settle this chicken-and-egg argument. Whatever the correct interpretation, it seems certain that, after more than two decades in which the growth of the market economy continued to reduce poverty, it no longer did so without government transfers after 1975. It is also indubitable that the eligibility criteria for numerous entitlement programs corresponded in effect to the imposition of marginal income tax rates on recipients that in many cases exceeded the marginal tax rates imposed on high-income individuals, thus contributing to work disincentives for the poor and, to some extent, the elderly (Greene 1981; Murray 1982).

There is also a strong perception that "government service delivery has been over-professionalized, and it has imposed unwarranted 'credentialing' requirements on alternative service delivery systems," thus frequently shutting out competition, or perpetuating wasteful practices and unnecessary overhead costs (Meyer 1982:4). Jordan Baruch and Ted Kolderie, in Chapters 4 and 5 of this book, provide examples of this feature of government programs. A similar element seems to be present in the failures of the "basic human needs" programs in Third World countries assessed by Orlando Patterson in Chapter 6 of this book.

Just as the widespread perception of the failures of private enterprise and the market system in the 1930s generated the political impetus for the creation of the welfare state, which reached its climax in the Great Society programs of the 1960s, so have the recent critiques of federal efforts gradually generated a new reaction back toward belief in the magic of the marketplace and the virtues of private sector dynamism and local initiative. These critiques have crystallized politically in the Reagan experiment, the most radical alteration in political direction in fifty years (Palmer and Sawhill 1982). They have also been an important underlying motivation for many of the private sector initiatives reviewed in this volume, as shown in Chapter 11 by William C. Norris. Whereas the last thirty years could be described as an era in which the public sector was increasingly called upon to redress market failures, we seem to be entering an era in which the private sector is increasingly asked to redress "non-market failures" (Wolf 1979). However, the emphasis on the choice between the private sector and the public sector may be misplaced, for in most practical situations they will be seen to be complementary. In this respect it is important to distinguish between private managerial and financial capabilities. Private managerial skills can often complement the public sector, but it would be a dangerous illusion to expect that "corporate billions will accomplish what federal billions could not" (Meyer 1982: 6).

THE BENEFITS OF PRIVATE INITIATIVES

The private sector may have an essential part to play in the rekindling of public support for governmental responsibility in the social area. As one observer has noted, "private sector initiatives—far from being a mean-spirited rejection of social obligation—may in fact be the only way to rebuild that obligation" in the aftermath of the disenchantment with the federal welfare state that is emerging. "By transferring some programs to the local voluntary level, we may begin to reconstruct the sense of obligation ultimately required to support those programs we would leave at the federal level" (Schambra 1982: 48). There is ample precedent for private initiative being used as a demonstration of public support for what later became large public programs. The classic example is biomedical research, which would never have been financed by government at its present scale without the continuing demonstration of broad public support through the funds raised by the voluntary health associations (Price 1965). Even the national agricultural research and extension system, which began with the Morrill Act of 1863, received a major impetus from the efforts of more affluent and progressive farmers to finance a voluntary cooperative research program (Peterson and Fitzharris 1977: 66). James Worthy (Chapter 10) cites the example of Sears, Roebuck in pioneering a model for what later became the Cooperative Extension Service of the U.S. Department of Agriculture. The great philanthropic foundations that began operation in the early twentieth century provided precedents and models for many of the large federal medical and scientific research programs that became important in the last half of the century, and of some of the more recent social welfare programs (Weaver 1967). The publicly funded International Agricultural Research Centers under the Consultative Group for International Agricultural Research (CGIAR) (Brown et al. 1977; Crawford 1977) also followed a model pioneered by the Rockefeller Foundation.

SOCIAL PROBLEMS, NEW AND OLD

What are the social problems with which we are dealing? There seems to be a consensus that they include at least the following elements:

1. Youth unemployment, particularly among certain minority groups
2. Deterioration of the public school system, particularly in the older central cities
3. Rising crime rates
4. General social disintegration in certain inner city neighborhoods where there is an increasing concentration of low-income and single-parent families belonging to disadvantaged ethnic groups
5. Deterioration of urban social services in the areas that need them most, together with disappearance of resources required to finance them
6. Inadequate investment in and maintenance of urban public infrastructures

Most observers would agree that jobs and employment are central in this complex of interrelated problems. Most, though not all, would also agree that "generalized policies directed toward further lowering of the aggregate unemployment rate cannot be the major vehicle for improving the position of youth in the labor market" (Anderson and Sawhill 1980: 148). On the other hand there is a bipartisan consensus in the country that "national economic prosperity is probably the most important contribution that the federal government can make on behalf of cities" (Gorham and Glazer 1976: 23). The conflict between these two quoted views is probably more apparent than real. While there is little question that the pathology of cities is heavily influenced by the state of the general economy, and therefore economic revival is a *necessary* condition for solving the problem of cities, the social problems listed are rooted in long-term shifts in the structure of the national economy and would not disappear with a general economic revival. In other words they have to be attacked at the microeconomic as well as the macroeconomic level (Renaud

1982), as indicated in Chapters 12 and 13 by Robert Reich and Peter Drucker.

DEMOGRAPHICS AND THE PLIGHT OF THE CITIES

During the 1970s the decline of central cities that had been occurring for at least two decades accelerated. Its causes were complex. Fundamentally they were related to changes in industrial technology, transportation, and communications whose effects had been cumulative since the end of World War II. These resulted in decentralization and dispersion of job opportunities and, with them, residential populations (Berry and Silverman 1980). Before the 1970s what had been going on was primarily a spread outward from core cities into the suburbs, with continued population growth for metropolitan areas as a whole. This could be regarded as a continuation of the classic urbanization of the U.S. population that had taken place throughout American history.

But in the 1970s the process became more complex. Many of the largest metropolitan areas began to decline in total population or to grow more slowly than smaller cities. There was some reversal of the classic pattern of net outmigration from nonmetropolitan areas, previously the hallmark of the urbanization process (Lang 1981). The resulting patterns of decentralization were not uniform, however. There was increasing differentiation among cities caused by the changing structure of the national economy. Some cities fared much better than others, depending on the relation of their local economies to growing or declining industrial sectors.

The decentralization trend produced two consequences, both detrimental to the economic vitality and sociocultural health of cities. First, it has resulted in differential outmigration of the more upwardly mobile segments of the urban population, leaving behind those least able to cope with the consequences of rapid technological and structural change in the economy. The rate of change has been enhanced by the internationalization of economic activity and the worldwide homogenization of markets, as exemplified most dramatically in the case of the automobile industry (Telesis Consultancy Group 1982: 44-63). Second, the escape of economic activity and the more affluent residents from the core cities created a growing imbalance between the need for urban public services and the tax base required to support them. This problem was aggravated by the fact that it was precisely in the cities experiencing the greatest decline that it was least feasible politically to alter old jurisdictional lines in order to equalize fiscal bases between inner cities and suburbs. Moreover, the growing gap could not be permanently covered from the federal treasury.

In the process what suffered most was investment in urban public infrastructure and the maintenance and renovation of this infrastructure. Furthermore, the problem was concentrated in older cities in which declining industries were overrepresented. As public revenues have plateaued or declined under the pressure of taxpayer revolts, rising transfer payments, and, most recently, declining federal subsidies, the capital structure of the public facilities of cities has tended to take the lowest priority. Maintenance or investment could, after all, always be postponed for yet another year (Choate and Walter 1981). But declining infrastructure reduced the attraction to those residents in a position to move, and made the environment less desirable for industry, especially those industries most dependent on highly skilled or professional labor forces sensitive to the quality of urban amenities. The result was a set of mutually reinforcing negative factors in the urban environment—precisely the social problems we are dealing with in this book.

BUSINESS AND CITIES

The plight of the cities has scarcely been neglected in the political process. The urban predicament has been high on the political agenda in the United States for more than a decade. One observer of the urban scene has remarked that "almost every idea that has had some modest level of sponsorship has been tried" during the last fifteen years (Gorham and Glazer 1976: 2). But today it is also true that "a smaller percentage of the population care about cities, while even fewer have confidence that the federal government (or any other level of government for that matter) knows how to make things better" (Gorham and Glazer 1976: 14). As mentioned earlier, there is increasing belief that government intervention, and especially federal intervention, has exacerbated rather than ameliorated the problems. Even many who still support a federal role believe that "the imposition of a great plan from outside cannot . . . be responsive to the complex, interlinked problems that are dragging these neighborhoods down" (Gorham and Glazer 1976: 31). For there is a strong recognition that the disintegration of neighborhoods, the loss of any sense of community, is at the heart of the social pathologies that afflict the inner cities. An encouraging factor is that many businesses have begun to recognize the degree to which the quality of life in cities, and the state of the urban infrastructure, affect their own viability in the long run (Federal Reserve Bank of New York 1981).

There is a growing disposition among business leaders to accept the alleviation of the problems of cities as a responsibility that they share with government and that in their own self-interest they cannot ignore. Although there is less agreement on the appropriate role for the private sector, most recognize that the resources of business, channeled only through the traditional medium of charitable contributions, will be grossly inadequate to the task.

COMPARATIVE ADVANTAGE

The private sector must undertake activities that attract larger resources than are available merely from skimming off a small percentage of corporate profits in prosperous years. Such leverage can come about in only two ways—either by attracting private resources through projects that promise a reasonable direct return on investment by more or less traditional business criteria, or by combining private entrepreneurial, managerial, and technological skills with public resources. Where these two approaches can be blended, the possibility of ultimate success will be increased.

Present urban configurations are the cumulative result of investments made over more than a half century in response to changing comparative advantage among locations as well as changing political priorities and influences. Thus the older cities frequently represent a capital stock that is more appropriate to the technologies and markets of the past than to those of the present. It is for this reason that they start with a severe handicap in the race to adapt to changing markets and technologies. In addition comparative advantage among locations and regions is much less tied to particular geographical or other location-specific factors than was true a generation ago. Whereas in the past economic advantages were determined by factors such as proximity to raw material sources, water transportation nodes, proximity to markets, or major transportation routes, these factors are now much less important because of reduced transportation and communications costs, the increased importance of value-added (by technology and skilled labor) relative to primary materials and energy, and the importance of cultural, educational, and environmental amenities in attracting a high-skill labor force. In short, the sources of comparative advantage are much more man-made than they were in the past.

This is, of course, almost equally true in the sphere of international trade. We have seen, for example, how countries like Japan, poor in natural resources, and far from major markets, have nevertheless been able to develop a huge comparative advantage in certain industrial fields through the skillful exploitation of their human resources and key man-made technologies such as the information technologies. What has happened in international trade has a parallel in the competition among cities and regions within the United States. Indeed the parallel goes even deeper. The older industrial economies are burdened with an obsolescent capital stock compared to the new capital stock of the rapidly growing economies of East Asia. Similarly, relative to the rapidly expanding regions of the country, such as the Sun Belt, the older industrial cities are burdened with an old capital stock. But we are reluctant to write off or abandon the cumulation of past investments or painstakingly learned human skills because it is very costly to do so, not only in economic terms, but even more important, in terms of the difficult human adjustments. Whether the type of nationally oriented industrial policy proposed by Robert Reich in this book can be sufficiently sensitive to these effects on local communities or subgroups of the population, such as racial minorities and recent immigrants, is a problem that has not been fully resolved.

THE IMPORTANCE OF COMMUNITY

Community is an important public value, and its loss due to shifts in economic activity is as serious a "negative externality" of economic growth as environmental pollution or industrial accidents or illnesses. Writing off historic capital investments is not the only cost of the "creative destruction" that Joseph Schumpeter equated with economic progress. The disintegration of communities has to be counted as much as economic efficiency in toting up the balance sheet of structural change in the economy. We have a national interest in preserving the health of local or regional economies as well as an international interest in avoiding the rapid deterioration of national economies. In our enthusiasm for economic efficiency we cannot overlook the fact that "community" remains a powerful value even in modern industrial societies, especially among the less educated, who are also less mobile. The educated elites, whose political perceptions often have a predominant influence on policy choices, tend to overlook these values because their own sense of community is more frequently tied to a national profession or to a multilocational organization or network. Yet the local sense of community in many cases outweighs purely economic motivations when individuals and groups make job choices (Bluestone and Harrison 1982: 67-72).

There are two facets to the changing nature of comparative advantage, one negative, the other positive. The negative facet is the obsolescence of the industrial and public infrastructure as well as the labor force skills in localities and regions, and the fact that these can no longer be compensated by natural advantages tied to location. Because of the strong coupling between the state of cities and the overall structure of the national economy, we must find a way of allocating society's scarce resources to cities that is not simply an attempt to reverse the tides of worldwide economic change. We have to learn how to work with existing trends in the evolution of the national and the world economies, not against them. Far too much of the federal investment in cities that peaked shortly after the mid-seventies was an attempt to turn back the tides of structural change rather than to facilitate adjustment to it. Federal urban policy was premised on a grossly exaggerated idea of what could be accomplished through public policy unless it worked with, rather than against, existing economic trends. Thus the task of a national urban strategy must be to "focus national concern on the allocation of capital to economic activities, to places, and to people, in a manner that not only contributes to overall economic efficiency and wealth, but provides for broad distribution of opportunity and avoids unnecessary waste of human and physical resources" (National Research Council 1983). Yet this task is easier to define in general terms than to translate into concrete choices for investment in the face of many conflicting political and economic pressures.

PRIORITIES FOR URBAN POLICY

The positive facet of the changed nature of comparative advantage lies in the very fact that it is to a much greater extent than in the past man-made. Our central cities can compensate for a loss of natural comparative advantage by human ingenuity and policy innovation. Although there are demographic factors such as age and ethnicity of local populations that can be changed only slowly by retirement, migration, and infrastructure investment, they *can* be changed over time by concerted local effort and sustained commitment.

What we are struggling for today is a way of setting priorities for urban revitalization that contains a built-in feedback mechanism to indicate more or less automatically whether our choices are consonant with, rather than in opposition to, larger social and economic forces acting through the whole national economy.

The experience with federal urban policy of the last ten or fifteen years has taught us that the system of interrelationships among different aspects of the economy and local communities and neighborhoods is just too complex to be comprehended by any centralized analytical process. Rather, we must devise simpler and more locality-specific measures to tell us how we are doing as we proceed on a much more experimental, incremental, and decentralized basis in individual situations. The search for quick-feedback mechanisms leads us naturally back to the market. This explains the sudden popularity of private sector oriented solutions to the intractable problems that massive federal programs have failed to solve. The dilemma is that we also know that many of the critical problems with which we are dealing were themselves the result of the uncontrolled operation of market forces, usually because of inadequate attention to the spillover effects or "externalities" of market decisions, a point stressed by William Baumol in this book (Chapter 8).

What is attractive about the approach to social problems advocated by Norris and others is that it seems to offer a bridge between the two partially conflicting requirements of a viable urban policy— the need for simple feedback measures with adequate signals for frequent midcourse corrections, and the need for sensitive responses to externalities, collective benefits, and the systemic effects of microeconomic decisions. Applying a business test of return on investment to urban investments seems essential if we are to concentrate our resources on activities that will work *with* larger trends in the national and local economy, not against them. We need a mechanism that ensures the prompt termination of failed experiments.

At the same time, however, the public sector must be involved because only it has the responsibility and the legitimacy to assess the spillover effects of private economic activity as well as to decide what public goods should be provided.[3] Private entrepreneurship with profit as the sole purpose is not enough. Projects must be selected with an eye to collective social needs, not simply as the sum of the needs or wants of individuals as consumers. The value of community is just one example of a public good that is not adequately captured in the unconstrained operation of the market.

RETURN ON INVESTMENT
IN SOCIAL PROGRAMS

The strict return-on-investment approach to the evaluation of social-problem investments is also questionable on other grounds. It can be a very misleading criterion even in the evaluation of more traditional corporate activities. In Norris's words, "the return-on-investment approach guarantees that long range, complex, and creative programs required to address major unmet needs will automatically be killed" (Norris 1981: 16). He correctly suggests that investment to develop new business opportunities in the solution of social problems is much more like investment in long-range research and development than it is like investment in new manufacturing facilities. To say that such investments must be required to show a return in the long run is quite different from asking that its proponents demonstrate a highly probable return prior to the undertaking of the project. As with many R&D investments returns can be assessed only in retrospect.

R&D investments and social-problem-solving investments are uniquely subject to what Albert Hirschman (1967) termed "the principle of the hiding hand." Although Hirschman illustrated his principle mainly by cases drawn from development economics in the Third World, it is equally or even more applicable both to traditional R&D activities of the firm and to the sort of social-problem solving addressed in this volume. In Hirschman's words, "since we necessarily underestimate our creativity it is desirable that we underestimate to a roughly similar extent the difficulties of the tasks we face, so as to be tricked by these offsetting underestimates into undertaking tasks which we can, but otherwise would not dare, tackle" (1967: 13). Hirschman goes on to point out that "entrepreneurs and promoters must long have been dimly aware of the hiding hand principle, for they have been most adept at finding ways in which projects that would normally be discriminated against, because they are too obviously replete with difficulties and uncertainties, can be made to look more attractive to the decision maker" (p. 17).

It may take the initial commitment to a project, undertaken in ignorance of its difficulties, to ensure the determination and ingenuity necessary to overcome obstacles that appear along the way. Thus one function of the entrepreneur is to announce the success of a project at the very time his colleagues and associates are working desperately to prevent him from being shown up as a liar. A major insight emerging from the discussions in this book is the importance of this hiding hand, which is as indispensable in converting social problems into business opportunities as in pioneering technological innovation. But for the hiding hand to manifest itself requires somebody with a vision well beyond that of the economist's model of the profit maximizer.

The criterion is much more than whether there is a profitable market. Rather, I suspect, the projects are selected in the first instance because of a vision of a social need and then configured in such a way as to provide a reasonable prospect of *some* positive return on the investment, though not necessarily the largest. I have argued elsewhere, in fact, that such a social vision or new concept of an unmet social need is much more important in the generation of all kinds of innovations, technological and social, than the traditional profit motive of the economist's model (Brooks 1982). Some return is all that is needed to provide the feedback that I mentioned earlier. The balance of the feedback is provided through the more intangible psychological rewards to the entrepreneur and his collaborators (the satisfaction of "doing good") and through the quasi-political process of working with the community constituencies affected by the project. Taking less than the maximum possible rate of return means, in effect, making a charitable contribution for a social benefit; but requiring *some* profitability in effect increases the chances that a given charitable investment will go much further in its social effects than would a simple gift. As pointed out by Ted Kolderie in Chapter 4, the view of reduced return on investment as a charitable gift is explicitly institutionalized in the programs of General Mills.

It is not hard to imagine a set of mixed investments in which the sum of social returns (not appropriable to the investor) and private returns (appropriable to the investor) would be maximized. The maximum ratio of the sum of social and private returns to the aggregate of private and public investment could in principle be used as the conceptual criterion of selection.

Experience suggests, however, that the more that people try to use social return (or its equivalent, aggregate cost-benefit analysis) as a criterion for public investment or a charitable giving program, the more personal biases and wishful thinking are likely to enter unconsciously into the evaluation process. Restricting the list of possible investments to those ultimately expected to produce *some* private return probably reduces the large errors arising out of these unconscious biases. Since private profit is a much harder criterion to argue against, using *some* private profit as a criterion of selection seems to ensure a more objective overall evaluation. There is no way to prove such a hypothesis. I put it forward only as a suggested rationale that could be used for public-private collaboration.

THE PROBLEM OF PUBLIC SUBSIDIES

If programs that deal with social problems involve public funds, then the return on investment for the private entity will depend on the magnitude of public subsidy. It could be argued that under those circumstances private return becomes a less meaningful measure of success than implied in the preceding discussion. Indeed, since profit represents a margin over cost, private investment might become even more sensitive to the politicization of public cost-benefit analyses than would a straight public or charitable program. How can public-private arrangements be designed so that the return on investment for the private partner remains a truly objective measure of performance for the private decisionmaker? Among other factors this requires that the ground rules for the public-private relationship be clearly spelled out in advance and not be subject to manipulation without challenge by any of the participating interest groups for their own advantage after the project is already underway. This demands a reasonable level of trust among the parties to any negotiated agreements but also among interest groups that are or might be affected by the program.

In his comparative analysis of the Model Cities program and the new Enterprise Zone legislation (Chapter 3), Charles Haar suggests that the most appropriate model for a public-private relationship is that of a limited partnership bound by a formal contract and judicially enforceable accountability of each of the parties. An important part of the role of a public, particularly a federal, participant would be to insert national goals and criteria into the localized process of interest group bargaining implicit in the formulation of the program. Haar points out that both the Model Cities program and the Enterprise Zone concepts are based on the assumption that the interplay of market incentives and local interest group pressures will lead to a substantive strategy to solve a problem, with the only federal role being to assure access to the process by all affected groups. In his view this is not enough because it fails to take into account broader interests, such as relationships to the structure of the national economy and the public value of community. A judicially enforceable contract between public entities and private firms may be used to measure the social benefit dimension of the return on the total investment. This social benefit must be clearly spelled out in the partnership agreement, and could be regarded as the equivalent to a return on investment to the public partner.

FORMS OF PUBLIC-PRIVATE AGREEMENT

How would Haar's proposal differ from the traditional contract between a public agency and a private firm or nonprofit group? For one thing the partnership might be multiple, with several public and private entities involved. The federal government might represent national interests and criteria. The legal framework for this kind of partnership has already been created through the Federal Grant and Cooperative Agreement Act of 1977 (PL 95-224, 1978), which enables entities at various levels of government to agree among themselves or with private entities to carry on an activity with joint governance and shared costs. The essential feature is that it provides for a true partnership rather than a client-supplier relationship. Thus it differs both from a contract, in which the client dictates what is to be done, and a grant, in which the grantee theoretically has complete discretion as to how to proceed with a very generally defined task. The key is joint decisionmaking according to criteria formally embodied in the agreement instrument. So far the authority granted to federal agencies under this Act has been employed primarily in R&D agreements between agencies and private firms or nonprofit institutions (Young 1978). But the Act opens up new opportunities for social invention and "creative negotiation." Government agencies are likely to be timid in the exploitation of this new instrument; the creativity will probably have to come initially from private entrepreneurs. It is to be hoped that private initiatives will stimulate hitherto latent entrepreneurial instincts from various actors in the public sector.

Another possible model for local economic development is provided by the industrial cooperative movement. According to conventional wisdom, government or cooperative ownership is incompatible with entrepreneurship. Nevertheless, the remarkable success of the Mondragon Cooperative Movement in the Basque region of Spain has demonstrated that entrepreneurship and rapid capital formation can be made compatible with collective ownership, within a legal framework that provides the proper incentives. The Caja Laboral Popular (CLP), the center of the cooperative movement, provides a model for cooperative entrepreneurship. Its Empresarial Division performs many of the functions of the traditional entrepreneur in combination with those of a venture capitalist (Ellerman 1982). In fact the services provided to start-up cooperatives by this Division are strikingly similar to those provided by the Business Technology Centers in combination with the Minnesota Seed Capital Fund, described by William Norris in Chapter 11. In both cases the survival rate of the new enterprises that are provided with entrepreneurial assistance far exceeds the rate characteristic of start-up enterprises on the average. The cooperative approach is attracting growing interest in this country and has even been the subject of a recent papal encyclical (Pope John Paul II 1981). Because ownership is tied to membership in the work force, capital and investment are rooted in the local community and cannot easily be shifted for marginal reasons. Worker ownership helps to ensure that the workers will share in the economic benefits of productivity gains resulting from the introduction of technology, giving them a positive stake in technological change. However, the corporate structure has to be carefully designed to preserve incentives for capital formation and reinvestment of profits in the business. In the past cooperatives have often failed because of the absence of such incentives embodied in the legal structure of the corporation (Industrial Cooperative Association 1983). The success of a few cooperatives demonstrates that it is possible to design a system that combines some of the strengths of private enterprise with the strong attachment to community characteristic of participatory membership organizations with strong shared political values.

Although the CLP is organized mainly to foster enterprises that would be privately owned in an ordinary market economy, it also runs schools related to jobs and supplies capital for infrastructure development in the communities in which its cooperatives are located. Thus in many ways the CLP acts like a business corporation trying to develop a profitable business out of social problems, with the difference that the intended beneficiaries are also owners.

CRITERIA FOR PUBLIC SUBSIDY

What criteria should determine the appropriate public subsidy in a public-private joint venture? The subsidy may be viewed as performing two separate functions. The first is to attract private managerial, technical, and financial resources to a task that would otherwise not appear sufficiently profitable to a private investor. The public contribution must be sufficiently large and reliable to assure the investor a return on his investment in the long run. The second function is to provide a contribution commensurate with the value of the social or collective benefit arising from the project that cannot be captured by the entrepreneur from the market.

These two criteria unfortunately do not always dictate the same size of public contribution. If the first criterion leads to a lower subsidy than the second, there is no problem. Difficulties arise only when the first requirement leads to much larger subsidies than the second, so that the subsidy to the private entrepreneur is so great as to make the project questionable in relation to the public or collective benefits derived from it. One could argue that the project was not worthwhile in these circumstances, except that very large uncertainty almost always surrounds estimates of collective benefits. This uncertainty creates an inevitable temptation for those who favor the project and private participation on ideological grounds to accept the larger estimate, and those opposed to accept the smaller, thus polarizing the decision along lines of general political ideology. In any event the size of the subsidy should be fixed in advance so that the discrepancy between the results of applying the two criteria is not too large. The participant firms should be permitted to retain at least a portion of any savings compared with initial estimates, subject to the judicially enforceable terms in the cooperative agreement.

The public subsidy could be provided in many different forms: direct cash transfers to the firms on the basis of performance, loans at concessionary interest rates, government loan guarantees, tax credits, equity participation in the project by public agencies, services or in-kind contributions by public agencies. The form it takes does not affect the size of contribution that is appropriate under the second criterion in the preceding paragraph, but it *does* have a substantial impact on the size of the subsidy required to attract private participation, the first criterion. For example, there is evidence that tax credits, while they may improve cash flow and accelerate recovery of the initial costs, seldom influence the decision whether or not to proceed with the project (Bendick and Egan 1982). The availability of "up-front" capital, repayable only if the project is profitable, guarantees much lower risk to the entrepreneur, and may be more effective than continuing subsidies, which are often viewed as unreliable by private decisionmakers because of the vagaries of the political process.

Private decisionmakers may also be more sensitive to possible large, though improbable, losses than to a somewhat more likely risk of less than expected profitability. This is especially true of firms like Control Data Corporation (CDC) or General Mills that already have a strong moral commitment to a project from motives of social responsibility. The "downside risks" that enter into such private calculations include not only large and unexpected financial losses, but adverse publicity or political "hassles" that are a threat to the public image of the corporation or of its chief executive officer. If a project requires a continuing public subsidy in order to provide a return on investment to the private partners, the more the public cash flow can be made to appear marketlike—that is, dependent on a diffuse decisionmaking process of many individual beneficiaries rather than on a commitment from one public agency—the less the perceived downside risk to a private investor. This is one reason that voucher plans, in which claims on private services are provided to individual beneficiaries through public subvention, are the most attractive form of continuing subsidy. Similarly, subsidies derived from earmarked tax sources or dedicated user taxes are more attractive to entrepreneurs than those derived from general revenues subject to periodic legislative appropriations or bureaucratic decisions. Examples are a national worker retraining program subsidy based on a dedicated value-added tax, or energy conservation services procured from private firms through vouchers subsidized by a "BTU tax" on energy consumption. In each of these, the source of the tax bears a logical relation to the purpose for which the revenues are to be used, as in the case of the federal gasoline tax and the Highway Trust Fund (Rose 1979).

THE IMPORTANCE OF JOBS
AND JOB MOBILITY

Two salient premises of much of the current discussion of the private sector role in social problem solving are that (1) jobs lie at the core of most of the problems, and that (2) jobs provided by the private sector are in some sense better—both for society and for the individual jobholder—than public sector jobs (Bendick 1982; Executive Office of the President 1981: 21). This philosophy has been explicit in the whole Reagan program, typified by its centerpiece initiative, the Enterprise Zone proposal (White House Press Secretary 1982).

While there may be some merit in this view, the evidence for it is mixed at best. There is little doubt that historically public employment has been a major route to upward social and occupational mobility for disadvantaged segments of the labor force (Harrison 1972: 193). The Great Society programs of the 1960s may have benefited the black population more by providing high-status, dignified professional or semiprofessional jobs in government for the administrators of the programs than by what they did directly for the intended beneficiaries. Moving from private to public employment raised earnings of urban ghetto residents by up to a factor of 3. In every occupational category blacks earn on the average more by working for the government than for private firms. Evaluation of the

Public Employment Program (PEP) under the Emergency Employment Act of 1971 showed that two of every three PEP workers were helped to find other employment after leaving the PEP programs, on the average their dependence on public assistance declined, and their average earnings increased 86 percent over their pre-PEP earnings.

Furthermore, public employment that helps maintain and improve public infrastructure and improves the quality and level of public services can be important to the general economic climate of a city for attracting private investment. The net cost of a well-managed PEP may be but a fraction of the gross cost when all the benefits in terms of reduced welfare payments, improved tax collections, and better and more urban services are taken into account (Palmer and Sawhill 1982: 254-58).

Furthermore, if one examines the restructuring of the economy due to new technology and to growth of nongovernmental services, there are disturbing indications that opportunities for upward mobility in the private sector labor force are declining and may decline even faster in the future. For example, the big growth in the nonprofit service sector has been in nonprofessional positions that do not allow for promotion to heavily credentialed professional ranks. The pay structure tends toward a bimodal distribution with a gap between better than average and poorer than average paying jobs (Stanback and Noyelle 1982: 29-51). This is notably true, for example, in the health services sector, one of the largest and fastest growing segments of the nonprofit sector.

Furthermore, both in services and in manufacturing that utilize high technology, there is evidence of a similar stratification into either entry-level positions with low advancement opportunities or high-qualification professional or semiprofessional positions that are filled from outside the organization on the basis of educational qualifications rather than by promotion from lower level positions on the basis of experience and skills acquired on the job (Stanback et al. 1981: 10-13; Noyelle and Stanback 1983: 13-17).

In a detailed analysis of the consequences of large-scale robotization of manufacturing industries, Ayres and Miller have suggested that the interaction of the introduction of robotized production with the seniority system in unionized plants will result in the creation of a "class of perpetually insecure, marginal workers," likely to be disproportionately racial minorities and women, and in any case early dropouts from the formal educational system. Furthermore, almost half of all unskilled and semiskilled jobs that could theoretically be replaced by robots in the next twenty years are concentrated in four metalworking industries, which employed about 6.7 million workers in 1980. Nearly half these production workers are located in the five Great Lakes states. These are the same sectors and states that have already suffered most from the restructuring of the national economy discussed earlier, and the Ayres and Miller projections indicate that we may be only in the initial phases of the problem (Ayres and Miller 1982: 188, 196 n. 2).[4]

In summary, in two major future growth sectors of the economy, nonprofit services and high-technology manufacturing and services (including office work), and in the metalworking industries, which face the highest degree of restructuring due to robotization, we may be seeing a similar trend: the bimodalization of the work force, and the consequent decline of traditional upward mobility. This upward mobility is probably a more important factor in maintaining social peace than the equalization of income distribution.

PUBLIC POLICY FOR LIFETIME LEARNING

These trends are by no means inevitable or inherent in advanced technology or the service economy, but without a conscious public policy to counteract them and without concerted collaboration by industry, organized labor, government, and education, they will almost certainly occur. Short-term pressures for cost reduction in highly competitive businesses and in nonprofit services will reinforce the tendency to subdivide jobs and create increasingly differentiated and rigid job structures. These structures may be economically efficient in a *static* sense; that is, they may offer the lowest overall costs in an environment of slowly changing technology and competition, but they are far from efficient in a *dynamic* sense in a business and technological environment that requires rapid adaptation and continuing reconfiguration of work tasks in order to meet changing competition or socioeconomic pressures (Klein 1977, 1979).

It is urgent that we move toward a division of labor that pays much greater attention to the continuous development and upgrading of "human resources" through constantly enhancing and diversifying the skill repertoires of the work force from bottom to top. This implies not only a system of lifetime learning within business, but also the organization of work to make learning and skill enhancement an intrinsic part of the production process. The shop floor and the office must undertake the functions of both laboratory and school in addition to their traditional functions. This also implies a pay structure based more on acquired skills and experience than on carefully drawn up job descriptions or formal educational credentials. Symbolically it means going back to the days when everybody in the firm started on the shop floor. In a day when education has become so important, it probably also means a much better integration of schooling with work. Above all it means an effort to reduce status differentials and layers of management and supervision in the workplace; probably in the long run a new work culture constituting something like a social revolution in working life will emerge that runs counter to much of the tradition in industrial management in the twentieth century (Sabel 1982: 194-231).

A vital and healthy small business sector may be able to provide more on-the-job opportunities for diversified skill acquisition than large organizations. The failure rate for the average start-up small business in the United States is now 80-90 percent in five years (Ellerman 1982: 37; Zupnick and Katz 1980). Such a degree of instability is incompatible with adequate job security or high-quality jobs. To the degree that future employment depends on small business, it is urgent that this survival rate be improved, and this will probably require the availability of better and more support services to small business, possibly partly subsidized by government, along the lines of CDC's Business Technology Centers.

INFORMATION TECHNOLOGY
AND LEARNING

Finally there is the role of information technology in restructuring and retraining the work force (Ayres and Miller 1982: 196). Information technology offers great opportunities for self-instruction and on-the-job training, as well as for privately marketed educational services for individuals, businesses, and schools. New educational technology is in fact central to the CDC strategy for cultivating business opportunities in the market of social-problem solving (Norris 1978; Office of Technology Assessment 1982: 128-133).

Computer aided instruction (CAI) was first touted in the early 1960s, and a number of electronics firms jumped onto this bandwagon as a potential growth business. But the glowing promises were premature; the technology itself was immature, expensive, and unreliable, and the institutional environment was uniquely unprepared to assimilate it. The whole field thus became discredited and fell into the doldrums.[5] Nearly two decades later the technology has matured and is becoming steadily less expensive and more reliable. Even earlier skeptics now believe that, in combination with other information technologies, computerization offers great promise both as a market opportunity for business and as a partial solution to the massive challenge of work-force retraining (Office of Technology Assessment 1982: ch. 4 and 7). Many observers foresee a day when continuing education for the adult public and the labor force, both professional and nonprofessional, will be an industry larger than the official educational establishment. The degree to which this new demand will be met by profit-making or nonprofit institutions is as yet unclear, but it *is* fairly clear that the business sector will be much more important as a producer of services and even of equipment than in the past. Continuing education may thus provide the ideal situation for public or collective provision combined with private production along the lines of the model proposed in this book by Kolderie. One could envision arrangements analogous to those in the health field, in which continuing education and retraining are provided for by employers as a fringe benefit like health insurance, possibly even with an insurance feature to take care of the uneven incidence on individuals of the need for retraining or "retreading" in the course of their careers.

On the other hand, if decisions about the accessibility and quality of educational technology and services are made in the market rather than the governmental arena, there could be large social costs. It could happen that "fewer social resources may be made available to support what have been regarded as the public benefits of education" (Office of Technology Assessment 1982: 67–108). Individuals and groups that can afford to purchase educational services in a competitive market may receive advantages in terms of occupational mobility and economic opportunity. Of course this is true today in our dual public-private educational system; the question is whether technology will enhance or reduce this differential. It is important to reemphasize that the problem applies only to private provision, not private production. If individuals who cannot afford private educational services are provided with publicly subsidized vouchers that give them access to the same markets as private purchasers (much as modern health insurance does for medical services), the differences in access to quality services can be minimized (though not completely eliminated because of differences in sophistication of the client about choices).

CONCLUSION

In conclusion, the American polity seems to be pointed toward new relationships between the private and public sectors, whose future shape cannot yet be foreseen. The Reagan experiment has administered a severe shock to the system of public and private roles and relations between levels of government that has grown up since the days of the New Deal. This shock is now pushing toward devolution and decentralization of decisionmaking and initiative, but also toward a serious undervaluation of the collective costs and benefits of the sum of individual decisions and actions. If the Reagan philosophy were the last word, the result might be rising conflict among and increasing alienation of large segments of our population and regions of the country.

The more likely outcome seems to be a shift toward a new balance among the public and private sectors, a new sorting out between market forces and "externalities," both beneficial and adverse. The public and private sectors have to be involved jointly in meeting needs. It is the function of the public sector to *identify* the needs and of the entrepreneur in the private sector to invent a market or a customer so the needs can be met at least partially through private modes of delivery. Experience suggests that private partners in this cooperation cannot be solely profit maximizers; they must have a strongly developed social conscience in *combination* with an eye for profitable business. The grounds on which they defend their decisions to investors or creditors may properly be different from their own motivations in embarking on the activity. In this sense neither social benefit nor private profit alone suffice to justify the activity. This is not so remarkable, for it is only in the abstract models of economic theory that corporations and entrepreneurs behave as pure profit maximizers.

The most optimistic outlook would be that in the future the Reagan shock will turn out to have produced the same kind of loosening of accumulated societal and institutional rigidities that occurred in this country as the result of the trauma of World War II, with a resultant unleashing of a new wave of social invention and experimentation, sparked by the private sector, but quickly drawing in the public sector at all levels. If this proves to be an excessively optimistic forecast, it will be at least in part because the private sector fails to produce enough entrepreneurs with the kind of social vision exhibited by such people as Alexander Graham Bell, Henry Ford, Julius Rosenwald, or W.C. Norris, each matched to the social needs and opportunities of his own era.

NOTES TO CHAPTER 1

1. For a typical exposition of this viewpoint, see Bruce R. Scott, "Can Industry Survive the Welfare State?," *Harvard Business Review* (September/October 1982).

2. For a broad-based critique of income transfer programs and their disincentive effects, see Leonard M. Greene, *Free Enterprise without Poverty* (New York: Norton, 1981).

3. For an excellent discussion of this last point, see Ted Kolderie (Chapter 4).

4. The four metalworking industries referred to are fabricated metals; machinery, except electrical; electrical and electronic; and transportation equipment. According to Ayres and Miller, "almost half of all the production workers in these four industries are geographically concentrated in the five Great Lakes states (Indiana, Illinois, Michigan, Ohio, and Wisconsin) plus New York and California. Within these same states, the metalworking sector also accounts for a large percentage of the total statewide employment in manufacturing. . . . The impacts of *not* improving the productivity and competitive standing of these same industries will also be concentrated in these same few states."

5. For a witty and acerbic account of the exaggerated claims and practical fiascos of CAI in this early period, see A.G. Oettinger, *Run Computer Run* (Cambridge, Mass.: Harvard University Press, 1969).

REFERENCES

Anderson, B.E., and I.V. Sawhill, eds. 1980. *Youth Unemployment and Public Policy*. Published for American Assembly. Englewood Cliffs, N.J.: Prentice-Hall.

Ayres, R.V., and S.M. Miller. 1982. "Robotics and the Conservation of Human Resources." *Technology in Society* 4, no. 3.

Bendick, Marc, Jr. 1982. "Employment Training and Economic Development." In *Meeting Human Needs: Towards a New Public Philosophy*, edited by J.A. Meyer. Washington, D.C.: American Enterprise Institute for Public Policy Research, ch. 8.

Bendick, Marc, Jr., and Mary L. Egan. 1982. "Providing Industrial Jobs in the Inner City." *Business* 32, no. 12 (January-March).

Berry, B.J.L., and L.P. Silverman, eds. 1980. *Population Redistribution and Public Policy*. Washington, D.C.: National Academy of Sciences.

Bluestone, Barry, and Bennett Harrison. 1982. *The Reindustrialization of America*. New York: Basic Books.

Brooks, Harvey. 1982. "Social and Technological Innovation." In *Managing Innovation: The Social Dimensions of Creativity, Invention, and Technology*, edited by S.B. Lundstedt and E.W. Colglazier, Jr. An Aspen Institute Book. New York: Pergamon Press.

Brown, Harrison, et al. 1977. *World Food and Nutrition Study: The Potential Contribution of Research*. Washington, D.C.: National Academy of Sciences, pp. 128-153.

Choate, P., and S. Walter. 1981. *America in Ruins, Beyond the Public Works Pork Barrel*. Washington, D.C.: The Council of State Planning Agencies, 1981.

Crawford, J.G. 1977. "Development of the International Agricultural Research System." In *Resource Allocation and Productivity in National and International Agricultural Research*, edited by Thomas M. Arndt, D.G. Dalrymple, and V.W. Ruttan. Minneapolis: University of Minnesota Press, pp. 281-294.

Ellerman, David P. 1982. *The Socialization of Entrepreneurship: The Empresarial Division of the Caja Laboral Popular.* Somerville, Mass.: Industrial Cooperative Association.

Executive Office of the President. 1981. *America's New Beginning: A Program for Economic Recovery.* Washington, D.C. (February 18).

Federal Grant and Cooperative Agreement Act of 1977. Public Law 95-224. February 3, 1978.

Federal Reserve Bank of New York. 1981. "The Economic Costs of Subway Deterioration." *Quarterly Review* 6 (Spring).

Gorham, William, and Nathan Glazer, eds. 1976. *The Urban Predicament.* Washington, D.C.: The Urban Institute.

Greene, Leonard M. 1981. *Free Enterprise without Poverty.* New York: Norton.

Harrison, Bennett. 1972. *Education, Training and the Urban Ghetto.* Baltimore: The Johns Hopkins University Press.

Hirschman, A. 1967. "Principle of the Hiding Hand." *The Public Interest* no. 6 (Winter).

Industrial Cooperative Association. 1983. *The ICA Report,* Somerville, Mass.: ICA, January.

Klein, Burton. 1977. *Dynamic Economics.* Cambridge, Mass.: Harvard University Press.

_____. 1979. *The Slow Down in Productivity Advances, A Dynamic Explanation.* Boston: MIT Center for Policy Alternatives.

Lang, John F. 1981. *Population Deconcentration in the United States.* Special Demographic Analyses CD S-81-5. Washington, D.C.: U.S. Bureau of the Census.

Meyer, J.A. 1982. "Private Sector Initiatives and Public Policy: A New Agenda." In *Meeting Human Needs: Towards a New Public Philosophy,* edited by J.A. Meyer. Washington, D.C.: American Enterprise Institute for Public Policy Research, pp. 3-32.

Murray, Charles A. 1982. "The Two Wars against Poverty: Economic Growth and the Great Society." *The Public Interest* 69 (Fall).

National Research Council, Committee on National Urban Policy. 1983. *Rethinking Cities: Urban Policy for an Advanced Economy.* Washington, D.C.: National Academy Press.

Norris, William C. 1978. *Via Technology in a New Era in Education.* Second in a series of perspectives on employing technology to solve the pressing problems of society. Minneapolis, Minn.: Control Data Corporation.

_____. 1981. *Technological Innovation and the Prudent Man.* Sixteenth in a series of perspectives on employing technology to address the major unmet needs of society. Minneapolis, Minn.: Control Data Corporation.

Noyelle, T.J., and T.M. Stanback, Jr. 1983. *Economic Transformation in American Cities: Conservation of Human Resources.* New York: Columbia University Press.

Oettinger, A.G. 1969. *Run Computer Run.* Cambridge, Mass.: Harvard University Press.

Office of Technology Assessment. 1982. "Case Study 2: Development, Production, and Marketing of PLATO." In *Informational Technology and Its Impact on American Education.* OTA-CIT-187 (November). Washington, D.C.: U.S. Government Printing Office.

Palmer, J.L., and I.V. Sawhill, eds. 1982. *The Reagan Experiment.* Washington, D.C.: The Urban Institute Press.

Pear, Robert. 1982. "How Poor Are the Elderly?" *New York Times*, December 19.

Peterson, Peter G. 1982. "No More Free Lunch for the Middle Class," *The New York Times Sunday Magazine*, January 17.

Peterson, Willis L., and Joseph C. Fitzharris. 1977. "Organization and Productivity of the Federal-State Research System in the United States." In *Resource Allocation and Productivity in National and International Agricultural Research*, edited by Thomas M. Arndt, D.G. Dalrymple, and V.W. Ruttan. Minneapolis: University of Minnesota Press, pp. 60-83.

Pope John Paul II. 1981. *On Human Work: Laborem Exercens.* Encyclical Letter. Boston, Mass.: St. Paul Editions.

Price, Don K. 1965. *The Scientific Estate.* Cambridge, Mass.: The Belknap Press of Harvard University Press.

Renaud, Bertrand. 1982. "Structural Changes in OECD Economies and Their Impact on Cities in the 1980s." Unpublished paper, Urban Development Department, World Bank, January.

Rose, Mark H. 1979. *Interstate: Express Highway Politics, 1941-1956.* Lawrence, Kan.: The Regents Press of Kansas.

Sabel, Charles. 1982. *Work and Politics: The Division of Labor in Industry.* New York: Cambridge University Press.

Schambra, W.A. 1982. "From Self-Interest to Social Obligation: Local Communities v. the National Community." In *Meeting Human Needs: Towards a New Public Philosophy*, edited by J.A. Meyer. Washington, D.C.: American Enterprise Institute for Public Policy Research.

Scott, Bruce R. 1982. "Can Industry Survive the Welfare State?" *Harvard Business Review* (September-October).

Stanback, Thomas M., Jr., and Thierry J. Noyelle. 1982. *Cities in Transition: Changing Job Structures in Atlanta, Denver, Buffalo, Phoenix, Columbus (Ohio), Nashville and Charlotte.* Totowa, N.J.: Allanheld, Osmun.

Stanback, T.M., Jr.; P.J. Bearse; T.J. Noyelle; and R.A. Karasek. 1981. *Services: The New Economy.* Totowa, N.J.: Allanheld, Osmun.

Telesis Consultancy Group. 1982. *A Review of Industrial Policy.* Dublin, Ireland: The National Economic and Social Council.

Vernon, Raymond L. 1982. "Technology's Effects on International Trade: A Look Ahead." In *Emerging Technologies: Consequences for Economic Growth, Structural Change, and Employment*, edited by Herbert Giersch. Institut fur Weltwirtschaft an der Universität Kiel. Tübingen, Federal Republic of Germany: J.C.B. Mohr (Paul Siebeck).

Weaver, Warren, ed. 1967. *U.S. Philanthropic Foundations: Their History, Structure, Management and Record.* New York: Harper & Row.

White House Press Secretary, Office of the. 1982. *The Administration's Enterprise Zone Proposal: Fact Sheet.* Washington, D.C.: March 23.

Wolf, Charles Jr. 1979. "A Theory of Non-market Failures." *The Public Interest* 55 (Spring): 114–133.

Young, John. 1978. *Application of R&D in the Civil Sector.* OTA-R-65. Washington, D.C.: U.S. Government Printing Office.

Zupnick, J., and S. Katz. 1980. *Case Study Profiles: Project NEED IT.* Worthington, Ohio: The Entrepreneurship Institute.

✳ *Chapter 2*

The Public and Private Spheres
in Historical Perspective

Thomas K. McCraw

Throughout American history, the proper relationship between the public and private spheres has been a theme of prickly debate. In our own time it underlies much research and commentary on such topics as regulation, industrial policy, and corporate governance. Proposals for deregulating industries, for "getting the government off the backs of the people," and for the "reprivatization of public functions" all reflect the characteristic belief of our time that the public-private relationship is somehow out of whack and must be restored to proper balance.

As soon as one begins to think systematically about this question, it becomes apparent that the ground is very slippery. Definitional problems abound. Does "public" mean simply governmental and "private" nongovernmental? If so, then in what sector should such entities as defense contractors be placed? When the Reagan administration increased the defense budget, did the public sector grow? Or did private companies such as General Dynamics merely record higher sales? And what is the impact on the public-private split when such "in-and-outers" as John J. McCloy, Cyrus Vance, Caspar Weinberger, and George Shultz change jobs? Is there any effect at all? Are these persons men of the public sector, or of the private?

Ambiguities of this sort are not new in our history. They have persisted from the beginning of the American republic, though in different forms at different times. For approximately the last century, Americans have been especially concerned about having a clear demarcation between public and private activities. During this same period, we as a people have developed certain abiding criteria for legitimacy that apply to both public and private behavior. These same criteria attach as well to that growing list of activities and organizations that cannot easily be classified as either public or private but which loom large in the mixed economies characteristic of modern democratic capitalism.

This chapter addresses these issues by orienting the American experience comparatively: first across countries, then within the United States itself across time. The premise is that we cannot see our present situation clearly without the light shed by the experience of other democratic market economies as well as by our own past. In the latter part of the chapter, I will explore the indexes of legitimacy within mixed public-private institutions in America, set forth some of the pillars of success in such undertakings, and comment on the performance of public functions by private corporations.

THE UNITED STATES IN COMPARATIVE PERSPECTIVE

One relevant index of American attitudes toward the public and private spheres is the extent of public ownership of industry. The United States at the present time is at one extreme among market economies, as shown in Figure 2-1.

The facts depicted in this chart speak mostly for themselves. The United States is the only country besides South Korea with a completely private airline industry. We are the only country with an all-private telecommunications network, and one of a handful with no public enterprises in oil, gas, and steel. Furthermore, the trend over the last decade in most countries other than the United States has been toward more state ownership. [1]

One perhaps unexpected characteristic of this chart is the absence of a clear correlation between extent of state-owned enterprise on the one hand and national economic performance on the other. Some economies that grew rapidly over the last twenty years (Germany, Brazil) had substantial public ownership, while others (Japan) relatively little. Some slow performers (Canada, the United States) had few state enterprises, others (Britain) a great many. [2]

Of course, public ownership in these industries, which include utilities as well as manufacturing, is only one measure of public involvement in a nation's economy. Another type of index is the degree and growth rate of government spending. Table 2-1 shows these numbers, which include all public spending on all levels.

Table 2-1. Government Spending as a Percentage of Gross Domestic Product.

Country	Government Spending as a Percentage of GDP, 1979	Increase in Government Spending as a Percentage of GDP, 1960–1963 Average to 1970–1973 Average	Increase in Government Spending as a Percentage of GDP, 1970–1973 Average to 1977–1979 Average
Sweden	59.7	13.1	14.4
Netherlands	57.7	11.9	10.2
Norway	51.3	11.3	8.0
Denmark	51.1	13.8	8.1
Belgium	49.2	7.8	10.5
Ireland	49.0	9.0	9.4
Austria	49.0	5.5	8.7
Germany	46.4	5.1	7.2
France	45.0	2.2	6.5
Italy	44.8	6.9	6.5
Britain	43.8	5.8	4.1
Canada	40.3	6.8	3.9
Switzerland	40.1	5.9	9.7
Finland	39.1	5.0	6.8
Greece	34.6	5.6	5.1
United States – – – –	33.4 – – – – – – – – –	3.5 – – – – – – – – – –	1.2
Australia	31.7	3.1	5.4
Japan	30.5	2.5	9.5
Spain	28.5	5.1	5.5

Source: Cameron (1982: 49), derived from OECD publications.

Here again the story is the same: the United States has a low percentage of government spending among the industrialized market economies. And by a very wide margin it has the smallest recent growth rate in public spending. Recent rhetoric about the rampant growth of government spending in the United States would seem to have little foundation when viewed beside statistics for comparable countries. Only if the United States is abstracted from the world economy and considered in isolation can the proposition of rapid growth in public spending be defended.

Government expenditures as a percentage of a national economy can be calculated in different ways, of course. One careful study using several methods was done in 1980 for the National Bureau of Economic Research. Each method pointed to the same conclusion: with the important exception of transfer payments, there has been no substantial growth of government spending in the United States as a percentage of gross national product since 1952. Government purchases of goods and services, as distinct from Social Security and other transfers, have followed a pattern characterized not by growth

Figure 2-1.   Extent of State Ownership.

	Posts	Tele-communi-cations	Electricity	Gas	Oil production	Coal	Railways	Airlines	Motor industry	Steel	Ship-building
Australia											NA
Austria											NA
Belgium					NA						
Brazil											
Britain											
Canada											
France					NA						
West Germany						NA					
Holland					NA	NA					
India											

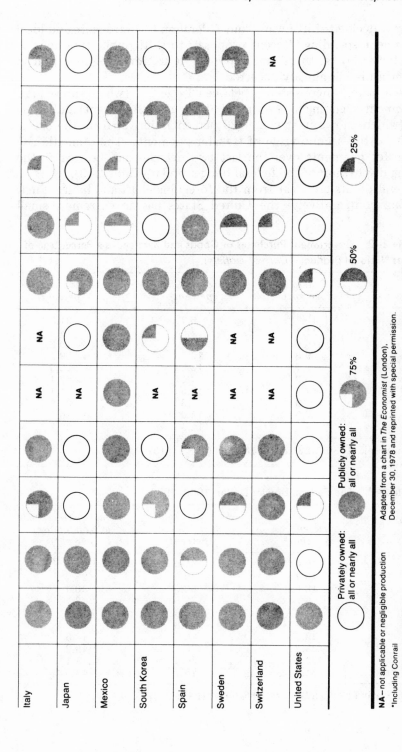

but by a decided shift away from federal and toward state and local government spending. Recent proposals to shift public functions to these lower levels, therefore, express a desire for something that in large measure has already occurred.

The apparent inconsistency between Table 2-1 (which shows total government spending in the United States at 33.4 percent) and Table 2-2 (which shows it at nearer 20 percent), derives from the exclusion from the second table of transfer payments. The dramatic rise in transfer payments over the last two decades can be seen in the shifting disposition of the federal budget dollar (Table 2-3).

Several points are clear from the foregoing chart and tables. First, speaking comparatively, the United States has an extremely small

Table 2-2. Government Purchases of Goods and Services as a Percentage of Gross National Product (*Current Dollars*).

Year	Federal (percent)	State and Local (percent)	All Government (percent)
1952	15.1	6.7	21.8
1955	11.1	7.6	18.8
1960	10.6	9.2	19.8
1965	9.8	10.3	20.1
1970	9.7	12.5	22.3
1975	8.0	14.1	22.1
1976	7.6	13.5	21.1
1978	7.3	13.3	20.6
1980	7.5	13.0	20.0
1981	7.8	12.5	20.3

Source: Break (1980: 622), *Stat. Abstract* (1982: 419).

Table 2-3. The Federal Budget Dollar, 1960-1979.

Year	Defense (percent)	Nondefense (percent)	Transfers (Included in Nondefense) (percent)
1960	49.0	51.0	24.8
1965	40.1	59.9	25.7
1970	40.0	60.0	30.4
1975	26.2	73.8	43.7
1976	24.4	75.6	45.7
1977	24.2	75.8	45.3
1978	23.3	76.7	43.3
1979	23.2	76.8	43.2
1980	23.6	76.4	43.1
1981	24.3	75.7	44.3

Source: Break (1980: 637); *Stat. Abstract* (1982: 250).

amount of state ownership of enterprise. Similarly, the size and recent growth rate of its government expenditure are quite small measured against those of other democratic market economies. As a percentage of gross national product, public expenditures in America have remained almost constant over the last two decades. But in two respects dramatic changes have occurred. One is in the rapid rise of transfer payments, as the United States—like other Western nations but unlike most Asian market economies—has determined that the welfare function will be a public responsibility with an extremely heavy call on public funds. The second change is a rapid shift from expenditures by the federal government to those by the states and local communities, largely through the mechanism of revenue sharing.

To be sure, a government's influence on a national economy cannot be measured solely by such percentages. Regulatory measures of many types cause private-sector expenditures that otherwise would not have occurred and that do not show up in calculations such as those outlined. Enormous investments in pollution abatement, reports to agencies, tax returns, and a host of other expensive requirements mandated by government constitute a hidden dimension of the public sector's impact on expenditures. In addition, tax laws often have decisive effects on private-sector investment decisions.

Here again, however, in cross-national perspective it is almost surely valid to say that the American private economy receives less direction from government than do the economies of most other countries. For example, to ignore government planning, promotion, and overall economic influence in such countries as Germany, Japan, and Brazil during their periods of "miracle growth" would be to leave out what most scholars regard as the most important elements. I can think of no serious scholar who would argue that the level of general government influence on the national economy is greater in the United States than it is in these other countries.

Many would argue, of course, that the kinds of influence and the goals of public policy differ dramatically across countries. The common perception that other governments tend to promote and encourage the development of business enterprise while we in the United States tend to regulate and restrain it is, by and large, an accurate position. Despite numerous exceptions, there is little question that in cross-national comparison the United States does not promote business enterprise to the degree that its international competitors do or that the United States itself did earlier in its history (Vogel 1981; Johnson 1982).[3]

A comparative framework for these questions is essential not only for the sake of intellectual perspective, but for immediate practical reasons as well. The economy of the United States has become so interdependent with others that we cannot isolate ourselves from economic tendencies elsewhere. Nor can others insulate themselves from events here. This is true whether the subject be interest rates in the United States, oil prices in the Persian Gulf, or export subsidies paid by other nations in order to make their products more competitive in international markets. Just as in the business world one company's actions tend to stimulate reactions by its competitors, one country's policies often compel responses by other countries. One country's promotion and subsidy of its exports, either through state-owned enterprise or by other means, can provoke competitive responses from foreign governments, because such promotion tends to steal market share. Export and domestic sales by the nonsubsidizing countries decline, and unemployment rises. The affected industries in those countries then exert political pressures on their governments to protect them from unfair competition abroad. When tens of thousands of jobs are at stake, the pressures can become irresistible. Thus a phenomenon such as the rise of state-owned enterprise turns out to be contagious. The quest for international market share in steel, automobiles, textiles, and many other industries tends powerfully to promote the rise of government influence within national economies, even those that stop short of substantial state ownership (Walters and Monsen 1981).

HISTORICAL BACKGROUND OF THE PUBLIC-PRIVATE SPLIT IN AMERICA

For the United States, these pressures pose extremely difficult problems. The need for decisive government action seems to point us in one direction, but our dominant ideology points in another. We almost desperately want to resist the further growth of government power, whether it be to combat unfair trade practices abroad or to improve our citizens' health and welfare at home.

In the context of this chapter, our national dilemma may be posed as a pair of questions. First, why does the public-private issue seem so much more important to Americans than to the people of other countries? Second, why is the American business-government relationship so much more adversarial? Some tentative answers to these questions might suggest ways in which our treasured but sometimes inconvenient ideology can be squared with the needs that are upon us at the present time.

At its birth, one of the traits that distinguished the United States from older Western nations was the conspicuous absence of established institutions. Here, unlike in Europe, there existed no established church, no standing army, no hereditary aristocracy, no clear locus of sovereignty. The trappings of feudal society, with its ordered strata and sense of organic unity, never took hold in America. Instead, ours was to be an open, mobile society, protected from absolutism by the division of powers so carefully written into the Constitution: the federal system of divided state and national spheres, the checks and balances of different branches of government. As if to underline their abhorrence of absolutism and privilege, the authors of the Constitution (Article I, section 8) expressly forbade the establishment of an aristocracy: "No Title of Nobility shall be granted by the United States." Compared with existing European models of the state, the American government, if not precisely weak, had sharply circumscribed powers (Hartz 1955).

One result of this decision by the Founding Fathers was that a large portion of political and economic power was left up for grabs. Because the society was so open and the continent so undeveloped, the scramble for wealth and shares of power did not unduly disrupt American life; instead it became the very essence of American life. The development of the country was so manifestly a positive-sum game that the growth of one person's wealth and power did not necessarily mean the shrinkage of another's. (It often did, of course, and in this respect as for so many others in American history, the issue of slavery was an enormously important exception.) But the openness of society and the manifold opportunities for the rise of new fortunes contrasted vividly with the situation in Europe, as a host of foreign observers remarked at the time.[4]

In such an atmosphere in America, the distinction between public and private affairs did not have the compelling quality it acquired later on. In a democratic republic, every citizen was private yet was also a member of the body politic, coequal with every other member. Most important, each citizen was free, and among his freedoms was his liberty to mix public and private functions without a sense of conflict. Several of the Founding Fathers, for example, made large sums of money speculating in western public lands. By later standards, their actions would have been scandalous. At the time, few objected.

It was not until the Progressive Era (1901–1914) that Americans at large began to take close and critical looks at such behavior. These years brought the high tide of journalistic muckraking, our first sustained period of obsessive preoccupation with thievery and betrayals of the public trust. The first glimmerings of insistence on the separation of public and private activity had begun late in the nineteenth century, for reasons discussed in greater detail below. But what happened in the Progressive Era brought into focus the issues at stake in the separation, as well as the assumptions underlying the conviction that the two must be kept separate.

A landmark in this new way of thinking was the historian Charles A. Beard's book *An Economic Interpretation of the Constitution* (1913). This influential work retrospectively muckraked the motives of the Constitution's authors. Beard argued that some of the delegates to the Constitutional Convention stood to profit personally from the adoption of such a document, and his book stimulated a host of similar studies of all periods of American history. Within a few years, this "Beardian" or "progressive" school of scholarship, as it came to be called, dominated the teaching and learning of history, political science, and other disciplines in the United States.

Progressive history told an exciting story. It recast the American experience as a continuous contest between public and private interests—that is to say, between right and wrong. Instead of the tale of uninterrupted glory narrated by Parson Weems and the McGuffey Reader, American history now became an ongoing struggle between good and evil. Most of the evil was found to reside in the business community. The banker Nicholas Biddle, it now developed, had provided a retainer to Senator Daniel Webster, who looked after the bank's interests in return. The young J. Pierpont Morgan, it was now discovered, had earned his first fortune by selling defective rifles to the Union Army.

These peccadilloes, progressive scholars wrote, were mere preludes to what happened in the last third of the nineteenth century. In that sordid era, such Robber Barons as John D. Rockefeller, Jay Gould, and James B. Duke rode roughshod over the public interest in pursuit of their private fortunes. Mark Twain had given this period its sobriquet, "The Gilded Age," in a spirit not entirely pejorative. Later on, one of the most eminent of progressive scholars, Vernon Louis Parrington, called it "the Great Barbecue." The cook at the Great Barbecue was big business, the carcass the American public (Josephson 1934).

In the 1920s, attacks on big business quieted down. But the Crash of 1929 and the ensuing Great Depression seemed to confirm the view that private business, which by common consent had caused the depression, was indeed rotten. Accordingly, it must be disciplined by an aroused people acting through a much enhanced public sector; as Franklin D. Roosevelt called it, "a New Deal for the American people." Along with banishing fear, FDR's first inaugural called for driving the "money changers" from the American temple. And by the middle of the twentieth century, the functional separateness of the public and private sectors had become a mainstay of the American liberal creed. Within the academy, the climax of progressive scholarship came with Arthur M. Schlesinger, Jr.'s great books on Jacksonian Democracy and on the New Deal. In the stirring prose emblematic of progressive writing, Schlesinger cast both these movements in terms of their resolute opposition to the business community. As he put it in a famous statement that by now was so self-evident in liberal circles that he hardly needed to make it at all, "Liberalism in America has been ordinarily the movement on the part of the other sections of society to restrain the power of the business community" (Schlesinger 1945: 505).

Self-evident in the middle of the twentieth century, such a generalization would have been incomprehensible in the middle of the nineteenth. The great leaders of that period—Clay, Webster, Calhoun, Jackson, Lincoln, Douglas—did not habitually posit a dichotomy between the interests of business and those of the American people. Instead, these were seen to go hand in hand. Granted there were plenty of quarrels between warring economic interests: southern planters versus northern textile magnates, industrialists versus labor unionists, merchants versus sharecroppers, shippers versus railroads. But there was no basic division between business on the one hand and the people on the other. In fact, the nineteenth-century political economy was characterized by widespread public assistance to business enterprise through the promotion of canals, railroads, and other "internal improvements" (Goodrich 1960; Heath 1954; Hartz 1948; Handlin and Handlin 1947; Scheiber 1969; Lively 1955).

What changed it all, what brought about the seismic shift in the American viewpoint toward the public-private issue, was probably the sudden rise of big business. This profound movement began with the railroads in the 1850s and matured with the revolution in manufacturing and distribution between about 1880 and 1910. Prior to this period, no single enterprise, indeed no entire industry, was sufficiently large to threaten a substantial number of people. Even major factories usually employed no more than a few hundred workers. Before the 1870s, even the largest manufacturing companies were usually capitalized at less than $1 million (Chandler 1977, pt. 1).

Within a single generation, all this changed. By 1890 each of several railroads employed more than 100,000 workers. By 1900 John D. Rockefeller's Standard Oil Company had grown into a huge multinational corporation capitalized at $122 million. James B. Duke's American Tobacco Company completed a series of mergers and internal expansions that took it from a capitalization of $25 million in

1890 to one of $500 million in 1904. And in 1901 the creation of the United States Steel Corporation climaxed a $1.4 billion transaction. This sum, far beyond the imagination of most contemporary citizens, became a symbol of the new giantism in the American economy (Chandler 1977, pts. 2-4; Moody 1904).

With the rise of big business, the term "private enterprise" acquired a different meaning. Where once it had meant liberty and freedom, it now meant danger as well. It menaced America. It brought, without any question, that very centralized power against which the Founding Fathers had fought their revolution. Small wonder that in its train came a new way of interpreting American history and a new insistence on separating the public sphere from the private.

As big business emerged, the size of the public sector was changing as well, though not nearly so rapidly. In 1871, on the eve of the creation of the first great business trusts, only 51,020 civilians worked for the federal government. Of these, 36,696 were postal employees. The remaining 14,324 governed a nation whose population exceeded 40 million. The subsequent trend in federal employment, further broken down with respect to those working in the national capital, was as shown in Table 2-4.

In the thirty years from 1871 to 1901, rapid growth is evident, but from a tiny base figure. Even by 1901, the year of the U.S. Steel merger, the ratio of federal employees to the national population was only 1 to 751, compared with 1 to 102 in 1980. As the table suggests, the largest absolute growth in federal employment occurred just where one would expect to find it: in the years of the New Deal, World War II, and the Great Society.

What do these numbers have to do with the relationship between the public and private spheres? Simply this: *In the United States, alone of all major market economies, the rise of big business preceded the rise of big government.* In Britain, France, Germany, and Japan, a substantial civil bureaucracy was embedded in the culture long before the appearance of big business. In addition, each of these other nations had a feudal heritage stretching back for several centuries, together with a well-defined locus of national sovereignty. In the United States, however, big business came first. And when it did come, no countervailing force existed to soften its impact: no aristocracy, no mandarin class, no guild tradition, no labor movement, no established church. This is one reason why the business revolution proceeded so much more rapidly here than elsewhere, why extremely large enterprises came so much earlier, and why the political reaction was so much stronger (Keller 1979; McCraw 1981: 1-19).

Table 2-4. Population, Federal Employment (Nonpostal), in Washington, D.C., and Ratios.

Year	U.S. Population (thousands)	Nonpostal Federal Employees	Located in Washington, D.C.	Population per Federal Employee	Population per Employee in Washington, D.C.
1871	40,938	14,324	6,222	2,858	6,580
1901	77,584	103,284	28,044	751	2,767
1925	115,829	268,495	67,563	431	1,714
1940	132,122	718,939	139,770	184	945
1950	151,684	1,476,019	223,312	103	679
1970	204,879	2,240,316	327,369	91	626
1980	227,700	2,215,852	366,000	102	654

Source: Bureau of the Census, U.S. Department of Commerce (1975: 8, 1102–1103); *Stat. Abstract* (1982: 6, 264, 266–7).

The United States was the only nation to enact regulatory legislation directed specifically against big business at very early dates. Congress passed the Interstate Commerce Act in 1887, the Sherman Antitrust Act in 1890, and the Federal Trade Commission and Clayton Acts in 1914. We were the only country to attempt such a thoroughgoing regulation of railroads as was contemplated under the Hepburn Act (1906). Elsewhere, such laws were regarded as unnecessary. In the case of railroads, either the government itself owned the enterprise or the size of the company was not so great as in the United States, with its vast distances and correspondingly large railroad corporations. And the antitrust laws were simply inappropriate for Europe. Although practices varied from one country to the next, in general the European polities encouraged guilds and cartels, both of which tended to protect small business and to aid those countries' efforts to promote their exports (Keller 1979; McCraw 1981: 1-19; Cornish 1979; Hannah 1979; Chandler 1980).[5]

In the United States, by contrast, small enterprises were often threatened, displaced, or even absorbed by the integrative measures typical of American big business, either through horizontal integration (absorption by merger and acquisition) or through vertical integration (displacement of small wholesalers and retailers by forward-integrating giant firms). The injuries suffered by small businesses in these often brutal procedures thrust the question of big business immediately into national politics. Bewildered owners of small businesses joined with angry farmers in demanding that the government do something about the new menace.

In this manner, a new political agenda emerged, and the adversarial business-government relationship in America was born. It is important to note that this adversarial character is strictly between American government and *big* business. Throughout the last century, small businesses have attempted to exploit the relationship as a means of protecting themselves. Their success has varied according to many different conditions: the ebb and flow of national prosperity, the involvement of the country in wars, and their own attitudes toward government (McCraw 1981: 25-55).

Of course, generalizations of the sort just set forth are very problematical. They require careful specification and are subject to many exceptions and qualifications. But the main point is simple and straightforward: The nature of the relationship between government and big business in the United States is difficult to specify in any absolute sense, but measured comparatively against the same relationship in other democratic capitalist countries, it is clearly more adversarial. Further, the character of this relationship derived in part from a reverse sequence of institutional growth. Whereas in most nations big government (or, more precisely, a powerful and well-developed state apparatus) preceded the coming of big business, in the United States alone, with its antistatist traditions, big business came first. The pattern resembled a three-stage evolution (see Figure 2-2).

Obviously, this chart is only a rough depiction of the differential growth rates of the public sector on the one hand and big business on the other. The size of the figures only crudely expresses their relative strength. And the chart leaves out other institutions such as the church, the aristocracy, and the military, all of which served in Europe and Japan as additional counterweights to undue influence by business. In the United States, where no such counterweights

Figure 2-2. Growth Rates of Government and Big Business.

STAGE	MOST COUNTRIES	THE UNITED STATES

1. Pre-Big Business (i.e., pre-1870)

2. Coming of Big Business (1870-1920)

3. Post-Big Business (1930-present)

existed, nothing appeared to stand between big business and the kind of centralized power Americans had so long abhorred. (A refinement of the chart might also show broad overlaps of the figures for the other countries. Business-government cooperation sometimes became so close that portions of the public and private sectors could enter relationships of symbiosis or even merger.)

In the United States alone, big business was seen as the initial threat to liberty, since it occupied the field uncontested and since many of the early railroads and "trusts" did indeed abuse their great power. They unilaterally decided questions that affected whole communities and often made little secret of their "Public be damned" attitude. The fact that they also brought technological innovations, economic growth, and low prices to consumers could not entirely offset the bad reputation they were making for themselves.

From the business perspective, on the other hand, when government finally did begin to grow, *it* was seen as the threat—as a new challenger and pretender to the power that business had grown accustomed to enjoying alone. Eventually, in a development full of irony, the rise of big government in stage 3 was perceived by both big and small business as an illegitimate incursion by Washington into the autonomy rightfully exercised by private enterprise. In the rise of big government, business saw, quite accurately, a reduction in its own freedom of decision.

Without the comparative perspective, it is difficult and perhaps impossible to understand this process. But in the differential growth rates between government and big business, the American experience has been more exceptional than we often think. In other countries, business executives seldom experienced the autonomy characteristic of their American counterparts. Few European or Japanese business managers took it for granted that they could make important investment decisions without consulting the state. American executives, by contrast, thought it outrageous when the U.S. government first did claim such a role during the New Deal. And within another generation, their feelings had hardened into a virtual ideology. As one student of this question has recently commented, "The most characteristic, distinctive and persistent belief of American corporate executives is an underlying suspicion and mistrust of government. It distinguishes the American business community not only from every other bourgeoisie, but also from every other legitimate organization of political interests in American society" (Vogel 1978).

To this day foreign business executives envy American managers their high social status, as well as the degree of autonomy they still possess in making decisions. Europeans would like very much to have the freedom their American counterparts enjoy from attacks by powerful Marxist groups and to some extent from claims by trade unions for a major voice in business decisions. Even the domestic cultures of Europe and the United States reflect the difference. Seldom in American history did business managers suffer the vaguely unseemly station characteristic of their counterparts in Europe, lower in the social pecking order than church officials, the landed aristocracy, or the military. Being "in trade" did not disqualify Americans from making a good marriage. Indeed, such American aristocracy as did develop grew primarily not from a landed gentry but from a business gentry.

European and Japanese managers emphatically do not, however, envy American executives their relationship with government. Instead, they often express wonder and bafflement at the adversarial character of that relationship. They have difficulty understanding the mutual hostility between two sets of players whom foreign executives tend to regard as natural allies.[6]

LEGITIMACY AND PERFORMANCE
IN THE MIXED ECONOMY

In Europe and Japan, both government and big business today enjoy a presumptive legitimacy that is simply lacking in the United States. Historically speaking, America's absence of a feudal heritage and its early conditions of openness and mobility meant that almost nothing except individualism and personal freedom did have legitimacy. In such a setting business enterprise, nearly all of which was small scale, appeared most often as a manifestation of individual autonomy, as well as the commonest means of upward mobility. It therefore shared in the legitimacy of individualism. But the rise of big business in the late nineteenth century partly undermined the presumptive legitimacy of private enterprise and separated business into two camps: small business, which retained legitimacy, and big business, which never quite acquired it. Whenever big business did seem to have gained legitimacy, some new scandal or other event undermined it once more.

The culmination came in the 1930s, when the Great Depression destroyed the legitimacy that big business had managed to gain through its remarkable record in promoting economic growth. At the same time, the initial failure of Herbert Hoover's government to deal with the economic crisis began to call into question the legitimacy of government itself. The issue of government legitimacy was complicated still further, though in a very different way, by the presidency of Franklin D. Roosevelt. FDR's New Deal appealed deeply to most Americans, but it angered corporate executives and wealthy shareholders more than any other event since the beginnings of big business itself. With the onset of the New Deal, the rise of big government began in earnest, and the whole question of the proper relationship between the public and private spheres took on new meaning.

The emergency of World War II temporarily mooted some of these issues, but the pattern had been set. Out of the combined upheavals of the Great Depression and the war emerged the modern mixed economy, in which the business-government relationship in America was far more complex than it had ever been before. The new situation did not offer a relevant setting for the old conceptual separation of the public and private spheres. The proliferation of huge government contracts—with defense industries, with private companies doing work unrelated to defense, and with universities both public and private—blurred the issue as never before. In the mixed economy nothing seemed purely public, nothing purely private. And within such a context, no status—public, private, or mixed—was in and of itself a route to legitimacy.

Instead, a series of new criteria arose that transcended the public-private question. Later in this chapter, these criteria or pillars of legitimacy are discussed in detail. First, however, the relevancy to the present discussion of both these criteria and the concept of legitimacy itself should be made more explicit.

The reason why the legitimacy question is so important is that it underlies whatever changes different groups may wish to make in the business-government relationship. These include, among other things, proposals for deregulation, for "getting the government off the backs of the people," and for the "reprivatization of public functions." In order to clarify such issues and estimate the likely degree of their fulfillment, it is appropriate not only to place the American experience in cross-national and historical perspective, as this chapter has done up to now. It is also necessary to examine the boundaries of legitimacy in some of the institutions that have been developed under the recent regime of the mixed economy.

A premise of this approach is that a question such as "Which types of activity belong in the public sector and which in the private?" is slightly off the mark. A better way to get at the important issues is to ask "What are the conditions of legitimacy in modern America for different types of public, private, and mixed undertakings?"

Often, new medical principles are discovered by researchers who look at uncommon pathologies or mutations. By much the same route, we can get a clearer idea of modern institutional legitimacy by examining the performance of organizations that combine public and private roles in some unusual way in the mixed American economy. It is likely that the American polity holds public, private, and mixed organizations alike accountable for the fulfillment of the conditions of legitimacy and that in some respects it makes little difference which of these institutions carries on a given activity.

For each, the conditions of legitimacy seem to be a complex amalgam of efficiency, fairness, and shared power. Often we tend to associate the first with the private sector and the next two with the public. But long-term legitimacy in America for any institution, whether public, private, or mixed, requires satisfactory performance on all three counts. To illustrate let us examine briefly the experiences of two mixed institutions that grew out of the New Deal. The examples are, first, the Tennessee Valley Authority, a public corporation with a variety of functions; and second, the public-private corporate regulatory system constructed under the aegis of the Securities and Exchange Commission.

THE TENNESSEE VALLEY AUTHORITY

The TVA was created in 1933 as a multiple-purpose river project intended to raise the standard of living in a depressed area of about 40,000 square miles and about 2.5 million population. The new agency was to construct dams, develop an inland waterway, control the river's chronic flooding, develop new forms of fertilizer, and bring electricity to farms, only 3 percent of which had it at the time in this region. The TVA was a controversial undertaking, primarily because of the provisions about electricity. Privately owned power companies were already serving the area, and they would have to be coopted or displaced. President Herbert Hoover had vetoed earlier legislation to do these tasks. His veto message expressed the characteristic American concern about keeping public and private affairs separate. For the government to enter into a competitive situation with private companies, said Hoover, "is not liberalism. It is degeneration" (U.S. President 1931).

President Franklin D. Roosevelt, on the other hand, regarded public ownership of utilities as a legitimate function of government, given certain circumstances. In the case of the Tennessee Valley, he showed no hesitation. Just before FDR signed the TVA Act, Senator George Norris of Nebraska, who had sponsored both this legislation and the bill Hoover had vetoed, put a question to him: "What are you going to say when they ask you the political philosophy behind

TVA?" Roosevelt answered with typical blandness, good humor, and unconcern about mixed enterprise: "I'll tell them it's neither fish nor fowl, but, whatever it is, it will taste awfully good to the people of the Tennessee Valley" (Goldman 1952: 339).

The TVA has remained controversial to this day. But in the years since 1933 it has also achieved an extraordinarily high reputation, both in the United States and even more so abroad, for the efficient performance of its multiple functions. Eventually it became the largest electric utility in the United States. It pioneered such innovations as the declining-block utility rate structure, the coordinated management of water reservoirs, and creative methods of personnel management. And it succeeded brilliantly in its overall strategy of a unified development of the Tennessee River system into a waterway whose flow can be controlled almost like a kitchen tap. That in the process of doing all these things the TVA forced a major privately owned utility out of business did not appreciably detract from the agency's overall reputation for success (McCraw 1971: ch. 8).

It was not until the 1960s and 1970s that the TVA ran into real trouble. In those decades, the agency's halo not only began to tarnish, but ultimately fell to the ground. The new problems had to do, first, with the pollution caused by its gigantic thermal power plants, which fouled the air and used huge quantities of strip-mined coal. Environmentalists protested against the spectacle of a government agency's doing no better on environmental issues than the privately owned utility industry was doing.

A second wave of problems struck in the 1970s, as the perceived dangers of nuclear power and the skyrocketing cost of both fuel and capital all hit simultaneously. When these blows fell, TVA's public-sector status afforded it no immunity. The agency was very adversely affected, just as were its counterparts in the investor-owned part of the industry. (The public sector accounts for about 20 percent of the electric power industry in America [McCraw 1976: 1372-1380]).

The significance of the TVA story to the present discussion falls into three parts. First, the multiple-purpose job accomplished by this public agency could not have been done by a private company or even a consortium of companies. Public ownership was sine qua non. Only a part of the enterprise was even potentially profitable, and this part initially was regarded as incidental to the harnessing of the river and the general uplift of living standards. There simply would have been no way to "privatize" all of TVA's multiple functions.

Despite its acknowledged success, the TVA experiment has never been duplicated in the United States. When Senator Norris introduced a bill in 1937 for "seven little TVA's" to be built in other parts of the country, the proposal did not even receive Roosevelt's support and did not come close to passage. In the American system, one TVA was enough, even in the depression atmosphere of the 1930s. The nation did not need additional yardsticks to measure the efficiency of the private utilities. Indeed, it is clear that without the crisis of the Great Depression, there would not have been even one.

Finally, when the TVA encountered intractable problems beginning in the 1960s, public-sector status not only failed to shield it from attack but actually compounded its problems. The pressures it received from environmentalists and from its own customers who were outraged at the rapid rise in its rates for electricity were all the stronger because TVA was perceived as part of the government.

In all these ways, the TVA's experience is a useful litmus test for the elements of institutional legitimacy in modern America. Its odyssey suggests that in some fundamental ways, it makes little difference whether an organization is wholly public, wholly private, or mixed in nature. If the organization is to maintain its legitimacy, it must be perceived as performing its tasks efficiently, fairly, and without too many unpleasant side effects. There is no immunity from these requirements.

CORPORATE CONTROL AND THE SECURITIES AND EXCHANGE COMMISSION

A second revealing story of a mixed system began with the passage of the Securities Act of 1933 and the Securities Exchange Act of 1934. In the years since this legislation, the Securities and Exchange Commission, which administers both laws, has developed a reputation as the most effective regulatory agency in the federal government (Heffron 1971:188; U.S. Senate 1977:I, 270; SEC Presidential Transition Team 1980:I, 9).[7] It might even be argued that without the SEC, business corporations in America would not now enjoy the legitimacy they do. The agency promotes the disclosure of information in an unusually thoroughgoing yet noncoercive way. Nearly all business executives have a well-founded respect for it. But it is the strategy behind the SEC's achievement in a mixed public-private system, in addition to the success itself, that is of interest here (McCraw 1982).

Confronted in the 1930s with a national economic depression and a discredited, moribund securities market, the SEC could easily have construed its mission as a punitive attack on unpopular giant corporations. Instead of wreaking vengeance, however, the agency set out to restore legitimacy to Wall Street's essential function of channeling investment capital into enterprise. In order to do this, the architects of the SEC's laws and policies emphasized disclosure and publicity of corporate affairs much more than the hunting down and punishing of miscreants. The strategy looked forward rather than back and focused on new reports rather than on past sins. The SEC did not, for example, dwell on corporate America's role in bringing on the Depression. The legislation, very carefully drawn (which was atypical for regulatory laws), required corporations to report annually to the SEC on a host of intimate details of their business.

In a crucial decision, the SEC opted for enforcement of these provisions not by a huge Washington bureaucracy but by a mixed public-private regulatory system. The agency worked hand-in-hand with the American accounting profession in order to promote accurate and useful reports. In effect, private-sector accountants were made the linchpin of the scheme of regulation. The accountants themselves cooperated enthusiastically once their panic over personal liability was assuaged. The size of their profession multiplied rapidly in order to meet the SEC-mandated requirements for accounting services. What is significant is that the SEC deliberately used private agents to serve public functions.

A similar strategy underlay the SEC's management of its relationship with the organized exchanges, especially the one in New York. Rather than take over the New York Stock Exchange, as it might well have done given the disgraceful record of Wall Street in policing itself, the SEC pursued a policy of encouraging reform-minded insurgents within the exchange organization. This approach achieved complete success within a few years, despite several contrary forces: opposition to cooperation from militant SEC staff members, stonewalling by the ruling oligarchs of the stock exchange, and frequent carping from the *New Republic* and other liberal organs, which argued that the SEC was contaminating itself by association with wrongdoers. Implicitly, the *New Republic* was insisting that the public and private spheres must be kept separate, that mixed systems of this nature were illegitimate.

The final brick in the SEC's edifice of public-private regulatory structures came in 1938, when the agency helped to organize a privately run regulatory body for the so-called over-the-counter portion of the securities industry. This new institution, the National Association of Securities Dealers, Inc., looked like an ordinary trade association. In fact it became an effective regulatory force for the industry. The association did not hesitate to discipline erring members through fines, suspensions, and expulsions. Expulsion from the association meant removal from the industry. And the beauty of the system was that as a private institution the association was not constrained by the procedural red tape that delayed implementation of sanctions by public regulatory agencies.

The SEC achieved its remarkable success primarily by encouraging and involving third-party groups from the private sector. These players, in turn, supported both the process and the SEC itself. The litigation, delay, and adversarial posturing so characteristic of other regulatory proceedings were thereby finessed.

Both the TVA and SEC stories are a good deal more complicated than suggested in these synopses, and the precise nature of bureaucratic "success" remains subjective and obscure. Such success as each of the two agencies did achieve was not gained without internal bickering within the organization, serious attacks from without, and perennial problems with Congress. In each agency, moreover, success could not have come without first-rate talent. Such men as Arthur E. Morgan and David E. Lilienthal of the TVA, James M. Landis and William O. Douglas of the SEC, were not just good public servants. They were topflight strategists who would have made their marks in many other lines of work in either the public or private sector.

To understand the likely fate of proposals for public-private partnerships or for the reprivatization of public functions, it is necessary to comprehend both the pillars of and barriers to success in mixed undertakings.

PILLARS OF SUCCESS

1. **A Sense of Crisis.** The most creative experiments in mixed undertakings have come during economic crisis, wartime, or intense international competition. The TVA and SEC during the Great Depression, the Manhattan Project and mobilization of the private sector during World War II, NASA and the moon shot during the post-Sputnik competition with the Soviet Union, all come to mind as instances of successful public-private collaboration in mixed institutions for the purpose of meeting some crisis. The perception of crisis is not a sufficient condition for success, and it may not even be essential. But it is certainly helpful. For example, a form of Medicare was introduced as early as the Truman administration, but not until the Great Society was the public perception of a crisis in health care sufficiently powerful to push through the required legislation.

2. **The Opportunity of a Positive-Sum Game.** In the examples just cited, almost every player ended up better off. There were few clear losers. Even in the TVA story, the principal loser on the private

side, Mr. Wendell Willkie of Commonwealth and Southern Corporation, parlayed his loss into the Republican nomination for the presidency in 1940. In the SEC case, Wall Street regained a measure of legitimacy, the accounting profession acquired new functions and hordes of new members, and the over-the-counter brokers and dealers gained power over the fly-by-night operators who were giving their industry a bad name. The Manhattan Project offered physicists and other scientists an enormous budget and relatively attractive working conditions. War mobilization presented the opportunity for the making of great private fortunes without profiteering. NASA was profligate with public funds during its heyday in the 1960s. And Medicare, with all its faults, finally passed Congress once the medical profession perceived it as an economic boon as well as an alternative to something more drastic.

3. **A Coherent Strategy Implemented by First-Rate Talent.** Most of these successful experiments were carried out by unusually able architects of the original strategies and by capable administrators who believed in the justice of the cause. The TVA and SEC leadership has already been described. In addition, there were Robert Oppenheimer and Leslie Groves of the Manhattan Project, James Webb of NASA, Robert Moses of the New York Port Authority, Lucius Clay of the interstate highway system, and Hyman Rickover of the Navy's nuclear power program. Each one of these leaders understood the necessity for a coherent strategy and for getting the right subordinates to carry it through.

4. **High-Percentage Initial Steps.** The first thing TVA did was build a great dam. Working round the clock, it employed four six-hour shifts of workers in order to alleviate unemployment in the depressed region. Given the engineering talent the agency was able to attract (in large part because private construction was languishing at the time), there was hardly any way its first project could fail. The initial success led to others and infused the whole organization with a spirit that became its trademark. Much the same thing happened with the SEC. And NASA took extraordinary pains to make its initial manned rocket launchings not only successful in the technical sense, but the occasions for national media spectaculars.

5. **An Identifiable Measure of Success other than Profit.** On a cost-benefit calculus, nearly all of the achievements listed so far become less clearly successful. Yet each project tended to be either self-justifying through its fulfillment of noneconomic criteria (making

the atomic bomb; reaching the moon), or was financially self-sustaining (the TVA power program through customers' revenues, the SEC though requirements that private accountants be paid by their corporate clients).

In the absence of severe crisis, this pillar is perhaps the most difficult of all to put in place. If no clear proof of success is available, the issue returns to the bottom line of the income statement. And if that is to be the criterion, then the very nature of capitalism's allocation of resources is not going to be helpful on a broad scale to any undertaking except the investments of first choice as defined by capital markets.

6. **Some Means of Controlling the Agenda and Limiting the Number of Players.** Almost any mixed-function enterprise or public-private collaboration depends, if it is to succeed, on the orderly implementation of a coherent strategy. If the agenda of a given undertaking is up for grabs and the number of participants is unlimited, then the likelihood of success is small.

Because of the upheavals in American society over the last twenty years, one can argue that insuperable barriers to the control of important public agendas now exist. The number of interest groups that now scramble for attention to their own narrow goals—whether economic, political, racial, social, sexual, or whatever—makes it clear that cozy bilateral business-government relationships, even on an ad hoc basis for admirable purposes, may often be doomed. The revolution in judicial standing, which makes it possible for all sorts of players to delay almost any new undertaking through exploitation of the court system, has already killed numerous projects that in an earlier time would have sailed through. One cannot avoid wondering whether some of the successes listed could have survived had they been born in the media-dominated, litigious atmosphere characteristic of American public life today. Several commentators have expressed doubt, for example, that the interstate highway system could have been built had it been proposed in the 1970s rather than the 1950s. Yet it is equally clear that without the revolution in judicial standing and the opening up of access to power, the civil rights movement and other social achievements of the last generation could not have occurred. The old dilemmas remain, and as usual there are no easy solutions.

Despite such problems (and the list could be much longer), one salient trend of the 1980s suggests that the barriers to successful public-private collaboration might be breached. This is the trend toward viewing countries as competitors, or toward viewing competition from abroad as a threat to domestic jobs. Today, as more and more of the American people begin to understand their economic vulnerability to the superior industrial efficiency of foreign producers, they might well begin to see that business-government hostility within the United States compounds the problem and delays the adjustment. As in the past, so too in the present: A sense of crisis can redefine legitimacy in any society. In the face of crisis, customs that seem entrenched or even sacred today might tomorrow become very flexible indeed. This is just the kind of thing that happened during World War II, when the issue of national survival made adversarial relationships within the American polity suddenly inappropriate, even irrelevant.

The history of the corporation itself illustrates the same point. That history began not in an adversarial but a cooperative context. It would probably surprise many American business managers today to discover that the roots of corporate development lie deep within the political state. The pattern in the early nineteenth century was to allow the incorporation of only those enterprises regarded as helpful to the public good. Bridges, turnpikes, and banks were the favored fields. The numerous special charters that characterized early nineteenth-century business history reflected a conception of the corporation as agent of the state. The chartered companies would perform functions that were necessary but that the miniscule state did not wish to perform for itself. In this sense proposals in our own time for private companies to assume public functions resonate with the origins of the business corporation in America (Handlin and Handlin 1945).

During the last part of the nineteenth century, however, state governments adopted laws permitting free incorporation without special legislative action. This ushered in the familiar modern era in which almost anyone could start a company for almost any business purpose. Yet neither here nor in the earlier period did a coherent theory of corporate legitimacy develop, aside from the original notion of incorporation as a privilege bestowed in exchange for the discharge of some public purpose. In the twentieth century, corporate legitimacy has rested almost entirely on the demonstrated ability of the device as a means of mobilizing capital for a growing economy. For good or ill, therefore, the legitimacy of the business firm has been entirely utilitarian. When it has performed poorly, as during the Great Depression, it has tended to lose legitimacy (Hurst 1970).

Seen against this complex historical background, the "reprivatization" movement raises perplexing issues. Suppose, for example, it is suggested that inner cities be revitalized through the employment of ghetto youth by profit-making corporations whose payrolls are to be subsidized by government. Such experiments have succeeded on a small scale, as we know. But consider the odds against widespread replication of these happy outcomes. Suppose that the arrangement became so successful in the financial sense that the corporation began to make a large profit. How long would the experiment be perceived as legitimate? For the public image of the undertaking, would it not be disadvantageous if the sponsoring company were a big business? But would not such a powerful company be the only kind able to afford the experiment in the first place? Assuming a large profit by a big business, how long would it be before an enterprising journalist wrote a convincing story that the company was enriching itself at the expense of taxpayers by taking advantage of loose public pursestrings? How long before "60 Minutes" brought the scandal to the attention of a national television audience?

Or consider the opposite financial performance. Suppose the undertaking lost money year after year. How long before complaining shareholders put a stop to it? Is it not illegitimate for companies deliberately to lose money, however worthy the cause? Given this damned if you do, damned if you don't situation, thoughts on the theme of "reprivatization" evoke a bit of hope, but some pessimism as well.

NOTES TO CHAPTER 2

1. Renato Mazzolini, *Government Controlled Enterprises* (New York: Wiley, 1979). The pie chart depicted in the present essay in some respects understates the extent of state-owned enterprise. Canada, for example, established a state-owned oil company in 1975 and has continued to nationalize elements of that industry, even though the chart shows no public ownership of oil in Canada. On the U.S. situation, see Annmarie Hauck Walsh, *The Public's Business* (Cambridge, Mass.: MIT Press, 1978).

2. The growth rates of national economies can be traced in the pages of the *Economic Report of the President* (Washington, D.C.: U.S. Government Printing Office), various years. For the 1982 *Report*, see Table B-109 on p. 355.

3. I do not wish to be misleading on this point. There is in America a long history of government-business interpenetration, occasionally even symbiosis. The relationship between the Defense Department and its thousands of contractors, the American system of price supports and research assistance to agriculture, and numerous other examples attest to the dangers of any easy generalization about American business-government relations. The many works of the historians James Willard Hurst and Ellis W. Hawley are especially helpful on this point. See also Harry N. Scheiber, "Law and Political Institutions," Gerald D. Nash, "State and Local Governments," Thomas K. McCraw, "Regulatory Agen-

cies," and Byrd L. Jones, "Government Management of the Economy," all in volume 2 of *Encyclopedia of American Economic History*, edited by Glenn Porter (New York: Scribner's, 1980). A useful and comprehensive text is H. H. Liebhafsky, *American Government and Business* (New York: Wiley, 1971).

4. I have in mind here Alexis de Tocqueville, M. G. Jean de Crevecoeur, Mrs. Trollope, and other articulate foreign observers of the American scene. For a sample covering a wide spectrum of time, see *America in Perspective: The United States through Foreign Eyes*, edited by Henry Steele Commager (New York: c. 1947, New American Library Edition, 1961).

5. The argument I am making in this section about the differential growth rates of big business and government in the United States, including some of the numbers about federal employment, was first articulated by Alfred D. Chandler, Jr., in an essay called "Government versus Business: An American Phenomenon," in *Business and Public Policy*, edited by John T. Dunlop (Boston: Harvard Graduate School of Business Administration, 1980), pp. 1-11.

6. These comments are based on my own conversations on this subject with European and Japanese business executives.

7. These favorable judgments of the SEC are typical, but such judgments are of course not unanimous. It is within the context of other regulatory agencies, not against some ideal standard, that I am positing the SEC's success.

REFERENCES

Beard, Charles A. 1913. *An Economic Interpretation of the Constitution of the United States*. New York: Macmillan.

Break, George F. 1980. "The Role of Government: Taxes, Transfers, and Spending." In *The American Economy in Transition*, edited by Martin Feldstein. Chicago: The University of Chicago Press.

Bureau of the Census, U.S. Department of Commerce. 1975. *Historical Statistics of the United States*. Washington, D.C.: U.S. Government Printing Office.

Cameron, David R. 1982. "On the Limits of the Public Economy." *Annals of the American Academy of Political and Social Science* 459 (January).

Chandler, Alfred D., Jr. 1977. *The Visible Hand: The Managerial Revolution in American Business*. Cambridge, Mass.: Harvard University Press.

_____. 1980. "Government versus Business: An American Phenomenon." In *Business and Public Policy*, edited by John T. Dunlop. Boston: Harvard Graduate School of Business Administration.

Commager, Henry Steele, ed. 1961. *America in Perspective: The United States through Foreign Eyes*. New York: New American Library.

Cornish, William R. 1979. "Legal Control over Cartels and Monopolization 1880-1914. A Comparison." In *Law and the Formation of the Big Enterprise in the 19th and Early 20th Centuries*, edited by Norbert Horn and Jurgen Kocka. Gottingen: Vandenhoeck and Ruprecht, pp. 280-303.

Goldman, Eric F. 1952. *Rendezvous with Destiny: A History of Modern American Reform*. New York: Knopf.

Goodrich, Carter. 1960. *Government Promotion of American Canals and Railroads, 1800-1890*. New York: Columbia University Press.

Handlin, Oscar, and Mary F. Handlin. 1945. "Origins of the American Business Corporation," *Journal of Economic History* 5 (May).

_____. 1974. *Commonwealth: A Study of the Role of Government in the American Economy, Massachusetts, 1774-1861*. New York: New York University Press.

Hannah, Leslie. 1979. "Mergers, Cartels, and Concentration: Legal Factors in the U.S. and European Experience." In *Law and the Formation of the Big Enterprise in the 19th and Early 20th Centuries*, edited by Norbert Horn and Jurgen Kocka. Gottingen: Vandenhoeck and Ruprecht, pp. 306-314.

Hartz, Louis. 1948. *Economic Policy and Democratic Thought: Pennsylvania, 1776-1860*. Cambridge, Mass.: Harvard University Press.

_____. 1955. *The Liberal Tradition in America*. New York: Harcourt, Brace.

Heath, Milton Sydney. 1954. *Constructive Liberalism: The Role of the State in Economic Development in Georgia to 1860*. Cambridge, Mass.: Harvard University Press.

Heffron, Florence Ann. 1971. "The Independent Regulatory Commissioners." Ph.D. dissertation, University of Colorado, Boulder.

Hurst, James Willard. 1970. *The Legitimacy of the Business Corporation in the Law of the United States 1780-1970*. Charlottesville: The University Press of Virginia.

Johnson, Chalmers. 1982. *MITI and the Japanese Miracle: The Growth of Industrial Policy, 1925-1975*. Stanford, Calif.: Stanford University Press.

Jones, Byrd L. 1980. "Government Management of the Economy." In *Encyclopedia of American Economic History*, vol. 2, edited by Glenn Porter. New York: Scribner's.

Josephson, Matthew. 1934. *The Robber Barons: The Great American Capitalists*. New York: Harcourt, Brace.

Keller, Morton. 1979. "Public Policy and Large Enterprise. Comparative Historical Perspectives." In *Law and the Formation of the Big Enterprises in the 19th and Early 20th Centuries*, edited by Nobert Horn and Jurgen Kocka. Gottingen: Vandenhoeck and Ruprecht, pp. 515-531.

Liebhafsky, H.H. 1971. *American Government and Business*. New York: Wiley.

Lively, Robert A. 1955. "The American System: A Review Article." *Business History Review* 29: 81-96.

Mazzolini, Renato. 1979. *Government Controlled Enterprises*. New York: Wiley.

McCraw, Thomas K. 1971. *TVA and the Power Fight, 1933-1939*. Philadelphia: Lippincott.

_____. 1976. "Triumph and Irony—the TVA." *Proceedings of the Institute of Electrical and Electronics Engineers* 64 (September): 1372-1380.

_____. 1980. "Regulatory Agencies." In *Encyclopedia of American Economic History*, vol. 2, edited by Glenn Porter. New York: Scribner's.

_____. 1981. "Rethinking the Trust Question." In *Regulation in Perspective: Historical Essays*, edited by Thomas K. McCraw. Boston: Harvard Graduate School of Business Administration.

_____. 1982. "With Consent of the Governed: SEC's Formative Years." *Journal of Policy Analysis and Management* 1: 346-370.

Moody, John. 1904. *The Truth about the Trusts.* New York: Moody.

Nash, Gerald D. 1980. "State and Local Governments." In *Encyclopedia of American Economic History*, vol. 2, edited by Glenn Porter. New York: Scribner's.

Scheiber, Harry N. 1969. *Ohio Canal Era: A Case Study of Government and the Economy, 1820-1861.* Athens, Ohio: Ohio University Press.

_____. 1980. "Law and Political Institutions." In *Encyclopedia of American History*, vol. 2, edited by Glenn Porter. New York: Scribner's.

Schlesinger, Arthur. 1945. *The Age of Jackson.* Boston: Little, Brown.

Securities and Exchange Commission. Presidential Transition Team. 1980. "Final Report." December 22.

Statistical Abstract of the United States, 1982-83. 1982. Washington, D.C.: U.S. Bureau of the Census.

U.S. President. 1931. *Veto Message Relating to Disposition of Muscle Shoals.* Senate Document 321, 71st Cong., 3rd sess: 1-3. Washington, D.C.: U.S. Government Printing Office.

U.S. Senate. 1977. *The Regulatory Appointments Process.* Committee on Government Operations, 95th Cong., 1st sess. Washington, D.C.: U.S. Government Printing Office.

Vogel, David. 1978. "Why Businessmen Distrust Their State: The Political Consciousness of American Corporate Executives." *British Journal of Political Science* January: 45.

_____. 1981. "The 'New' Social Regulation in Historical and Comparative Perspective." In *Regulation in Perspective: Historical Essays*, edited by Thomas K. McCraw. Boston: Harvard Graduate School of Business Administration, pp. 155-185.

Walsh, Annmarie Hauck. 1978. *The Public's Business.* Cambridge, Mass.: MIT Press.

Walters, Kenneth D., and R. Joseph Monsen. 1981. "The Spreading Nationalization of European Industry," *Columbia Journal of World Business* Winter: 62-72.

✤ *PART II*

PATTERNS OF PUBLIC-PRIVATE RELATIONS

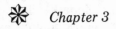 *Chapter 3*

The Joint Venture Approach to Urban Renewal: From Model Cities to Enterprise Zones

Charles M. Haar

The mixed society is upon us. More and more, the solution to complex and difficult social problems is sought through a combination of public and private energies. In order to understand the implications of the homily, "Let's all put our shoulders to the wheel," it becomes necessary to examine the separate values of the public and private sectors, the distinct contributions each can make, the mutual attractions and antagonisms, and the divergent forms in which these forces can best be combined in order to attain the objectives of the joint endeavor. One area of public policy where a combination of government and private efforts has long been envisioned—and attempted— is the revitalization of central cities. This has been true since the Housing Act of 1949, passed by a coalition of Taft Republicans and Truman Democrats, called for a "decent home and a suitable living environment for every American family." It has remained an uninterrupted theme through subsequent administrations—albeit with varying emphases. What have we learned from this sustained effort at bringing the two sides together?

COMPARING MODEL CITIES AND ENTERPRISE ZONES: SIMILAR GOALS, DIFFERING PHILOSOPHIES

In its basic thrust, enterprise zones are the direct opposite of the model cities programs of the 1960s.

President Ronald Reagan
March 23, 1982

In his message introducing his Urban Enterprise Zone legislation, President Reagan, falling back on political memory, chose to contrast the proffered program with the (presumably) nefarious Model Cities program. But is this characterization accurate? In several ways, it is true, Enterprise Zones are quite different from past federal efforts to help the cities: they connote a reduced federal role, greater private initiative, increased reliance on the free market. Upon closer inspection, however, the Enterprise Zones are not so much the opposites of Model Cities as a skewed reflection of them.

Private-Sector Participation

Enterprise Zones emerge naturally from historical and political trends in this country and from ongoing national urban and housing policies. Inducing the private sector into the revitalization of deteriorating urban areas, the most troubling physical environmental problem of the twentieth century, has been at the heart of even the boldest federal programs initiated by the Democrats, who nevertheless are keenly aware of the limitations of public funding and public expertise. The construction industry is the stated beneficiary of much housing legislation. Again, the private sector has been continuously encouraged to employ the disadvantaged through the jobs program in 1968 and the targeted jobs tax credits under the Carter administration.

Even the epitome of New Frontier legislation, Model Cities, aimed strongly at private participation, both in the formulation of the plan for a distressed urban neighborhood and in its implementation. The legislative history abounds with references to private industry (Haar 1975). Clearly, the Model Cities program was founded on this congressional stance: "fullest utilization possible of private initiatives and enterprise."

Because of the intent to use private initiative, it is not surprising that Model Cities, the diamond in his crown, as President Johnson tended to call it, managed to survive under President Nixon. Floyd Hyde, assistant secretary of the U.S. Department of Housing and Urban Development (HUD) was able to persuade Secretary George Romney that the Model Cities program meshed with the new administration's general stress on voluntarism. "Priority considerations will be given," HUD announced, "to those cities that successfully enlist the participation of private and voluntary organizations in their Model Cities grants."

Unfortunately, the involvement of the private sector proved minimal in practice. Cities responded routinely by putting a chamber of commerce representative on the policy board or by plugging in a private agency or two. There was emphasis, in many comprehensive program proposals, on minority group entrepreneurship and also on securing private investment. But here, too, the follow-through was disappointing.

President Carter's urban policy, echoing this private enterprise rhetoric, pivoted on what he termed a new public-private partnership. Its major representative is the Urban Development Action Grants (UDAG) program where eligibility requires that the local government show that the federal aid would trigger at least five times the amount of the grant in additional private capital.[1]

The Ideology of Public and Private: A Federal Ostrich. While both Model Cities and Urban Enterprise Zones envision a mingling of the private and public sectors, each stresses different aspects of the common goal. Both programs attempt to address the private-sector decision not to invest in central cities. Model Cities emphasizes social control and social incentives; the major concentration of the Enterprise Zone program is the dynamics of the private sector. The earlier Model Cities approach anticipated that improved infrastructure, aided by the coordinated panoply of federal grants and subsidized loans, would produce business decisions that coincide with governmental objectives. Now, specific financial incentive and encouragement are required to thwart a "redlining" practice. Businessmen, after all, are rational end-seekers. So the question to ask of Enterprise Zones is whether with tax incentives and deregulation, investment and location within these zones will become a rational choice for business.

Both the Democrats and the Republicans can cheer on a "partnership" and urge concentrated efforts to save the cities. But if the Democrats insist on creating an unattractive atmosphere for business (*pace*, "Taxachusetts"), or if the Republicans ignore an overall strategy of public investment, then the two wings cannot be brought together to create an effective urban strategy. Hence the conclusion that both programs are prisoners of ideological bonds, each neglecting an essential component of the joint undertaking.

The urban Enterprise Zones can be seen, like Model Cities before them, as the logical and consistent end of a long and sturdy heritage of wishful thinking—the belief that without too much institutional turmoil or sacrifice, fundamental urban malfunctions can be remedied and primary inequalities redressed. The ghetto poor will be lifted up. Wary business will be enticed to reenter the urban jungle, dilapidated cities restored with minimal disturbance. Neither program, however, addressed the fundamental structural and institutional changes required to strengthen the urban environment—where the market does not function, or fails to achieve optimal public welfare.

In neither case have levers powerful enough to deal with the structural weaknesses the programs pinpoint been forthcoming. The shortcomings of the free market and land ownership patterns, the inadequacies of local government bureaucracies, the fumblings of federal management, even the flaws in the way Congress perceives and acts on problems of the central city are incorporated into both solutions. When compared to the nature and extent of the problems, such programs as Urban Enterprise Zones and Model Cities act more as a federal pea-shooter than a federal bulldozer.

The failure of Model Cities to turn around poverty or to halt the decline of inner cities is a dangerous warning about the new form of joint venture that is presently being undertaken; the failure is a confirmation of the insight that the ills are ingrained, their source deep within the nature of the American society and economy: the private market economy, the pattern of allocation of resources and distribution of income, the complex interdependencies of land financing and ownership of metropolitan areas. These structural obstacles will not be removed by Model Cities, or by Urban Enterprise Zones. No more successful will be any program that focuses on the entities of cities as the sole determinant of solutions to the urban dilemmas, or seeks to influence businesses to perform economic activities, which in turn will further social goals, by a program that tinkers with tax expenditures and regulations. The centrifugal forces of the metropolitan market (better jobs, cheaper land, more available infrastructure, and absence of deterioration in the suburban areas) will not be overcome by any program that concentrates on providing aid to targeted areas within central cities and fails to confront the larger issues involved.

To deal with these issues, some kind of overall strategy is required. A formula for an appropriate public role in renewing the inner city would encompass at least the following: develop a program to effect needed institutional changes, consider the costs and benefits of revitalization efforts impinging on various population groups, lead and coordinate an appropriate strategy, and achieve public goals by creatively manipulating private investment.

The Plan: Involvement by the Public Sector. The role of planning in revitalization of the city is a prominent difference between Model Cities and the Urban Enterprise Zone. Model Cities called for cities to create a goal-oriented plan and a set of measures to reach those goals. Although a strategy is essential, the requirements of the Model

Cities program proved too onerous in their prescriptive regulations and in administration. Such a total strategy was obviously of professionals, by professionals, for professionals; the classroom fully entered the political arena and grandiose social science concepts of planning overwhelmed tactics and consequences. Model Cities was based on assumptions, possibly overambitious, about the capacities of cities to carry out broad-range planning on a grand scale. How could local government, as the Model Cities regulations so loftily required, prepare a "systematic analysis of all the relevant social, economic and physical problems?"

This credibility gap around planning requirements was never bridged. It may have been the sharp disappointment in the results that led Congress to give up on comprehensive planning. It would seem in the case of Urban Enterprise Zones that legislators imagine that somehow invisible hands will weave a seamless web and the need to plan can be jettisoned. The Reagan ideology reacted against the overplanning of Model Cities—but in doing so abandoned both comprehensive analysis and strategy.

Decentralization

The linking of Urban Enterprise Zones with state and local aid and governance rather than with a federal presence is the culmination of a decentralization mood in this country, and not a departure from past urban programs. The federal government since the days of President Johnson has been reducing its emphasis on highly structured and directed programs. The supplemental grant of Model Cities can be fairly described as a forerunner of revenue sharing and block grants. The Carter Community Development Block Grants, for example, were developed in order to reduce the federal presence, relying instead on local initiative and supervision. Therefore, the federal role is seen more and more as a purely ministerial one. Federal expenditures are to be made to locally sponsored projects that conform to proper procedures; only to the extent that goals are written into the procedures, however, can federal agencies affect substantive policy and implement national goals.

Process: The Lawyer's Solution. In defining the federal role in urban revitalization, both Model Cities and Urban Enterprise Zones share the same outlook that Tocqueville described as the "law domination of American society." It is given a special curlicue in legislation concerning urban matters. Lawyers are primarily occupied with the process of how the ends embodied in a statute are arrived at and with the prescribed methods for transacting business. Too often, as a result, details of process overwhelm the contents. In Model Cities, the Washington initiative was to be limited. A federal agency would simply review plans, accepting the determination of the initial decisionmakers on the local level unless clearly arbitrary or manifestly unreasonable. This procedure parallels judicial review of administration actions; there would be no *de novo* review, no analysis of what Washington would have decided had it made the original assessment itself. The prevailing attitude was that substantive goals should be eschewed—partly because there was no agreement as to what should be the national goals for urbanism and cities. Instead, contending urban forces would be given an objective forum with due process, including notice to all affected parties and appropriate hearings. Decisions would be hammered out through the bargaining and mediation processes of the local democracies. But Model Cities added one novel provision: these processes were to be improved by bringing the poor and minorities to the interest group bargaining table. There was faith that wise actions would emerge as a result of the interaction—a faith reinforced by lack of agreement on any single approach to the revitalization of American cities. To take a substantive course requires a consensus on national aspirations and probably a radical transformation of housing and urban policies. The mood in 1966 hardly merited so extensive a shakeup.

Cannot the same be said of 1983? The diffusion of decisionmaking to the local level and to the private sector was a natural choice, not only for the Reagan administration but for the predominantly Democrat House of Representatives. People in Washington can avoid the searing sequence of arriving at a decision in a context of uncertainty. In the American legal tradition, agreement on process supplies an appearance of neutrality and becomes acceptable as a fair and pragmatic way to solve troubling social issues. While there is an agreement on the appropriate process, there is no similar consensus on the substantive problem—how urban renewal can be fostered. As a result, the central city problem under both Model Cities and the Urban Enterprise Zone has been masked in process. Legitimizing a solution has become the goal rather than arriving at the correct one.

If process is thus to be elevated as the kingpin of both programs, as it may have to be in the vortex of conflicting interest groups and forces, then process needs to be clarified and implemented in a way that allows all viewpoints to be presented. It is probably more difficult to have an effective negotiation in an Urban Enterprise setting, where the joint venture is dominated by the private sector, than in the Model Cities case. Yet the approach is basically the same and, unless modified suitably, may suffer the same fate as did Model Cities.

Targeting and National Goals. One way to clarify the process of urban revitalization and to stir in an element of strategy is to focus the efforts on the urban poor. The initial Urban Enterprise Zones are destined to be set up in neighborhoods targeted for special assistance. But the link is tenuous; can it safely be assumed that the benefits to business automatically beget benefits to the poor and unemployed? Should not the purpose of the zone be to target people, to direct the benefit of the program to those most in need? Another troubling issue is that the first zones to be activated will be selected on the basis of local efforts. The poorer communities—the Newarks and the Detroits—are less likely to be able to provide matching funds, tax abatements, or other incentives for the private sector, and hence are less likely to be chosen as enterprise zones.

Parallels with the history of revenue-sharing programs can be drawn. The earlier enthusiastic support for revenue sharing, (now drummed up for Urban Enterprise Zones) came from those who saw it as a means to terminate the interference, delay, bumbling, and politically timed actions of the federal bureaucracy. Much can be said for this goal. On the other hand, it should be recognized that both revenue sharing and Enterprise Zones not only insulate cities from the federal executive, but also act to undercut the historic role of Congress in the design of urban programs. In light of this perspective, the clearest contrast with Urban Enterprise Zones, in terms of national targeting, is not Model Cities but the categorical grant programs. With the latter, Congress chooses the subject area, lays down the program design, and is brought in again in the reauthorization, as well as in the appropriation, cycles. Additionally, Congress is drawn by the grants into the day-to-day detailed work of responding to the needs and claims of constituents of the individual program. In contrast, both geographically oriented programs, Model Cities and Enterprise Zones, would reduce Congress to nothing more than a one-time check writer. By minimizing the federal presence, they impair (often as an unintended consequence) the congressional function of setting policy and priorities in urban affairs.

This defederalization, of course, is sharper in the Urban Enterprise Zones, for it relies on tax expenditures. Oversight of this program is given to the Appropriations and Ways and Means Committees, which deal with tax legislation, and is taken away from the banking, housing, and urban affairs committees, which have acquired experience with the programs that may and may not work in central cities. Public scrutiny of urban policy is removed from those members of Congress whose chief expertise has been developed in urban problems—and whose national leadership and reelections spring from a displayed knowledge of these affairs—and is lodged in the hands of the general financial people experienced with the tax structure (gross and net income and depreciations) rather than the substantive problems of the inner cities.

Hence the issue arises whether the fate of urban policy, the future of our deteriorating cities, should be stripped from a forum in which national goals can be argued and sought and left in the hands of local officials, or as a more extreme step, in the hands of the private sector alone. To the degree that one believes that there are national goals at stake here, then there needs to be a continued federal presence—through sanctions and grants, as well as through incentives, credits, and delegations to the private sector and to local government. Otherwise the objectives and the strategies necessary to achieve them may be accorded so low a priority on both the local and private sector scales that they can be considered to have been abandoned.

Clearly, such ideals and commitments as the concept of progressive expenditures to help the poorest the most, or the elimination of discrimination in the expenditure of public funds, or efforts to prevent the encapsulation of central cities and to make them an organic part of urban America are questions deserving serious consideration in the rush toward the use of taxation as a means of dealing with frustrating local and physical problems. Decentralization, important in implementing many goals, should not mean disengagement and disavowal. More important, the sum total of local policies need not add up to a rational national policy.

Tax Incentives

Even the use of tax incentives as a major instrumentality of national urban policy is not novel. The Section 235–236 (of the 1968 Housing Act) programs introduced by President Johnson, as well as the Section 8 housing program of President Carter, are primarily tax devices: the amount of accelerated depreciation permitted the private developers proved far more an inducement than the subsidy represented by the reduction of interest rates that the programs formally provide as the incentive for development. It can be concluded fairly that it was the returns of tax shelter that induced the private sector to invest in or to build moderate- and low-income housing.

Exclusive reliance on tax devices for urban development policy provides a politically easy source of federal funding but neglects the need for improving public facilities and services. Moreover, it does not sharpen the public policies to be furthered by such incentives. By concentrating on the individual building's financial package, it overlooks what is essential to city health, and, ultimately, to the well-being of industry located there: the general area and neighborhood of which these buildings are but individual components, and the fit of an individual development into overall strategy.

The Effectiveness of Tax Breaks and the Nonsupply of Public Goods. The major difference in the technical implementation of the Model Cities and Enterprise Zones programs comes down to the form of subsidy. Model Cities relied on its supplemental grant and on the coordination of categorical grants, while the Enterprise Zones provide the carrot of Internal Revenue code dispensations to induce activity. And this difference may be the determinative factor. For the effectiveness of the more recent approach of tax expenditures to meet the Enterprise Zone goals turns out, on examination, to be questionable, unfortunately.

If the major thrust of the Enterprise Zone concept is to attract business through tax credits, then it first becomes important to examine business operations and what makes them move. After all, the theory runs that private enterprise is wise using its own economic calculus; hence it has not invested in inner cities because it sees no profit potential. So the program's success will depend upon whether taxation is a current obstacle to business locating in cities or, alternatively, whether the reduction of taxes makes an Urban Enterprise Zone more attractive.[2]

But limited research now available yields a negative response. Location decisions are not made on a tax basis. Small retail, wholesale, and service firms are more concerned with start up and operating capital, markets, sources of raw materials, and labor supplies than they are with taxes, either income or property. Furthermore, quality-of-life considerations, rather than tax incentives, are what attract job-generating businesses.

Critical factors that render an urban center unattractive to business, such as lack of major growth markets, inadequate seed capital for business formation and expansion, absence of trained labor, and the lack of capable managers are not addressed by Enterprise Zone legislation. Equally crucial is the inattention given constraints on public services. Enterprise Zones will not be able to spur economic development unless the new enterprises have access to adequate public facilities, and that will require massive expenditures on someone's part (apparently not on the Reagan administration's part); the federal government is looking to reduce expenditures in urban areas, not to increase them. Moreover, a usual source for such infrastructure expenditure, local revenues, will be drained by the tax concessions granted to these same zone businesses.

And this is the fact of urban existence today. Half of the nation's communities cannot accommodate major expansions to existing firms or new plant locations because waste water and water treatment facilities are operating at or near full capacity; another quarter of the nation's communities are unable to accommodate new economic activity because of worn-out, obsolete, or overburdened roads, streets, and waste disposal sites. Without a general overhaul the dilapidated urban infrastructure will be unable to support the new private activity that is being targeted to save our cities. The input by the public partner will be lacking. This can defeat the ends of the common venture.

The Use of Tax Expenditures: A Government Free Market Intervention? Enterprise zones are supposed to be unplanned and spontaneous examples of free enterprise; presumably that is why the tax mechanism is the selected form of government aid. The invisible hand continues to determine what economic entities will locate within the zones, what their makeup will be, the type of industry, location, number, and nature of workers. But it is presumed that the desired entities will locate in the designated enterprise zones.[3]

This underplayed part of the Reagan program represents a major break from the past, a fundamentally different philosophy of public-private relations: financing from foregone tax revenues rather than by the route of direct grant or loan or loan guarantee. Thus the country is faced with the dilemma of how best to attain urban policy goals—through direct federal expenditure or through indirect tax subsidies.

The Congressional Budget Act of 1974 requires a listing in the budget of tax expenditures, defined as "revenue losses attributable to provision of the federal tax laws which allow a special exclusion, exemption, or deduction from gross income or which provide a special credit, preferential rate of tax, or a deferral of tax liability."[4] The use of the term "tax expenditures" came as the culmination of a long battle for reform; they are so designated and listed because they are a means by which the federal government pursues public policy objectives, as an alternative to a budget outlay. Indeed, precisely similar ends can be pursued either by a tax expenditure or by a direct appropriation.

The use of tax incentives has one overwhelming advantage, which the Reagan administration has stressed time and again: They do not require a bureaucracy. The only administration required is by the private parties and their lawyers and accountants, who are left to make their own planning decisions and file the appropriate income tax returns. There is no regional administrator of HUD who comes around to ascertain whether the cities are building mandated housing, enforcing building codes, or accomplishing legislative goals. All that happens is that a building is constructed and depreciation and credits are taken thereon in accordance with the schedules prescribed by the IRS.

Further, as housing reformers found in setting up tax shelters to produce low- and moderate-income housing, it is always easier to get public monies for a program through a tax expenditure rather than through a direct appropriation. Psychologically it is easier to accept the nonreceipt of revenue into a pocket than it is to spend that same money once it has been lodged inside the pocket. Realistically (and as sophistication grows this will be recognized) the identical pain and harm result from either type of subvention; yet the fact remains that tax expenditures are not a line item and are not included in the budget at all. Thus tax incentives prove highly popular, politically, and unsurprisingly become the essence of the federal role in the Urban Enterprise Zone.

But tax expenditures have crucial weaknesses. First of all, the tax revenues lost may be far more expensive than a grant or subsidy. One typical study indicates that for a particular industrial park in Indiana, Enterprise Zone tax benefits would have cost the government 45 percent more than the amount of the UDAG grant actually given for the project (Wenzel 1982). Second, there is no limit or overall cap on tax expenditures. Just as no one knows in advance the tax loss from accelerated depreciation on historic properties, so Congress cannot predict how many industries will move into an enterprise zone, and hence what the total tax expenditure bill from the wage incentive device will be.[5] Neither does the local government retain control; it cannot determine the appropriate subsidy on a project-by-project basis or limit overall participation in the program. The only weighing of costs and benefits performed at all is that inherent in Congress's passage of the program.

Finally, there is no continuous supervision of tax expenditure programs. In the case of appropriations, the reviewing committee and the executive agency in charge of the program will do their utmost to learn what is happening in the real world, to improve the program, to amend it, and to spell out new concerns. With tax expenditures, in the absence of any watchdog, there is a definite shift in the orientation of control.

TWO EXAMPLES OF THE JOINT VENTURE APPROACH TO URBAN REVITALIZATION: FINDING AN APPROPRIATE PUBLIC ROLE

Eminent Domain: The *Poletown* Case

National concerns and Congressional programs designed to spur urban renewal are the first focus of inquiry. But, as is nearly always true in our republican system, the "laboratory of the states" is a breeding ground for local experimentation. Two key examples will be presented here, instances in which the two other branches of government—the judiciary and executive—have attempted to structure an effective and productive public-private urban joint venture.

Central to any plan designed to link the public and private sectors in a joint development effort—and essential to the concept of urban renewal from its initiation—is the sorting out of "public" from "private." In defining the proper role for the two sectors when they join together for urban redevelopment, it is helpful to consider the distinctions drawn by the judiciary. Because of the Fifth Amendment to the Constitution, "nor shall *private* property be taken for a *public* use without just compensation," this mediating branch has been called on continuously over history to classify these two broad categories.

The contribution of the judicial process can best be appreciated by considering a provocative eminent domain case that received an unusual amount of press coverage during the spring and summer of 1981: the *Poletown* controversy,[6] which pitted residents of a mixed-race inner city neighborhood against a formidable public-private partnership, the City of Detroit and the General Motors Corporation. Although in many ways the decision is a natural extension of a long line of cases in which courts have allowed a public taking in the name of economic revitalization, on closer inspection *Poletown* signals that courts may no longer reject government action performed under the guise of public benefit.

The area of Detroit known as Poletown dates back to the 1870s, when, according to the testimony of one observer, "Within two or three years about fifty Polish families have settled by themselves . . . and have stores and shops of their own so that they need not trade out of the community." In the next century, the automotive revolution affected Poletown in a significant way with the establishment, in 1910, of the Dodge brothers' giant assembly plant. The population of the neighborhood increased fivefold during the first three decades of the twentieth century and, despite the ravages of the Great Depression, Poletown emerged in the 1940s economically and socially buoyant.

Like other industrial inner city neighborhoods, Poletown lost much of its wealth to the suburbs in the decades following World War II. As the community lost its economic base, its population became more ethnically and racially diverse; in 1980 Mayor Coleman Young described the neighborhood as "Afro-Poletown." Although devastation of the automobile industry after 1973's oil embargo and subsequent oil price increases took its toll on what remained of the area's factories, the neighborhood could not clearly be labeled a slum or blighted area. A microcosm of the depressed city, state, and region that it represented, Poletown was considered ripe territory for the reindustrialization and redevelopment program conjured up by General Motors (GM) and its partner, the City of Detroit.

Anxious to relocate its Cadillac and Fischer Body plants, GM favored a large horizontal structure, typically found in suburban "green field" locations. Equally anxious about losing such a prominent corporate resident, Mayor Young's administration developed and presented to GM a list of nine possible sites, only one of which was found acceptable—a site that included 250 acres in Poletown.

With the convenience of Michigan's "Quick Take" Act, allowing municipalities to take property for industrial relocation within sixty days even though no price agreement has been reached, costly delays would be avoided.

On April 30, 1981, the agreement between GM and the Central Industrial Park Project Joint Venture (the economic development corporations of the cities of Detroit and Hamtramck) was signed. The terms represent a culmination of the concessions municipalities have granted to large industrial taxpayers over the past two decades—the cities would provide site preparation (at a cost of $200 million) and twelve years of 50 percent tax abatements. The only specified quid pro quo (outside of any tax revenues) was a promise by GM to employ "at least three thousand (3,000) employees within four (4) years . . . economic conditions permitting."

The price, in human terms, for these anticipated revenues and "guaranteed" jobs was high—the displacement of 1,500 households, several churches and schools, over 100 businesses, and a hospital. The Dodge factory was one of several structures of more than passing historical and architectural significance that were to be leveled for the new expansive plant. Harder to measure is the cost of the loss of a neighborhood, the disappearance of a community. *The Village Voice* pulled no punches in its front page headline: "A Neighborhood Dies So GM Can Live."

While most Poletowners offered no opposition—some were anxious to take the relocation money and flee to the suburbs—a significant number were angered and embittered over the plans. Their resistance took several forms: complaining about compensation offers, refusing to move, organizing and enlisting the aid of Ralph Nader to challenge the city's actions, and filing three lawsuits to halt the project. In one of the more ironic twists of the controversy, in a reversal of traditional racial positions, a black mayor (Coleman Young) labeled Nader, supporter of a predominantly white neighborhood marked for destruction, a "carpetbagger."

One suit alleged that the city had abused its discretion in including the Poletown parcels in the site; a second argued a violation of federal environmental laws. It is the third action, a constitutional lawsuit asserting that the plant proposal was not a true public use, that is most relevant to and significant for the consideration of public-private development partnerships.

The briefs and opinions all the way up to the Michigan Supreme Court wrestled with the assertion that the arrangement among the parties was merely a governmental taking for private purposes. Ultimately, the state Supreme Court found that the project was a valid governmental undertaking.

The Poletown litigation was set against a background of centuries of case law and legal commentary. "Public use," a limiting phrase found in the federal and state constitutions, has long been recognized by American law as an independent prerequisite for governmental condemnation.[7] Yet the law of eminent domain over the last few decades is a witness to a gradual withering away of "public use" as a legal barrier to development. Courts tend to accept legislative determinations of what constitutes public use. Three rationales have emerged as justifying a taking: blight removal, private benefit that is only incidental, retained public controls. Each of these categories has a bearing not only on eminent domain cases, but also on consideration of the latest efforts toward urban revitalization—Urban Enterprise Zones—as well. The three rationales thus warrant more than passing reference.

It is well established that the public use requirement is met when the purpose of the planned venture is to clear a slum or blighted area. Pittsburgh's downtown "Golden Triangle" is a prominent example of condemnation of a blighted area for extensive redevelopment. Provisions in the most recent Enterprise Zone proposal that seek to pinpoint depressed regions as target areas echo this public concern for slum clearance. Despite Poletown's precarious economic and social position, however, the court did not consider labeling the community as blighted.

Instead, in a form of sensitive judicial balancing, the *Poletown* majority—as many other jurists confronted with the public-private dilemma have done—weighed the resultant benefits. In times of recessionary cycles and high unemployment, especially in the depressed Northeast industrial arc, many courts are satisfied that additional jobs and increased tax revenues are clear and significant public uses that outweigh any incidental private benefits that may accompany them. So, in a 1963 case that set the standard for more recent cases, the New York high court helped clear the way for the World Trade Center by finding a valid public use in "the gathering together of all business relating to world trade that is supposed to be the great convenience held out to those who use American ports and which is supposed to attract trade with a resultant stimulus to the economic well-being of the Port of New York."[8]

It is not surprising, therefore, that the Supreme Court of Michigan—a state with pockets of unemployment hovering around 20 percent—should find that the jobs and tax revenues resulting from a major plant site of the world's largest automobile company were sufficient to establish a public use. The *Poletown* dissent's jeremiad— "there is virtually no limit to the use of condemnation to aid private businesses"—is spoken against the strong winds of prevailing jurisprudence. In fact, the only exceptions to the trend to find takings for economic growth invulnerable to a public use challenge come from courts in the still-growing Sun Belt. And it is questionable whether even those judges would continue to disapprove of public-private joint ventures "with no assurance of more than negligible advantage to the general public," if their jurisdictions were faced with double-digit unemployment and severe budgetary straits.

As a replacement for, or in conjunction with, the weighing of interests, other courts have inquired as to the nature and extent of legal controls retained and guarantees secured by the governmental parties in the joint venture. Assurances of continued regulation and the setting aside in perpetuity of public areas are two common elements of public control that have found judicial favor. In the case before the Michigan Supreme Court, the majority deemed itself satisfied with the "promises" of increased employment and revenues from the GM–Detroit joint venture, promises the critics found insubstantial indeed.

Poletown, Public Use, and Lessons
for the Joint Venture

The public-private relationship with which the court wrestled is one of the hardest lines to draw in constitutional law. There is a continuum that represents the values and aspirations and objectives of the polity that will change over time. It is impossible to pinpoint with precision where any given item belongs, but a range of activities cluster around either pole.

What is interesting about *Poletown* and other eminent domain cases is that the term "public use," whether for manipulative ends or for hortatory or inspirational purposes, is not a device monopolized by any one interest group. It may be more often invoked by the middle classes to their own advantage and by the business groups for their needs to assemble land, but it has also been the rallying cry for public housing reformers, who have asserted successfully that the power to exclude others should not be held to render the project a private use for which public funds cannot be expended.

Yet public use, as we examine the various public endeavors to attract private enterprise into the central cities, is clearly more than the sum of competing interests or the political compromises of divvying up a portion of the goodies to each interest group. The concept holds the ultimate ethical and moral justification for the demands that the state may make on the individual.

While eminent domain for land assembly is sharply visible as a public action and thus exposed to public consideration of its public and private benefits, other exertions of public power, such as the tax expenditure of the Urban Enterprise Zone, are not so apparent. The public role and public purpose in Urban Enterprise Zones, then, must be carefully considered.

For concessions to the difficulties of separating out public from private advantage do not mean that the concepts are disappearing, even from ordinary usage. Indeed if the distinction were legally abolished today, some other term would be coined to contrast the selfish goals of the few—the takings that the courts have called "ancillary"—with the more general community interest.

Can we take the public-private distinction and find a standard susceptible to empirical verification? *Poletown* and other eminent domain cases suggest several criteria: a process that encompasses participation by broad groups of the population, a weighing so that public benefits can be said to be primary and the private gains ancillary, and an imposition of public controls to make the benefits real. It was this last factor, retention of control, that Detroit and the *Poletown* court failed to nurture. Other courts have declared that the govern-

ment role, reduced to its bare minimum, is to ensure all of these protections, to retain these controls. In an Enterprise Zone, even if affirmative government functions are eliminated, the protective role of
local government must remain.

Property Tax Incentives: The J-51 Program

Once the judicial imprimatur has been granted to a revitalization
program, it is up to the executive branch to administer the details
and to ensure that the proper public-private balance is maintained.
Perhaps the most successful and well-publicized urban renewal program, New York City's J-51, serves as an interesting case study. It
exhibits many of the problems and pitfalls associated with the type
of incentive package of which Urban Enterprise Zones are the last,
and most far-reaching, extension.

J-51 was established in 1976 amendments to a 1955 safe housing
upgrading program. It extended housing rehabilitation incentives to
rent-stabilized apartments, conversions of nonresidential buildings,
improvements to cooperatives and condominiums, buildings with
dwelling units over commercial space, and specified repair and replacement efforts.

There are two major components to the program, both based on
the real estate tax: (1) an exemption from taxation for any increase
in assessed value that results from qualified improvements; and (2) an
annual tax abatement of up to $8\frac{1}{3}$ percent of the certified reasonable
costs of such improvements.

Participation in the program is widespread: 800,000 dwelling units
have been admitted to the program since 1955; more than $96 mil-
lion was expended on over 82,000 units in fiscal year 1980 alone.
As is inevitable, however, such marked success has not escaped unscathed from those prone to believe that the private partner has unduly profited.

Critics of J-51—the most prominent of whom is City Council
President Carol Bellamy—have focused on serious drawbacks of the
widely used program:

1. Displacement of commercial or industrial interests
2. Reduced revenues for the city
3. Windfalls to luxury developers
4. Fraud in qualifying for and taking abatements
5. Lack of targeting of both individuals and geographic areas

Not unlike the judiciary in *Poletown* and similar public taking
cases, the administrators of the J-51 program are concerned with the
character and extent of control retained throughout the designation

and abatement process. Verifying and approving qualified conversions and improvements are ongoing processes that, along with random fiscal audits, are designed to eliminate fraud and to ensure full compliance with the regulations (that is, the terms of the partnership arrangement between the city and the developers).

Amendments in 1979, 1981, and, most recently, in 1983, sought to eliminate wasteful subsidies to developers who would have converted or improved their properties even without the tax incentives provided. Thus areas on the east side of Manhattan, by the far the hotspot of J-51 activity, were excluded from eligibility for abatements, in an effort to redirect development to other parts of the island and the other boroughs.

Accusations surfaced that there existed a privileged group of developers. In the report most critical of the program, Carol Bellamy's office stated, "J-51 is nothing less than a raid on the public treasury by a greedy and powerful real estate industry." Governor Cuomo expressed other reservations, while pressing for the program's reauthorization. In short, the experience in New York points up one crucial fact in incentive programs: The free market alone is not up to the task of "directing" the most beneficial and deserving redevelopment; the honing and fine tuning of J-51 testifies to the need for and difficulties with a sensitive, equitable, and effective targeting process. A system as comprehensive as Urban Enterprise Zones requires that governmental attention be directed to where the benefits will flow, when, and to whom.

The public controls, which courts have stressed as important to the finding that a taking is for a public use in eminent domain proceedings, emerge as equally important in any joint venture of public and private energies. The moment legislation diverges from the classical Adam Smith model of laissez faire and admits that government exists to pursue policies—even tax incentive and tax subsidy policies—then some sort of societal overview becomes requisite. As Justice Robert Jackson pointed out as early as the *Everson* case, the federal presence requires that once tax money is given it must be expended in the public interest, for it "is hardly lack of due process for the government to regulate that which it subsidizes." [9]

This justification for the public intervention allows continuity of supervision. As in the J-51 situation, targeting of the benefits (in that case, geographical as well as income targeting) avoids the dissipation of public funds. Total return to local decisionmaking, or to the private sector, is a pious intonation by mayors and by chief executives of corporations, but one that, when pressed, these officials do not espouse on a practical level. For they themselves need the reinforcement of checks and balances, the ability to take certain actions under compulsion, in order to divert pressures onto other branches of government or onto the public sector in the case of the businessman. Thus the goal should be to reform and improve the social review process, not to abandon it or the responsibility it reflects.

The Private Joint Venture Agreement as an Exemplar for Urban Enterprise Zones. As viewed by central city governments, the Enterprise Zones are a bright star in an otherwise bleak horizon composed of fading federal urban programs. The Zones' initial aura, however, will dim if they are expected to shine alone as self-sufficient programs or if their implementation fails to provide a substantial role for local government. Other urban aids need to be provided and the roles of the various parties within Enterprise Zones solidified if a genuine joint venture is to get off the ground.[10]

The private sector must recognize that effective urban policy requires public sector involvement even for Urban Enterprise Zones. A balanced public-private approach can improve their efficacy, eliminate areas of market imperfection and ensure that benefits are targeted to those in need.[11] Public sector participation is needed to provide basic infrastructures such as roads, water, and sewers, and basic services such as police and fire protection. Such government supports, on the basis of the empirical research thus far undertaken (Birch 1979; McMillan 1965; U.S. Department of Commerce 1975), are more vital than tax incentives in attracting business to the city.

While joint ventures of public and private enterprises are much deliberated, even verbally embraced, the form of this arrangement is still clouded and evolving. Analogies from the world of private land developers are illuminating in structuring an appropriate public role in the Enterprise Zone process. One helpful precursor is the form of business organization used to combine different interest groups—lenders, builders, developers, packagers—in the private sector itself: the traditional joint venture in real estate syndications. In many ways the joint venture of government and business is most analogous to a limited partnership, a form of organization popular in the world of property development.

In a limited partnership, the parties can demand the maximum from each other. Each general and limited partner contributes what it is best at providing: money, marketing, management, or other specialized skills. In return, each party retains defined powers, rights, and remedies for breach. No one participates unless a potential profit is seen.

In the public-private venture, the private interests can be said to fill the role of general partner: they are responsible for construction of the project (after site clearing) and day-to-day management of the completed structures, and also remain accountable for business losses and liabilities incurred. The public sector serves as a sort of limited partner, a "money person" who provides the funds for site clearance and advances the "costs" of foregone revenues, in anticipation of increased employment, a revitalized urban area, and the possibility of future tax revenue. Like any other limited partner, the public needs to retain two basic rights: (1) the right to keep informed as to progress on the project, and (2) the right to an accounting of the return which it is due. These private and public rights and responsibilities should be articulated through negotiation and recorded in a written agreement for each redevelopment project.

Further, if a joint venture is to address the structural problems underlying the urban crisis, the need for overall evaluation becomes pressing. Equity considerations demand that this evaluation reflect all viewpoints, something missing, for example, from Detroit's decision to provide GM with a site in Poletown. Goals of the program should be delineated, target populations defined and measured, and before-and-after conditions of zone areas compared. As a consequence, there will be increasing pressure on the public sector to seek creative solutions to the difficulties of public cost-benefit analyses. Ways will need to be found to assign—indeed, to quantify—newly emergent values; as, for example, the social benefits of integrated neighborhoods. In the evaluation process, the costs of the zone should be accounted for in terms of local expenditures, federal tax dollars uncollected, and the possible adverse impacts on neighboring areas. This is reminiscent of the court's decision process in *Poletown*; however, local government may be able to bring more specialized expertise to the analysis needed.

Thus the public sector should prepare an urban impact or public benefit statement that attempts to describe the net benefit to the public springing from the proposed urban redevelopment project. Such a document, prepared prior to the signing of the formal agreement, can force all parties to consider the costs and benefits to those not officially a party to the deal but whose interests are ultimately at its core. Significantly, rigorous cost-benefit analysis can place the city in a strong negotiating stance to demand the maximum contribution from the private sector.

The outcome of these two documents—a written contract defining public and private rights and responsibilities and an impact statement—may be seen together as a form of constitution, setting out rules for the exercise of powers by the public and private sectors within the confines of the joint venture. The ambiguous nature of public benefit can be dispelled in the negotiation process, highlighted by cost-benefit analysis and public participation, and formalized by written documents. At a minimum, the procedure could endow the term "public use" with more depth and reasonableness (and, ultimately, acceptability) than it has been accorded in recent eminent domain judicial cases or in the legislative revisions of the J-51 program. For the private sector, such a process is common; for the public sector, such an explicit costing is somewhat less usual.

Even the presence of formal writings, in the final analysis, cannot guarantee the validity and worth of the arrangement. For example, in the *Poletown* case the dissenters were justifiably concerned that GM would "be accountable not to the public, but to its stockholders." To these jurists, simply put, the public's agents had made an unenforceable deal. The line separating public and private was irrevocably crossed the moment the majority gave its blessing to the partnership agreement. Local government gave up too many of its rights and powers; once power seeped out of the public's hands, it would be unable to supervise the actions of the general partner—General Motors.

This result suggests the proper role of the court in evaluating a "public" use. It should verify that the local government secures a good deal, one in which a balance of responsibility evolves from the negotiation process. In Poletown, the public sector used its condemnation powers, launched the quick-take provisions, and expended other resources without exacting countervailing consideration. New York City may also have made some poor bargains in its J-51 program; critics charge that developers who would convert a building without the subsidy provided by the program nevertheless take advantage of its tax breaks. Courts are traditionally concerned, in challenges to police power regulations, that a city is regulating a private interest too heavily, hovering at the unconstitutional brink of a taking. When considering joint ventures, the courts should be concerned with the converse: whether the city is helping an individual business too much, failing to obtain a balance of responsibility.

Another major lesson for Urban Enterprise Zone purposes is that, when formulating or passing judgment on joint public-private urban redevelopment projects, municipal officers and judges must ensure the inviolability of the public's interests. It is not enough that those interested in and affected by the joint venture be heard—the rudiments of due process (which were only minimally addressed by the Michigan quick-take procedure). Nor is it sufficient to remind the vehement advocates of privatization that (as is the case with any partner in an ordinary joint venture) the private parties will be held to the terms of their agreement. It must be beyond peradventure that, in the event the joint venture agreement, owing to lax supervision or even collusion, becomes a facade for "pure" private action, the courts will both scrutinize and step in on behalf of the public, to hold the general partner to the terms of the agreement.

Under this analysis, the Enterprise Zones program, as currently visualized by the Reagan administration does not demand enough of either the public or private sector. It fails to exploit adequately the strengths of each party or to balance power and responsibility. There is much more each party can contribute in the process of revitalizing the inner cities of this country. The private sector should be responsible for coordinating the efforts of individual firms and providing necessary market information. The city should furnish the infrastructure necessary to attract business and should develop a comprehensive plan to synchronize the diverse private and public investments. The federal government should supply the services at which it is most experienced, those that it is best equipped to provide: first, funding—be it for grants, loans, or guarantees—for infrastructure improvements and small business assistance; and second, a national clearinghouse for ideas and experiences.

Unless these protections are embodied in the kind of documents proposed here, however, the Enterprise Zone concept cannot validly bear the sobriquet of joint venture. A negotiated contract, setting forth the mutual commitments, is needed to articulate the rights and responsibilities. As in any joint venture, the bargaining process, in which drafts of clauses and paragraphs are hammered out, is crucial. Unless public officials are aware of the shoals threatening urban joint enterprises—in which terms are the essence of the agreement—the venture will be shipwrecked. An impact statement, setting forth the costs and benefits to the public at large, is needed to articulate the broader issues. This sort of evaluation by the public partner can ensure that the government has struck a deal fair to itself and the other venturers. Casting the arrangements for urban revitalization in the form of private market limited partnership agreements, which will be specifically enforced, can be significant in formulating public policy, and writing the rules for power sharing can be equally important in implementing the joint venture society that is fast becoming the dominant form of twentieth-century capitalism.

NOTES TO CHAPTER 3

1. UDAG grants are federal funds used to leverage private economic development projects in distressed areas. Job creation, economic development and neighborhood revitalization are the program's main objectives. In 1979, UDAG funded projects in 239 cities, and, it is claimed by HUD, the average UDAG dollar leveraged six private-sector dollars.

2. Ironically, the similarity of the Enterprise Zone's tax incentives to the national tax reduction programs that have been passed by the Reagan administration makes them less of an effective lever. To the degree that tax losses can be sold to IBM under the safe-harbor lease provisions of the 1981 tax act, for example, the lure and magnet of lower taxes within the enterprise zone becomes weakened. Further, there are many special state acts that will "compete" as incentives for business locations: relief from property taxes and capital gains taxes and rent control laws, with tax credits being given for hiring zone residents and business development.

3. To the degree that the present bill is rewritten and made more specific and purposed (for example, as the earlier Kemp-Garcia bill would have targeted to encourage only small business), then there is more social engineering, pointy-headed or not. And as its purpose is made more specific in the legislative and committee process, the bill will resemble categorical programs more closely and look less like a reduction of federal government involvement.

4. The Reagan administration has defined "special exclusions" and "special credits" to minimize the seeming expense of the Enterprise Zone tax expenditures. In reading the special analyses of the budget of the U.S. government for the fiscal year 1982, and then reading that same report for 1983 issued by the same executive office of the President, the Office of Management and Budget, one finds a startling contrast in the definition of tax expenditures. The legislative history of the Congressional Budget Act defines them as exceptions to the "normal structure of the individual and corporate income taxes." That is, they are tax measures that reduce tax liabilities for particular taxpayers in order to encourage certain economic activities. Now, the normal structure is nowhere defined in the tax code. This means that the tax expenditures in principle might be defined as departures from the theoretical income tax base. Although a theoretically pure, "normal" structure for an income tax base can be specified with reference to general rules of income measurement, there is no similar point of reference for regarding as theoretically pure and normal any particular structure of income tax rates. The structure of tax rates depends on how you define the normal income tax structure. If a deduction or credit is not regarded as normal, it becomes counted as a tax expenditure and in effect a budget outlay.

The difference in the two budget reports lies in determining the amount of tax expenditure, in other words how much additional tax liability would be incurred by taxpayers if a given preferential tax rule were not enforced. The second report defines the normal tax structure more broadly, including within it some of the tax incentives built into Urban Enterprise Zones. Since these are then normal rather than "special" exclusions or credits, they automatically do not represent tax expenditures.

Previously, the philosophy behind tax expenditures was that all the resources of the normal tax base belong to government, hence only by its dispensation (and, presumably, its kindness) is money left to the taxpayer, resulting in a loss or "expenditure" to the government. The Reagan administration rejects this philosophy; hence the use of tax incentives does not seem to them to be so extraordinary an incursion into the private decisionmaking. They would say that most of the tax exceptions for Urban Enterprise Zones are "normal," belonging to taxpayers, and hence should not be regarded as a government outlay. But this is a Humpty Dumpty play on words. Whether one regards one's income as belonging totally to the new joint venture of the federal government with oneself being left to keep the residue, or whether one regards all the income as one's own and then as a good, decent citizen paying part of it over to the sovereign, the fact remains (unless one is an ethereal philosopher like Justice Oliver Wendell Holmes, who was ready to render up taxes as the price for civilization) that paying taxes hurts the pocketbook and not paying taxes affects federal revenue. The Reagan administration's new view of the philosophy of taxes and the command of the resources of the individual does, however, permit them to press before Congress the Urban Enterprise Zone with its reliance on tax expenditures rather than on grants.

5. The exact amounts will of course depend on how vigorously the program is pushed and how acceptable it turns out to be. The Treasury's educated guess in 1982 was that the tax relief granted to businesses that locate in designated inner city areas could cost $3.6 billion over the next five years.

6. *Poletown Neighborhood Council v. City of Detroit*, 304 N.W. 2d. 455 (1981).

7. One author in the 1940s spoke of the "wondrous elasticity" of the doctrine. While this elasticity reflects the judge's ability to accommodate technological, economic, and social changes, it also challenges the popular notion that doctrinal law can independently discern public from private uses.

8. *Courtesy Sandwich Shop, Inc. v. Port of New York Authority*, 12 N.Y. 2d 379, 190 N.E. 2d. 402 (1963).

9. *Everson v. Board of Education*, 330 U.S. 1 (1947).

10. Furthermore, Enterprise Zones need to be recognized as demonstrations, as Model Cities once were called (before that term, in the turbulent 1960s, brought along with it many odious connotations). Enterprise Zones *are* experimental by definition—after all, no one knows whether or how much they will contribute to staunching the deterioration of many of our great cities. Thus Enterprise Zones should be tested and treated explicitly as demonstration projects before they are implemented comprehensively across the nation. Central city problems have not been well served by programs that promise too much and deliver too little.

11. That the intractable nature of inner city problems requires public action is more and more apparent. The British, from whom we borrowed the Enterprise Zone concept, also recognize this principle. In a letter describing a proposal for a new urban program modeled after our UDAG program, Britain's then Secre-

tary of State for the Environment, Michael Heseltine, stated "I wish to encourage co-operation between the public and private sectors in regenerating our urban areas by giving special emphasis in the distribution of urban programme resources to projects where the local authority's input attracts substantial private sector investment." Just as the United States is borrowing the Enterprise Zone concept to combat urban decay, the British—who have experimented extensively with such zones—have chosen to combat their inner city problems with a UDAG-like program calling upon local authorities and private interests jointly to design investment projects for urban centers. See Department of the Environment Press Notice, April 6, 1982, Grants to Help Investment in Urban Areas.

REFERENCES

Birch, David. 1979. *The Job Generation Process*. Cambridge, Mass.: MIT Press.

Haar, Charles M. 1975. *Between the Idea and the Reality: A Study in the Origin, Fate, and Legacy of the Model Cities Program*. Boston: Little, Brown.

Haar, Charles M.; Michael Allan Wolf; Sarah L. Sheon; and Jill Friedlander. 1983. "Urban Enterprise Zones: Inner City Panacea or Supply-Side Showpiece?" Cambridge, Mass.: Lincoln Institute of Land Policy, Land Policy Roundtable Basic Concept Series, Number 105.

McMillan, Thomas. 1965. "Why Manufacturers Choose Plant Location," *Land Economics* 41: 239–246.

U.S. Department of Commerce. 1975. *Industrial Location Determinants*. Washington, D.C.: U.S. Government Printing Office.

Wenzel, David. 1982. "UDAGs Are Better," *Planning* 48 (April): 14.

 *Chapter 4*

Business Opportunities in the Changing Conceptions of the Public Sector Role

Ted Kolderie

Looking toward business for help in meeting social needs is of growing interest as the United States rethinks both the definition of "social needs" and its approach to social action. Businesses attracted by the challenge of working on problems traditionally handled by the public sector can no longer count on the older model of public-sector action: clear national policy objectives, adequately funded with grants to states and cities, appropriations to public agencies, and contracts to private industry for the execution of work. Today the national government is less the leader. People disagree about the objectives. Resources are scarce. And there is disillusionment about the effectiveness and concern about the costs of large-scale, centrally (and politically) directed programs and projects.

The opportunities for the private sector—both for-profit and nonprofit organizations—are not necessarily reduced by efforts to redefine our problems and to rethink the way in which they should be attacked. In fact, they may very well be increased. The social needs, after all, remain. As the country moves away from large national programs and federal government contracts, it becomes necessary to find new and appropriate approaches. But the private sector will not find its opportunities unless it understands the changes taking place.

NEW CONCEPTS

What do we mean when we talk about government "doing something"? As Elinor and Vincent Ostrom (1977) noted, there are two quite separate decisions involved. First there is the policy decision about whether or not something will be made available, the decision that some good or service will be consumed collectively: "provided," as we shall say. Second there is the decision as to the way in which that good or service shall be "produced."

Having decided that a service shall be provided publicly, the government may then go on to produce that service itself. But equally it may not. The federal government, for example, provides certain services for eligible veterans of the military service: medical and hospital care and higher education. There is a policy decision that these shall be made available, that they shall be paid for publicly. The government produces the medical and hospital services through its Veterans Administration hospitals. The government does not produce the college education but pays a wide range of colleges and universities, public and private, to produce this service for eligible veterans.

This same distinction can also be seen at the state and local levels. Government provides a system of roads, but contracts for their construction with private, for-profit firms. Governments frequently contract for the collection of refuse and cleaning public buildings. In social and human services (including education) it is much more common for the government to produce what it has decided to provide. But even here government may secure the service from an independent producer. Minnesota law, for example, requires a public school district only to "furnish," not to operate, a school; and there are nonoperating districts that pay tuition for their students to be educated at some nearby school operated by another district. Fire protection is normally thought of in terms of the municipal fire brigade, but contracts with other municipalities are common and there are cities (Scottsdale, Arizona being the best known example) where the service of fire suppression is produced by a private company on contract to the city.

And, of course, the government can provide a service without paying for it directly. The policy decision may be to induce producers to supply the service by making available to them indirect financial support, such as loan guarantees, insurance, franchises bearing a guaranteed rate of return, or regulations protecting the producer from competition. Minnesota has done this extensively by bringing a variety of personal services under the umbrella of health care reimbursement. The Legislature requires, for example, that every insurance company doing business in the state must offer a specific number of days of coverage for treatment of a particular problem, such as alcoholism and drug abuse; insurers are allowed to pass the costs into the premiums charged to employers; and institutions for treatment appear. Thus in the 1970s both free-standing and hospital-based programs for what Minnesota uniquely calls "chemical dependency" quickly expanded and new ones appeared.

The government may also provide a service simply by requiring individuals and organizations to produce it at their own expense. So city governments provide the public with walkways by requiring homeowners to build and maintain sidewalks, and they provide clean restaurants by requiring owners to meet health and sanitation standards and closing down those that do not (the government paying only for the cost of the inspection). Other "public goods," such as clean air, accessibility to public (and private) buildings for the handicapped, or the clean-up of waste-disposal sites are commonly provided by regulations compelling the private sector to produce the services in question.

THE CONFUSION BETWEEN "PROVIDING" AND "PRODUCING"

Though providing and producing are distinctly separate in concept they are, unfortunately, often linked in popular discussion. It is the production function that is the most visible, accounting for most of the employees, budget, and the contact the citizen has with the government. So, understandably if incorrectly, the idea develops that government is what it does rather than what it decides.

Part of the problem is the way this idea has come to shape the thinking of elected officials in the system. Gradually many if not most have come to see themselves primarily as the members of the board of directors of an operating service (or even as its managers and administrators!). This was perfectly illustrated at a meeting in Minneapolis early in 1982, at which a Ramsey County commissioner spoke at length about the way the rising cost of health care was cutting into the funds available for welfare and income support. When she finished someone asked her where the medically indigent go for care in Ramsey County. "Why, to Saint Paul/Ramsey medical center," she said. It was observed that, after University Hospitals, Saint Paul/Ramsey was probably the most expensive place in town to get doctor and hospital care. The county could get the same care for less money at any number of other clinics and hospitals. She did not disagree. She said, "But it's our hospital."

It forces the central question. Is a school board a seller of education or a buyer? Is a transit authority a seller of bus service or a buyer? Is a county board a seller or a buyer of hospital care? In truth, of course, they are frequently trying to be both at the same time. The important questions are: When the two roles conflict, as they surely will, which is primary? And: Why is it that this duality of roles, with all its potential for conflict, is so seldom challenged?

It is astonishing both how little this duality of roles is seen as the central issue and how powerful an idea it becomes once it is seen. Especially in human services and especially at the state and local levels, government has frequently been operating as monopoly seller to itself as monopoly buyer. When money was fairly freely available and when government production could easily expand, this was not much questioned. But when resources are not growing and when the need is for more effective and efficient service production, it takes very little effort to show people both inside and outside the government the inherent conflict of interest and to persuade them that some separation of these roles—even a partial escape from the commitment to its own bureau as a sole source of supply—would be a feasible and prudent change.

Similarly, it should require very little effort to show people in the private sector the importance to them of this change in thinking about what the government does. At all levels government has long turned to outside producers, including business, for equipment and supplies. It has traditionally used nongovernmental, commercial contractors to construct the buildings, roads and other public works it has decided should be provided. But in the area of services, especially at the state and local levels, the dominant view has been that the government is and ought to be a producer, frequently the only producer, that whatever the government decides to have done it should do itself.

Clearly, the opportunities for the private sector and for business would be enlarged by a change in the traditional conception of what makes a public service public, and by understanding that the essential function of government is providing—deciding what services should be available to what groups of citizens at what level of quality and cost.

A MIXED SYSTEM

Up to this point we have been thinking of public services provided by government. Similarly, the social need can still be met when a service is provided privately—that is, when it is left to individuals and to private organizations to decide what should be available, to whom, and at what quality.

Think about what might be called the "life support systems" whose successful operation is vital to a metropolitan area, a state or a nation. Think about health, housing, transportation, education and learning, protection and security, communication, recreation. In none of these is the function either of providing or of producing purely governmental or purely nongovernmental. Every such system is a combination of governmental decisions about what to provide (such as how many roads to build) and private decisions about what to provide (such as how many automobiles to own and how many miles to drive). There is also a mixture of governmental and nongovernmental producers.

In each of these systems there is both government and nongovernment money, government personnel and nongovernment personnel, government and nongovernment facilities. In almost all, the government element is the smaller. But in all, there is a public character to the private operations: their facilities are for the most part open to the public; and their accessibility and availability, price and quality and safety are affected with a public interest. Government provides (decides that some of us at least shall have, and decides to pay for) some health care, some housing, some transportation and some education; but so do business firms, nonprofit organizations and families.

Provision and production can be organized in different ways. A service can be governmentally provided and governmentally produced (like the "public schools"). It can be governmentally provided and privately produced (like Medicare). It can be privately provided and governmentally produced (as when a private, commercial hockey arena contracts with the city police department for security). It can be privately provided and privately produced (like a golf course "open to the public"). And there are curious mixtures; an airport, for example, is built as a result of a decision by a quasi-governmental special district, financed by charges to users (with payment according to use), and operated largely by private concessionaires on contract to the airport authority.

THE GROWING IMPORTANCE OF CHOICES

There are, in a word, choices to be made about how we have a service produced and how we have it provided. The exercise of these choices can be the key to change and improvement.

A governmental body need not be eternally committed to its own bureau as the sole source of supply for a service it is committed to provide. It can use several producers at any given time, one of which may be its own bureau and several of which may be other organizations (which may in turn be other governments or nongovernmental organizations, commercial or noncommercial). About 20 percent of the Minneapolis school district bus routes are run by district-operated buses and about 80 percent are run by seven different contractors. In Denmark about half the municipalities operate the fire service with a municipal brigade; about half contract for the service from a private company, Falck. Fire protection for one city, Aarhus, is divided: half to the municipal brigade, half to Falck.

When providers leave themselves no choices, producers are in control. They may agree to improve their service or product, but cannot be forced to do so. With choices, the providers have greater control. If one producer does not agree to change, the provider can move to another. The loss of work, or even the prospect of the loss of work, can give the current producer a new view about the desirability of doing things differently and better. Incentives are more effective than exhortation.

This is more and more likely to be the strategy for a public sector under fiscal pressure. Governments will recognize (as private organizations have) the danger in being caught with a sole source of supply. Over the years many governments have become skillful at creating and maintaining competition among vendors, construction being the most conspicuous example. Personal services, on the other hand, have been the conspicuous exception, and it is in this area that the new interest in the potential for choice and competition is beginning to develop.

Choices do not necessarily have to be made by the governmental body. They can also be made by the users for themselves. For example, in a number of central city districts the school boards and administrations (sometimes quietly) are setting up "options" or "alternative" programs that let parents choose among different schools within the district in an implicit voucher arrangement. This arrangement is limited, however, as a device for change. The individual schools continue to be financed directly by appropriations from the central district office, and usually they have little if any discretion to change their programs. If these decisions were made by the schools themselves, it would be necessary to expand the more popular schools and to close or reduce in size the less popular schools. This would obviously create political problems for the central school board and administration. So in this situation so-called options, while permitted, tend to be carefully controlled.

Matters would be different (and the pressure for change greater) if the user had a broader range of choices that included producers in the private sector. Some programs have been set up on this basis. The best known are the GI Bill and Medicare, both of which have operated on the principle that the eligible user has free choice of vendor. Other programs could also work on the same principle. For example, voucher systems have been proposed for education. But these are difficult to introduce. Organizations that have been receiving appropriations from the government to deliver services are unlikely to respond enthusiastically to the suggestion that they should now begin to earn their revenues instead. Where the transition can be made, the opportunities for change and improvement can be significant, not least because the users of a service may know more about a service and make better market-type choices about quality and costs than the elected officials and the administrators in the central office who are subject to political pressures.

But there are problems with choice. Choosing depends on information. People need time to absorb information even when it is organized and available; and in the case of public and professional services, information is normally not organized and readily available. So frequently there is a fear that poor people, especially, will be disadvantaged and will not make "good decisions." This objection comes from people who are entirely disinterested and who have only the welfare of the users at heart. Unhappily, it comes also from the existing producers who have their own welfare at heart and are fearful of the competition that will result from freedom of choice. However, people do not have to be well-educated to be smart; they do by and large seek quality and value; and they may in fact make better decisions for themselves than other people (or institutions) make for them. Information is of limited use when choice is absent. Quite rationally, nobody invests much effort to describe or to understand the public education system so long as the district tells students what schools they will attend. When people can choose, however, information begins to appear. And government usually intervenes to remove fraudulent and incompetent producers and deceptive advertising.

THE GROWING USE OF FEES AND CHARGES

There is a trend toward user charges, as state and local governments find federal aid declining and access to tax revenues blocked by voter resistance and limits on what the economy can afford. User charges have traditionally been resisted. The essence of a public service was that it was provided free. Zero prices (or even low prices) stimulated demand. They served both the interest of the elected officials in accomplishing the policy objective and the interest of the professionals and government managers in increasing the demand for their services. Now, however, attitudes are beginning to change. To the government manager revenue from user fees seems better than no growth in revenue at a time when a financial crisis forces a cutback in service and raises the prospect of layoffs. And the public, observing the reduction in the level of services, begins to see low prices as an unnecessary subsidy to users who could afford to pay more of the real cost themselves.

One striking and important feature of the current discussion is the way the concern for equity in the system is playing out as pressure to use limited tax dollars for those who genuinely cannot afford to pay, and to ask those who can afford to pay to do so. Think, for example, about the discussion over the financing of higher education, where tuition is being increased and aid targeted toward students in greatest need; or about the debate in transportation, where consideration is being given to raising fares for long-distance suburban commuters and introducing "transit stamps" for low-income riders.

The concept of the "means test" has entered the discussion about Social Security and public pensions and has even begun to appear in programs traditionally financed entirely by charges to users. So now we have programs (both state and national) to help low-income households pay their winter heating-fuel bills. It is a dramatic change, which has scrambled many traditional ideological alignments.

The rise in prices for public services also expands choices by inducing nongovernmental organizations to enter the field as producers. Think, for example, about the growth of United Parcel Service and the various new forms of message-distribution that have appeared during the last fifteen years as the price of mailing a letter has been raised from 5 cents to 20 cents, and as the price and convenience of the delivery of parcels have changed, or about the way the rise in bus fares in major cities has drawn private bus operators into commuter service, especially for long-distance commuters, for whom fares are well in excess of $1 a ride.

Once again, the implications of this transformation in the public sector should be clear. The opportunities for new—and new kinds of—service producers is growing. Increasingly, they will be able to enter not the political competition for contracts, but the nonpolitical business of selling service directly to individuals.

THE REDEFINITION OF "SERVICE"

A service is something done for a person by some other person (increasingly, someone professionally trained), sometimes on a volunteer basis, but usually not. Now we want to look at the possibility that, increasingly, social needs may be met in ways that do not use large amounts of professional service. This is important, for it is in this trend toward a reduced use of professional service that many challenging opportunities for new entrepreneurial private-sector producers will be found.

The assumption that more professional service must be the response to social needs is now under attack. Increasingly it is being argued that the relationship has been turned upside down, that needs are being manufactured in order to create a demand for the employment of trained professionals. The idea of a service "delivered" by a professional to a client is more and more resisted. Partly this is because professional services are so expensive, for the family and for the society. Partly it is because they are now seen to diminish or discourage the self-reliance of the individual, family, or neighborhood.

This view is still much debated, but a new attitude based on the notions of conservation and prevention is clearly visible. There is a growing feeling that solving problems and delivering services may be two distinctly different things.

Health care is again a useful example. So long as the ills that befell people were diseases and unavoidable accidents, an increased supply of personal medical services could reasonably be seen as an unquestionable good. But when the leading causes of death come to be automobile accidents, interpersonal violence, suicide, and a variety of ailments caused and preventable by individuals themselves, redefinition is needed both of the problem and of the appropriate response. There is a changing conception of the "social need" in health care, away from more personal medical services and toward "health maintenance"; away from medication and surgery, for example, and toward programs of diet-and-exercise and the elimination of cigarette smoking as a strategy for controlling heart disease. There is a growing sense that prevention is a better strategy than repair, and that the dominant social need is now for mechanisms that will encourage maintenance and conservation.

A related idea gaining recognition is that although services can be performed by professionals, they will not succeed without the participation of the client. Doctors cannot keep a person well who will not take care of his own body; teachers cannot educate a child who is not trying to learn; sanitation crews cannot overcome a community determined to litter its streets; and the police by themselves cannot keep a community safe. There is, as a result, an interest in what is coming to be called, inelegantly, "co-production": an effort to draw the citizen and user into the solution of a problem, in the hope that this will minimize the incidence of the problem and the cost of dealing with it.

This opens up important opportunities for innovative people to introduce new and less costly—and perhaps more effective—ways of meeting social needs. Would it be possible, for example, to capture part of the stream of payments now going to professionals, for use instead in alternative ways, such as improved preventive programs? And one step further, could the innovative producers keep any savings as personal income? Most important: What changes in the organization of a public service system would best stimulate ideas about alternative, nonservice, and less expensive approaches to meeting social needs?

THE COMBINATION OF PREPAYMENT AND DEREGULATION

One approach now being tried in an effort to make constructive use of these new perspectives is to change the method of payment—that is, to move away from paying for a service and to offer the producing organization instead a given amount of money to accomplish a defined result in a defined period of time, with the understanding that the producer may then keep whatever money is not spent. Doctors are being encouraged to reduce the amount of "sickness care" and to emphasize "health care," and specifically to reduce the amount of expensive hospitalization they prescribe. The essential idea is to shift from payment based on inputs to payment based on outcomes and in the process to stimulate producers to think about new and different ways of doing things. The goal is to reward and therefore to stimulate innovation.

It is important, obviously, that new approaches not be obstructed by requirements and prohibitions set up by existing producers precisely to prevent innovation. So the growing interest in competition and in prepayment is accompanied by an effort to reduce the volume of regulations and the authority of the existing regulatory mechanisms. Some regulation is essential, to protect both workers and consumers. Some requirements for credentialing and certification protect the public. But there are too many of them. Many have been put in place over the years by professional groups that prefer to define competence in terms of training and work experience and that are uncomfortable with the idea that their competence should be judged by their customers. Finally, remember that the government officials who write regulations (and who decide whether new regulations are "needed") are interested parties, as well.

DECENTRALIZATION AND THE
PRIVATE SECTOR

As a part of the current reappraisal there has been a growing interest in the potential of state and local governments and of the institutions of the private sector. Partly this is because the national government will not or cannot continue to expand its financial responsibilities for meeting social needs; therefore the expectations of the states and localities and of the private sector are inevitably enlarged. It also results from a recognition that local and private institutions may be better equipped than the national government for the jobs that now need to be done. It is not that they have more money. The philanthropic giving of business firms and foundations cannot substitute for the reduced resources from the national government. Nor can the state and local governments do so. They face an array of statutory and constitutional restrictions on taxing and spending imposed by the voters of the 1960s and 1970s and are further constrained by the interstate competitive effects of their financial policies.

But the delegation of responsibility downward to local governments and outward to the private sector may stimulate new approaches to meeting social needs. By and large the major public service systems are owned and operated by local government and controlled by a framework of law established by state legislatures. Unable to expand their financing, officials at these levels may redesign and restructure service systems, using ideas and people from the private sector. This is presumably the basis of the recent interest in public-private partnerships—an appreciation, as much as anything, of the talent and the flexibility within nongovernmental organizations and of what they can contribute to the solution of problems in the public sector.

POSSIBLE APPLICATIONS OF THE CONCEPT
OF SERVICE REDESIGN

In the complex model of the public sector we now have in front of us, there can be found a variety of opportunities for business, as provider and as producer of service.

Government as Market
Government has traditionally bought materials, equipment, and supplies from outside (usually private) suppliers, and supplied the

personnel (labor and administration) itself. Sometimes it does buy the *management* of personal services. One of the remarkable businesses that has taken advantage of this opportunity in the public service field is ServiceMaster Industries, of Downers Grove, Illinois. Founded in 1929 as a mothproofing business, it moved into carpet cleaning after World War II, and in the 1960s into housekeeping services for hospitals. Gradually it took on the management of other support services in hospitals (the management of the physical plant, inventories and materials, laundry, equipment, and food service) and more recently has been expanding these services to schools and colleges, as well as to commercial and industrial establishments. American Transit Enterprises (ATE) of Cincinnati, Ohio runs a similar business. In the Minneapolis–Saint Paul area the buses are owned and the drivers and mechanics hired by the Metropolitan Transit Commission, but the management is retained on contract with ATE.

Contracting presents great potential for improvement of the public sector. But it remains controversial, and its expansion will depend on a better understanding of several points. First, "contracting" may, but need not, mean "contracting *out*." It is possible for a public body to have a contract arrangement with a group of its own employees. Second, "contracting out" may, but need not, mean the use of private and commercial vendors. Governments frequently contract with other governments. Third, it is possible and usually desirable to contract out only a part of a service (say, only its management). These options would reduce the criticism inevitably directed against contracting—that it will hold down wage rates and reduce the level of employment in public services.

Nothing will eliminate this criticism entirely, of course, because the purpose of the strategy of choice, competition and innovation is to introduce into the public-service sector some of the same element of risk that falls on producers selling to private individuals and organizations.

It is important to say again, however, that the essential idea of contracting is not to replace one monopoly producer with another or to replace a governmental producer with a private producer, but rather to develop competition. The best arrangement is permanently mixed, containing elements of in-house production and elements of contract production, so that the provider has at all times an opportunity to shift work back and forth between the two, using this as leverage to encourage producers toward better performance. Choice and the potential for improvement are the goals. Contracting by government is simply a means to this end, not an end in itself.

The New Market of Private Buyers

Mentioned earlier are the opportunities for business to sell to individuals, groups of individuals, and private organizations that are buying services either with money (or vouchers) provided by government or out of their own private resources. In almost every city there are firms selling security services to private buildings, to neighborhoods, and sometimes to households. (In one Twin Cities area suburb the municipality pays Pinkerton's $9.50 an hour for security at the public arena where the high school teams play hockey, while down the street the professional team is paying $30 an hour for "hard" security from the city police.) Other producers—business firms and nonprofits, large and small—are selling transportation services to neighborhoods and to businesses. Interesting new organizations, formed to contract with homeowners associations for the management of condominium and townhouse developments, are beginning to take on the character of small city administrations. Hospital corporations (increasingly hard to distinguish from business firms) are moving into the field of contract management. And while public education remains firmly in its public-bureau model, nonprofit organizations and business firms interested in the market for education are working with children and adults directly, especially in computer-aided instruction.

The U.S. Postal Service is one of the oldest and largest public services. The national government has been both provider and producer (though in rural areas it is increasingly contracting with individuals to carry the mail on a part-time basis). In recent years much more of its costs have been charged to users. A part of its business is protected by the law which gives it a monopoly on the delivery of letter mail. But now the new technology of electronic communications is giving competitors a way around the Postal Service monopoly on the delivery of messages by "letter." And it is experiencing stiff competition from other producers in the delivery of other-than-first-class mail: parcels, newspapers, magazines. Of these, the courier companies are best known, from their television advertising. But within local areas, too, there are private firms that deliver; and some companies (such as the Wall Street Journal and Knight-Ridder) have been testing their own delivery services, for their own publications as well as for others. Already, in California, entrepreneurs have set up private "post offices" that offer many of the services found at the government station (and after 4:30 P.M.). This competition is changing the operations of the Postal Service, so its role (at least as producer of service, as letter-carrier) could be very different in the not-too-distant future.

Research and Development in the Internal
Corporate Market

Some business firms have found ways to test and develop new services internally, using their own organization or employees as a test market, and later selling the service either to public agencies or to other private buyers. For a larger business firm this can be an important way to move into the public service industry. Day care centers, health care plans, employee transportation systems, in-house educational programs, and similar services—originally started to meet purely internal needs—may gradually be expanded to include employees of other firms and eventually offered for sale to the public.

In many such cases the firm has not recognized or has not taken advantage of the innovation. Frequently some outside party sees the potential in one of these internal services and adopts and adapts it for use in the larger setting. On occasion, however, a service developed in the business firm moves out in really striking ways: The Kaiser–Permanente health plan, originally conceived as a way of getting medical care to the workers in the Kaiser shipyards during the war, is an important example.

One of the most interesting features of Control Data Corporation has been its use of its own organization and employees as a market for the design, testing, and start-up development of new forms of services. Those having to do with health improvement and counseling are perhaps best known, but a similar pattern has been followed with temporary help services and is being attempted with commuter transportation, in which the company introduces into the general market a service originally developed in-house. Control Data (which operates more than seventy plant and office locations in the Twin Cities area) began by announcing it would not pay mileage in privately owned cars for travel between company locations, except where specific permission had been granted. This created a demand for group travel, which the company then undertook to supply by organizing an internal transportation service with commuter vans and shuttle buses, both for the home-to-work and interplant trips during the day. From the beginning the explicit aim was ultimately to serve riders beyond Control Data.

Business is reluctant to pay for a service itself, believing this to be appropriately the role either of government or of individuals themselves. Sometimes, however, it will do so. The 3M Company had a congestion and parking problem at its huge main corporate headquarters. In order to defer construction of an expensive parking ramp, the company decided to spend money to reduce the number of vehicles arriving. Its traffic engineer, Robert Owens, "crossed" a school bus with a carpool and produced the commuter van. It was remarkably successful because it offered a combination of better service and lower cost, and was subsequently expanded greatly by 3M and copied by other companies and cities across the country. (3M did not, however, treat it as a business opportunity.)

Business firms have found opportunities to become creative and even entrepreneurial buyers of service, as well as creative and entrepreneurial producers. The best known and most important case has to do with health care. Not more than a decade ago the typical business firm did not see itself as a buyer of health care. In 1970 representatives of Honeywell described the company as simply paying compensation—either cash or benefits. A decade later that attitude had almost completely disappeared: Acutely conscious of the rapidly rising costs of medical and hospital care, business executives had come to see themselves clearly as buyers; and in an effort to become more prudent buyers, they were giving strong support in their companies and communities to the movement toward prepaid health care plans (health maintenance organizations) and to efforts to develop a competitive marketplace for the health care industry. Their support was leading, in turn, to the emergence of new producers, offering new kinds of services (freestanding centers offering minor surgery on an outpatient basis, for example) and stimulating traditional producers to control their costs (as well as to broaden their search for new markets). Furthermore they were influencing the government also to buy health care in a price-conscious manner.

OBSTACLES TO INNOVATION AND WAYS TO OVERCOME THEM

Social needs may exist. Business firms, large and small, may have good ideas about innovative ways in which to meet them. Government may be eager to try these ideas, and willing to finance them. Still, the introduction of new ideas may be frustrated, opposed, and blocked by the individuals and the organizations who consider that meeting social needs has been their job in the past, is their job, and should be their job in the future.

Whether they are public employees, a nonprofit organization, or a business firm working under contract, those threatened by change almost always resist. Jobs, work rules and wage rates will not be yielded easily. Existing public-sector producers are often powerfully supported by the users. Users can intervene to influence the hours at their local library or the refuse collection in their alley ("Will the man please come up to my house to get the can so I do not have to take it out to the curb?") and, understandably, will not be eager to see decisions turned over to the managers of a private firm on contract. Some users, too, place a high value on participation and control, especially where the service affects their personal life or their neighborhood. They do not want professionals making all the decisions for them.

In some circles there is also a fear that business involvement will introduce a profit-maximizing ethic in place of a real service ethic and that business will lobby even more effectively than public employees for increased financing for professional services, even where these are neither effective nor efficient. The current situation in the health care industry lends some support to these concerns.

SOME POSSIBLE RESPONSES

Clearly, the opportunities for new service producers (business or nonprofit) will not be realized unless there is an effective strategy for dealing with this opposition. Probably it is best not attacked frontally, by seeking a political decision to displace the existing producer and substitute a business firm to perform the same service, even if it might do so more effectively and efficiently. General arguments for the superiority of private over public producers are not persuasive. Seeking total system change, no matter how valid the reasons, will probably lead to endless debate. Success is more likely to come through changing the nature of the service, or changing the identity of the buyers or decisionmakers, or changing the methods of payment in such a way as to introduce the incentives for innovation. A constituency for new and different ways of doing things—ways that would utilize the business firm as a major and legitimate producer of service—must be developed. This problem has not yet been successfully addressed by business.

Demonstration projects can encourage similar activity by others in the private sector. Another approach would be to seek arrangements in which the business firm joined forces with the governmental agencies and nonprofit organizations now handling programs in the area of human and social services, under which each organization does what it does best. Existing producers often know the job and how to do it. But they are likely to be less good at management, especially if they have a monopoly position that deprives them of the incentive to learn good management techniques. For the business firm the reverse is often true; it is typically quite good at finance and management, but may know relatively little about the substance of the public-service field. The potential exists for a joint venture, utilizing the strengths of each partner.

Public schools present an intriguing opportunity for a joint venture approach. They remain an almost classic public-service model: a governmentally provided service, financed partly by the state and partly by the local district; produced in local districts by a school administration with strong centralizing tendencies developed over the years; and actually "delivered" in local schools by professional teachers working for the district on salary. These systems have been highly resistant to change. In recent years, however, declining enrollments, an increasingly critical attitude on the part of the public, and a shortage of revenues have developed a willingness to think about basic changes.

Suppose, for example, a school were able to develop a contract relationship with its district, under which it was given funds to carry out the educational objectives of the district but left free to decide at the school site how that would be done—free to decide how many professionals would be hired, how many nonprofessionals, and where supplies and support services would be procured, and free to use teachers, students, and parents (and computers!) in new and creative ways. It would also be free to carry forward from year to year any funds it could find a way to save.

Suppose further that "the school" were conceived of not in conventional ways, as "the principal and staff," but rather as a partnership of professional teachers, required, like a partnership of lawyers or doctors, to set up its own office and administration. With the principal selected and hired by the faculty, the normal pyramid would be inverted and administrative management would operate (as in a law office or medical clinic) from the bottom. Most important, both an incentive and an opportunity would be created to use enough administration but not too much, to differentiate staff, and to substitute technology for labor wherever that improved efficiency, because savings would accrue to the partnership of teachers that is the school.

Where would the school secure the skills to run on an efficient and businesslike basis? (Currently only districts have business managers.) One possible answer would be to staff the school with the management skills required. But another, surely, would be to retain those skills on contract, if a business were available to supply management support for teacher partnerships. (Subsidiary, but equally interesting, questions are whether a department—the science department, say, or the math department—might seek the same kind of contract with the school as the school had with the district; whether a school that succeeded on this model might seek a second contract with the same or with a different school district; and whether a department that became successful as an independent partnership of scientists and professionals might arrange a contract with a second school.)

Similar opportunities exist for "group homes." Today these are typically free-standing institutions, run by local nonprofit organizations, with foundation grants to buy an old house and a van and hire a staff that is interested mainly in program rather than administration. They take purchase-of-service contracts with public agencies for the care and treatment of runaways, disturbed children, battered women, former felons, or recovering alcoholics. Not surprisingly, both the foundations and the public agencies often become concerned about management and operating problems.

Why couldn't a business firm form a "support services corporation" that would organize and produce all of the nonprogram services for these group homes? It would own and maintain the physical properties, and handle (perhaps by subcontract) the food service, bookkeeping, benefits, procurement of supplies, transportation, and personnel administration. Nonprofit organizations, like most other organizations, prefer to handle and control their own operation. But as their funding declines (and as their foundation sponsors press for outright mergers in an effort to secure efficiencies in operation) a joint venture with a private support services corporation might prove an attractive way of maintaining programmatic and organizational independence while achieving economies of scale in administration.

WHAT KIND OF "BUSINESS FIRM"?

Nothing in this points toward any particular kind of private organization to form the joint venture with the existing service producer. The need to have services handled on a businesslike basis, with more careful attention to costs and results, could lead to the expansion of such nonprofit but businesslike institutions as hospitals, which may in fact soon be broadening into the social-services field. For-profit business organizations represent the largest supply of such organizations if they can be induced to venture into the public sector to tackle the challenge of social needs.

What sort of for-profit enterprise will venture into this area and should be encouraged to do so? Much of the discussion about "business" has centered on corporations, particularly large corporations. However, many of the most interesting examples of social entrepreneurship occur among the small (and very small) firms, new and (at least initially) local. ServiceMaster Industries is an important example.

It would be interesting to explore whether the more successful companies most inclined to move toward social service activities do their major business in consumer markets, are suppliers to other producers, or sell to government and whether they are engineering or manufacturing firms, or in a service business. These are important questions for any firm that is considering a venture into the public sector ("Is it right for us?"), and for any group considering a third-party effort to encourage business to take a more active role in the search for a solution to social problems.

A BUSINESSLIKE USE OF CORPORATE PHILANTHROPY

One effort to put business (and corporate business) skills to work on problems of the public sector, which will bear watching, is the demonstration organized in 1983 by General Mills. In the sophistication of the concept, the nature of the objective, and the method of implementation, this breaks new ground.

General Mills, one of the old Minneapolis companies and once the world's largest miller of wheat, has broadened into a consumer products company. Its executives have a long tradition of involvement in the public affairs of the Minneapolis area.

In the early 1970s some of its executives—less than fully satisfied with the traditional "social responsibility" roles of giving money, lending executives, and endorsing worthy causes—began to think about a new form of corporate involvement. Because their real strength was in the organization as an organization, their greatest contribution would be to put that organization to work on socially useful activities. Most important, they decided to operate these activities on a businesslike but zero-profit basis, hoping to recover at some point the capital invested, with the thought that another organization might replicate successful demonstrations on a for-profit basis.

This concept was combined with the experience gained from the company's commercial business. General Mills officials had become skeptical about initiating successful new ventures within a large corporate organization and much preferred to find an individual entrepreneur who had already developed an innovative idea into a successful business. The goal was to combine the corporation's financial and management skills with the entrepreneur's knowledge and drive.

In 1973 the company bought a majority interest in a local apartment-rehabilitation business that was working in an older but essentially sound residential area just south of downtown Minneapolis. Over the next few years General Mills invested about $9 million in that business, learning a great deal about the risks and rewards of social involvement. Stevens Court Properties, as it came to be known, had been doing a good job of renovating apartments, with nonunion labor, and putting them back on the market at prices the occupants (mainly, younger single persons and couples moving into the city) could afford. Soon after the company became involved, union labor protested and threatened a boycott of General Mills' products nationwide. The company yielded and found itself hit from the other side by a protest from the residents against the higher rents required by the higher cost of renovation by union labor. In 1981 the company, having contributed to the improvement of the neighborhood, sold the properties, losing more than originally planned, but still recovering about $8 million of the original investment, which continued to be earmarked as its social responsibility money.

That year General Mills assigned Verne Johnson, former director of strategic planning (and long involved personally in the public affairs of the community), to develop a program for the reinvestment of these funds. In 1982 he proposed several ventures into the public service field, built on the same principles that had gone into the design of the Stevens Court project. Essentially at risk would be the amount that would otherwise have been the growth of giving from the corporate foundation. The first was a venture in central city housing. The second proposal concerned education. The third, and the one selected by General Mills, addresses the growing problem in the care of the elderly. It is an effort to test and demonstrate alternatives to institutionalization. Minnesota has a high proportion of its elderly in nursing homes, especially in expensive "skilled" nursing homes that are frequently debilitating and dehumanizing for the residents.

Private-Private Partnerships
General Mills and the Amherst H. Wilder Foundation, a nonprofit operating foundation in Saint Paul that has run health care, social service, and housing programs since 1906, have formed a jointly owned corporation known as Altcare. The new corporation will stimulate a variety of service groups, including doctors, hospitals, nursing homes, adult day care centers, recreational and social service programs, transportation systems, and housing projects, to join in providing support

for individuals who need help but who want to maintain as independent a life as possible. The idea is to pull together the separate streams of money now financing the care of older individuals (personal resources, family resources, private insurance, and Medicare and Medicaid) under new management to offer a continuum of services and facilities and to accept responsibility for older persons on a prepaid basis. The first such service center has been formed. Known as Senior Health Plan, it will utilize services from Wilder, Saint Paul/Ramsey Medical Center and a Twin Cities area hospital group known as Health Central.

The joint venture involves two corporations. One, Altcare Capital, will finance the development and early operation of these new organizations as a Small Business Investment Corporation; the other, Altcare Development, will work to arrange new systems of service delivery and reimbursement. Changes will be needed in the way the care of the elderly is now paid for and occasionally in the regulations covering the production of service (as, for example, in city zoning restrictions governing the number of unrelated persons who may share a dwelling). General Mills and Wilder will share equally in the basic financing. If the program moves successfully the two organizations will contribute about $5.3 million over a five-year period. Most of the money will go to Altcare Capital. A line executive of General Mills will be chairman of Altcare. A former executive of Wilder was the first chief executive officer. In August 1983 he was replaced by Verne Johnson.

The Objectives and the Strategy

The General Mills venture depends on cooperative arrangements with an organization that knows the public service field and the community, and has credibility in both. It is a private-private partnership. Because most such efforts do not earn profits, it has not been cast as a for-profit enterprise for General Mills. Instead, the objective is to develop and demonstrate new and effective ways of attacking public problems. The hope is that a successful project will challenge other business firms to try similar ventures, as well as to stimulate the government to change the way it buys long-term care. There is a conviction that the way to proceed is by taking the more manageable problems, rather than the more intractable problems, first; and to move gradually toward the tougher cases as experience and resources build up. Finally, there is a disposition in the company not to talk a great deal about what is being tried before it has actually been done, and to keep its nonprofit partner out front.

CONCLUSION

Business firms that venture into the public sector hope to find commercial opportunities there and may very well succeed. But few are likely to take the risk without deeper motivation and a greater sense of purpose. Meeting a particular local need for housing, or the improvement of a school or rehabilitation of a neighborhood, or retraining some of the unemployed may be sufficient for many. But there is a social need that runs even deeper. This is the need to help adapt the public sector to the situation it now confronts.

Governments at all levels are caught between the increased demand for services and the shortage of revenues. They must become more productive—more effective and more efficient. But governments cannot do this simply or quickly. So they do what they can quickly, which is to raise taxes if possible and cut back the level of benefits and services, year by year giving the public less for more.

The public sector needs the stimulus of visible examples of better ways of defining social needs and organizing social action. Models are beginning to emerge from the demonstrations of alternative methods of delivering and paying for public services. Some are being conducted by private nonprofit organizations, some by business firms, some by governments. But the stimulus will have to come from the private sector. The challenge, and the opportunity, for business is to take a stronger lead, to become a competitor to the public sector as well as a partner.

REFERENCE

Ostrom, Elinor and Vincent. 1977. "Public Goods and Public Choices." In *Alternatives for Delivering Public Services*, edited by E.S. Savas. Boulder, Colo.: Westview Press.

✳ *Chapter 5*

Structuring Markets for Public Goods and Services

Jordan J. Baruch

THE NATURE OF PUBLIC GOODS
AND PRIVATE OPPORTUNITIES

Much of this book is concerned with the philosophical and political questions associated with private profit-making firms addressing social needs. Social needs can indeed provide corporations with profitable opportunities, and corporations can satisfy many social needs. Having stipulated those two points, we face two questions: How can a corporation realize the opportunities to make a business out of satisfying social needs? And how can society utilize the corporation's skills in meeting social needs?

Experienced business executives and managers have learned how to satisfy private needs through business activities; at least those who are successful have done so. They have learned to assess consumers' needs and desires, create products and services that meet them, and deliver those products at a price that facilitates purchase and use.

If industry does so well at satisfying private needs at the consumer and industrial level, what is so different about satisfying social or public needs? The answer is like the Maine sailor's attitude toward wind, "A gale and a breeze are the same, except in a gale there's a lot more of it." The experienced corporate manager will recognize that many of the problems in connection with public marketing exist in private marketing as well, except that here too there seems to be a lot more of it.

Let's start by examining the technical difference between public and private markets. Because companies satisfy needs by supplying goods and services, it will be easier to talk about social *goods* and private *goods* than social *needs* and private *needs*. Economists differentiate between private goods and social or public goods largely in terms of the transactions in which they figure. An apple, for example, is considered a private good because the transaction between buyer and seller of the apple is a private transaction. All the benefits of selling the apple accrue to the seller. He will use the proceeds to pay the costs of growing the apple and is free to use any surplus for his own enjoyment. All the benefits of acquiring the apple accrue to the purchaser. Within the limits of reasonableness, no other party has an interest in the transaction, and the apple is thus considered a private good.

Compare the purchase of the apple to the purchase of national defense. The M1 tank, B1 bomber, or MX missile are considered part of our national defense structure. The seller may well be a private organization, but the purchaser is the vaguely defined "public." Indeed, I benefit from my neighbor's purchase of such goods. Were each of us left to our own resources, we would be perfectly willing to let neighbors and friends pay for the totality of our national defense, resting assured that we would be protected through their generosity. This characteristic of a public good—that there is no way of excluding nonpayers from enjoying them—has led to some of the complex social and economic structures developed for defining, procuring, and using such public goods equitably.

Many goods, of course, fall between the purely public and purely private. These are goods whose procurement and use satisfies some private needs and some public needs. Left to our own devices, each of us would procure some level of education, although the amount might differ widely among different segments of society depending on each individual's perception of the benefits to him or his offspring of procuring education and of his resources. In addition to my interest in my own education, however, I am better off if my neighbors are educated; they become more effective citizens and producers. Thus I have an interest both in my own education and in my neighbor's education. To put it differently, some of the benefits of his education are appropriable to me. Generalizing that situation throughout society, we find that each individual has an interest in procuring some education, and society has an interest in the education of each individual. Under such circumstances, economists would say that the individual left to his own devices would "underinvest" in education.

To satisfy the public need for education, the total quantity of education produced and purchased is generally increased by society—that is, the government—paying part of the bill. We have then what economists refer to as a mixed good.

While theory, in pursuit of economic efficiency, has much to say about who should pay for mixed goods or public goods, it has nothing consistent to say about who should produce them. Whether the production should be undertaken by the private sector or the public sector and whether it should be part of a for-profit activity or a not-for-profit activity is and will remain a subject of ideological dispute for many years. It is my belief, and one widely held, however, that private organizations that are forced to survive under intense competition tend to produce better goods and services more efficiently than public organizations that do not face Darwinian pressures for survival.

THE TRANSACTION

One difference between transactions involving private goods and public or mixed goods is identifying the customer. In private selling, the customer is generally easily identified and the successful corporation is sensitive to his needs. Things get much more difficult in a private-public transaction. Let's examine the characteristics of a "public buyer" and a "private seller."

Who is the customer? One problem in a public-private interaction is that we can see the need, we can see the market, but we cannot find the customer. First, there must be an individual or an assemblage of individuals responsible for meeting a set of social needs. An acid test of whether these needs are actually identifiable is that money is being spent to meet them; another is that there is a significant amount of publicity about how much is being spent by *not* meeting them.

Second, we need an identifiable body that controls the expenditure of the resources necessary to meet those needs. If a customer does not have the money, he becomes a hypothetical market rather than a customer.

Third, the customer must have the authority to change the means for meeting those needs and to enforce that decision. He has to be able to say, "Yes, we've been doing it this way; now we're going to do it *this* way," and to make the system behave accordingly.

Last, for the customer to act, he must be convinced that the new means of meeting the social needs represents a benefit to him—political, emotional, economic, or ecumenical benefit—but he must perceive a benefit from the change.

Note that we are talking about a decisionmaker as a customer. In the public sector, the decisionmaker may be many-headed—a group of public employees, a congressional committee, presidential appointees, and even a judge or two. In that complex group, however, there must be one or more people who can persuade the rest to reach a collective decision. Clearly, a major task of the creative entrepreneur selling public goods and services is to identify and convince those influential few.

The creative entrepreneur, the "private seller," must also identify a set of needs that the prospective customer sees as important and develop a credible case that he can deliver the goods and services to satisfy them. Most important, he must convince the prospects that their private goals as well as the public goals will be satisfied.

Finally, the entrepreneur needs patience—in André Gide's words, "Nothing to do with simple waiting . . . more like obstinacy." For the creative entrepreneur will engage in long negotiations, often with minority members of the customer group, who have an implicit veto. The negotiations will require skillful juggling of individual desires and prejudices; but patience, creative approaches, and understanding can indeed prevail.

Examination of some actual cases can give a feel for how the absence of one or more of these factors can prevent a transaction from taking place. First, however, let us look at a technique that has proven useful in analyzing the kind of decisions on which private-public transactions depend.

A TOUCH OF DECISION ANALYSIS

In the field of industrial marketing, Edwin Mansfield and others have done extensive research on the economic factors leading to the diffusion of an innovation within an industry. The capture of an increasing share of the market by a good or service is the result of a series of individual buyers' decisions to procure the innovation in question. Mansfield's analysis demonstrates clearly that the primary determinant of the decision to buy is the perceived economic return from that purchase. This conclusion, of course, comes as no surprise to those engaged in designing, making, and selling producer goods, although it is frequently surprising to them how accurately a quantitative analysis can predict such things as the relation of price and performance to market penetration.

Unfortunately, transactions in public goods to meet social needs are rarely amenable to such precise economic analysis. Despite the growing penchant in the U.S. Office of Management and Budget and its state and local level offshoots for cost-benefit analysis, its accuracy in the policy area remains largely unproven. One reason for its ineffectiveness is that public authorities are often concerned with the distributional effects of services: *who* gets them rather than simply how well they are provided. Public policy and distributional considerations are, however, likely to be embedded in the individual decisionmaker's calculus. Fortunately, tools are available for estimating the decisionmaker's reaction when he is influenced by considerations outside the purely economic sphere. One such tool is an adaptation of the "payoff matrix."

Basically, the payoff matrix is a simple way of answering the question, "What's in it for me if I make the change, considering that the change may or may not be successful?" Figure 5-1 represents such a matrix.

The rows represent the two possible decisions, and the columns show the two outcomes. In each of the cells there is a letter that represents the net personal value to the decisionmaker of that combination of decision and outcome. *A* represents the reward to the decisionmaker (or the cost if *A* is negative) of making a change decision and being successful. *B* represents the value of an unsuccessful change decision. *C* and *D* represent the values of deciding not to change if the change would have been successful or unsuccessful, respectively. Note that the matrix differs from the more elegant deci-

Figure 5-1. The Payoff Matrix.

		The Outcomes	
		Successful	Unsuccessful
The Decisions	Change	*A*	*B*
	Don't Change	*C*	*D*

sion-tree analysis in that it does not include a priori estimates of the probability of the two outcomes. In general, however, assigning those probabilities often is so difficult that we avoid any analysis at all.

We will take the value of each decision to the decisionmaker as being the simple sums along the rows. $A + B$ is thus the value of a decision to change and $C + D$ is the value of a decision not to change. That simple summation works when the probabilities of the outcomes are equal or when they are arbitrarily assumed to be equal because there are no data to indicate otherwise, which in public selling (and public buying) is most often the case. Clearly, in some very simple public transactions, where probabilities can be assigned, the values in each column can be multiplied by those probabilities to yield a more precise analysis.

The matrix assumes that a decisionmaker will act in his own perceived best interest. Note the carefully chosen reference to the quantity in each cell as the "value to the decisionmaker." While the apparent selfishness implicit in that formulation of the decisional calculus may be decried, self-interest can be extended to include altruistic as well as selfish motives—whatever enhances the individual decisionmaker's objective function. It could in practice be a complex mix of altruistic and self-interested motives of which the decisionmaker himself may not be completely conscious. In any event, experience tells us that the decisionmaker is assessing rewards in terms of his personal values, and that for each of the cells in the matrix he is asking, "What's in it for me?" In turn, our ability to use that matrix analysis depends heavily on our ability to get inside the decisionmaker's skin and evaluate his matrix as he would. Indeed so persistent is the question, "What's in it for me?", that the payoff matrix, when applied to the innovation field, has come to be called the WIIFM matrix, from the initials of that question.

Despite the fact that the values to the public decisionmaker are rarely in dollar terms but are usually a mix of incommensurate political, economic, emotional, and social values, we must choose a simple scale that implies that they are, in fact, reduceable. The best we can hope for is a simple ±5 point scale as follows:

-5	0	+5
Very Unfavorable	Neutral	Very Favorable

Clearly, there are many other tools that can be used by the private entrepreneur selling to the public market. We, however, will use the WIIFM matrix in this chapter. A simple tool, however, does not mean the task is simple. Let's use it, nevertheless, to uncover why the job is so difficult.

WHO IS THE CUSTOMER?

In our list of requirements for the successful seller, the first was the ability to identify the public buyer—the customer. Although that problem often exists in private markets, it is far more difficult in the world of public-private transactions. The customer we're looking for must have all four characteristics listed above.

In describing the plight of corporate ventures into the education market, Professor Theodore Levitt, one of the true marketing sages of our time, points out that they failed because, while there is a huge education market, customers are hard to find. How neatly put. In those few words he points out that there are many potential beneficiaries for new technologies in education; there are many educational authorities who agree that the new technologies would fit well in their schools; there are few or none, however, who can simultaneously make the decision and commit the resources necessary to bring about those technological changes. There is a huge market, but there are few customers.

This situation is repeated in many areas where private action can satisfy public needs. For example, consider the shoe industry in this country in recent years. Using highly labor-intensive technologies that were appropriate when labor costs were cheap, the U.S. shoe industry was no longer competitive with foreign manufacturers. Hence unemployment was high and urban areas dependent on the industry deteriorated. The public cost of unemployment is enormous. It has been estimated that each person joining the unemployed rolls costs the government about $20,000 in payments and lost tax revenues, to say nothing of the personal and noneconomic social costs.

There were, however, technologies available that could restore some of the industry's competitive edge. But those technologies required extensive development before they could be adapted to the problems of the shoe manufacturer. The question was, "Who would pay for the development?" Note that the technologies were in the private sector, as were the buyers of the ultimate tools. The purchase of the development, however, was necessary to meet a public need. Since both the public and the manufacturer would benefit, this was a classic case of a mixed good—but a mixed good with no customer, despite the existence of a market. The market was too small and too uncertain to warrant the investment by the supplier firms in the development of the technology, and the shoe industry was too dis-aggregated to have any mechanism for supporting the effort. As a further complication, some of the equipment—such as a computer-controlled mold-maker—would be so expensive that no one company had a sufficient market for its products to justify exclusive purchase and ownership of the equipment.

In this case, the shoe industry and the federal government, work-ing together, literally created a customer where none had existed. The Philadelphia shoe center was created with joint funding to de-velop the new technologies and, where necessary, to own the new equipment and rent it to shoe manufacturers. To the market had been added a customer. Development is proceeding.

Whether in shoe-producing equipment, fire-fighting equipment for a group of towns, or computer services for small communities, the supplier must be able to recognize a market without a customer and must then be able to help create a customer. Dealing with this prob-lem requires great creativity on the part of the supplier! Not all the problems in the public marketplace are soluble, however, at least not without more effort than they are worth to any supplier. Indeed, there are segments of the public market that are intentionally struc-tured to ensure that they can effectively withstand unwanted change.

THE ORGANIZATIONAL FORTRESS

In the list of characteristics for the public buyer, the third deals with the power to enforce a change. In most cases this happens because the served public is simply not knowledgeable enough to make in-formed choices, so society establishes a body of professionals to make choices on its behalf. In order to isolate them from undue out-side influence, they are often given a high degree of autonomy. As the public becomes better informed or as developing technology makes those professionals less necessary, these organizations fre-quently use the autonomy that once functioned well in the public interest to ensure their own continued employment or power posi-tion. Their constituency shifts from the public to their own member-ship. That shift changes their WIIFM matrix, and their autonomy prevents society from shifting the WIIFM matrix back to satisfying the public interest.

Consider, as an example, the effort to sell to a school system cartridge-loaded audiovisual equipment. The equipment had been well designed and proven in industrial use. In a school it makes it possible for the student to set his own pace, to use the equipment at odd times, to review, and so on. When the originally enthusiastic board sought testimony from the school system's audiovisual experts, the results were uniformly negative. Tales of equipment breakage, burned fingers, and too few titles were supplemented by huge estimates of the cost to replace pilfered cartridges. When a casewriter examined a school where the new equipment *had* recently been introduced, she found a high degree of satisfaction on the part of the students and the faculty. However, the audiovisual specialists, once consultants to the faculty on audiovisual matters and professionals on a par with the faculty, were most unhappy. Although their salary was the same and their jobs seemed in no danger, they had been reduced to librarians and custodial supervisors of an equipment inventory. Word had spread and the audiovisual ranks had closed.

The school board considering the adoption in the first town was stymied. They had the authority to make the decision but, in fact, as an elected body they lacked the power to enforce it. The board recognized that any forced override of the veto would result in the testimony becoming a prophecy. The equipment *would* break, cartridges *would* get lost, the project would fail, and the cost to the school board of such a failure after having gotten a "fair warning" would be high.

Let's look at the two WIIFM matrices in Figure 5-2 to see what happened.

The audiovisual specialist's matrix is most peculiar. If the change is implemented and succeeds, he suffers a major status loss, which we have rated -5. If it fails, his wisdom is reinforced, but little other advantage accrues. If, however, the decision is made not to adopt the cartridge system, then independent of the income, he is satisfied to stay where he is. Indeed, the cells conservatively labeled zero may

Figure 5-2. The Cartridge Film Case.

	The School Board				The Audiovisual Specialist	
	Succeed	Fail			Succeed	Fail
Change	+3	-3		Change	-5	+2
Don't Change	-3	0		Don't Change	0	0

have some positive value—but even the conservative rating causes him to testify in favor of no change.

The school board, on the other hand, by the assignment of values shown, is moved to adopt the cartridge system. Again, conservative values have been used in the cells. What brought about the vote not to adopt? To answer that, we must look at the audiovisual specialist's matrix differently. Up to now we have summed rows in order to assess the decision. Now, however, force majeur is threatened in the form of a school board vote; the audiovisual specialist does not have decision power. Unfortunately, because of tenure and its long-established role of guardian, the specialist *can* control the outcome—and now the probabilities we earlier ignored must come into play. Summing the *columns* of the specialist's matrix, we see that failure has a value of +2 and success a value of –5!

Now let's look at the school board's matrix. Even if success and failure were even odds, the decision to change would have a zero value, while not changing would be worth –3. The difference, however, quickly changes as the board recognizes the audiovisual specialist's ability to change the odds. Were the odds of failure 2:1, the two decisions would have equal value (+3 plus –6 versus –3 plus 0), and the board intuitively recognized that the audiovisual specialist's self-fulfilling prophecy powers made the odds worse than that. Clearly, options did exist for the board, such as abolishing the specialist jobs entirely, but such a decision would have required more support from the private supplier in terms of educating the voters than it was worth.

The options for dealing with closed systems range from brute-force use of power to establishment or encouragement of a competitive service organization (e.g. the frequently proposed educational voucher system). In most cases, however, the game is rarely worth the candle to the private business manager. There are other sales that are not so tough. The identification of closed systems and the potential for collaboration between the public sector and the private sector in dealing with them deserves significant further exploration. Such costly monopolies are probably more prevalent in the public sector than in the private sector.

The astute entrepreneur will realize that if a closed system can enforce a "no" vote over what seems to be the public interest, it may be able to enforce a "yes" vote as well. Such is indeed the case, as shown by the following illustration. In recent years authorities have been impressed and disturbed by the rate at which the cost for in-hospital medical care has risen. Justifiably or not, much of the blame has been attributed to the proliferation of advanced medical technology. Often cited as an example of the culprit is the computer-aided tomograph, or CAT scanner. A CAT scanner typically costs on the order of $300,000, and the charge for the typical brain scan is approximately $200-$300, despite the fact that it takes only a few minutes. There is little question that the CAT scanner can uncover brain lesions too small to be uncovered by traditional means and that the early discovery of some of those lesions will lead to extension of some patients' lives. There is also, however, little doubt that the use of the CAT scanner far exceeds reasonable expectations. To understand the system that has led to the explosive use of this technology, we might well look at the WIIFM matrices of the beneficiary (the patient), the user (the doctor), and the buyer (the hospital).

For the patient (who is covered by a third-party payer in more than 85 percent of the cases) the decision is straightforward, as shown in Figure 5-3.

In the case of the doctor's WIIFM matrix, shown in Figure 5-4, the positive side of the decision has been reinforced not only by the ethics of the medical profession but through changes in the way professional liability cases have been decided in recent years. The liability judgments likely to be levied because of the doctor's failure to use the best available technology can be very high. Similarly, the positive reward of being able to treat the patient if something is discovered is high. This is tempered, for the doctor, however, by the knowledge that not everything discovered is treatable. The precise values in the other two cells are unclear, but their direction, caused by reassurance to the patient, is such that they will reinforce the doctor's "Use" decision.

Does the hospital buy one? Let us assume that two hospitals in the area already have CAT scanners, but that they are busy only 20 per-

Figure 5-3. The Patient.

	Something Discovered	Nothing Discovered
Have the Procedure	+5	+3
Don't	-5	0

Figure 5-4. The Doctor.

	Something Discovered	Nothing Discovered
Do the Procedure	+3	+?
Don't	-5	-?

Figure 5-5. The Hospital Administrator.

	Succeed	Fail
Buy	-1	X
Don't	-4	X

cent of the available time. As far as the public is concerned, the "Buy/Don't buy" decision comes down hard on the "Don't buy" side. Will the administrator and board of a third hospital impose the veto that reflects the public interest? Hardly—at least not in this closed system. Let's see why not.

Let's look at the net cost of the two decisions to the administrator (Figure 5-5). Consider first the cost of the "Buy" decision. In most modern hospitals, the depreciation of the CAT scanner appears in the hospital's cost base and hence is reflected in the price negotiated for its service with third-party payers. As a result the cost to the hospital is small. How about the "Don't buy" decision? It is often assumed by those new to the medical field that the role of the hospital is to provide a place for patients to receive treatment and recover from illness. In part that is true, but, in fact, the primary role of the hospital is to provide a theater with infrastructure supports in which a doctor can practice his profession. The physicians are thus both the hospital's primary resource and its primary constituency. If the hospital fails to provide certain support services, better physicians will practice elsewhere and the average level of competence of its physicians (and the reputation of the hospital) will drop. Hospitals must compete for physician affiliation far more than for patient occupancy. Given one, the other will follow. There is little difficulty then in understanding the penalty for making the "Don't buy" decision. "Buy" carries only a modest cost and a bit of nagging conscience, but "Don't buy" has a direct, negative impact on the heart of the hospital—its reputation. What a nice system for the manufacturers of *some* medical equipment. If the equipment serves the physician's needs and if its costs are borne by the third-party payer, there is no negative pressure to keep it from propagating explosively throughout the system. Note that we used the matrix even though the second column has zero probability. We know the CAT scanner works.

Unfortunately for the public, however, if a new piece of equipment is efficacious, but its goal is cost reduction, it will only propagate if it produces no *negative* impact on the doctor or administrator. Cost reductions benefit the third-party payer, but the veto power of the other two, the doctor and hospital, will kill any decision that requires them to bear part of the cost! Any pressure to adopt a system that reflects society's view of appropriate resource allocation will have to come from outside the system itself. For the corporation seeking to meet social needs through marketing in such closed systems, however, the foregoing analysis may serve as a useful tool for product selection, design, marketing strategy, and pricing. In the end, it may also lead to strategies for circumventing power or information monopolies.

This discussion of the power of the potential customer to enforce or block change has been so extended because of its importance in public compared with private sales. While it shows up in forms, such as labor resistance to innovation, in most *private* sales the buyer either is the user or effectively controls the user's behavior. In the world of public sales, this is rarely the case. My example of the closed group and its hidden veto is convenient because it is easy to analyze. In many other cases, however, where multiple decisions are required for change to come about, the players are not so clear.

DEFINING THE SERVICE

Recall that it was said that the buyer is responsible for meeting a set of public needs and that the seller must be able to identify them. A "set of needs" was mentioned rather than a single need because public services can rarely be neatly unbundled. This is illustrated by the following examples.

The Post Office Department (predecessor to the current U.S. Postal Service) was, for many years, charged both with delivering the mail and serving as the federal government's employer of last resort. No leader of a veteran's organization, congressman, or other politician of influence ever had to turn down an urgent plea to "get Uncle Henry a job." The Post Office was always there. With its million-person employment roll and its 100,000 annual turnover, it could always come to the rescue—and postal rates could often be raised. As might be expected, tradeoffs were made. The quality of mail service (with the general public as constituency) was often sacrificed in favor of employment (with the Congress and the employees as the constituencies). The more numerous, but disaggregated, members of the public were less influential in affecting the decisions of the Congress than the postal employees who acted en bloc. Thus, as in the case of the audiovisual specialists, the postal employees could heavily influence the introduction of any new technology. It is little wonder then that technological change until recently proceeded so slowly in the Post Office.

Yet clever entrepreneurs have been able to bring about dramatic changes in our mail service. We mentioned earlier the use of competitive services; in the case of the mails those are proving most effective. Private services, such as Federal Express, despite their cost, compete effectively with small segments of the first-class and fourth-class postal services. Private lock box facilities, open twenty-four hours a day, which also sell stamps and money orders and even deliver mail, compete with still other segments of the Postal Service's business.

Using its political clout, the Postal Service has been able to throw up barriers to these new services, such as prohibiting the use of the recipient's mail box for delivery. Private entrepreneurs have flourished nonetheless. More important, they have forced a new responsiveness in the Postal Service, which now understands that the Congress is not interminably manipulable. Express mail, a resurgence of automatic sorting equipment, and a new general responsiveness in the Post Office bear silent testimony to the effectiveness of competition.

This development, however, raises serious distribution questions for the policymaker. Local mail delivery revenues have long subsidized the higher cost of providing rural mail service. Sound arguments can be made that allowing private suppliers to "skim" the delivery services acts to the disadvantage of the rural recipient of mail. The basic question to be decided by society, of course, is: Who shall pay for the expensive mail-delivery service? That question is still unanswered, but if, under present conditions, the private sector is allowed to expand its skimming behavior, rural or other customers in low-density markets will bear the increased cost. Of course, that need not be so. The Congress can appropriate funds out of the general treasury to subsidize the service previously subsidized by the urban customer. It could even directly tax the private postal suppliers in order to return to the original subsidy situation.

It must be recognized that cross-subsidization and "natural monopoly" are often cited as reasons for resisting change. Rarely, given congressional power to tax, can those excuses stand scrutiny. All too often, because of the politicians' fear of making existing subsidies explicit, rather than allowing them to remain hidden, they remain unchallenged. In fact, such excuses should only be accepted when significant economies of scale can be proven to outweigh the potential benefits of competitive sources of supply. Enough is known about innovation under competition and its absence under monopoly to render such proof exceedingly unlikely!

There is little doubt that successful private purveyors of mail services meet public needs and that, by stimulating efficient responses from public and private competitors, they produce a far greater impact than their own services do directly. Yet not all efforts to design competitive responses to existing providers of services succeed as well.

Consider the following example from a New England city. A new automated sweeper was proposed to the sanitation department. The manufacturer estimated that, for normal roads, the sweeper could do the work of thirty men and be highly cost effective. Since high taxes had long been a problem in the city, the manufacturer expected his cost-saving equipment to be quickly adopted. The director of sanitation, however, was a prominent local political figure whose prestige among the elected politicians was enhanced by the number of patronage jobs that he controlled in the sanitation department. Indeed, the rolls of his department often read like family trees of the local ward and precinct leaders.

When the new equipment was to be tested, the manufacturer found that the test course laid out consisted of three blocks of badly pot-holed roads where the brushes had to be continually interrupted, two blocks of roads with unpaved shoulders where the cleaning attachment had to be deactivated, and a long stretch with no hydrants so that the dust-suppressing water tanks could not be refilled. After what can only be described as a disastrous test, the director of sanitation "regretfully" explained that it would be some time before machines could compete with men in a highly individualized service like street cleaning. No mention was made of the fact that the test course was representative of less than 1 percent of the town roads; nor is it clear even now that the selection of such a nonrepresentative sample was made consciously. The department merely decided to give the new equipment a "tough test" to see if it could stand up and perform as claimed.

CREATIVE NEGOTIATION

There is little doubt that the most important tool of the entrepreneur who wants to sell goods or services in the public arena is that of creative negotiation. Why? Transactions aimed at satisfying public needs, as we have seen, generally involve several players. The purchaser, the user, and the beneficiary of the transaction are usually different individuals or groups. In national defense, for example, the purchase of a new fighter aircraft will, in general, represent a decision made by people who will never pilot it and, indeed, who may be gone from the service by the time the first unit is delivered. The user of the aircraft will be the pilot, while the direct beneficiary may be the ground troops for whom it will provide cover. The ultimate beneficiary, of course, is intended to be the public. Some such spread may also exist in transactions involving private goods. For example, rarely is the executive purchaser of a new machine tool its user. Despite this apparent similarity, however, the divergence of interests among the buyer, the user, and the beneficiary in the public market is much more dramatic. It is, therefore, far more important to eliminate or neutralize that divergence if a transaction in the public market is to take place.

We saw, in the case of cartridge films, how the WIIFM matrix of the decisionmaker was distorted by the power of the specialist. For major social innovations, however, there are many more than two players and many more kinds of interaction. The private sector organization seeking profitably to meet social needs had, therefore, best recognize that it is, in fact, initiating social change—and social change never comes easy. Yet to increase the effectiveness and efficiency of providing for society's needs, social change is often necessary. Consider a purely hypothetical example.

At the present time, there exists a set of technologies capable of revamping the way transfer payments, such as welfare, Social Security, and even tax refunds, are administered. Most of us are already familiar with the automatic teller, that almost ubiquitous robot that accepts our plastic card, identifies us through a secret code, permits us to draw real money from its store and then debits it from our accounts. Indeed, soon many of those machines will have been interconnected so that we can perform the same feats away from home.

Let us now suppose that entrepreneurs in the public and private sector decide to institute a technologically facilitated social change. Plastic cards with the necessary coding will be issued to everyone who makes or receives payments to or from any governmental entity. Everyone will receive a card at a local point where he will be photographed or fingerprinted to ensure that one and only one card is issued per person. Simultaneously, an account will be created and attached to that card, with the secret code that the recipient enters on his first transaction. From then on, all governmental payments will be made to that account and, similarly, governmental withdrawals, such as tax payments, may also be authorized at the time of filing. It is not necessary to develop the system in further detail to see that it would probably involve some controls. The amount that could be withdrawn in cash on any day might be limited (as banks now do). It would be possible to insist that some portion of any deposit could not be withdrawn but only spent at a food store equipped with a special terminal. Problems such as stolen checks and the burden on the Postal Service would be eliminated.

What would happen if such a system were adopted? Consider some of the affected constituencies. The Postal Service would lose a significant source of revenue. The American Civil Liberties Union would object to the potential for misuse of the unique account number. Welfare recipients would object to the loss of freedom of choice in using *their* funds. Banks, equipment suppliers, and card manufacturers would welcome the new markets for their wares. The general public would benefit from reduced costs of certain transactions and a more effective system. What an opportunity for creative negotiation! Before the reader—of whatever persuasion—pounces on me for even suggesting such a scheme, let me assure you that it appears here for illustrative purposes only.

The role of the creative negotiator in selling any new service, product, or system can be broken down into a set of tasks:

1. Identify the various constituencies, but beware of assumptions of homogeneity.
2. Evaluate the power of each constituency and the extent of their potential loss (a good use for the WIIFM matrix).
3. Starting with the most powerful constituency, redesign the system in a way that changes their WIIFM matrices from no to yes.

The three tasks of the creative negotiator are interrelated. Identification of a constituency permits evaluation of its potential loss and hence modification of the rules—resulting in new losses, gains, and even new constituencies. (Consider the reaction of the Lottery Commission to the foregoing suggestion!) Of course, there is no book that lists the constituencies (positive or negative) of any proposed system. Nor is there a table of their losses and gains. It is generally through the probing effects of negotiation that they are uncovered, and this is a long and arduous task. The rewards to society and to the successful entrepreneur can, however, be great. The creative part, of course, consists of conceiving potential solutions during the negotiation process, tendering them, evaluating reactions, and redesigning the system or service. Negotiation thus often becomes a part of defining the service.

Let's look briefly at this system. Identifying the interested constituencies is clearly the most important task. Whoever coined the expression "Divide and conquer" understood the advantage of disaggregating opponent constituencies. Without making social judgments, let's see how appropriate identification opens the way to system design strategies. Why will welfare recipients object to the restriction of their spending choices in exchange for a system that protects them from theft? Let us suppose that some subset wants cash in order to gamble. The thought of hitting the lottery is an enticing one. If that subset seemed important, a creative entrepreneur might suggest a playerless lottery. Each day thousands of randomly selected accounts would receive deposits over and above their normal level, paid for by small reductions in the overall payments and from other savings. The creative negotiator could balance the political consequences of additions to some accounts against the cost to many others.

Or consider the proposal to have corporations run our schools. We fool ourselves when we categorize the service provided by the school only as "education." Our public schools provide multiple services. They impart vocational and life skills, they keep young people out of the labor market, they babysit for busy parents, they pass on the traditions of a society, they stimulate young minds to explore and take risks, and more. Which of those functions does the corporation want to take on? How will we measure its performance? What is it worth? Who will carry out the functions for which the corporation does not contract? Defining a work statement, performance measures, and appropriate payment is a creative task. Indeed, without such creative activity the transaction would not materialize.

Another illustration of defining services through negotiation arose when the private sector offered to take on the task of the National Technical Information Service. The NTIS is charged with disseminating technical information created by or for the government and creating and maintaining an easily accessible archive of this information. Both functions are currently paid for by those who use the dissemination system, while federal funds supplement the creation of new information products. During negotiations, several companies wanted to contract only for the dissemination task which, they correctly claimed, they could do more cheaply than the NTIS. Unfortunately, that would have left the Congress to support the archival function from the general coffers or to charge prohibitively high fees for access to the archives. The Congress believed that the public was better served by taxing those who used the dissemination service to cover the archiving costs. Since none of the companies would contract to undertake both archival and dissemination services, they could not satisfy the Congress, and the negotiations failed.

What set of services do our schools, garbage collectors, prisons, and fire departments provide? How can the creative negotiating process unravel them, quantify them, and lead to better systems for carrying them out? The rewards for private business would no doubt often be worth the effort.

WHERE DO WE GO FROM HERE?

Although many of the illustrations used in this chapter referred to information management tasks, it is important for entrepreneurs to recognize that private opportunities for providing mixed or public goods exist in many other areas. For example, some of the reactions to the problem of U.S. industries that are no longer competitive arise from a recognition that those industries supply mixed goods. A domestic steel industry is important to national defense, as are domestic automobile and heavy chemical producers, and oil refineries. Government policymakers struggle with subsidy schemes, tax measures, and research programs without recognizing explicitly that they are paying a price for national preparedness. It is probably time now for creative joint public-private negotiating teams to unravel and price the public and private needs those industries meet and, in the interest of efficiency, to develop arrangements that facilitate their separation.

A look at the government section in the phone book shows many agencies that are providing public goods and services that might more effectively and efficiently be supplied by private industry. Unfortunately, many of them, such as the Agricultural Marketing Service and the Forest Service (looking just under the Department of Agriculture), benefit only a small portion of the population directly—although all of us indirectly—and yet are paid for by our tax funds.

Under those conditions, there is little incentive for efficiency. As long as narrow constituencies consider themselves well served, the functions will continue as government-supplied services. In my experience with the National Bureau of Standards, and the experience of others in trash collection, however, once a publicly supplied service is converted to a fee-for-service basis, the users demand efficiency and the system can quickly convert to a private supplier.

The fact is that *every* good and service now created by government is a fair candidate for private suppliers. Why? If we believe (as do most economists) that a monopoly will always operate less efficiently than competitive firms, except in valid cases of "natural monopoly," where there are significant economies of scale, we must recognize that any service provided by a government monopoly can be more efficiently provided by private competitive firms.

Those of us who are convinced of the effectiveness and efficiency of the private profit-making organizations, tempered by the heat of competition and honed by the abrasive of forced reexamination, are convinced that there is a greater role for them in meeting public needs. Similarly, those of us who are convinced of the need for publicly responsible bodies to monitor the quality, quantity, and cost of social goods and services, are equally convinced that there is a role for them in meeting public needs. Clearly, full responsibility for more effective provision of public services cannot be laid at the private sector's door. Federal, state, and local governments are responsible for developing creative, knowledgeable individuals who are effective customers for the private sector and who can negotiate to produce congruence between the goals of the individual and those of the organization. This calls for internal incentives.

Redefining the role of government away from producing social goods and services to monitoring the supply system in the public interest is a difficult task that will be with us for a long time. Entrepreneurs—creative entrepreneurs—exist in public and private sectors. I hope this chapter helps them join forces to bring about needed social changes.

 *Chapter 6*

The Realities of Intervention
in Alienated Cultures:
A Jamaican Case Study

Orlando Patterson

What are the basic social needs in Third World societies? What role
can the private sector play in meeting them? Can private enterprise
ever hope to make a profit in such endeavors? And is there a role for
foreign firms in meeting these needs?

The first question has been implicitly answered by the recent
major shift of emphasis in development thinking toward the so-called
basic human needs approach. But there is no easy response to the
other questions, largely because there is so little concrete experience
to rely on. In this chapter I draw on my own experiences in a typical
Third World society, Jamaica, during the 1970s, when there was an
unusually strong commitment to the basic needs approach. Based on
this experience I will illustrate the formidable sociocultural problems
associated with efforts to alleviate basic human needs among the
poorest elements of Third World populations. Some of these problems probably have their counterpart among the poorest groups in
developed societies as well. These problems may be summarized as a
profound sociocultural mismatch and conflict of interest between
the needy and those who attempt to help them. The mismatch is
acute where public-sector personnel are the change agents and even
greater when local entrepreneurs with a free-enterprise orientation
are involved. Foreign entrepreneurs, with far less awareness of local
realities, are faced with problems of sociocultural accommodation
that would seem to be even more formidable.

THE BASIC SOCIAL NEEDS APPROACH

An unusual consensus has emerged in recent years among specialists in economic development. They agree that a policy aimed directly and immediately at the problems of absolute poverty is essential, not only as a painfully obvious end in itself, but as a means of achieving overall growth in national product. Until the early 1970s the conventional wisdom among development specialists was that Third World countries should concentrate on increasing their national product before attempting to tackle directly the problems of distribution and social welfare. The pie was simply too small to provide resources for redistribution or for social programs, such as health, education, and housing, without diverting capital needed for growth. Planners were urged to concentrate on capital accumulation to increase the aggregate rate of growth. With increased wealth would come either a trickling down of the benefits of development or the opportunity for meaningful redistribution of the increased national wealth.

The early 1970s saw a drastic departure from this approach for many reasons. The most obvious was the clear failure of earlier strategies to make a dent in the welfare of the mass of people in Third World countries, even when there were impressive rates of aggregate growth. Unemployment remained high, absolute poverty continued at unacceptable levels, and in most cases relative poverty increased rather than decreased with increased growth rates (World Bank 1980; Chenery 1979; Young, Bussink, and Hasan 1980).[1] Recognition of the failure of the traditional approach, reflected, for example, in a UN report in 1971 (United Nations 1971a), was accompanied by a new conception of basic needs in the development process (International Labor Office 1977; Hicks 1979; Streeten 1979).[2] While structural economic change was still recognized as necessary, it came to be realized that improvement of the human condition of the poorest segments of the population would contribute both directly and indirectly to accelerated socioeconomic development. A healthy, better educated population with a sense of belonging to the larger society would be more productive.

Specifically, the basic needs approach called for a direct assault on problems of nutrition (especially childhood nutrition), education (especially primary literacy and day-care facilities, as well as preschool education for the poor), family planning, inadequate health facilities, and unsatisfactory housing and care for the elderly.

This emphasis entailed new programs and implementation techniques. First, there was a shift in focus from the aggregate population to targeted population groups; the neediest groups are now clearly specified, and the success of any given program is measured in terms of its impact on the welfare of those groups. Second, and closely related, was the partial shift of focus from the nation and regions to specified communities—for example, a particular village or cluster of villages, rather than the rural poor in general, a particular slum community rather than all urban slums, and so on.

Thus the basic needs strategy saw the emergence of the community development approach, and at the same time attention to improvement of the individual.[3] Several elements underlie this strategy. One is that people are more motivated to engage in new productive activities if their immediate neighbors are also involved and if they see tangible benefits for themselves and their community. Second is self-help: the best way to improve the conditions of the poor is to help them to help themselves. Third, local resources that go untapped in traditional macroeconomic planning can now be mobilized for the common good. In particular the so-called informal economy, which provides the livelihood for most of the Third World poor, can now be integrated into formal planning and change. Finally, broader community participation is seen as a key factor in any successful program (Cohen and Uphoff 1980; Goldsmith and Blustain 1980; Patterson 1977).

Where the United Nations with its strong input from Third World planners led the way, the World Bank eventually followed. The World Bank had been the major institutional purveyor of the traditional macroeconomic aggregative approach to planning, so its recent acceptance of the basic needs approach means that the latter has achieved, if not dominance, at least respectability in development circles. To be sure, the World Bank still insists on traditional growth strategies and sees what it calls the "human development" approach as complementary. It also cautions that such programs must be carefully chosen and efficiently carried out. Human resource development "is an end as well as a means of economic progress," which integrates the traditional approach with a concern for "increasing employment, meeting basic needs, reducing inequalities in income and wealth and raising the productivity of the poor" (World Bank 1980: 32, 96–97).

One important aspect of a basic needs approach is the complementarity and mutual reinforcement of the different components: "Health, nutrition, education and fertility all affect each other." Thus, to be effective, these programs must be applied simultaneously within a given community.

In an excellent recent paper, the social anthropologist M. G. Smith (1983) has identified other important factors that must be kept in mind in designing a basic needs program. The first is that social needs are culturally determined and require social legitimacy gained through participation of the intended beneficiaries within the community. Second, the basic needs approach focuses on individuals and families and should not be confused with the provision of social goods such as prisons, courts, and other institutions designed to meet the needs of society at large. And, third, the needs of individuals within the community "vary with categories and conditions of persons," such as sex, age, and state of employment.

FAILURES OF ECONOMIC "DEVELOPMENT" IN JAMAICA

When the People's National Party won office in 1972, it inherited a socioeconomic situation that was almost a textbook case of the failures of traditional neoclassical strategies of development. During the 1960s the conservative Jamaica Labor Party did all the "right things" in terms of conventional neoclassical doctrine. It planned carefully, invested heavily in an import-substitution light industry program, and encouraged foreign investment in its booming bauxite and tourist industries. It also achieved the predicted success, measured in neoclassical terms; the rate of growth of gross domestic product in real terms between independence (1962) and 1970 was 4–5 percent per annum. With a rate of population growth of 1.6 percent per annum, per capita output grew at the rate of almost 3 percent. Investment between 1961 and 1967 was a striking 20 percent of gross domestic expenditure, rising to 31 percent in 1969. This was financed by external loans and local savings, which together amounted to a savings rate of 17 percent during the decade (World Bank 1971; Girvan 1971; Jefferson 1972).

In spite of this impressive record of growth there was clear evidence of serious social and economic problems. On the economic front the largest failing was in agriculture, where a rise of only 1.5 percent a year in the value of agricultural output from 1963 to 1969 meant a decline in real output, increased dependence on foreign sources of basic foods, and rising rural unemployment and underemployment (Beckford 1972). A second major problem was overall unemployment. Including the estimated effects of underemployment, the national figure for unemployment was put at between 25 percent and 33.3 percent of the available labor force.

Most serious of all was the island's third major problem: massive overurbanization. The urban population, which was 22.4 percent in 1943, was projected to rise to over 50 percent by the early eighties; 63 percent of this urban population lived in the Kingston metropolitan area in 1970, the vast majority in low-income areas varying from dilapidated working class districts to horrendous shanty towns and squatter settlements. A 1973 study estimated that over 70 percent of the Kingston population lived in households with an annual income below the poverty level (Patterson 1973). The problems were not confined to the poor, because the entire urban population faced the consequences of the deplorable social situation in terms of an unusually high crime rate, exacerbated by the alienation and desperation bred of poverty.

When the People's National Party gained office in 1972, it immediately recognized this urban pathology as one of its major problems. As with previous governments, the standard reaction was to institute slum-clearance strategies. However, by the early 1970s it was already well established, through experience in both the Third World and advanced societies, that such schemes could only benefit a tiny, favored minority of the most prosperous workers who, despite government subsidies, are the only ones able to qualify financially for new housing. Except for this favored few, slum clearance merely worsens the already dismal condition of the abject poor by destroying and dispersing the communities on which they have relied for mutual aid. Since the number of new units rarely exceeds 10 percent of units destroyed to make way for them, rents that the poorest pay rise so that they are less able to compete for the available units. Because the rents in the newer units occupied by the better off are already subsidized by taxes, the poorest are indirectly forced to support the more fortunate. Finally, slum-clearance schemes, by concentrating on housing structures, neglect the other major problems of the slums, stemming from lack of participation in the money economy.

The slum-clearance approach was too ingrained, however, to be easily abandoned for alternate strategies. When I was appointed special advisor to the prime minister in 1972, I lobbied strongly for a different approach to the problems of the urban slums and, with the prime minister's support, the Cabinet agreed to an urban upgrading program on a pilot basis in one area of the south central slum. The first step in this program in 1974-75 was a socioeconomic survey of the proposed project area, whose results are described in the next section.

The Project Area

Southside is one of Kingston's worst slum areas, notorious throughout the city for its political violence, gang warfare, and high incidence of crime. The project area occupied a total of 71 acres. 5,732 persons lived in the area. It was an extremely youthful population; the mean age was 20 years—18 years for men, 22 for women. Over 30 percent were under 10 years of age, 45 percent under 15, and 50 percent under 20. Over 70 percent of all households lived in single-room dwellings, while 19 percent lived in two-room apartments. A detailed physical survey of 402 of the 521 residential buildings in the area revealed that 169 were in need of minor repairs, 79 required moderate repairs, 23 major repairs, and 131 were irredeemable and should be demolished. Further, over one-third of all households lived in dwellings with 4 or more persons per room. Forty-three percent of households were headed by women, 44 percent by men.

A depressing feature of the households was the fact that the larger the household, the smaller the mean individual and household income. The combined mean weekly income was only $16.22 (Ja.) Approximately 78 percent of all individuals lived in households where the head was unemployed. Only 40 percent of the population over 15 were employed and only 30 percent were working for wages. Over 33.3 percent of the unemployed were seeking a job, and 12 percent had taken themselves out of the labor market. In the age group 20-24 the unemployment rate was 49 percent. A growing proportion of persons became self-employed with increasing age. Of the surveyed population, males had an average of 7 years of schooling, females 8 years. Years of schooling only slightly influenced a person's employment status, and more so for men than for women. Apart from the overall record of depressed social conditions, a striking general finding indicated by the foregoing figures was that women bore the major burden of poverty. Since they also were the major providers for children growing up in the area, it is evident that the situation was even worse for the children than the already dismal figures suggest.

THE PROGRAM

The pilot program in south central Kingston began in the summer of 1975 and continued until the end of 1980. The major goals of the program for the area were

1. To improve the physical condition of life
2. To improve the general level of social welfare
3. To improve the sense of community in the area through self-help and local leadership
4. To generate special employment and training

5. To construct and demonstrate a model urban strategy for other low-income areas in Kingston and other urban areas of Jamaica

The pilot program was based on three main strategies: rehabilitation of the physical environment, provision of essential services, and reduction of unemployment.

Rehabilitation of the Physical Environment. The first objective of the program was upgrading the entire environment, rehabilitation and new construction being simply one component. The plan was to proceed in three phases. Phase 1 would involve the rehabilitation of buildings requiring minor and moderate repairs, along with the improvement of environmental sanitation services in the entire area. Phase 2 would begin with the construction of a transition center where residents of buildings requiring major repairs could reside while their dwellings were being repaired. Phase 3 involved the construction of a second transition center, which together with the first would house residents of buildings that had to be demolished. New low-cost units would then be built in situ to compensate for the demolished units.

It must be emphasized that it was not the intention to build new units that were in any way comparable to those in a typical housing scheme. Households of four or five persons would still be found in a single room, if that was all they could afford, but the room would be secure and invulnerable to intruders, with walls and ceilings not likely to fall on children and floors that were not breeding grounds for roaches, rats, scorpions, and other pests.

It was agreed by all concerned that this was the fairest way to proceed, entailing the minimum of displacement while improving the living conditions of the maximum number of persons. It was easy to demonstrate from the income data that, even with subsidies of over 50 percent, fewer than 10 percent of the residents of the area could afford a unit in a traditional housing scheme. The survey also made it clear that the new approach was favored by the overwhelming majority of the residents of the area.

Provision of Essential Services. The project was to provide certain services for the residents of the area (many of them indicated by the socioeconomic survey). These were located in the Community Service Center that housed the administrative offices of the project and an information and service center, that provided, for example, small loans to operate in the informal sector, legal aid, poor relief, and assistance in procuring help from the public sector; a demonstration day care center, with satellite centers throughout the area; a basic school for up to 100 children; adult literacy classes; a community council of elected block leaders to ensure community participation in the project's activities; a public library; and cultural activities, such as dance and drama classes and a brass band for the area's youth.

In addition, the project also established a separate day care center in another part of the area, and jointly sponsored a health clinic with the Ministry of Health, and a geriatric center. The clinic, located behind the community center, was designed to provide comprehensive clinical service, dental care, nutritional and public health service, and family planning and health care demonstration services.

Reducing Unemployment. The third major objective of the project was to improve the desperate unemployment situation in the area. The rehabilitation and the construction activities of the project provided some immediate relief, but this was temporary. Increased employment was to be generated in three ways. First, small capital loans of up to $50 were made to hawkers and others in the informal sector. Second, were more substantial loans of up to $5,000 to local self-employed persons, such as cabinetmakers, tailors, and shop owners, who, with improved and expanded facilities and operations, would create additional jobs in the area.

The third and most ambitious effort involved the rehabilitation of an old garage as a small industries complex. The plan was to introduce between seven and twelve small firms, chosen on the basis of the available pool of underutilized skilled labor in the area and a feasibility study of the market. These firms included an aluminum casting works, a radiator repair shop, a mechanic shop, and a pottery operation. The Small Industries Development Division of the Jamaica Industrial Development Corporation agreed to provide technical and managerial help, and financial support was to be secured from the many government agencies already established for this purpose.

Financial Support for the Project

How was the program to be funded? When I originally developed the program, I won approval from the prime minister, in whose constituency it was physically located, and the minister of Local Government, in whose ministry the program was administratively placed, for two basic principles. First, the program would be self-supporting, as far as possible. Second, every effort would be made to engage the private sector where there were business opportunities.

Four types of funding would be involved. First, direct government grants would fund the administrative costs of the project, as well as the community services. No tangible return was expected on these grants. In keeping with the basic needs philosophy, we considered such expenditures an investment in human resources, with returns of a public, long-term nature.

The second type of funding involved government aid for self-supporting activities. This aid took the form of loans to build the small industries complex (to be repaid on a noninterest basis from the rent paid by the small enterprises participating in the scheme); loans to small businesses and individuals working in the informal sector, from government agencies that already existed for this purpose; and start-up matching funds, provided by government in the form of mortgages to landlords participating in the rehabilitation scheme. It was anticipated that some landlords would refuse to participate, in which case government would compulsorily rehabilitate and charge the costs to them. Another group of landlords, while willing to participate, were shown by the survey to be clearly incompetent to manage the rehabilitation loans. In such cases the project officer would rehabilitate with government funds and arrange for repayment from the incompetent landlords (mainly old and infirm people living, often in no better condition than their tenants, on their own premises). Finally, government funds would be used as direct subsidies for the transition centers until they were converted to permanent dwellings.

In the third and major source of the rehabilitation funds, we saw the greatest opportunities for the private sector—second mortgages to all landlord-owners in the area. A technical survey had specified required repairs and the costs, and mortgage funds were to be used only for the repairs approved by the project's housing officer.

Finally, the landlord, of course, was free to make additional repairs with funds of his or her own. There were several incentives to the landlord. The most important was that it was impossible to obtain second mortgages, or any kind of home-improvement loans, through the normal commercial channels for any dwelling in the slum areas of Kingston. Mortgage houses and banks considered the risks too great, at any rate of interest. A second incentive was the fact that the entire area was to be developed, increasing the locational value of the premises. At the same time the landlord had certain obligations. The objective of the program was to assist all the residents of the area, most of whom were tenants. The landlord would therefore have to negotiate with the project's housing officer the appropriate rent after the rehabilitation. This, as one would expect, proved to be the most sensitive and difficult part of the program. In some cases we anticipated no increase in rent, since the rent was already too high. The landlord would then have to bear the full cost of the rehabilitation. In other cases a modest increase in rent would be allowed, depending on the tenants' ability to pay. The survey, incidentally, had indicated that almost all the residents were willing to pay as much as 20 percent more rent if the improvements promised were actually undertaken. Thus we expected that the costs of rehabilitation would be borne jointly by landlords and tenants.

Landlords are, of course, businessmen. Their role in the program constituted one important business opportunity to meet a basic need. But the principal involvement of the private sector was providing mortgage funds. With the project providing continuous monitoring and with funds guaranteed by the government, I expected that risks would be sufficiently reduced so that private sector financial institutions would no longer avoid the slums as bad risks.

In the summer of 1975 I approached several private institutions with my plan and received favorable responses from two of them. The chairman of the association of building societies (as Jamaican mortgage houses are called) put the idea to his board, which accepted it in principle. One of the building societies agreed to participate on an experimental basis, and the managing director, after negotiating with me and his board, made an informal commitment of one half million dollars for the program. This was to have been confirmed later at a meeting of his full board.

The second source of private funding was the Workers Loan and Savings Bank. As its name implies, this bank was originally established to make funds available to working-class borrowers. However, it was run on strict commercial lines and over the years had become simply another commercial bank, no more involved with workers than its counterparts. With a democratic socialist government in power, the bank's departure from its original objective had become something of an embarrassment to its board. My proposal was therefore quickly embraced as a risk-free way of helping the poor. The bank immediately voted to set aside an initial one-quarter million dollars of its mortgage funds for the project, one-half of which was put on stream immediately.

The bank also offered to play another vital role in the project. The experience of the Ministry of Housing indicated that the risk of bad loans was much greater when government agencies directly disbursed and collected mortgage money. It was decided therefore that the disbursement of the rehabilitation loans and the collection of repayments would be on a strict commercial basis. The project's housing officers would determine the upgrading to be done, its cost, and the qualified landlords. They would also monitor the work. Other than that, the whole transaction would be a private matter between the landlord and the bank.

The bank, however, agreed not to apply the same stringent rules it used when dealing with other clients. It would, for example, run a credit check but drop a few of its usual criteria concerning levels and sources of income; it would not demand standard fire insurance, since no insurance company was prepared to insure against fire in the Kingston slums; and it would omit its customary 1 percent development fee.

Thus, between the Workers Bank and the Building Society, we thought we had secured a sufficient commitment of funds from the private sector to finance the first two phases of the rehabilitation. By the end of the summer of 1976 all seemed set for an innovative joint venture between government and the private sector in meeting some of the most pressing basic needs of the country's urban area. Developments, alas, proved otherwise.

Evaluation of the Program

Three years later the Urban Upgrading Program had achieved only the first of its three major objectives: the delivery of improved social services. It failed in the generation of employment, and the rehabilitation of the environment.

Provision of Social Services. All the social services offered were eagerly accepted by the residents of the area. Within a couple of years 45 infants were being provided care in the two day care units; over 60 preschool children were being educated in the basic school; there were 1,002 registered users of the library, 238 of them adults, 764 children. The clinic was completed in the third year and was immediately swamped with patients who would otherwise have gone unattended. The geriatric center was also enormously successful. Not only had it rescued several of its original members from premature death, but as the first such center in the island, possibly in the entire Caribbean, it was a model for other projects.

By the middle of the second year of operation, the project social workers had a caseload of 45 persons from the area to whom they offered a variety of services. These included help to persons who were destitute, terminally ill, or in need of emergency loans or help in getting around red tape.

Perhaps the project's greatest success was the reduction of crime, especially crimes of violence. In the early 1970s the area was notorious for its youth-gang warfare and frequent political maimings and killings. The project staff was able to negotiate a formal truce between the warring gangs. It became possible for outsiders to enter the area without risking their lives. In 1977 President Carter's wife visited the area with security precautions no more than usual for other areas.

The few disappointments arose in areas where construction costs and standards set by the health coordinator conflicted with the other objectives of the program. In particular the yard-type day care centers to be run by local women never materialized for this reason.

Increasing Employment Opportunities.   The small-scale industrial project failed to get off the ground for three main reasons. First, the elaborate and expensive cluster of agencies that had long existed for this purpose proved to be fraudulent. Though staffed with "experts" with economics or business degrees, these agencies had not a single person capable of setting up a small business in a low-income area. The project staff eventually abandoned all efforts to mobilize existing agencies and instead secured funds to hire its own specialist in small-scale industrial development. No one on the island could be found with the right combination of managerial, community, organizing, and entrepreneurial skills. An attempt was made to attract former businessmen with a proven record of running successful businesses. Such persons, however, were either afraid of entering the area or felt that the salaries were much too low for such demanding and "hazardous" work.

Rehabilitation.   The failure of the rehabilitation program can be attributed to three kinds of problems—funding, political, and administrative. Analysis of this failure suggests several basic dilemmas that all programs aimed at meeting the basic needs of the poorest residents of urban areas face.

In relation to funding, our experience with the building societies was a great disappointment. After the initial expression of enthusiasm, the society assigned to assist the project lost interest. Instead of candidly stating so, their representatives delayed matters by demanding one concession after another from the government to guarantee the security of their investment, until they finally backed off after a demand for a new parliamentary law could not be met. Later I learned that the real reason for the loss of interest in the project was hostility to the government on the part of many of the board members of the building society, which intensified after the elections of 1976—a violent, partisan event—in which the "socialists" won by a landslide. In this climate, almost no board of directors was prepared to become involved with a government that they regarded as socialist and hostile to their basic political and economic interests.

As it turned out, however, availability of funding was not the major problem. The Workers Bank continued to lend support. Furthermore, the Agency for International Development (AID) made a positive evaluation of the project and in record time negotiated a $15 million (U.S.) load for a national program. After three years, however, not even a fraction of the original small credit of $125,000 offered by the Workers Bank had been used, and less than 10 yards had been rehabilitated.

To some extent the failure was due to the resistance of landlords. There were three classes of landlords: those living in their own residences in the area, those who lived in the area but on other premises, and absentee landlords. The first group, owner-occupants, was by far the largest. They were the ones most willing to cooperate. Their dwellings, however, were the ones with the least problems. Many in the second group were not interested, but substantial numbers did express an interest, although they had reservations concerning the rate of interest charged on the loans and the rents that could be recovered afterwards. The absentees presented the biggest problem. Many of them could not be found and, when they were, they were rarely interested. Unfortunately, the dwellings of these landlords were the ones in greatest disrepair.

Other problems also got in the way. Of these the biggest turned out to be the extraordinary difficulty of working out a negotiating procedure for the disbursement of the home-improvement loans. Although every one involved was mindful of the need to simplify the loan procedure, nonetheless safeguards were necessary. No matter how hard it tried, the bank simply could not go beyond a certain point in relaxing its credit-worthiness criteria or the formality of the negotiating procedure. Nor, for that matter, could the project officer in charge of this aspect of the program, an experienced accountant with a strong commitment to the ideals of the program. After months of fine pruning, he and his staff handed me a procedure manual for processing loan applications that left me flabbergasted. Processing each loan required seventeen forms and a sequence of twenty-seven activities. Yet on reflection, it became clear to me that circumstances made these complicated procedures necessary.

The urban poor in Jamaica (like similar groups in other parts of the world) live by their wits in a highly informal and unforgiving economic environment. This is a world in which trust simply does not exist. In the urban slums the trusting person, as even every preschooler will cheerfully acknowledge, is fair game for the "scuffler," who will seize any opportunity to get something for nothing. Thus we were faced with the first of several dilemmas that all programs aimed at meeting the basic needs of the poorest members of urban areas must come to terms with.

Dilemma 1: The Delivery Crisis of the Underclass. The poorer the urban population to which one wishes to deliver "self-help" services, the greater the security risks in delivering such services. The greater the security risks in delivering self-help services, the greater will be the administrative costs. Thus self-help services cannot be implemented in a cost-effective manner, for if necessary administrative precautions are not taken, the program will suffer losses through fraud or theft, but if adequate precautions are taken the services will cost too much.

Dilemma 2: Disinterest of the Ablest. Very often, landlords who were the best able to participate, those with alternative sources of income, were precisely the persons who felt they were doing well on their own and thus had little interest in the development of the area. Either they were absentee owners or interested in getting out. Thus many of them offered their properties for sale to the project, while declining the offer of a rehabilitation loan. My experience with these landlords led me to formulate this second dilemma of basic needs programs, namely: Those most able to participate are usually those least interested in participating.

Dilemma 3: Inability of the Neediest to Participate. The tenants of the least cooperative landlords were usually the most desperately poor, with no skills, and essentially unemployable. Any direct assistance to them had to take the form of direct grants and subsidies. We could only involve them in the self-help rehabilitative scheme indirectly through their landlords and by helping the better-off in the area to increase employment opportunities, which would trickle down to the poorest. A third dilemma of the basic needs approach was suggested by this experience, the counterpart of the second dilemma stated above, namely: Those most in need of basic needs are those least able to participate directly in a basic needs program.

The political problems of the project came from two sources: outside the area, from the Ministry of Housing, and from within the area. From the very start the minister of Housing and his staff opposed the project despite, or perhaps because of, their strong political commitment to the poor. First, helping the poor meant bringing their standard of living up to the level of the middle classes as fast as possible. If this was impractical for the great mass of the poor, it should at least be held out as an ideal. The minister felt that any program, no matter how equitable as compared to alternatives, that assumed that the poor would continue to live in slums, was an insult to the masses. To others he frequently referred to the program as "Patterson's African yard concept."

Second, the traditional slum clearance and housing scheme approach offered political pay-offs that few politicians could resist. There was patronage: not only massive building contracts to business supporters, but substantial employment for local supporters during the construction period. The negative political response of the many displaced people is diffused by their dispersion elsewhere in the city. At the same time the new housing estate provides a golden opportunity to carefully select and concentrate the party faithful. It also allows for closer monitoring of voting behavior. These advantages more than compensate for the negative votes of the disgruntled few who remain in the area. And a housing estate is also a more politically exploitable asset than a basic needs community development program.

Furthermore the counterpart to the absence of trust among the very poor is their strong propensity to gamble. Since life offers so little, people are strongly motivated to place their hope on the lucky break. It is the poorest who engage most in lotteries, as every astute politician knows. A housing scheme has the same effect on the fortunes and legitimacy of politicians as a lottery winner from the poor has on the legitimacy and success of the lottery. Community-based basic needs programs have no such dramatic political pay-offs. Indeed their very emphasis on equity, on smaller marginal gains for all as opposed to major gains for a lucky few, gives them little political appeal. And politics, especially in Third World countries, not to mention democratic ones, is above all drama.

Dilemma 4 is thus the following: *The Fundamental Incongruity Between the Most Effective Means of Meeting the Needs of the Poor and the Most Effective Means of Maintaining Power on the Part of their Political Leaders.* A depressing corollary is that the more democratic the polity the greater the incongruity.

Another political problem springs from one important segment of the population of low-income areas. The members of the community most willing and able to cooperate with the program were also those who were better off. Many of them simply wanted to leave the area. However, a few did want to stay and upgrade the community. These were the natural local leaders, whom we eagerly sought out and who just as eagerly sought us out. Invariably they turned out to be persons already well locked into the political structure, who saw the program as a way to expand their influence in the political process. But the local leadership had a different conception of basic needs than the developers of the program. Their aspirations were more those of the petit bourgeois. Their commitment to living in the area was conditioned on implicit understanding that their leadership would be rewarded with a petit bourgeois life-style. This translated into a housing scheme. Thus there was pressure to shift the focus of the program away from environmental rehabilitation to the construction of new dwellings from the very people within the area on whom we were relying most for support in achieving our objectives.

Dilemma 5 is, hence: *Incompatability of Goals of Local Leaders and of Basic Needs Programs.* Those residents best able to provide leadership in achieving the objectives of the basic needs program and outwardly most committed to it are the very persons likely to emphasize goals which, if they do not undermine the program's objectives, at least entail a drastic shift in its priorities. (Indeed the local leadership, ably assisted by a key member of the project staff, successfully lobbied the prime minister for a housing scheme behind my back.)

In addition we faced three important administrative problems. The first was the difficulty of getting qualified personnel to work in the area. The second was the failure to find a first-rate director of the project. The post demanded two different kinds of skills: the ability to manage a multimillion-dollar budget and coordinate many different activities, on the one hand, and the social skills of a first-rate community organizer, on the other hand. These rarely go together. The problem was compounded by the unrealistic pay scales imposed by the government's personnel office and the incredible difficulty of redefining job descriptions. The result was a high turnover for this most important position.

The third major administrative problem was what can only be described as the subversive role of technical experts from the private sector. What we learned, quite simply, was that if you hire an architect-planner you get an architect-planner, no matter what his rhetoric, and that architect-planners, like other people, are inclined to do what they do best—in their case, to design and supervise the construction of buildings (United Nations 1973).[4]

After the architect-planner joined the team, he rapidly broadened the scope of his activities. Many activities that should have been per-

formed by the director or one of his officers were soon being performed by the architect-planner, at exorbitant professional fees.
Second, the construction aspects of the program quickly ran ahead
of other developments, which should have preceded them. The building to house the small-scale industrial program, for example, was well
under way before the director of the project knew what industries
were going to occupy it. Third, there were large cost overruns.

But the worst was yet to come. The planner quickly sensed the
political pressures favoring a housing scheme. At about that time the
downturn in the economy, reflected most dramatically in a slump in
the private construction industry, meant that the architect-planner
had a largely unemployed staff. He therefore had a powerful personal
interest in mobilizing support for a housing scheme, justifying it on
the grounds that his technical survey showed that 131 units in the
area were unfit for habitation and had to be demolished. To replace
them, he designed a housing scheme of 168 two-bedroom units. His
argument was utterly spurious. With the most generous subsidy
these units were estimated to cost (in 1977 Jamaican dollars) $8,700
each, resulting in a monthly mortgage payment of approximately
$41.00. Assuming that 25 percent of total household income went
to housing, this meant that only families earning a total household
income of $164.00 per month could afford these highly subsidized
units. The socioeconomic survey of the area had shown, however,
that only 3 percent of all households earned this income. This, incidentally, is typical of the proportion of low-income families capable
of participating in slum-clearance housing projects and is one of the
main reasons for preferring an urban upgrading program.

Dilemma 6. So it was that I learned the last of the many dilemmas
that beset any basic needs programs: *Incompatability Between Goals
of Technical Experts and of Basic Needs Programs.* All such programs
are caught on the horns of a technical dilemma. If they proceed without technical expertise they are likely to fail, because certain minimum levels of engineering, architectural, and other skills are required
in even the most basic programs. But the moment professionals are
employed, they tend to reorient programs toward traditional modern-
sector thinking with its physical and capital-intensive biases. In so
doing they will be abetted by interest groups, within and outside the
target area, best served by traditional modernization programs. The
propensity for subversion is further enhanced by the inexperience
and political weakness of many of those who direct projects. Thus
unless basic needs programs are directed by forceful, well-paid directors with strong political backing the original objectives will almost
certainly be subverted by the needed technical experts.[5]

CONCLUSION: BUSINESS OPPORTUNITIES
AND BASIC NEEDS

This case study of urban upgrading in Kingston illustrates the enormous difficulties that any attempts to meet the basic needs of the poorest sectors of a Third World society are likely to encounter. Even with a democratic socialist government strongly committed to a basic needs approach, the political and administrative leadership faces complex cultural and economic problems. There is a profound lack of congruence between the political and social interests of leadership and those whose problems it attempts to alleviate.

We have demonstrated, also, how serious the problem of what M.G. Smith (1983) calls "social recognition and legitimacy" can be. It was assumed by a socialist minister of Housing elected from an urban slum community that the most urgent housing need of his constituents was a modern two-bedroom unit. My surveys, and anthropological field studies by others, indicate that this level of housing improvement is not given high priority by the urban poor for the very sensible reason that they consider it wildly unrealistic and attempts to achieve it highly disruptive. Yet the minister of Housing, like those before and after him with quite different ideological persuasions, persisted in the pursuit of wasteful and inequitable slum-clearance policies.

This case study also points to the even greater problems of the private business sector in meeting those needs. Business cannot make a profit where potential customers have little or no income. Over a third of the poor in most Third World countries are in this situation. It could be argued that businessmen can deliver services more efficiently than government and that profits potentially exist in the difference between the cost to government and the lower cost to business. Experience leads us to doubt this. Where it was successful—in the mobilization and delivery of existing government services—the project staff was actually highly efficient, and it is highly unlikely that a private concern could have performed such tasks more efficiently. Nor, and this is the crucial issue, is it likely the private sector would be interested in such ventures. The work involved is complex, often risky, and entails a great deal of human interaction that cannot be assigned a cost. And the returns are often difficult, if not impossible, to quantify in monetary terms, and therefore cannot be rewarded objectively.

However, it was my hope that there was a role for business in the financing services required by the project. I still think that the private sector can participate in financing such projects, but only if it is understood that the funding must be guaranteed by government and supplemented by public subsidies. Our experience shows that there is no way in which a private firm alone can take on such risks. The security and administrative costs are simply too great.

Perhaps the most important point is that most of the problems faced by the Kingston project were not peculiar to the public sector. Exactly the same problems would have been faced by private businessmen—the difficulty of securing competent staff, the status problem of working in the slums, the political pressures to subvert project goals from both inside and outside the area, and, most critical of all, the fact that those most in need are the weakest source of political support for the goals of the program.

The private sector may have a role in one area: the construction of buildings. Governments, especially Third World governments, should have as little as possible to do with the provision of new housing stock. Building should be left entirely to the private sector, and government should intervene only through the provision of subsidies, where necessary. Housing, like education, employment, and other needs, means different things to different people. To the extent that the private sector can construct modern housing more efficiently than the public sector, it can participate in providing basic needs. But whose needs? We have seen that even with enormous subsidies new housing is well beyond the reach of all but 5 percent or less of the residents of poor areas. The question then is not simply, what are basic needs and who can best provide them, but basic needs of what kind and for whom?

When I speak of businessmen, I mean indigenous businessmen. It should be obvious that multinational firms face the same problems (but greatly magnified) as do indigenous firms. The most important factors accounting for the success or failure of basic needs programs are political will or commitment and acumen. Next is a thorough understanding of the cultural patterns, needs, anxieties, hostilities, and vulnerabilities specific to the populations targeted for improvement. One cannot expect representatives of foreign firms to have these skills and knowledge.

In fact, it is precisely the things that multinationals are good at providing that a basic needs program is least likely to need, namely, capital-intensive technologies and products. For example, over the years that I served as a consultant for the Jamaican government, I examined numerous so-called breakthroughs in low-cost housing for the poor in the Third World. In every case the "breakthrough" turned out to be impractical, expensive, culturally inappropriate, and, even if transferable, would become a heavy drain on already desperately low foreign exchange reserves.

I do not oppose the participation of multinational firms in the development of Third World countries. With adequate knowledge, supervision, sensitivity to local needs on the part of foreign personnel, flexibility for the host country to renegotiate contracts, and other safeguards cited by the United Nations (United Nations 1978: chs. 4 and 5), it is possible for multinational firms to participate constructively in the development of the more advanced sectors of a Third World economy. But the difficulties faced by the public sector and indigenous private entrepreneurs in meeting basic needs in one area in Jamaica suggest that initiatives undertaken by a foreign firm would require knowledge and sensitivities that would be extraordinary, even for the most experienced and adroit companies.

NOTES TO CHAPTER 6

1. For a thorough documentation of these failures see the World Bank, *World Development Report, 1980* (New York: Oxford University Press, 1980). For a general analysis from the neoclassical viewpoint see Hollis Chenery, *Structural Change and Development Policy* (New York: Oxford University Press, 1979) ch. 11. And for a good case study of a country that experienced high growth without significant change in its level of poverty, see Kevin Young, William Bussink, and Parvez Hasan, *Malaysia: Growth and Equity in a Multiracial Society* (Baltimore: Johns Hopkins University Press, 1980), especially pp. 3-9, and chs. 4, 5, and 8.

2. Attempts by econometricians to measure the effects of basic needs programs on national income are conceptually spurious, methodologically flawed, and socially irrelevant, especially when such needs are interpreted from the demand side. For a typical collection of such approaches see Everett M. Kassalow, ed., *The Role of Social Security in Economic Development* (Washington, D.C.: U.S. Department of Health, Education and Welfare, 1968). For a good short critique see Benjamin Higgins, "Planning Allocations for Social Development," *International Social Development Review* 3: 53-54. As Higgins bluntly puts it, "as long as the sole guide to benefits is social demand, the whole question of costs becomes irrelevant. The implication of the social demand approach is that the demand must be met, whatever the costs. And when one comes right down to it, there is no reason to suppose that the electorate, or the general public, is less able to judge costs than it is to judge benefits." (p. 54)

3. The track record of community development programs is hardly an impressive one. For a good critical appraisal of this approach and the essential prerequisites for success see, United Nations, *Popular Participation in Development: Emerging Trends in Community Development*, ST/SOA/106, 1971. For an assessment of the policy issues for both urban squatter settlements and rural areas see *International Social Development Review* 2, 1970.

4. On this problem see, United Nations, *Self-help Practices in Housing: Selected Case Studies*, ST/ECA/183, 1973. An important finding of these five case studies from around the world was that "some level of technical know-how must be present before self-help housing or mutual aid housing can be given a better than average chance for success" (p. iv).

5. For an excellent comparative study of several similar programs that strongly emphasizes the role of power and the problems of internal subversion see Gayl D. Ness, "Planning and Implementation: Paradoxes in Rural Development," in *The Sociology of Economic Development*, edited by Ness (New York: Harper & Row, 1970) pp. 577–593.

REFERENCES

Beckford, George. 1972. *Persistent Poverty: Underdevelopment in Plantation Economies of the Third World.* New York: Oxford University Press.

Chenery, Hollis. 1979. *Structural Change and Development Policy.* New York: Oxford University Press.

Cohen, John M., and Norman T. Uphoff. 1980. "Participation's Place in Rural Development—Seeking Clarity through Specificity." In *World Development Report* (World Bank) 8: 213–235.

Girvan, Norman. 1971. *Foreign Capital and Economic Development in Jamaica.* Kingston, Jamaica: Institute of Social and Economic Research.

Goldsmith, Arthur A., and Harvey S. Blustain. 1980. *Local Organization and Participation in Integrated Rural Development in Jamaica.* Ithaca, N.Y.: Rural Development Committee, Center for International Studies, Cornell University.

Hicks, Norman. 1979. "Growth versus Basic Needs: Is There a Trade-off?" *World Development Report* (World Bank) 7: 985–995.

Higgins, Benjamin. 1971. "Planning Allocations for Social Development." *International Social Development Review* (United Nations) 3.

International Labor Office. 1977. World Employment Conference. *Meeting Basic Needs: Strategies for Eradicating Mass Poverty and Unemployment.* Geneva: International Labor Office.

Jefferson, Owen. 1972. *The Post-War Economic Development of Jamaica.* Kingston, Jamaica: Institute of Social and Economic Research.

Kassalow, Everett M., ed. 1968. *The Role of Social Security In Economic Development.* Washington, D.C.: U.S. Department of Health, Education and Welfare.

Ness, Gayl D. 1970. "Planning and Implementation: Paradoxes in Rural Development." In *The Sociology of Economic Development*, edited by Gayl D. Ness. New York: Harper & Row.

Patterson, Orlando. 1973. *The Condition of the Low Income Population in the Kingston Metropolitan Area.* Kingston, Jamaica: Office of the Prime Minister.

_____. 1977. *Community Councils in Jamaica: A Critical Appraisal.* Kingston, Jamaica: Office of the Prime Minister. Restricted circulation,

Smith, M.G. 1983. "The Study of Needs and Provisions for Social Assistance." Unpublished. Department of Anthropology, Yale University, New Haven, Conn.

Streeten, Paul. 1979. "Basic Needs: Premises and Promises." *Journal of Policy Modelling* 2: 136–146.

United Nations. 1970. *International Social Development Review* 2.

_____. 1971a. *International Social Development Review* 3.

_____. 1971b. *Popular Participation in Development: Emerging Trends in Community Development.* ST/SOA/106.

_____. 1973. *Self-Help Practices in Housing: Selected Case Studies.* ST/ECA/183.

_____. Economic and Social Council. 1978. *Transnational Corporations in World Development: A Re-Examination.* New York: UN Economic and Social Council.

World Bank. 1971. *Current Economic Position and Prospects of Jamaica,* vol. 1.

_____. 1980. *World Development Report, 1980.* New York: Oxford University Press.

Young, Kevin, William Bussink, and Parvez Hasan. 1980. *Malaysia: Growth and Equity in a Multiracial Society.* Baltimore: Johns Hopkins University Press.

✳ *Chapter 7*

Privatization of Public Services:
Recent Experience

Marc Bendick, Jr.

One way that government can mobilize the business sector to contribute to the solution of social problems is by creating a market that provides a profit opportunity. That market can be created in direct and explicit ways, as when agencies "contract out" public service delivery to private firms. Or government may enhance market demand at one remove, as when it issues vouchers to citizens for purchasing goods and services from firms. Or, still more indirectly, government can create opportunity not by increasing market demand but by subsidizing production costs on the supply side of the market.

Such actions will advance the public welfare only if the markets thus created function efficiently—indeed, more efficiently than the "nonmarket" alternative of government agencies themselves directly producing a good or service. In particular, four aspects of market efficiency are important to examine:

- In producing the goods or services to meet the social need, do the private sector's production processes and input costs allow it to generate output at lower total cost than could the public sector?

- Are the administrative costs incurred by government to mobilize and control the private sector less than the cost savings from more efficient production?

- Is the supply side of the market sufficiently responsive that private firms enter markets rapidly and smoothly?

• Are purchasers (be they individual citizens or public agencies) sufficiently rational and careful, and the quality of the goods or service sufficiently definable and measurable, that effective, informed consumer sovereignty can be exercised?

Empirical evidence can be mustered to answer each of these questions, and that is the purpose of this chapter. It reviews the recent experience of federal, state, and local governments in utilizing each of the three approaches mentioned above for creating profitable market opportunities in social problem solving: contracting out, consumer vouchers, and production cost subsidies. It evaluates the evidence concerning the extent to which efficiency and effectiveness are achieved.

This empirical evidence generally provides an affirmative answer to the four efficiency questions in cases where the good or service demanded is relatively straightforward, simple, and technological. However, the evidence justifies only a very cautious and skeptical stance when the public need being addressed is complex, long-run, and sociological. Thus, the chapter will conclude that various approaches to the mobilization of the private business sector in meeting social needs have a generally promising record in meeting many clearly definable social needs. However, past experience does not suggest that such approaches offer large advances in meeting some of society's most complex and persistent social problems.

CONTRACTING OUT FOR PUBLIC SERVICES

Contracting out for public services is defined as provision of goods or services through issuance of contracts to private firms instead of having those goods or services produced directly by a government agency. The contractual arrangement itself may involve a single agreement with a simple structure (e.g., a fixed-price or cost-plus-fixed-fee contract). Or the arrangement might be embellished by such features as cost-sharing penalties, financial bonuses for good performance, or multiple competitive contracts within one jurisdiction.

Contracting out is in widespread use, although in few types of services and in only rare localities has it become the dominant mode of service delivery. Table 7-1 reports the finding of a 1973 survey of 2,248 municipalities concerning their use of contracting out. Twenty-six services—those listed in the table—were reported to be contracted out in at least 1 percent of reporting municipalities. Four services—refuse collection, street lighting, electricity supply, and engineering services—were reported to be contracted out by some-

Table 7-1. Municipal Services Most Frequently Provided by Contracting Out, 1973.

Services	Proportion of Municipalities Reporting Contracting Out for this Service (percent)
Refuse collection	13.7
Street lighting	12.5
Electricity supply	10.4
Engineering services	10.4
Legal services	7.7
Ambulance services	6.7
Solid waste disposal	5.7
Utility billing	4.4
Animal control	4.1
Planning	3.7
Water supply	3.4
Mapping	3.0
Water distribution	2.7
Payroll	2.7
Street construction and maintenance	2.5
Hospitals	2.4
Cemeteries	2.0
Special transportation services	2.0
Microfilm services	1.8
Nursing services	1.5
Property assessment	1.4
Public relations	1.2
Industrial development	1.1
Bridge construction and maintenance	1.1
Treasury functions	1.0
51 other services	a

a. Less than 1 percent.

Source: Adapted from Kirlin, Ries, and Sonenblum (1977: 116-119). Data are from a survey of 2,248 municipalities throughout the United States conducted in 1973 by the International City Management Association.

what more than 10 percent of municipalities. If these responses are taken as representative of those of all municipalities in the United States with a population of 2,500 or more, then an average of about 420 municipalities across the country contract out for a typical service.[1]

A few examples (Hatry 1982: 22-40) will indicate the variety of uses of this approach:

- Scottsdale, Arizona (population 95,000) and several adjacent cities have for more than twenty-five years purchased their fire protection services from Rural/Metro Fire Department, Inc., a for-profit firm. The company asserts that it provides these services at approximately half the per capita cost in cities of comparable size, and independent evaluations have confirmed these claims (Ahlbrandt 1973, 1974, 1977).

- In 1979, the city of Poughkeepsie, New York contracted out for operation of its wastewater treatment plant. The contract incorporates both performance standards for effluent characteristics and annual compensation adjustments based on price changes for such inputs as labor, industrial chemicals, electrical power, and fuel oil. The city has estimated its annual cost savings from the arrangement at $250,000 or approximately 25 percent (Breuer and Fitzpatrick 1980).[2]

- In Minneapolis, Minnesota two intertwined service areas were established for solid waste collection. One has been assigned to a city department, while the other has been allocated to a private firm. The service costs for the two areas are similar, but this appears to be true only because of determined efforts by city officials to bring their own costs down to the level of the private firm.

- Eight of California's thirty-nine county hospitals are operated by private firms under contract from counties. A study by the School of Public Health of the University of California at Los Angeles concluded that no cost savings were realized and no significant quality changes were observed but that significant revenue gains were achieved from improved accounting and billing procedures (Shonick and Roemer 1982).

- La Mirada, California, a suburb of Los Angeles with a population of more than 40,000, operates its entire city government with fewer than sixty employees. More than sixty service contracts with private, for-profit firms provide such services as data processing, traffic signal maintenance, park maintenance, refuse collection, recreation, social service counseling, employment development, legal counseling, and probation services.

These examples indicate that cost minimization is the primary objective and primary effect in many cases of contracting out. The potential for cost savings arises from several sources: competition among firms that may produce pressure for efficiency not present in a monopolistic municipal department; a relative freedom in private firms from hindrance by red tape and other procedural constraints; and the ability of private firms to hire, fire, compensate, and therefore motivate and utilize workers with greater flexibility than can government departments constrained both by civil service rules and strong unions. On the other hand, the costs of providing a service could be increased in a contracting out arrangement if the administrative costs of letting and monitoring contracts are large; if private bidders are so few that little competitive pressure exists; if union, civil service, or other constraints prevent the city from reducing its own labor force and costs when the private sector is hired to take over some of its former duties; or if corruption arises in the contracting process (Hanrahan 1977).

The empirical evidence on cost savings is also illustrated in the examples presented above. Where careful, controlled evaluations have been undertaken, verifiable cost savings were observed, if not universally, more often than not. For example, two careful studies have been performed of contracting out in solid waste collection, one examining the experienced 315 local communities nationwide and one examining the experience of 130 communities in Connecticut. Both studies identified a cost savings of about 25 percent, although one study concluded that this result held only for communities of over 50,000 in population (Kemper and Quigley 1976; Savas 1977, 1979).[3] Similarly, a 1981 survey of California local governments conducted by the California Tax Foundation found that 69 percent of local governments surveyed felt that contracting out led to reduced costs, while only 17 percent felt that it led to increased costs. The results of this survey are summarized in Table 7-2.[4]

Interestingly, the findings in Table 7-2 suggest that improved service, as well as reduced costs, frequently resulted from contracting out. In that survey, 76 percent of local governments agreed that contracting out led to the availability of more specialized equipment or personnel, and 41 percent reported improved service, as opposed to 18 percent who reported poorer service and 33 percent who complained about contractor unreliability. Thus for the sorts of services listed in Table 7-1, the preponderance of experience has been favorable in terms of cost, quality, or both.

The sorts of service listed in Table 7-1, while important to the efficient operation of government and the well-being of citizens, are predominantly straightforward, immediate, measurable, monitorable, and technical in nature: refuse collection, data processing, street paving, and so forth. As one moves from such examples to (relatively rare) examples of contracting out for more complex, undefinable, long-range, and "subjective" services, the record of successful experience thins.

The largest single experience with contracting out for the delivery of complex services comes from the experiments with educational performance contracting during the early 1970s (Peterson 1981: 14-16; Carpenter and Hall 1982; Gramlich and Koshel 1975). The

Table 7-2.   Opinions of California Local Governments Concerning the
Advantages, Disadvantages, and Problems of Contracting Out, 1981.

Characteristic of Contracting Out	Proportion of Local Governments Agreeing (percent)
Advantages	
Reduced cost of labor, material, or overhead	69
Improved services	41
Ease in measuring or monitoring contractor performances	24
Ease in adjusting program size	53
Avoidance of start-up costs	57
Availability of special equipment and skilled personnel	76
Other	18
Disadvantages	
Increased costs	17
Poorer service	18
Difficulty in monitoring contract	38
Displacement of employees	11
Unreliability of contractor	33
Other	2
Problems Encountered	
Legislature constraints	25
Unions	21
Public resistance	15
Other	9

Source: Adapted from a 1981 survey of eighty-seven local government agencies
(cities, counties, school districts, and special districts) in California conducted
by the California Tax Foundation and reported in Hatry (1982: 25).

concept of educational performance contracting is to delegate classroom instruction in regular elementary and secondary schools to
private firms, allowing these firms freedom in instructional methods.
Typically, firms implemented a variety of proprietary learning systems, computerized instruction, incentive payments to students, and
other techniques not in widespread use in public schools. Then these
firms were paid not on the basis of costs but rather on the basis of
students' educational gains as measured by standardized achievement
tests.

More than 100 local school districts experimented briefly with
educational performance contracts using their own funds, and the
federal government financed a more carefully controlled study in
twenty localities. The experience was universally disappointing. In
the carefully controlled studies, test scores for subjects on which
firms were paid showed only modest gains for experimental students
compared to controls (e.g., 0.04 of a year's achievement in language
or mathematics in one year, approximately 7 percent). At the same
time, scores fell in other subjects for which firms were not paid. Consistent with these results, none of the participating school districts

chose to renew their contracts; the private firms lost money; and relations between contractors and school boards often closed on an acrimonious note.

A second pool of experience with contracting out of complex services is to be found in "purchase of service" arrangements for social services (Fisk, Kiesling, and Muller 1978: 52–59; Gutowsky 1979; Gurin 1980). Some use is made of for-profit firms for such services as child day care, homemaker or chore assistance services, and vocational rehabilitation, and a few studies have indicated some cost savings from this use. For example, officials in Hennepin County, Minnesota have estimated that they could cut their cost per service-hour for homemaker services about 25 percent by use of competitive bids among for-profit firms, without loss of quality. However, the majority of contracts for social services are with nonprofit firms; rigorous competitive bidding is avoided; and the objective, in most cases, for contracting out is not efficiency in the sense of cost reduction. Indeed, "too efficient" or "too low cost" private operations are viewed with suspicion by some social service agencies on the grounds that service quality is being compromised in some way not easily captured in contract specifications or performance monitoring. The typical motivation for contracting out for social services is to obtain the services of a delivery system with particular characteristics needed for program effectiveness (e.g., one acceptable to clients or with established roots in the community). The goal is to thus obtain unique services that, social service officials typically believe, cannot be obtained from the for-profit sector.

CONSUMER VOUCHER ARRANGEMENTS

In the context of public programs, a voucher can be defined as a transfer of income to a citizen to enhance that person's ability to purchase a specified type of good or service. Vouchers can thus be distinguished from general redistributions of income with no attempt to restrict the use of the funds (for example, cash public assistance payments). The rationale for vouchers in place of cash payments is that the taxpayers making a donation have a right to restrict their donation to uses that the donors believe is meeting a social need. The rationale for vouchers in place of direct government provision of the good or service is, first, that recipients should be allowed some consumer choice over goods and services and, second, that goods can be obtained at a lower cost than by direct public provision.

The voucher approach has become increasingly popular over the past twenty years. Over the decade 1965 to 1975, for example, the proportion of total federal social welfare expenditures accounted for by voucher programs rose from 3 percent to 20 percent (Lynn 1977: 88). Over that period, food stamps—vouchers that can be used only for the purchase of food—replaced distribution of surplus commodity food from government warehouses; Medicaid and Medicare— voucherlike reimbursements for health care expenditures—largely replaced (or were used to finance) health care provided by publicly run clinics at county hospitals; the purchase of home heating fuel has become covered in part by special energy assistance payments; and working parents came to be eligible for voucherlike refunds (via tax credits) for the purchase of day care for young children, rather than simply having publicly funded day care centers available to them. Other examples of voucher approaches include transportation vouchers and even cultural vouchers for museums, zoos, libraries, and the performing arts (Bridge 1977; Kirby 1981).

One recent demonstration program can be used to illustrate both the strengths and weaknesses of this approach. The Experimental Housing Allowance Program (EHAP) was a $160 million social experiment (complete with control group) conducted with 30,000 households in twelve cities over the early and middle 1970s. The system studied involved housing allowances—vouchers intended to increase housing consumption by low-income families. Empirical questions addressed in the EHAP study included: How did housing allowance vouchers compare with direct government provision of housing services (e.g., public housing projects) in terms of cost and housing quality? Are low-income families capable of efficient shopping in private housing markets? And would private landlords and builders prove responsive to the market demand created by vouchers and increase the supply of decent-quality housing without inflating rents (Bendick 1982; Struyk and Bendick 1981; Bradbury and Downs 1981; Frieden 1980)?

On questions of cost, quality, and market responsiveness, the findings from EHAP were highly encouraging. For example, the mean annual cost of providing a standard-quality two-bedroom housing unit in Pittsburgh in 1974 was estimated to be $4,155 per year if that unit was provided through government-operated public housing. The identical unit purchased with a housing allowance from the private housing market cost $1,869 annually, only 45 percent as much (Bendick 1982:14; Struyk and Bendick 1981:286). Low-income families generally proved to be efficient shoppers, obtaining units at good value for their money and needing little assistance in searching for or negotiating for units. Housing suppliers proved generally cooperative, and no supply bottlenecks or price inflation were evident. Public control of the program could be maintained for relatively modest administrative cost (between 10 and 20 percent of total program costs). In the majority of housing markets at least, vouchers for purchase of housing services from the private market seem better for everyone—taxpayers, recipients, and housing suppliers—than public construction and operation of low-income housing.

While housing vouchers thus seem a success in terms of cost, efficiency, and straightforward aspects of housing quality, the story becomes more complex, and the lessons more cautionary, when considering other objectives of the voucher program. In particular, we must remember that the reason housing vouchers rather than cash were selected as the instrument for transferring purchasing power to the poor was that taxpayers wished the additional purchasing power to be used only to improve their housing. In practice, the recipients of housing allowances elected primarily to substitute their vouchers for money they would otherwise have spent on rent and thus, in effect, to spend the newly acquired resources on goods other than housing. Only about 20 percent or less of their increased purchasing power went toward increased rental expenditures (Bendick 1982: 4–6; Struyk and Bendick 1981: 142). This substitution was perfectly legal. The uses that the recipients made of their new purchasing power were even the sorts of things of which taxpayer-donors might well approve (additional food, clothing, health care, and dental care, for example). Nevertheless, the elaborate process of calling the transferred purchasing power a *housing* voucher and believing that was how it was spent was largely a charade.

The general principle this example illustrates is that provision of a social good through the voucher mechanism is a double-edged sword. On the one hand, harnessing the efficiency of private markets may well lead to better quality goods and services, lower costs, or both. On the other hand, the more consumer control that is placed in the hands of voucher recipients, the less taxpayers are able to impose their own preferences that only a specific social need be met. In particular, it is a vain hope that simply labeling a transfer payment (calling it a housing voucher or a food stamp) will lead to complex behavioral change on the part of recipients such as alteration of their consumption patterns. Use of the private market through vouchers may thus be efficient in narrow terms but ineffective in more ambitious terms.

Other voucher experiences parallel the pattern illustrated with housing vouchers:

- The Special Supplemental Food Program for Women, Infants, and Children (WIC) is a federal program that provides a limited set of highly nutritious foods to pregnant women, nursing mothers, infants, and young children. The food may be distributed in several alternative ways, including direct distribution by a government health clinic or issuance of vouchers by the clinics for clients to purchase items at regular supermarkets. Compared to the cost of government itself running its own warehousing and food distribution system, the voucher approach saves 10 percent of total program costs. On the other hand, the voucher system provides less control of the foods clients receive and is less successful in generating contact between poor families and the health care system and opportunities for nutrition education, which are major objectives of the program (Bendick 1978: Bendick et al. 1976: 147-149, ch. 3 and 4).

- The National Health Service Corps is a federal program placing young physicians on salary in medically underserved locales. Comparisons of cost per medical encounter and annual physician productivity suggest that health care delivery via this mode is less efficient than is delivery by private practice physicians working on a fee-for-service basis in the private market, by perhaps as much as 40 percent. On the other hand, Service Corps physicians provide health services in locales unable to attract private market physicians, even with Medicaid (voucher) financing. Hence, the private market failed to be sufficiently responsive for privatization (at least at the same cost savings) to be feasible (Hadley 1980: 268-272).

- A large-scale demonstration of the concept of educational vouchers for elementary and secondary schooling was conducted in the Alum Rock, California school district for four years in the early 1970s. This demonstration suffered from numerous shortcomings, among them a limitation of parental choice to a variety of public school offerings but not private schools. On the other hand, the public schools were placed on a market-competitive basis in the sense that if they failed to generate revenues from vouchers to cover operating costs, they would go out of business. Interesting results were observed even within this limited trial. On the favorable side, parents did seem to increase their involvement in school decisionmaking, and parents of limited education (slowly) achieved some ability to act as informed consumers. Also, improvements were observed in pupils' attitudes toward school. On the other hand, the voucher system did not raise pupil achievement scores, and it increased the clustering of students by race and class. Neither educational productivity nor social mobility was significantly enhanced by introduction of market competition (Bridge 1977: 83-85).[5]

Incomplete and imperfect as these various pieces of evidence are, the consistency is striking. If the goals of a public program are stated modestly—to deliver a well-defined product to an easy-to-reach clientele in a cost-minimizing way—then redistribution of purchasing power to the clients themselves and allowing consumer choice in private markets seem, in many cases, to offer greater efficiency than direct public provision of a good or service. But such modest goals are not at all characteristic of many of the social programs in which governments have become involved. To change the life chances of the disadvantaged; to break down racial, class, or cultural ghettos; to alter traditional patterns of living—these are often the long-run objectives of public activities, with the simple delivery of goods and services merely part of a broader goal. Whatever gains there might be in efficiency from a privatization strategy such as vouchers must be weighed against possible losses in effectiveness in terms of these larger goals.

GOVERNMENT PROVISION OF PRODUCTION SUBSIDIES

The two types of initiatives we have considered so far have both involved government enhancing demand. The approach we will now examine involves government subsidization of inputs to private firms' production, creating a profit opportunity by lowering their cost of production. Two major examples of such subsidies are wage subsidies to encourage the hiring of disadvantaged workers and capital subsidies to encourage plant locations in economically distressed locales.

Providing wage subsidies to encourage private employers to hire hard-to-employ workers is asserted to be a cost-effective alternative to having these workers idle and dependent on unemployment insurance, public assistance, or other taxpayer-provided sources of income. And it is asserted to be preferable to creating jobs for these workers in the public sector through such programs as the Depression-era Civilian Conservation Corps or the recently terminated Public Service Employment Program under the Comprehensive Employment and Training Act (Palmer 1978; Haveman and Palmer 1981).

The most current experience with a large-scale wage subsidy program is that of the federal Targeted Jobs Tax Credit (TJTC). Under TJTC, private firms can claim a credit against corporate income tax liabilities for wages paid during the first two years of employment (up to a maximum of $4,500 per worker) for workers drawn from such difficult-to-employ groups as ex-convicts, welfare recipients, the handicapped, and disadvantaged youth. The objective is to expand employment opportunities by making these individuals more attractive to hire compared to other workers, as well as compared to the purchase of capital equipment to substitute for labor.

Despite the fairly generous size of this subsidy and despite fairly extensive (although spotty) efforts over a number of years by the federal government to advertise the availability of these cost-reduction opportunities, the response of the business sector has been persistently disappointing. Only a small proportion of firms bother to participate at all, and credits are claimed for only a small proportion of potentially subsidized workers. More significantly, the majority—approximately two-thirds—of those claims for credits that are filed are retroactive, in the sense that firms first hire workers without determining whether they are TJTC-eligible and then later have them certified. In such circumstances it is presumed that the subsidy had no effect on the hiring decision (Ripley 1982).[6]

There are many reasons why employers are reluctant, despite a subsidy, to hire workers judged to be unattractive. They can all be summarized, however, by saying that employers evidently feel the costs outweigh the benefits. Employers may fear an unreliable, unproductive, or even disruptive employee (for example, a ghetto teenager). They may also anticipate extra training or supervisory costs, or union opposition. In some cases these fears may be justified. Even when they are not, they are extremely difficult to overcome. Even larger subsidies—and the political and budgetary feasibility of these is not high—would face a predominantly unresponsive business community.

This same pattern of unresponsiveness to financial incentives in situations tied to social objectives is also characteristic of local, state, and federal experience with programs designed to encourage businesses to locate in economically distressed locales. Virtually every one of the fifty states actively solicits new business locations and the retention and expansion of existing firms with a rich variety of economic development incentives. These include tax-exempt industrial revenue bonds; various tax exemptions, credits, or moratoria; and free or below-market provision of goods and services ranging from prepared plant sites to worker training. Many local governments (often using federal funds, such as Urban Development Action Grants) have become financial partners in new business ventures located in downtown areas they seek to revitalize (Committee for

Economic Development 1982). The federal government, through such agencies as the Economic Development Administration, Office of Minority Business Enterprise, and Small Business Administration, has made similar efforts, particularly with respect to urban and rural regions of long-term economic decline.

The general experience with such incentives has been that their cost-effectiveness in eliciting significant change in business behavior is quite low. For one thing, the fact that the majority of states and localities offer competing incentives means that competitors' offers largely cancel each other. Then too, many of the goods or services that firms are offered without cost or at a subsidized price would be tax-deductible operating expenses if they were purchased at full price. For firms typically facing corporate income tax rates of 46 percent, this deductibility cuts the net value of the offer approximately in half (Rasmussen, Bendick, and Ledebur 1982). But, most important, in making locational decisions, firms typically are much more concerned with the production costs, risks, and convenience associated with a plant location than they are with special incentives. If they perceive that, for example, an inner city plant site is too small to allow construction of a modern, single-story industrial building; or if they fear for the security of their goods, employees, or facilities; or if the site is too far from the firm's markets, raw materials, or skilled labor pool; then typically no special locational incentives can overcome these disadvantages (Schmenner 1981). Little evidence is available showing significant amounts of job development or job relocation in declining regions or distressed inner cities as a result of the extensive federal, state, and local attempts at industrial location incentives.

These two examples illustrate that locations (in the one case) and potential employees (in the other case) that private firms have largely chosen to abandon are not easily made attractive. A profitable market opportunity is not easy to create. The drawbacks of these locations and workers are substantial; thus the size of an effective compensatory incentive would be very large; finding ways to provide subsidies is not always easy; and even when offered large subsidies, many firms will not cooperate.

CONCLUSIONS

The most disappointing finding that emerges from this review of recent experience with harnessing the private sector to solve social problems is the prevalence of unsubstantiated claims. The U.S. Department of Labor recently asserted that efficiency will be enhanced by phasing out publicly run Job Corps training centers in favor of centers run by private contractors; and yet no documented data were presented to support that assertion. Fingers are pointed at publicly run hospitals in large cities for costing more per case than private hospitals; and yet no definitive study has dissected these cost differences into those due to differences in efficiency in performing identical functions and those due to differences in the types of patients treated and types of treatments provided. Since the empirical evidence is incomplete, conclusions must modestly be phrased as probability statements.

One statement that seems justified by the evidence reviewed here is that there are enough documented success stories with privatization that government should seriously examine market-based approaches whenever undertaking a major initiative. There is no basis in experience for automatically assuming that direct government provision of a good or service is the only feasible way, or the most efficient and effective way, to meet a social need.

This same evidence suggests, however, that the probability that privatization will be successfully implemented and preferable to government service delivery is strongly associated with certain factors. Among them are

- Relatively narrow objectives, readily defined and easily measured
- Specifiable tasks and familiar production processes, monitorable at modest cost
- A number of willing and able competing private sector suppliers
- A competent, honest government to enforce the rules of a fair market

A substantial number of social needs seem to fall within the boundaries set by such prerequisites. These include refuse collection, street maintenance, data processing services, and activities subject to voucher purchases, such as food distribution and housing. In such cases there have been some (although not universal) impressive cost savings and other favorable outcomes.

But some aspects of even these straightforward services and the dominant aspect of many others do not meet these prerequisites. As the mix of objectives in a program shifts toward more complex, long-range, holistic, and unmeasurable outcomes, and when the state of the art is more primitive concerning how to achieve those outcomes, the record of experience is barren of success stories. Indeed, the historical landscape becomes strewn with negative findings, aborted demonstration projects, and unfulfilled expectations. In seeking to educate or train the disadvantaged, transform ghetto communities or economies, improve individuals' living patterns, health, or social functioning, or meet other complex objectives, the record of past privatization initiatives is not impressive.

This is not to say that the record of direct government service programs seeking such objectives is any better, of course (Aaron 1978; Bendick 1982; Haveman 1977). It is simply to say that privatization per se seems to offer no panacea. The challenge for the future thus seems to be one of discovering more effective ways to address persistent, elusive, complex social problems, whether they are eventually to be implemented by the public or private sectors. There is little evidence that privatization alone would contribute significantly to their solution.

NOTES TO CHAPTER 7

1. Contracting out arrangements were half again as prevalent in western states as in eastern or southern states (Kirlin, Ries, and Sonenblum 1977: p. 116).

2. However, according to Hatry (1982: p. 30), the local employee's association fought the layoff of city workers when the services were shifted to the private sector and has won a judgment from the New York State Employment Relations Board ordering city officials to offer alternative jobs and back pay to laid-off employees. This ruling will reduce these cost savings somewhat.

3. The sources of these savings were technical and managerial efficiency in the private firms, including smaller crew sizes, more efficient vehicles, and lower absenteeism. These same studies showed that private refuse collection under competitive *multiple* supplier arrangements tended to be more expensive than public provision, due to the costs of duplicated routes.

4. This table is adapted from Hatry (1982: p. 25). A less sanguine verdict was rendered by Fisk, Kiesling, and Muller (1978). They concluded that costs tended to fall whenever municipal services were switched from the public sector to the private sector or vice versa! This was true because the typical circumstances in which a municipality makes such a shift is when the current mode of service delivery is grossly inefficient.

5. "The G.I. Bill" is sometimes cited as a more positive experience with a voucher educational program (O'Neill 1977). For proposals to implement the concept of educational vouchers through tuition tax credits, see West (1978, 1981).

6. For (not necessarily representative) examples of success stories in business initiatives to help the hard-to-employ, see Committee for Economic Development (1978). For an analysis of one case of success with a ghetto manufacturing facility—virtually without government subsidy—see Bendick and Egan (1982).

REFERENCES

Aaron, Henry J. 1978. *Politics and the Professors: The Great Society in Perspective.* Washington, D.C.: The Brookings Institution.

Ahlbrandt, Roger. 1973. *Municipal Fire Protection Services: Comparison of Alternative Organization Forms.* Beverly Hills, Calif.: Sage Publications.

_____. 1977. *Alternatives to Traditional Public Safety Delivery Systems: Civilians in Public Safety Services.* Berkeley, Calif.: The Institute for Local Self-Government.

Ahlbrandt, Roger S., Jr. 1974. "Implications of Contracting for a Public Service." *Urban Affairs Quarterly* (March).

Bendick, Marc, Jr. 1977. "Education as a Three-Sector Industry." In *The Voluntary Nonprofit Sector: An Economic Analysis*, edited by Burton A. Weisbrod. Lexington, Mass.: Lexington Books, pp. 101-142.

_____. 1982. "Employment, Training, and Economic Development Programs." In *The Reagan Experiment*, edited by John Palmer and Isabel Sawhill. Washington, D.C.: The Urban Institute Press.

_____. 1982. "Vouchers versus Income versus Services: An American Experiment in Housing Policy." *Journal of Social Policy* (July).

_____. 1978. "WIC and the Paradox of In-Kind Transfers." *Public Finance Quarterly* 6(3): 349-380.

Bendick, Marc, Jr., and Mary Lou Egan. 1982. "Providing Industrial Jobs in the Inner City." *Business* 32 (January-March): 2-9.

Bendick, Marc, Jr.; Toby H. Campbell; D. Lee Bawden; and Melvin Jones. 1976. *Toward Efficiency and Effectiveness in the WIC Delivery System.* Washington, D.C.: The Urban Institute.

Bish, Robert L., and Robert Warren. 1972. "Scale and Monopoly Problems in Urban Government Services." *Urban Affairs Quarterly* 8 (September): 97-120.

Bradbury, Katharine C., and Anthony Downs, eds. 1981. *Do Housing Allowances Work?* Washington, D.C.: The Brookings Institution.

Brettler-Berenyi, Eileen. 1980. "Public and Private Interaction Patterns in the Delivery of Local Public Services." *Governmental Finance* (March): 3-8.

Breuer, Daniel B., and Daniel W. Fitzpatrick. 1980. "An Experience in Contracting Out for Services." *Governmental Finance* (March): 11-13.

Bridge, Gary. 1977. "Citizens Choice in Public Services: Voucher Systems." In *Alternatives for Delivering Public Services*, edited by E.S. Savas. Boulder, Colo.: Westview Press, pp. 51-110.

California Tax Foundation. 1981. *Contracting Out Local Government Services in California.*

Carpenter, Polly, and George R. Hall. 1971. *Case Studies in Education Performance Contracting: Conclusions and Implications.* Santa Monica, Calif.: The RAND Corporation.

Committee for Economic Development. 1978. *Jobs for the Hard-to-Employ: New Directions for a Public Private Partnership.* New York.

_____ . 1982. *Public Private Partnership: An Opportunity for Urban Communities.* New York.

_____ . 1978. *Training and Job Programs in Action: Case Studies in Private-Sector Initiatives.* New York.

Davies, David G. 1971. "The Efficiency of Public versus Private Firms: The Case of Australia's Two Airlines." *Journal of Law and Economics* 14 (April): 149-165.

Edwards, Franklin R., and Barbara J. Stevens. 1978. "The Provision of Municipal Sanitation Services by Private Firms." *Journal of Industrial Economics* 17 (December): 133-147.

Fisk, Donald; Herbert Kiesling; and Thomas Muller. 1978. *Private Provision of Public Services: An Overview.* Washington, D.C.: The Urban Institute.

Fitch, Lyle C. 1974. "Increasing the Role of the Private Sector in Providing Public Services." In *Improving the Quality of Urban Management,* edited by Willis D. Hawley and David Rogers. Urban Affairs Annual Reviews, vol. 8. Beverly Hills, Calif.: pp. 501-559.

Frazier, Mark. 1980. "Privatizing the City." *Policy Analysis* (Spring).

Frieden, Bernard J. 1980. "Housing Allowances: An Experiment That Worked." *The Public Interest* 59: 115-133.

Ginzberg, Paul. 1981. "Medicare Vouchers and the Precompetition Strategy." *Health Affairs* (Winter): 39-52.

Gramlich, Edward M., and Patricia P. Koshel. 1975. *Educational Performance Contracting: An Evaluation of an Experiment.* Washington, D.C.: The Brookings Institution.

Gurin, Arnold, et al. 1980. *Contracting for Services as a Mechanism for the Delivery of Human Services: A Study of Contracting Practices in Three Human Services Agencies in Massachusetts.* Waltham, Mass.: Florence Heller School for Advanced Studies in Social Welfare of Brandeis University.

Gutowski, Michael. 1979. *Rehabilitation in the Private Sector: Changing the Structure of the Rehabilitation Industry.* Washington, D.C.: The Urban Institute.

Hadley, Jack. 1980. "The National Health Service Corps." In *Medical Education Financing,* edited by Jack Hadley. New York: Prodist, pp. 260-273.

Hanrahan, John D. 1977. *Government for Sale: Contracting Out, The New Patronage.* Washington, D.C.: American Federation of State, County, and Municipal Employees.

Harris, C. Lowell. 1975. "CUNY, SUNY, and the Independents: New Directions for Higher Education in New York City." *City Almanac* 10 (December).

Hatry, Harry P. 1982. *Alternative Service Delivery Approaches Involving Increased Use of the Private Sector.* Washington, D.C.: The Urban Institute.

Haveman, Robert H., and John L. Palmer, eds. 1982. *Jobs for Disadvantaged Workers: The Economics of Employment Subsidies.* Washington, D.C.: The Brookings Institution.

Kakalik, J., and S. Wilhorn. 1971. *The Private Police Industry: Its Nature and Extent.* Santa Monica, Calif.: The RAND Corporation.

Kemper, Peter, and John M. Quigley. 1976. *The Economics of Refuse Collection.* Cambridge, Mass.: Ballinger.

Kirby, Ronald F. 1981. "Targeting Money Effectively: User-Side Transportation Subsidies." *Journal of Contemporary Studies* (Winter): 45-52.

Kirlin, John J. 1973. "The Impact of Contract Service Arrangements upon the Los Angeles Sheriff's Department and Law Enforcement Services in Los Angeles County." *Public Policy* 21 (Fall): 553-581.

Kirlin, John J.; John C. Ries; and Sidney Sonenblum. 1977. "Alternatives to City Departments." In *Alternatives for Delivering Public Services*, edited by E.S. Savas. Boulder, Colo.: Westview Press, pp. 111-145.

Krashinsky, Michael. 1978. "The Cost of Day Care in Public Programs." *National Tax Journal* 31 (December): 363-372.

Levenson, Rosaline. 1976. *Government by Private Contract: Experimentation in South San Francisco*. Davis, Calif.: Institute of Governmental Affairs of the University of California at Davis.

Lynn, Laurence E. 1977. "A Decade of Policy Development in the Income-Maintenance System." In *A Decade of Federal Antipoverty Programs*, edited by Robert H. Haveman. New York: Academic Press, pp. 55-117.

Meyer, R.A. 1975. "Publicly Owned Versus Privately Owned Utilities: A Policy Choice." *Review of Economics and Statistics* 57: 391-399.

O'Neill, David. 1977. "Voucher Funding of Training: Evidence from the G.I. Bill." *Journal of Human Resources* 12 (Fall).

Ostrom, Elinor; William Baugh; Roger Parks Guarasci; and Gordon Whitaker. 1973. *Community Organization and the Provision of Police Services*. Beverly Hills, Calif.: Sage Publications.

Palmer, John L., ed. 1978. *Creating Jobs, Public Employment Programs and Wage Subsidies*. Washington, D.C.: The Brookings Institution.

Peterson, George E. 1978. "The Distributional Impact of Performance Contracting in Schools." In *Redistribution through Public Choice*, edited by Harold Hochman and George E. Peterson. New York: Columbia University Press.

_____. 1981. *Pricing and Privatization of Public Services*. Washington, D.C.: The Urban Institute.

Rasmussen, David W.; Marc Bendick, Jr.; and Larry C. Ledebur. 1982. "Evaluating State Economic Development Incentives from a Firm's Point of View." *Business Economics* (May): 23-29.

Ripley, Randall, et al. 1982. *The Implementation of the Targeted Jobs Tax Credit*. Columbus: Mershon Center of the Ohio State University.

Savas, E.S., ed. 1977. *Alternatives for Delivering Public Services, Toward Improved Performance*. Boulder, Colo.: Westview Press.

_____. 1977. "An Empirical Study of Competition in Municipal Service Delivery." *Public Administration Review* 37 (November-December): 717-724.

_____. 1981. "Intra-City Competition between Public and Private Service Delivery." *Public Administration Review* (January/February): 46-52.

_____. 1974. "Municipal Monopolies versus Competition in Delivering Urban Services." In *Improving the Quality of Urban Management*, edited by Willis D. Hawley and David Rogers. Urban Affairs Annual Reviews, vol. 8. Beverly Bills, Calif.: Sage Publications, pp. 473-500.

_____. 1977. *The Organization and Efficiency of Solid Waste Collection*. Lexington, Mass.: Lexington Books.

_____. 1976. "Policy Analysis for Local Government: Public vs. Private Refuse Collection." *Policy Analysis* 23 (Winter): 49-74.

_____. 1982. *Privatizing the Public Sector: How to Shrink Government.* Chatham, N.J.: Chatham House Publishers.

_____. 1979. "Public versus Private Refuse Collection: A Critical Review of the Evidence." *Urban Analysis* 6: 1-13.

Schmenner, Roger. 1981. *The Location Decision of Large, Multiplant Companies: A Summary.* Washington, D.C.: U.S. Department of Housing and Urban Development.

Schultze, Charles L. 1977. *The Public Use of Private Interest.* Washington, D.C.: The Brookings Institution.

Shonick, William, and Ruth Roemer. 1982. *Private Management of California County Hospitals: Expectations and Performance.* Los Angeles: School of Public Health of the University of California at Los Angeles.

Sonenblum, Sidney; John J. Kirlin; and John C. Ries. 1977. *How Cities Provide Services: An Evaluation of Alternative Delivery Structures.* Cambridge, Mass.: Ballinger.

Stipak, Brian. 1974. *Citizen Evaluation of Municipal Services in Los Angeles County.* Los Angeles: University of California at Los Angeles Institute of Government and Public Affairs.

Stocker, Frederick P. 1973. "Value Determination: The Assessor's Staff vs. The Private Appraisal Firm." In *Property Tax Reform: The Role of the Property Tax in the Nation's Revenue System.* Chicago: International Association of Assessing Officers.

Struyk, Raymond J., and Marc Bendick, Jr., eds. 1981. *Housing Vouchers for the Poor: Lessons from a National Experiment.* Washington, D.C.: The Urban Institute Press.

U.S. Senate. 1981. *Alternative Service Delivery, Hearings before the Subcommittee on Intergovernmental Relations, July 1981.* Washington, D.C.: U.S. Government Printing Office.

Wedel, Kenneth R. 1976. "Government Contracting for Purchase of Service." *Social Work* 21 (March): 101-105.

West, E.G. 1981. "Choice or Monopoly in Education." *Policy Review* (Winter).

_____. 1978. "Tuition Tax Credit Proposals." *Policy Review* 3: 61-75.

Wildhorn, S., et al. 1980. *Rediscovering Governance: Using Non-Service Approaches to Address Neighborhood Problems—A Guide to Local Officials.* Palo Alto, Calif.: SRI International.

NEW FUNCTIONS FOR
THE CORPORATION?

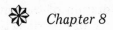 *Chapter 8*

Matching Private Incentives
to Public Goals

William J. Baumol

[Competition] has the effect of rendering . . . inhumanity compulsory.
George Bernard Shaw, 2nd Fabian Tract

We have inherited from the upheavals of the 1960s the view that private firms must assume a wide-ranging set of social responsibilities going well beyond their traditional missions—production, efficiency, and responsiveness to consumer desires. This view holds that corporations and other firms must *actively and voluntarily* undertake to improve environmental quality, help the underprivileged, support education, public health, and the arts, and promote a number of other goals, many of them neither well defined nor universally agreed upon.

There have long been voices emanating from the business sector itself urging industry to accept the challenge. But the members of the business community who take this position predominantly stress the role of voluntarism that underlies the concept. Business people, like the members of any other group, are not uniform in their dedication to virtue. There is no doubt justice in the contention that *some* business advocates of voluntarism are more concerned with public relations than with substance and that their espousal of a voluntary approach represents a cynical attempt to escape measures that really would constrain them to act in a manner more closely consonant with the dictates of the public welfare. But it would be a serious mistake to ascribe all or even most of this position to cynicism. The great bulk of business persons have strong consciences, and they also live in the communities that are beset by deterioration of the environment, underfinanced schools, and unavailability of artistic activity. Many of them expend great amounts of their own time and energy in the voluntary support of worthy causes. There simply is no question that these persons mean what they say.

The question is what can industry be expected realistically to accomplish? This chapter offers four main conclusions on this subject:

1. There is, indeed, *some* scope for completely autonomous business contributions, unstimulated by any outside agency. Indeed, intelligent dedication to the social interest *can* be good business.
2. However, the market mechanism imposes very severe limits upon business voluntarism. Paradoxically, the very invisible hand mechanism, which, where it is successful, enforces good business behavior in terms of efficiency, product quality and reasonable prices, at the same time severely restricts the scope for voluntary contributions to other social goals by business firms, no matter how good the intentions of management.
3. In that case it becomes appropriate for government not to *impose* behavior upon industry but simply to weaken in an appropriate manner the inhibiting effects of the invisible hand. The chapter will explain how this can be done; it will examine the consequences and show how all affected groups may benefit thereby.
4. Finally, the more competitive an industry is, the smaller the scope it offers to voluntarism. Paradoxically, the greater the market power of a firm (however defined) and consequently, the more suspect its behavior should be to the antitrust authorities, the more capable it is of contributing voluntarily to the achievement of social objectives.

An important question is what can be done by the public sector to stimulate business activities that contribute to the public welfare. Some things firms do in their self-interest also contribute to the social welfare (and not just to gross national product). For example, corporate contributions to basic research or to the support of orchestras may be induced by the profit motive. The basic research support may constitute an investment in pertinent future knowledge and the training of future personnel, and the purpose of the orchestral support may be public relations, or the attraction of specialized personnel to the community. Yet both of these, incidentally, benefit the community. In the language of the economist, they constitute beneficial externalities.

Similarly, government can and does directly contribute a great deal to the public welfare. But here we are concerned primarily neither with the role of industry nor government, taken by themselves, but with the role of the public sector in facilitating or stimulating business activities undertaken to fulfill its social responsibilities.

OVERLAP OF SOCIAL AND BUSINESS GOALS

Anyone who believes that business activity is an enemy of the social welfare suffers from a total misconception. Both business firms and business people have always made major contributions to the public's well-being. This is worth illustrating and discussing briefly because the most vehement critics of business are all too apt to proceed as though the opposite were true, even if no one seems willing to take so manifestly false a position explicitly.

The statement that "What is good for General Motors is good for the country" elicited the amusement it deserved when it was first uttered. But while it exaggerates the degree of coincidence in the interests of the firm and the community, it surely has considerable validity. The primary contribution of industry to the social welfare surely is its production of goods and services, a fact that seems curiously neglected in discussions of the obligations of business to society. In its ability to produce, business enterprise is unsurpassed in human history. Its accomplishment even moved Karl Marx to wax poetic: "The bourgeoisie . . . has accomplished wonders far surpassing Egyptian pyramids, Roman aqueducts, and Gothic cathedrals. . . . The bourgeoisie during its rule of scarce one hundred years has created more massive and more colossal productive forces than have all previous generations together" (from the *Communist Manifesto*).

Marx was, of course, right. Business provides consumers with an abundance that is unparalleled. Its products adapt themselves to consumer preferences and to changes in their tastes with speed and reliability. It produces these outputs efficiently, minimizing the value of the social resources used up in the process. This, clearly, is the primary responsibility of business, and a diversion of its activities that exacts a high social cost in terms of the efficiency of its productive operations and the abundance of goods and services it provides may well be considered questionable.

But business finds other social goals appropriate to pursue, goals more immediately in line with the items commonly included among its social responsibilities. For example, some firms have undertaken investments to control pollution going well beyond the requirements of current regulations. In some cases this was induced by the discovery that emissions control processes generate by-products such as useful chemicals or recycleable items that are of considerable value in themselves. Indeed, any commercial recycling firm that reprocesses waste oil or paper or steel incidentally serves as an emissions control device, which is no less desirable socially because it happens to generate a profit.

A second inducement for firms to contribute to improvement of their environment is that an unacceptable environment can be an impediment to its operations. It may make it difficult for the enterprise to acquire able management. Poor air quality can impede the productivity of its work force. Deterioration of the environment of an urban enterprise can increase its vulnerability to crime and reduce its accessibility to a skilled work force. Poverty in the neighborhood of a local merchant may cut into his sales. Good business practice, driven by enlightened self-interest, may call for investment in environment by the firm to a degree that is not negligible.

Similarly business support of education and academic research may augment the firm's supply of skilled personnel and technological improvements. The same sort of explanation may account for business support of the arts, whose availability near the location of the company can help it to attract scientific and technical personnel as well as management and which may often be considered effective advertising as well as an instrument of personnel relations.

This suggests that self-interest can go a long way in driving firms to serve the interests of society. Not only does it drive them to produce abundantly and efficiently in the manner Adam Smith explained so eloquently, but it may lead them to devote attention to socially beneficial activities such as the training of unskilled members of minority groups, pollution control, and support of the arts.

This argument should not be misinterpreted as denying that business people are capable of altruism. There is, indeed, abundant evidence to the contrary, from the early support of the black colleges by the Rockefellers to the enormous outlay of time by business people on the training in business skills offered in a number of ghetto areas. Perhaps the most telling piece of evidence is the fact that our largest private foundations, on which so much socially beneficial activity relies, bear the names of the business leaders of the past— Ford, Rockefeller, Sloan, Mellon, and the like—the names of the persons who voluntarily provided their funding. But while individual business people can, if they wish, transcend self-interest in their contributions to the social welfare, it is far more difficult for a business enterprise to do so.

ON INDUCEMENT OF INCREASED
INDUSTRY CONTRIBUTIONS

The social contributions of business that have just been described are undeniable. But it is obviously not the purpose of this essay to congratulate business for its accomplishments any more than to denigrate them. Rather, the pertinent question here is what may induce business to do *more* than it has been doing previously.

Leaving until later the possibility of initiatives on the part of government, three obvious possibilities arise. First, management may perhaps discover opportunities of which it was not previously aware to serve its own interests by serving those of society. Second, exogenous changes may occur, perhaps fortuitously, which render profitable socially beneficial activities that previously were unprofitable. Finally, public discussion of issues such as environmental deterioration, racial discrimination, and the like may stimulate the consciences of business persons and induce them to increase the magnitude of their voluntary efforts and, if necessary, to sacrifice a greater quantity of profit for these purposes than they were prepared to sacrifice before.

Though what can be expected along any of these lines is rather limited, a few illustrations will confirm that all three of these possibilities have played some role. For example, firms have indeed discovered some activities whose primary goal is the social welfare but that turn out to be profitable despite earlier beliefs to the contrary. The extraction of valuable chemicals from pollutants reportedly has, in a number of cases, turned out that way. A number of employers who have gone out of their way to hire women either as a public gesture or to salve their consciences have finally learned that women can be as competent as men. As word of the associated profit opportunities spreads, such business activities can be expected to expand simply as a matter of self-interest. Thus discovery of additional opportunities for profit through socially beneficial activities can indeed expand the magnitude of business contributions in this domain.

Fortuitous exogenous developments that change the range and character of profitable opportunities may have contributed still more. There is an abundance of evidence that rising prices of various raw materials have increased the profitability of methods that reduce waste of these materials in the production process as well as the profitability of recycling. Both of these have helped to reduce the amount of waste requiring disposal and that, in turn, has helped to contain the emissions of pollutants. The most noteworthy example, of course, is the series of fuel crises of the 1970s, which led industry to adopt all sorts of fuel conservation measures such as increased use of insulation and the employment of more economical engines,[1] all of which helped to reduce the use of fossil fuels and thereby even decreased the imminence of the threat of the earth-warming greenhouse effect.

Casual observation suggests that public concern over issues such as equal opportunity and the health effects of pollution has stirred the consciences of people in business along with persons in other fields of endeavor (Committee for Economic Development 1974). What has already been done in this respect can doubtless be carried further in the future. Management's concern over public issues can perhaps be stimulated still further and some whose consciences have not yet been aroused may perhaps be recruited to the cause.

In short, if we feel that more should be expected of future business performance than it is currently doing in contributing toward fulfillment of its social responsibilities, all three avenues that have just been examined must be judged to offer room for further accomplishment.

Yet there are limits to the degree to which one can depend on such manifestations. Each relies at least to some extent on chance developments, but happenstance, of course, need not always work in society's favor. The avenue that is most obviously vulnerable is the exogenous change that makes it profitable to perform socially beneficial acts that previously were unprofitable. Several examples of such changes have been cited, but it is just as easy to provide illustrative cases in which events have moved in the other direction. Recession characteristically brings with it declines in the prices of raw materials, and a fairly sure sign of its effects is a spurt in the number of abandoned cars to be seen by the side of the road, it not having been worth the owners' while to have them towed to a junkyard. The lag in real oil prices that accompanied the "glut" of 1981-82 undoubtedly was an impediment to industry's continued investment in fuel-economizing equipment. The recession also delayed the airlines' purchase of a new fleet of airplanes that promise to reduce fuel consumption as well as noise.

It is equally plausible that public pressures for measures such as environmental protection, rather than constituting an interminable crescendo, will spend themselves after the first flush of enthusiasm has abated. Certainly, President Reagan's withdrawal of resources from the environmental authorities has not been greeted by a deafening chorus of disapproval. That being so, we can hardly expect the social pressures upon industry to grow without interruption.

The point is that autonomous increases in industry's attention to its social responsibilities are indeed to be expected, at least intermittently. But it is difficult to think of grounds that would justify reliance upon them as the mainstay of a program to increase the welfare of society contributed by sources other than the abundance of consumers' goods and services. Something more will surely be needed if the end result is to constitute an effective partnership of industry, government, and the general public, aimed at the achievement of social goals.

THE INVISIBLE HAND AS AN IMPEDIMENT TO BUSINESS GENEROSITY

In the twentieth century Adam Smith's invisible hand doctrine is widely misunderstood. First, the term itself is taken as a metaphor and the doctrine is consequently interpreted as a purely secular and matter-of-fact analysis of market behavior. In fact, in the eighteenth century "the invisible hand" was a commonplace term, used, with no need for explanation, to refer to the workings of Divine Providence— the hand of God. The doctrine, in other words, is religious, not secular (Viner 1972.) This use of the term "invisible hand" occurs frequently in eighteenth-century letters, those of George Washington, for example.

More germane to our purposes is the fact that Adam Smith's doctrine is the culmination of some three centuries of discussion of the compatibility of human passions and pursuit of self-interest with the divine purposes. How, in other words, can one reconcile human selfishness with goodness of society as a whole? Many answers were proposed over the years, with contributions offered by Bacon, Pascal, and Montesquieu, among many others (Hirschman 1977). Adam Smith's contribution may be considered the culmination of this literature, and he offers what is perhaps the first convincing answer to the riddle.

Smith tells us that the competitive market mechanism is the marvelous instrument of the deity that does not *merely* succeed in curbing the evils of human selfishness. For this brilliantly conceived mechanism of the deity actually transforms selfishness into a prime instrument of social welfare, serving the economic interests of nations as no other arrangement can. "Every individual necessarily labors to render the annual revenue of the society as great as he can ... by directing that industry in such a manner as its produce may be of the greatest value, he intends only his own gain, and he is in this, as in many other cases, led by an invisible hand to promote an end which was no part of his intention" (Smith 1937: 423).

Today, of course, we have adopted a more secular interpretation of the competitive process. But we still accept Smith's logic. Competition is an extremely powerful mechanism that severely constrains business managers' freedom of decision. It does not permit them to overcharge for their products. It prevents them from delaying innovations or taking advantage of the latest productive techniques. It forbids them the luxury of inefficiency and waste. All of these types of misconduct carry the severest economic penalties that can be imposed upon a firm: loss of markets to rivals and, ultimately, insolvency.

The point in all this is that the market mechanism, like a mindless computer, makes no distinctions among types of expenditures that are unnecessary for the firm's central purposes. All of them, whether they serve the most despicable forms of self-indulgence or the most commendable social purposes, are condemned equally as unpardonable waste, which carries with it the extreme penalty, if carried beyond the most negligible proportions. The firm that voluntarily devotes substantial funds to the support of the arts or to training the unskilled subjects itself to a fatal handicap in the struggle for its markets. A competitor who chooses not to indulge in this sort of "wasteful outlay" can afford to undercut the philanthropic business firm and steal away its customers. The pressures of competition simply do not distinguish between egregious waste and commendable philanthropy but treat them both with equal severity. In short, the invisible hand is an instrument that precludes all significant acts of benevolent voluntarism on the part of competitive industry. It is ironic that only firms with the sort of market power decried by the antitrust authorities are permitted the luxury of making voluntary contributions to the social welfare.

It may well be objected that industry has an alternative—that by mutual consent of the pertinent competitors business people may undertake to suspend competition in this arena. They can attain immunity from the inhibiting market forces if they agree simultaneously to undertake programs promoting social goals—if they engage in a sort of program of tacit cooperation, of virtuous tacit collusion. If every firm in an industry undertakes to do so, none will find itself at a competitive disadvantage and the blockade of the invisible hand will thereby be withdrawn.

Anyone who proposes such a solution must not underestimate the difficulties it faces. The difficulties are very much akin to those that beset the organization and monitoring of a cartel no one of whose members can observe perfectly what the others are doing and each of whom has something to gain by cheating secretly. Such cartel arrangements are notoriously unstable and few of them have, apparently, achieved their purpose for very long.

The difficulties of maintaining such coordination have long been recognized in the economic literature and confirmed by an extensive body of analysis and empirical evidence. Recently the nature of the problem has been brought out in a remarkable paper describing a set of experimental simulations of market transactions (Plott 1982). Groups of twelve students were given money with which they were permitted to conduct purchases and sales of a "commodity" whose price was determined by a supply-demand process. The participants kept all the profits they obtained from the transactions. However, a "tax" was also levied on each participant, with the magnitude of the tax dependent on the *total* number of transactions that took place in the market. In other words, a decision by any one participant to undertake a profitable trade increased the tax imposed on each and every participant, including himself, by a prespecified amount. This is a situation that involves what economists call "externalities," in which a transaction between two individuals incidentally harms other persons who are external to it. In these circumstances, if every participant selfishly were to carry out every trade profitable to himself alone, the group as a whole would end up earning considerably less in total than if they had all been able by some process of tacit collusion to restrain their purchases. In the experiment in question it was possible to calculate in advance the number of transactions that could be expected to occur if each participant took advantage of every opportunity for personal profit without regard to the welfare of the others, disregarding the effects upon everyone else. That number was 24. On the other hand, the optimal number of transactions— which would have maximized the net income of the group as a whole—was only 13.

Reports indicate that the participants were well aware of the damage each of their transactions was imposing on the others, and that, at first, they sought to hold back, expecting others to do the same. But this self-policing state rapidly broke down, as the data confirm. In successive trials the number of transactions formed the following pattern (there were two different groups of participants in this particular phase of the experiment):

	Trial 1	Trial 2	Trial 3	Trial 4	Trial 5
Group 1	17	25	24	26	24
Group 2	17	21	24	24	24

It should be noted that in each case only 17 transactions occurred the first time the market operated; tacit collusion yielded a number of transactions only slightly higher than the optimal 13. However, the understanding broke down rapidly and from the third trial onward the number of transactions, with one exception, actually equaled exactly the 24 predicted if each participant felt it necessary to disregard completely the effects upon others.[2]

The moral of this study and of the extensive economic literature examining the difficulties of tacit cooperation (collusion) is not that people are devoid of concern for the welfare of others and will act only upon selfish motives. Rather, the conclusion should be interpreted to imply that the market mechanism allows little scope for the exercise of altruism by participants in competitive markets. With the best of intentions, tacit collusion is a feeble instrument to hold the market forces at bay, a weak means to make effective voluntarism possible. Even if every participant in the market is equally dedicated to the welfare of others, the fact that any one participant does not know how much he can depend on the appropriate behavior of others makes it very difficult for him to hold out. Moreover, his own incentives for indecision and retreat are only apt to increase his unwillingness to rely on the others. How much more forlorn is the hope for virtuous tacit collusion in a world in which *some* businesspeople surely are driven primarily by self-interest and will give short shrift to any proposal that their firms devote very substantial resources to social purposes.

THE NECESSARY INGREDIENT: PUBLIC SECTOR PARTICIPATION

In order then for industry to be able to do substantially more than it does already to promote the goals of society, some force will have to intervene from the outside to do whatever is necessary to suspend the inhibiting effects of the invisible hand mechanism. The object is not to impede competition, but to prevent the competition from rewarding the firms that get away with the severest degradation of the environment or the smallest outlays on safety of employees, for example. There appears to be only one outside power capable of achieving such a circumscribed reduction in the forces of competition: the government. This is the prime reason the public sector is probably an indispensable partner in any effective program for business contribution to the attainment of the pertinent social goals.

The general outlines of the role that the public sector must play here are not difficult to describe. The details are, of course, much less obvious. In broad outline, the nature of the problem dictates the remedy. The fatal inhibition besetting the social contributions of any one firm is fear that its competitors will not contribute commensurately and that it will, therefore, find its generosity to have become a dangerous competitive disadvantage. With each firm threatened by the severest penalties if it turns out to be among a minority that contributes, none but the most foolhardy will venture beyond token contributions.

The remedy for this problem therefore consists of any rule that assures each firm that it will not be alone in what it does for society, that it can make its contribution in full assurance that its rivals will also do their part. There are obvious ways in which this can be done, though they often have rather unfortunate consequences. For example, a regulation requiring *all* firms that emit smoke to install smoke-stack scrubbers means that no one enterprise need be put at a competitive disadvantage by this outlay on pollution control. For the rule imposes a similar obligation on all of its competitors. Such a rule may be unacceptable for other reasons, for example, because it imposes inefficiencies and excessive costs, or because it inhibits freedom of decisionmaking unnecessarily and subjects management to heavy bureaucratic burdens. There are far better ways of going about the achievement of the requisite inhibition of competitive impediments to the social contributions of industry. But before we turn to these subjects two general remarks are appropriate.

The first is that if business is to be taken seriously when it expresses its dedication to social goals, it must not attack every proposal for a governmental role in the arena. Without some government participation the competitive mechanism renders business powerless to contribute significantly toward the attainment of social goals, no matter how good its intentions may be. It must, therefore, reconcile itself to a partnership with the public sector here. A constructive business attitude must avoid predictable rejection of every proposed measure by the public sector. Rather, it is appropriate for business to participate in the design of those measures, using management's experience and judgment to help in improving their effectiveness and in reducing to a minimum their economic cost and interference with business initiative.

The second pertinent remark relates to the choice of priorities, what sorts of social goals are to be selected for immunization from the inhibiting market forces. Public sector participation inevitably means that this sector will have a voice in the determination of these priorities, that it will not be left exclusively to the judgment of business persons.

But that is hardly deplorable. After all, one may well question whether business executives are uniquely qualified to determine what is best for society. They have not been chosen for this task in anything resembling a democratic election, nor have they received any special training for that role. Surely, it is not inappropriate for the public sector to have a hand in determining the priorities in the use of the nation's economic resources for the promotion of social goals.

TOWARD UNINHIBITING FORMS OF PUBLIC SECTOR INTERVENTION

The form of government intervention used as illustration was deliberately chosen to be of the most obvious and most objectionable type. Clearly, an inflexible rule requiring all firms to install smokestack scrubbers or forcing all of them to use low-sulfur coal, while it may handicap all competitors commensurately, introduces a number of inefficiencies. Most obviously, it gives management no voice in the decision over choice of emissions control technique. Along with this, it precludes differences among plants, firms and industries from being taken into account. Any imposition by fiat of uniform control techniques is virtually certain to be poorly suited to some of the affected organizations. Third, the apparent equality in the treatment of different plants precludes the economy from taking advantage of savings opportunities presented by differences in abatement costs. Thus, suppose in one plant, A, because of the high cost of equipment installation, a reduction of emissions of sulfur costs $17 per ton, while a second plant, B, which is newer and more flexible, can achieve the same reduction at a cost of $2. Is it really efficient from the viewpoint of the economy to require both plants to reduce emissions by equal amounts by the installation of control equipment of equal capacity?

Various steps can be taken to reduce such inefficiencies. Two imaginative programs with this purpose were introduced by the U.S. Environmental Protection Agency (EPA) in recent years, with rather unlikely labels: the bubble concept and the offsets program. The bubble concept undertook to treat an entire plant, or even a complex of plants owned by one company at a given location, as a single entity. Conceptually, it encased such a complex in a giant plastic bubble with a single vent through which emissions must pass from the plants into the atmosphere. Plant managers were, in effect, told by the authorities, "We don't care how much sulfur is emitted from this smokestack or that one, in particular. We only care about the *total* emissions from your plants. Therefore, *any* method you choose to reduce their *total* emissions to an acceptable level will be considered satisfactory." Thus management was given freedom and, indeed, encouragement to select the most economical combination of techniques, plants, and processes to be used with industry, in exchange, being assigned responsibility for demonstrating that emissions *overall* had been cut to the required degree.

The program clearly reduces bureaucratic impediments to freedom of business decisions. In addition, it can be a source of substantial savings. Finally, and most important for our purposes, because it can be applied in a similar manner to all firms that emit pollutants, it assures each enterprise that it will be joined by its rivals. In that way it does indeed hold back the inhibiting influence of the invisible hand.

While the bubble concept thus represents a significant and imaginative improvement in the means the government can use to help business to meet its social responsibilities, the offsets approach constitutes a giant second step that carries the approach to its logical culmination. Society, as we have noted, has no stake in the choice of plant or the choice of process from which a reduction in emissions is obtained. But if it does not matter to society whether a given firm obtains its emission reductions from its plant A or its plant B, surely it is equally irrelevant to society whether that reduction is contributed by Company Alpha or Company Beta. As was noted earlier, considerable savings can be obtained by assigning the bulk of the task to those firms that can do it most cheaply and efficiently. For example, a beet sugar plant can reduce its discharges of BOD (biochemical oxygen demand) far more cheaply than it can be done by a petroleum refinery, and a new paper plant can generally do it far more cheaply than an old one.

The issue, of course, is whether a government agency is in a position to pick and choose among firms to whom the task of emissions control is assigned. The very question shouts its own answer: Any such attempt would certainly stimulate a nightmare of information requirements, arbitrary decisions, and unfairness, and it would clearly give rise to a mass of litigation.

But another approach is possible—the market mechanism, operated through the voluntary decisions of the affected enterprises. Suppose firm A, a petroleum refiner, can reduce emissions of BOD at a cost of 6 cents per pound, while a neighboring beet sugar plant can do so at a cost of 2 cents. If each is requested to reduce its emissions into a given waterway by 1,000 pounds per day, the petroleum refinery can, of course, do the job itself. But under the offsets program it is free to offer the beet producer a fee of three or four cents per pound to do the job for it. That is, the beet company is encouraged to reduce emissions by 2,000 pounds per day, thereby leaving the refinery to operate exactly as before. The waterway's pollution would then be reduced by precisely the selected amount, but under the offsetting trade there would be financial benefits to both firms and substantial savings to the economy. The procedure thus constitutes neither more nor less than a free market in pollution rights in which trades are voluntary and prices are set by supply and demand in accord with abatement costs.

Economists have long advocated this sort of free market in emission rights, though they had envisioned the use of a slightly different instrument. They had proposed that the government print coupons to be purchased by any emitter, each coupon constituting an entitlement to a certain quantity of emissions of a prespecified variety, all presumably clearly printed on the face of the coupon. By its decision on the number of coupons it would issue, the government would determine their supply and hence the total quantity of emissions to be permitted in the area, say, during that month. The coupons would be freely salable and resalable on an open market where their price would be fixed by supply and demand.

The experimental results, part of which were reported earlier, have a bearing here. In that experiment, besides testing how the groups of subjects reacted to the presence of externalities, the effects of various policies were also investigated. It will be recalled that the externality in the experiment did not, of course, consist of the emission of pollutants that damage persons other than the polluter, but was injected in the form of a tax on all participants whose magnitude depended on the total number of trades undertaken by all participants together. Thus, if participant A decided to undertake an additional trade, this increased the tax bill paid by B, C, and all other participants. The group's welfare would, then, have been served by a restriction in number of trades in just the same way as, in reality, public welfare may be served by a reduction in noxious emissions.

The experiment stimulated three policy arrangements: no corrective policy, direct controls, and a market in trading coupons. These were evaluated by seeing how close each of them brought the group to its maximal welfare (earnings) level, which theoretically ideal behavior would have yielded.

The results were extremely clear. Leaving out the first two sessions for each experimental group (which could be treated as training periods), without any corrective policy, average earnings were only 33.9 percent of their maximum. With direct controls this figure rose to 56.6 percent. But with the market in coupons the groups of subjects earned, on the average, 98.3 percent of the maximum! The actual numbers should not have great weight imputed to them, because they depend so much on the terms of the experiment. However, the relative magnitudes are suggestive. And given the astonishing degree to which the pricing behavior in each and every experiment approximated that which economic behavior predicts, the results should surely not be taken lightly.

What the experiment confirms, then, is that with a little thought and flexibility it is possible to design a role for government that is very effective in stimulating improvement in the quality of life, yet is at the same time highly circumscribed and not very onerous. It also demonstrates how the market mechanism can be used to correct one of its own defects—the constraints it imposes upon substantial voluntary contributions by industry to quality of life.

GOVERNMENT AND THE PROFITABILITY OF SOCIAL GOALS

Many social goals represent what economists refer to as "beneficial externalities." For example, a firm that engages in unpatentable basic research, while it may benefit itself, incidentally provides valuable new information to others; that is, there are benefits external to the firm that generates them. Or an enterprise that provides on-the-job training to members of a deprived minority thereby incidentally improves the pool of workers from which other firms may derive their labor force.

The problem is that while enterprises that engage in activities yielding such economies automatically provide benefits to the community, if they are driven exclusively by the profit motive they will not engage in these beneficial activities to the extent that is optimal for society, because they are not compensated fully for their contribution to the social welfare. It is desirable, then, to induce firms to do these things to an extent greater than they would if impelled by the profit motive alone.

The economist's standard proposal in such cases is that the activities in question be encouraged by means of Pigouvian subsidies.[3] Such subsidies are payments to the firm by the public sector, with each unit of basic research or each minority worker receiving training accompanied by a subsidy to the firm that carries out the activity. The Pigouvian subsidy per unit (e.g., per worker trained) is equal to its marginal social contribution—the savings to future employers that the training of one such minority worker promises.

The basic point of this arrangement is that it increases the profitability of social contributions by the firm. Pigouvian subsidies make it more profitable for a company to provide beneficial externalities, and so they will induce profit-maximizing firms to increase the quantities of such beneficial externalities that they generate. In the examples, they will be led to carry out more basic research or to provide on-the-job training to more minority workers.

Thus the profit motive can be used to induce private enterprise to do more to help in the achievement of social goals, and economists have long advocated this use of the pursuit of profits. Indeed, it is possible in principle to set the subsidy payments at such a level that firms will generate the optimal amount of social benefit, as judged by a benefit-cost criterion. It has been proved many times in the economic literature that this will be so if the subsidy for a beneficial externality is exactly equal to its marginal social contribution. That is, the analysis indicates that profit-maximizing firms will find it in their interest to provide the socially optimal quantities of the socially beneficial externalities if the subsidies are set exactly in the way called for by the Pigouvian formula. If this is done, any action by the firm that benefits society will also increase the profits of the firm by a commensurate amount, and so the profit-maximizing firm will be induced to extend its activities just to the point that maximizes their benefits to society.

The conclusion is clear: There is considerable scope in the economy for prosocial behavior by firms to be induced to an optimal degree by the profit motive, provided the public sector provides just the right financial incentive for the purpose. The magnitude of the optimal subsidy for this purpose is equal to the marginal social benefit of the activity—the amount it contributes to groups and individuals other than the firm that carries it out. This approach, widely advocated by economists, then, represents a generally applicable use of the profit motive to elicit maximal net social contributions from the economy's enterprises.

COMPLEMENTARITY AND SUBSTITUTION AMONG SECTORS

This chapter has focused primarily upon the roles of profit-making industry and the public sector. However, there are other groups highly important for the social welfare, most of whom are private, nonprofit institutions. These include the foundations, hospitals, groups advocating improvements in the environment, and an enormous variety of other organizations. It is hardly necessary to document their contributions here. The roles of the three sectors—private industry, private nonprofit, and government—have, often for good reasons, been very different. For example, the nonprofit sector has often served as the conscience of government and has helped to induce the public sector to undertake valuable programs that might otherwise have been delayed, introduced in weaker form, or never have been introduced at all. Some differences in the roles of the private sector and government have already been discussed.

But the differences in these roles should not obscure the complementarity of the three sectors, the fact that the work of each can improve the performance of the others, so that the whole is, indeed, much more than the sum of the individual parts. This observation has been implicit in the preceding discussion of the role of government as a facilitator of industry's contributions to the social welfare.

The other side of the coin is the scope this area offers for substitution of one sector for another. Many tasks that have traditionally been considered the responsibility of government can be carried out, sometimes more effectively, by private organizations, profit-making or nonprofit.

The literature of economics has traditionally singled out a set of goods and services, called the "public goods," that benefit the general public, but that private industry cannot be expected to provide by itself. These include such disparate items as lighthouses, national defense, and basic research. Two common characteristics render them unsuitable for supply by private industry, unaided by government. The first of these characteristics is that it is difficult, indeed, economically infeasible, for their supplier to charge a price for their use. How does a lighthouse collect a fee from the ship that passes at a distance, protected by its warning signal? How do those who carry out basic research, that is, by definition, research whose ultimate product is unknown, charge a fee to the unidentifiable future users of its unpredictable products? The second defining property of such public goods is that, once they are available, their costs are not increased by an expansion of number of users. It costs the same to build and operate the lighthouse whether it is passed by 10 or 100 ships per day. The basic research uses no more resources if the knowledge it yields is used by 1 million persons rather than 20. This means that, once provided, additional use of such a product is costless to society; it uses up none of the economy's resources. Consequently, from the social point of view it is perverse to charge a price for such a service, a price that discourages its use by anyone.

The point in all this is that a public good is a good for which it is impractical to charge a price, and for which such a price is, in any event, undesirable. In short, it is the one type of good that should be provided "free," meaning that payment for the item by any individual should not be increased when he chooses to use more of it. Obviously, free goods are not the natural terrain of private enterprise, which survives and prospers, ultimately, on the revenues it derives from the sale of its products.

That is why the provision of public goods generally is and must be financed by government. It alone has the tax powers that enable it to pay for them without charging a price for additional use of their products. Many of these public goods, for example environmental protection and public health measures (such as control of infectious mosquito populations), are intimately related to the social welfare. The public goods, then, constitute a distinctive role for the government sector in provision for the welfare of society.

Yet, even here, room exists for significant participation by the other sectors. While no group outside the public sector can afford to *finance* the supply of public goods to any significant degree, the actual work often is carried out in other sectors, thereby contributing to overall efficiency.[4] True, basic research is carried out predominantly in the nonprofit universities. Military hardware and waste treatment equipment are produced by private industry, although all of these are funded to a considerable degree by government. The government *can* do all of these by itself, but experience and judgment suggest strongly that the public interest is served by having much of it carried out elsewhere. Thus, while each sector has its appropriate role, the three sectors together can serve the social interest most effectively. In this sense, then, the optimal arrangement is, indeed, a partnership involving both specialization and interaction.

ON THE ROLE OF ECONOMIC ANALYSIS

It is worth digressing briefly to note what illumination has been provided by economic analysis in the course of our discussion. It has offered two main types of contribution. First, it has explained why private industry is not able to do much more than it has done without suitable participation by the public sector. The inhibiting role of the market mechanism here is not generally understood and, as a result, business is apt to find its limited contributions misinterpreted as deliberate evasion of its responsibilities.

It is important to understand the relationship between the market mechanism and industry's freedom to adopt social goals not only to protect the latter from accusations that may be unfounded, but, more important, in order to enable society to do something about it. This is the second major area in which economic analysis can be and has been helpful. For it can help in the design of appropriate measures and in the evaluation of the measures that are derived from this source and others. The policies that emerge are sometimes rather unconventional and not of the sorts to which the general public is habituated. And the systematic evaluation of proposed policies can, as we have seen, yield somewhat surprising and surprisingly definitive results.

The moral is that in the arena with which we are dealing, common sense, while valuable, as it is everywhere, may suggest conclusions that, on more careful investigation, turn out not to be quite so sensible. Here, formal economic analysis can shed some additional light where it is needed and can buttress the foundations for rational policy decisions.

CONCLUDING COMMENTS

The issues that fall within the rubric of the social responsibilities of business are prone to give rise to responses based on emotion more than on reason. At one extreme, it is tempting to impute complete free will to the business community and, consequently, to interpret a limited response on its part as a cynical disregard of the interests of society. Alternatively, it is tempting to solve problems by fiat, in the belief that any difficulty can be disposed of simply by declaring it illegal. Both these extreme attitudes are misguided, unproductive, and can impose heavy costs upon society.

The analysis here has shown that matters are more complex and has delved into the character of at least some of the complexities. It has also shown the subtlety and delicacy required for the design of policy arrangements that are effective and do not waste society's valuable resources. Such programs inevitably must assign a role to the private sector and to government. And a primary task of government here is simply to make it possible for industry to play its part.

NOTES TO CHAPTER 8

1. A delightful example of the substitution of labor for fuel, according to newspaper reports, was a reversion to the employment of cowboys, who have resumed driving cattle to market on the hoof to economize on the use of petroleum by the trucks that normally transport the animals.

2. Other results of the experiment are equally remarkable. For example, prices converged almost precisely to the figure predicted by supply-demand analysis on the assumption that each participant gives up any attempt to serve the interests of others.

3. Named after their inventor, the late A.C. Pigou of Cambridge University, who first proposed them in 1911.

4. The relationship is not without its complications. For example, when funding is supplied by government, it is difficult to offer the incentives for efficiency that the market mechanism provides so well. There is the danger that compensation will employ arrangements such as cost-plus contracts that pay the supplying firms an amount equal to the costs they incur, plus a margin for profit. Such a contract is, in principle, an invitation to waste, and has often proved so in practice. Economic analysis has suggested devices for the purpose that are rather more promising. But as Leonid Hurwicz has pointed out in his comments on this chapter, the problem is far more fundamental than is suggested by the preceding remark on cost-plus contracts. If firms do not operate under some sort of profit-sharing arrangement, their motivation for efficiency is lost. In Professor Hurwicz's words, "If you have some form of profit sharing . . . you create the same incentive for the management to take advantage of monopolistic position that you have under [purely] private [operation]."

REFERENCES

Committee for Economic Development. 1972. *More Effective Programs for a Cleaner Environment.* New York.

Hirschman, Albert. 1977. *The Passions and the Interests: Political Arguments for Capitalism before Its Triumph.* Princeton, N.J.: Princeton University Press.

Plott, Charles R. 1982. "Externalities and Corrective Policies in Experimental Markets." Social Science Working Paper 180. California Institute of Technology.

Smith, Adam. *Wealth of Nations.* Modern Library. 1937.

Viner, Jacob. 1972. *The Role of Providence in the Social Order.* Princeton, N.J.: Princeton University Press.

 *Chapter 9*

What Is the Proper Role
of the Corporation?

Robert C. Clark

This chapter discusses the business corporation's role with respect to objectives that traditionally have been thought to be the responsibility of governmental units. The focus is on actual and possible legal norms that define what the purposes of a business corporation are. Examined first are some conceptions of the corporation's role and what can be said for and against each of them. In the second part of the chapter a different analytical approach to the concerns that underlie these traditional debates is suggested.

EXISTING CLUSTERS OF VIEWS

Five major clusters of views can be discerned concerning the corporation's proper role in relation to governmental tasks. For ease of analysis and reference, they can be given the labels usually applied to major strands of thought in philosophy: dualism, monism, modest idealism, high idealism, and pragmatism. In each case, I will first present a statement of the view, then describe its legal status, and then consider reasons for the viewpoint and objections to it.

It is only in a limited, special sense that these views are about the corporation's role. In a larger sense, the corporation's role in society depends on one's social philosophy. For example, if one is a utilitarian, as many people seem to be, one will see the corporation's role as being to aid in maximizing total welfare or happiness. One would not accept assertions that the corporation's sole purpose is to maximize profits for shareholders, or gains to consumers, or the welfare of any special group. A utilitarian legislator would insist on considering the net effects of the corporation on all affected groups of people. If corporations are generally maximizing the welfare of their consumers but harming other groups, for example, such a legislator would ask whether there were a way to rearrange things so as to increase the surplus of benefits over harms.

But there is also a more limited sense in which the phrase "the corporation's role" is meant: as a shorthand way of referring to the affirmative, open-ended goals that a particular corporation's ultimate decisionmakers should try to pursue. (In the current system, this decisionmaking group consists of the corporation's managers—its directors and officers.) Granted that these decisionmakers should cause the corporation to abide by specific legal duties imposed by lawmakers (who have, let us hope, taken a fully comprehensive viewpoint); how should they conceive their residual duty? Should they adopt the legislator's stance, or some other? These are the questions to which the following views relate.

Dualism: The Norm of Strict Profit Maximization

The dualist, who is also the traditionalist, regards the private and public spheres as having distinct functions that ought to be kept distinct. Accordingly, from the traditional legal viewpoint, a corporation's directors and officers have a fiduciary duty to maximize shareholder wealth, subject to numerous duties to meet specific obligations to other groups affected by the corporation.

Several comments about this norm are needed to forestall some common misunderstandings of it. First, under appropriate conditions and definitions, different formulations of the thing to be maximized—"profits," "the company's net present value," "the market value of the company's common shares," and "shareholder wealth"—turn out to be equivalent to one another. Similarly, the profit-maximizing norm does *not* imply a commitment to short-run profits at the expense of long-run profits. All intelligent formulations of the norm, such as the "net present value" or "stock market value" ones, implicitly assume that a wealth maximizing balance should be struck between long- and short-run profits. In any event, for my purposes most of the alleged differences in formulations can be ignored.

Second, the profit-maximizing norm does *not* imply that corporations and their managers have only minimal legal obligations to persons other than shareholders. Quite the contrary is true. Every major relationship between the corporation and persons or groups it affects is subject to vast and intricate bodies of legal doctrine and to legal enforcement mechanisms. These legal controls are ineffective in some instances and suboptimal in others, but they exist. Almost all of the relationships between the corporation and other groups are governed by contract and tort law. The relationship between a corporation and its creditors is ordinarily governed also by provisions of the Uniform Commercial Code, fraudulent conveyance law, the state laws on collection and enforcement of debts, and the federal bankruptcy and reorganization laws. The relationship between a corporation and its employees is governed by the labor laws, various civil rights statutes, the Occupational Safety and Health Act, the Employee Retirement Income Security Act, and numerous other statutes. The relationship between the corporation and its customers is affected or governed by the federal and state antitrust laws, consumer protection statutes, product liability rules, truth in lending laws, and many others. The relationship between the corporation and the general public is massively affected by major regulatory statutes, such as the pollution laws and numerous regimes of more industry-specific application. The relationship between a corporation and various governmental entities is heavily controlled by tax statutes of all kinds. And so on.

If the legal system as a whole imposes so many duties to so many constituencies and thus mandates a wide-ranging (though perhaps inadequate and not ultimately coherent) accommodation of diverse interests, what, if anything, is the real meaning of the profit-maximizing norm? The answer is that it tells corporate managers what their *residual* goal is—or, in financial management jargon, what the company's "objective function" is. The duties to all other groups need simply be satisfied, they function as constraints. But the duty to shareholders is open-ended: Profits should be made as large as possible, within the constraints.

Perhaps surprisingly, the state business corporation statutes under which corporations are chartered generally do not say explicitly that the purpose of a business corporation is to make or maximize profits. When the statutes do refer to the corporation's purposes, they usually mean its lines of business. The general profit-maximizing purpose has nearly always been assumed by courts and lawyers, however, and legal authorities sometimes state and use the general purpose as a basis of decision. In the famous case of *Dodge* v. *Ford Motor Co.*,[1] for example, the Michigan Supreme Court viewed as bad faith and a breach of fiduciary duty Henry Ford's use of his power to withhold corporate dividends, over the objection of minority shareholders, in order to be able to sell cars more cheaply and benefit the American public at the expense of corporate profits. The court told Mr. Ford that the corporation was not an eleemosynary institution, and that, though his objective was laudable, he should not be generous with other people's money. In addition, the statutory[2] and case law[3] formulations of the directors' and officers' duty of care can easily be read to imply profit maximization as the ultimate goal.

Perhaps the most notable justification of the strict profit-maximizing goal is Milton Friedman's essay entitled "The Social Responsibility of Business Is to Increase Its Profits" (*New York Times* 1970). I will present a similar but differently structured argument. The argument has a positive and a negative side. We gain a lot from strict profit maximization in terms of private-sector performance, but we do not really jeopardize the attainment of public policies.

More specifically, the argument proceeds as follows. A single, objective goal like profit maximization is more easily monitored than a multiple, vaguely defined goal like the fair and reasonable accommodation of all affected interests. It is easier, for example, to tell if a corporate manager is doing what she is supposed to do than to tell if a university president is doing what she is supposed to do. Since shareholders do have some effective control mechanisms—the proxy context, the takeover bid, and the derivative law suit—better monitoring means that corporate managers will be kept more accountable. They are more likely to do what they are supposed to do, and do it efficiently. Better accountability thus encourages people to participate in large organizations, in which claims on the organization and the power to manage it are necessarily separated; it helps such organizations exist and function well. Large organizations are in turn often desirable for everyone. They increase social welfare, for without them certain large-scale business ventures would be impossible or would be carried out in a wasteful way.

And on the other side, no one need be made worse off by the corporation's having a single goal of profit maximization. The interests of nonshareholder groups like employees can be protected by contract, common law developments, and special legislation. Negative externalities like pollution can be corrected by tort law or pollution laws telling companies not to pollute or taxing them when they do. The production of public goods and the redistribution of wealth from rich to poor can be better accomplished by actual governments, which have a more legitimate claim to do these things. And corporate resources can still be diverted to these governmental activities—in small or great measure, as elected representatives see fit—because governments can tax both corporations and their shareholders. Profit maximization is therefore a legitimate and desirable goal for business corporations.

Objections to the preceding line of argument should be considered in two parts. The first concerns the dualist view that strict profit maximization promotes better monitoring and enforcement of the corporation's economic performance. No truly persuasive critique of this view has been offered. Though it is difficult to make any definitive comparison between the relative tightness of controls on managerial performance as between business corporations and governmental units, and though the total set of market and legal controls on corporate managers clearly leaves them with a significant amount of slack or uncontrolled discretionary power to deviate from strict profit maximization, the evidence for the power of capital market controls on managerial behavior is very strong, and getting stronger (Easterbrook and Fischel 1981). Earlier writers like Galbraith and Marris, who in the 1960s proposed that corporate managers maximize size or sales rather than profits, have been seriously challenged by later empirical work (McEachern 1975).

That leaves us with the negative side of the dualist argument. The most serious criticisms of the dualist viewpoint are those that attack the notions that external governmental regulation of corporations can be an effective way of correcting market failures and that strictly profit-maximizing corporations will not seriously distort political mechanisms for deciding collectively about the size and nature of redistributive programs. So much evidence of governmental and regulatory failure has accumulated in the last decade or so that many critics have urged that corporations must be involved more directly in setting and pursuing public goals, if we are to achieve them at all well. As the committed dualist would quickly point out, however, even massive regulatory failure does not necessarily imply a change in the corporation's residual goal of strict profit maximization. It does so only if (1) an alternative to external regulation were available that would result in better achievement of the legitimate public goals behind regulation, (2) the alternative would necessitate a change in the profit-maximizing goal, (3) the cost of the alternative (in terms of reduced monitoring and control of corporate managers' performance, for example) would not outweigh the gains, and (4) no other alternative reform strategy exists that would yield a better cost-benefit ratio but not involve a change in the corporation's goal.

Many analysts have pressed vigorously for regulatory reforms that do not impinge on the dualist norm. An example is the call to greater deployment of market-mimicking incentives like user fees on polluters rather than simple prohibitions against effluents exceeding a single standard (Schultze 1977). But others, like Elliott Weiss (1981), have bitten the bullet and argued, in effect, that the four conditions just listed do obtain.

Monism: Long-Run Identity between Public and Private Interests

The monist viewpoint is that many types of corporate activities that appear to be profit-reducing voluntary expenditures for the public good are really conducive to profit maximization in the long run. Virtually no one is a strict or absolute monist; that is, one who believes that all public spirited tasks a corporation may engage in will conduce to long-run profits. The typical monist believes rather that there is some set of socially responsible corporate activities that it is good for corporations to foster, because doing so will eventually create a "better climate or culture" in which business can operate. The set of socially responsible activities is usually understood (not defined) in an extremely conventional sense to include contributions to recognized charities and nonprofit organizations, modest investments in blighted urban areas, employment of minority or handicapped workers, and the like.

Limited monism has been sanctioned by both courts and legislatures. In an earlier time, a board of directors that caused a corporation to make a gift to a university might find itself sued in a stockholder's derivative action based on the theory that there had been a waste of corporate assets. After some initial uncertainty, courts were inclined to accept at face value managerial arguments that, in their honest business judgment, their corporation's charitable contributions would promote its long-run profitability, and so did not constitute waste.[4] State corporation statutes now routinely allow boards of directors to make charitable contributions,[5] and the Internal Revenue Code facilitates them to the extent of allowing a limited deduction for such contributions.[6] Notice, however, that these statutory authorities deal only with conventional charitable contributions. If directors are attacked for causing their corporation to embark on other kinds of socially responsible activities that take away from tangible short-run opportunities to increase profits, they have to invoke the business judgment rule.

With a possible exception or two,[7] courts have not retreated from the assumption that the primary or residual purpose of a business corporation is to make profits for its shareholders. Accordingly, it is important for managers to make the right noises—namely, some version of the monist argument—when they cause their corporations to embark upon some socially responsible activity. On the other hand, if they are at all careful to do so, it is almost impossible for shareholders to attack their actions successfully.

The abstractly stated monist view is logically consistent with the dualist viewpoint, as defined earlier. In practice, of course, some observers will disagree with the judgment that the sorts of activities that monists like to foster really do promote long-run maximization of a corporation's profits.

The basic argument for the monist view is that received notions of profit maximization were too narrow minded, because they were overly biased toward tangible short-run payoffs, and ultimately self-defeating, because they led corporations to behave in a way that caused society at large to be permanently suspicious of corporations.

The main argument against monist views is that they are a facade for the illegitimate accumulation and exercise of managerial prerogatives. This argument can be broken down into four steps. First, managers almost always enjoy some slack or freedom to deviate from strict profit maximization, because market and legal controls are never perfect. Second, because of the differential effectiveness of controls on different kinds of deviation from profit maximization, managers do not capture the value of slack only in the form of excessive pay; they also secure perquisites of many kinds (Williamson 1967). Third, one kind of perquisite is managerial power to direct corporate resources toward nonbusiness goals that suit the managers' political preferences. Fourth, these managerially chosen public goals often do not have much to do with long-run profit maximization by the particular corporation, do not reflect their shareholders' preferences, and do not reflect the public policy preferences of citizens at large. And the more readily managers' monist arguments can be shielded from challenge by the business judgment rule, the more likely it is that these disparities will occur. In short, monism is plutocracy in disguise.

Less sophisticated arguments against monist activities are that they do not in fact create a significantly better climate for business; they cannot do much to solve social problems, given current and foreseeable levels of monist activities; and they may deflect governments from adopting much needed taxing and regulatory measures.

Modest Idealism: Voluntary Compliance with Law

The essence of modest idealism is that corporate managers should cause their corporations to comply with applicable laws and regulations even when noncompliance would increase the corporation's net present value. Consider, for example, a complex water pollution statute and the elaborate administrative regulations that implement it. For a given corporation that has long been accustomed to discharge pollutants into rivers next to its factories, the estimated cost of compliance is $10 million. There is no honest doubt, let us assume, about which regulations apply to the corporation, whether they are legally valid, and how they are supposed to be met. There is only a small probability, however, that if the corporation fails to comply with the regulations, its noncompliance will be both discovered and corrected (through successful legal proceedings) by the regulators. The corporation expects that, if there is discovery and successful enforcement, it will incur additional legal fees, a modest fine, and delayed expenditure of $10 million for compliance. Using their best business judgment, the managers discount these costs by their probability of occurrence and by their futurity, and they conclude that the estimated present value of these costs of noncompliance is only $2 million. Thus, compared to compliance, noncompliance has a net present value of $8 million. From a purely profit-maximizing point of view, the managers may decide not to comply with the pollution regulations, unless and until the regulators bring legal proceedings specifically against their corporation. The modest idealist would say that the managers should not be guided by a cost-benefit analysis that takes the probability of successful enforcement into account but should cause their corporation to comply with the regulations promptly.

Two cautionary points are worth noting. First, modest idealism is only modest in its conception of idealistic behavior; the corporate manager is not asked to create public policy but only to help carry it out. But to its proponents, modest idealism is not at all modest or trivial in its economic significance. Christopher Stone (1975), for example, has argued vigorously and persuasively that the main problem in making corporations socially responsible is the problem of enforcement of defined public policies. Many of the most shocking examples of corporate misbehaviors involve conduct that violates existing law.

Second, as with monism, modest idealism is not logically inconsistent with the traditional dualist viewpoint, as it was defined earlier. Dualism holds that managers should maximize shareholder wealth, *subject to* the constraint that the corporation meet its specific legal obligations to other persons. In a sense, modest idealism merely postulates that the constraint should not be interpreted as containing an implicit qualification that managers may or must take the likelihood and cost of enforcement activities into account when deciding whether to meet specific legal obligations.

Though clear and explicit legal authority is hard to come by, it seems obvious that modest idealism would be acceptable to the courts. For example, suppose a shareholder brought a derivative action for waste against his corporation's directors, claiming that they caused the corporation to spend $10 million to comply with (valid and clearly applicable) water pollution regulations even though any rational cost-benefit analysis would have led them to opt for noncompliance. It is difficult to believe that any court would give more than short shrift to such an argument. Nor is this prediction a function of the business judgment rule. It should make little difference if the plaintiff offered clear and convincing evidence to show that the directors completely neglected to make any sort of cost-benefit analysis of compliance versus noncompliance. Indeed, if corporate managers did commission and act upon an explicit cost-benefit analysis of this sort and left a written record of it that later came to light in a legal proceeding to enforce the pollution laws, it is likely that their activity would be a target of judicial condemnation rather than a recognizable excuse.[8]

These intuitions are consistent with the rhetoric that corporations actually use when resisting regulation. When challenged, noncompliers never say they made a rational decision to run for it in the hope that they would not be caught. Typically, they try to argue that the regulations do not apply to them, at least not in the manner alleged; that the agency followed improper procedures in adopting or enforcing the regulations; that the regulations exceeded the agency's statutory authority (here cost-benefit analyses do come into play); and so forth. All of this seems to assume the legal validity of modest idealism.

Outside of litigation settings, one does sometimes hear corporate managers and attorneys try to rationalize corporate noncompliance with regulatory statutes by complaining that the devil of fiduciary duties to shareholders made them do it. What they are complaining about is not corporate law, which certainly does not tell them to break other laws in order to make their shareholders richer, but the unfortunate fact that, if they do not take advantage of lax legal enforcement, they may be ousted by aggressive managers who will.

One major argument for modest idealism is that, if corporate managers lived up to its mandate, the bad side effects of profit-seeking activity in the private sector would be greatly mitigated. If corporations voluntarily complied with the antitrust laws as interpreted by the courts, more of the surplus from economic transactions would go to consumers in general rather than to strategically situated clumps of investors, managers, and employees. If corporations voluntarily complied with the environmental laws, they would greatly curtail important negative externalities of modern business enterprise. If corporations fully complied with workplace safety regulations or drug testing regulations, they would curtail other kinds of bad side effects of business activity. And so forth. This argument assumes that the antitrust laws, the environmental laws, and other major laws whose implementation would benefit from voluntary compliance are socially desirable on balance. The modest idealist may postulate this assumption as reflecting his own best judgment or may appeal to the idea that the laws reflect the outcome of a more or less legitimate political process, and should not be second-guessed in the enforcement context.

A major part of the modest idealist's first line of argument is to convince everyone that noncompliance with regulation is a major problem and compliance would have important and desirable effects. I submit that they have had more success with the first premise than with the second.

A second line of argument for modest idealism is that voluntary compliance reduces the transaction costs generated by the legal system. When law is internalized; when citizens follow the rules even when the policeman isn't looking; when, in short, law becomes morality—then the costs of enforcing law will drop.

A third line of argument is that, if most business leaders act as modest idealists most of the time, society at large will upgrade its estimate of the legitimacy of the modern business corporation, and there will be a truly better climate for business. This is because the corporate manager who acts as a modest idealist is bound to be seen by the public as a nobler and more trustworthy figure than the calculating opportunist.

One drawback of modest idealism is that it is subject to the familiar difficulties of voluntary collective action, such as the free rider problem and the prisoner's dilemma, and so is only likely to be possible within a range of action that corresponds to managerial slack. In short, it is not likely to work very well; its economic effects are likely to be modest after all. For example, if any one corporation's board of directors decides to comply voluntarily with an expensive regulatory statute, but their competitors do not, their company may take a beating in the market for its products. In addition, when the company's actual stock market value drops (because of its reduced earnings) relative to its potential value (as revealed by comparison to the stock market values of noncomplying competitor companies), the company may well become the subject of a takeover bid, after which the idealistic managers will be replaced. To be sure, these adverse reactions from the product and capital markets would not occur if managers of all firms in the industry acted as modest idealists. But how, short of coercive collective action of some sort, is this state of affairs going to come about? Any individual corporation will observe that the best of all possible worlds would be for the other corporations to act as modest idealists while it acted as a calculating opportunist; for then it would gain an enormous competitive advantage.

A second major objection to modest idealism is the same as one raised against dualism: the laws and regulations that are actually adopted do not reflect optimal public policy, for there are systematic imperfections in the traditional lawmaking process. Accordingly, corporations should be enlisted in the work of defining public policies, not just in pursuing them.

High Idealism: Interest Group Accommodation and the Public Interest as Residual Goals

High idealism holds that the business corporation's residual goal, and not just its specific, externally imposed legal obligations, should be defined to include a much wider set of interests than those of the shareholders. One variation is that the purpose of the corporation and the general residual duty of those who hold decisionmaking power over its activities is to achieve a reasonable accommodation of the interests of all groups affected by the corporation. Another version is that the basic purposes of a corporation include not only the objective of making profits but also that of furthering the public interest, as conceived by its decisionmakers.

Other variants could also be stated. Most of them avoid the concept of maximization (of an interest, of a variable, of a sum of interests or variables, or anything else), and in effect they reject or ignore the concept of an identifiable group of owners of the corporation's residual value. Consequently, they are inevitably vague and do not imply an operational meaning or measure of good corporate performance. Unlike the other views considered here, high idealism *is* logically inconsistent with the traditional dualist viewpoint.

A prototypical example of how the interest-group variation of high idealism might apply is a proposed plant closing. Suppose a corporation in a northeastern city operates a factory that is losing money, and its directors are considering whether to close it and open a substitute plant in a Sunbelt town where taxes are lower, labor is cheaper, energy use would be less, shipping facilities are more modern and convenient, and the surrounding environment is more pleasant. The workers at the old factory, as well as some activists who reside in the city, protest the proposed plant closing, claiming that it will cause a hardship to the workers and will lead to all the bad consequences of increased unemployment in a declining local economy. The high idealist would say that the directors should consider the interests of the employees and of the neighborhood, and they might justifiably decide to continue operating the old plant, even though it continued to lose money or made a subnormal rate of return. Perhaps the high idealist would draw a line at operating losses and say that they would almost always justify a plant closing, although inability to maximize profits would not. The important conceptual point, however, is that the corporate decisionmakers might properly consider the interests of the affected workers even though they were not bound to do so by contract or by the labor laws.

An example of the application of the public interest variant of high idealism would be the cigarette manufacturing company that voluntarily ceases to make cigarettes even though business is highly profitable, because its decisionmakers have finally become convinced that cigarette smoking does indeed cause some 350,000 premature deaths per year in the United States. Once again, the important conceptual point is that the corporate decisionmakers would not be acting to fulfill an explicit governmental command. Instead, they would be making their own determination as to what was a negative externality or "public bad," and voluntarily adopting a policy to reduce it.

These examples suggest an important caveat. The corporate actions involved might also be justified in traditional, nonidealistic terms—specifically, within the monist framework. The directors might decide that not closing a currently unprofitable plant would promote the company's long-run profitability by improving labor relations. This need not be a disingenuous or mistaken judgment. Observers of Japanese companies have long suggested that a policy of lifetime employment can have sizable benefits, such as fewer strikes and a more loyal work force, for the sponsoring corporation. Similarly, though perhaps less persuasively, deciding to cease production of a major health hazard might improve public relations and solidify long-term profitability. Thus, though in theory the monist and high idealist positions will result in radically different actions in some situations, it is difficult to assess beforehand how their implications will differ in practice. And it is misleading to assign particular classes of apparently socially responsible activities exclusively to one or another of the theoretical viewpoints.

More acutely than the other viewpoints, high idealism raises the question, *Who decides* how the corporation's general purpose is to be accomplished? The traditional view, as embodied in the business corporation laws of all states, is that the business of the corporation is to be managed by (or under the supervision of) its board of directors, who are elected by shareholders.[9] Logically, the high idealist might want decisionmaking power over particular corporate activities to reside in shareholder-elected directors, or directly in shareholders, or in a board composed of directors elected by members of a number of different constituencies, or in a board containing representatives appointed by an explicit governmental unit. Let us call these options managerial decisionmaking, investor decisionmaking, interest-group decisionmaking, and government-influenced decisionmaking, respectively.

In practice, idealists of the interest-group variety tend to support reforms that would promote interest-group decisionmaking. The most common, yet the most limited, proposal of this sort is to have employee representation on the board of directors, as is done in some other countries (Vagts 1966; Steuer 1979; Olson 1979). More ambitious interest-group representation has been urged by the Nader group (Nader, Green and Seligmen 1976; Engel 1979). For the high idealist of the public interest variety, such as Elliott Weiss, government-appointed directors seem to be a more natural reform proposal (Weiss 1981: 41834).

High idealism, as defined previously, is not embodied in current statutes and case law. Its various formulations are to be found in the writings of reform-oriented commentators. Occasionally, corporate managers will say that what they are trying to do, what they ought to do, and what they think the law allows or requires them to do is to effect an accommodation of the whole family of interests in their corporation, not to maximize profits. But such statements seem to reflect either ignorance of specific legal authorities or a bid for greater discretionary power.

Perhaps the main reason for high idealism is government failure. Explicit lawmaking and regulatory activities are said to be flawed in many ways. The legislatures and agencies suffer from informational problems, perverse agenda-setting processes, capture by vested interests, nonrepresentation of diffuse interests, poor incentive structures and role definitions for the lawmakers and regulators, and more (Weiss 1981: 37893; Breyer 1982). In view of these failures, it seems prudent to encourage private enterprise, perhaps only on an experimental basis, to participate actively in the definition and execution of public policies. Since the setting and implementation of public policy is in such bad shape, so the argument goes, we must try something new.

A second argument for high idealism is that it would help to disperse governmental power and responsibility, thus reducing the likelihood of a wholesale abuse of that power and promoting participatory democracy. For this argument to work, reasons should be furnished why the thousands of local governmental units in the federal system do not provide an adequate dispersal of power and responsibility.

Another argument sometimes offered for interest-group variations of high idealism is that a large corporation always has powerful impacts on the lives of certain groups of people, such as employees, consumers, and neighbors, and the latter therefore ought to have a direct voice in determining how the corporation runs, in order both to protect their interests and to develop participatory decisionmaking as an end in itself. To the extent that this argument is not based on simple romanticism or deep confusion about the nature of decisionmaking in a complex economy, it seems to reflect a belief that the kinds of controls on corporations that affected groups do have are either impotent or inadequate and cannot be made adequate at reasonable cost. These currently available controls include market forces (corporate behavior is powerfully affected by consumer choices); legal mechanisms (consumers can sue under existing tort law and consumer protection laws); and the right to lobby governments to tax and regulate corporations in certain ways. To this combination of opportunities for "exit" and "voice" (Hirschman 1970), the interest-group idealists would add an opportunity for a more direct voice in ordinary business decisionmaking.

One main argument against high idealism is that, to the extent it would make a difference, it would have a very high cost in terms of decreased economic performance by corporations. It might impair overall allocational efficiency. For example, the corporation that quickly accedes to demands not to close an unsuccessful plant may be adding to immobility in the flow of resources to more productive uses; it may be merely putting a costly drag on changes that eventually ought to be made. Indeed, high idealism may lead to a low level of managerial performance even in terms of its own, partly noneconomic objectives. This point is the reverse side of the main positive argument for dualism. Since corporate decisionmakers would not be assigned the task of maximizing a single, objective, easily monitored goal, it would be very difficult to keep them truly accountable to a vague statement of purposes.

A second argument is that high idealism might be largely ineffective. Consider this point under three assumptions. (1) If the idealist viewpoint were implemented by some form of managerial decisionmaking, the managers might well lack the incentive or the slack to pursue the more broadly defined goals to a significant extent, unless they were somehow shielded more effectively than they now are from takeover bids, derivative lawsuits, and competition in their product markets. A deliberate governmental weakening of these present controls, in order to give managers more discretionary power to serve the general good as they saw fit, would probably do more harm than good. Among other things, the newly increased discretionary power might in fact be used by managers for their own benefit, just as existing amounts of slack seem inevitably to be turned into perquisites or excessive compensation.

(2) Could high idealism be implemented by shareholder decision-making? It seems unlikely that shareholders would often sacrifice their self-interest to the interest of other affected groups. The poor voting record on corporate social action proposals under the federal proxy rules supports this prediction.

(3) If high idealism were implemented by interest-group decision-making of some sort, it might indeed have real effects. But caution is needed even here. Labor representation on boards of directors, in countries where it has been tried, seems not to have made nearly as much difference as early proponents thought it might. Partly this is because corporate behavior must often bend to other controlling forces, such as consumer choices in the product markets. If a company keeps a relatively inefficient plant in operation, for example, it may have to charge more than competitors, lose business, and eventually be forced to change its practices or seek a governmental bailout. This need not happen if competitors are following similar policies of accommodating nonshareholder interests. But, once again, one must realize the limits of voluntary collective action.

A third argument against high idealism (the main one, in the eyes of some observers) is that it would constitute an illegitimate form of government—a case of oligarchy in disguise and on a very grand scale indeed. When implemented by managerial or shareholder decision-making, the high idealist's brand of social responsibility will reflect mostly upper class preferences. Consider, for example, that over half of the corporate stocks and bonds owned by individuals (or estates, trusts, and the like) in the United States are held by the wealthiest 1 percent of the population (U.S. Bureau of the Census 1979: 544, table 897; 470, table 775) and that managers of large, publicly held corporations are paid incomes that send them into orbits far above the ordinary ground-level income (Forbes 1982). Policies defined by such persons will have a very different scheme of priorities and effects than policies made by democratically elected representatives of the entire population. This is true even though democratically elected bodies are in fact heavily influenced by elite interest groups.

If high idealism is implemented by some form of interest-group decisionmaking, it may or may not be legitimate from the point of view of one who insists on broad representation and participation. Unless great care is taken in the institutional design, some groups who ought to have power (or "direct voice") may not get it. Consider, for example, the possible implications of a board composed of directors elected by shareholders and employees. The interests of these groups may conflict seriously with those of consumers and governmental units. For example, featherbedding may be desired by employees but may raise prices to consumers and result in lower profits, thus reducing corporate income tax revenues to certain governments. Unless there is some good reason to think that these latter groups already possess adequate controls on corporations, whereas labor does not, the premises of interest-group idealism seem to suggest that they also be given "direct" voice.

A fourth argument against high idealism is that, with so many thousands of minigovernments (namely, the newly transformed business corporations) acting independently to define and implement public policy, overall public policy is likely to be even more incoherent and uncoordinated than it is now. The strength of this argument varies with one's estimate of the importance of overall coherence in public policymaking and may be different in different substantive areas—for example, more important for health care policy than for land use policy.

Despite these many objections, it should be stressed that no one knows with certainty that corporations transformed in accord with some leading version of high idealism would fail to make a net improvement in the overall welfare of our society. The hard questions are ultimately empirical ones, and high idealism has not yet been tried on a significant scale in the American setting.

Pragmatism: Contracting to Provide Public Services

Pragmatism holds that governmental units should make much greater use of business corporations to implement public policies and that business corporations should design, develop, and seize opportunities to perform public services on a profit-making basis. For example, the typical pragmatist wants the realm of government contracting to expand well beyond traditional activities like making weapons for the Defense Department and office buildings for other governmental units. He envisages more contracting by business corporations to provide job training for members of minority groups, to redevelop urban areas, to educate children, and to run municipal hospitals. Like its counterpart in academic philosophy, pragmatism in this sense is as American as apple pie.[10]

Nothing in corporate law encourages or restrains the pragmatist viewpoint, which is logically quite consistent with the traditional dualist viewpoint. Such legal norms as exist that bear on the possibility of realizing pragmatist hopes are to be found in the numerous laws that influence when governments may or may not contract with private, for-profit corporations.

A major argument for pragmatism is the claim that business corporations can bring more expertise and more efficient management and production techniques to bear on the solution of social problems and the provision of social services. This effect is seen as flowing from the fact that private corporations are more tightly disciplined by product market forces and capital market forces than are government bureaucracies.

Another argument for pragmatism is that it may ultimately reduce the "we-they" feeling that now exists between persons who work for business corporations and those who work for governmental and nonprofit organizations. That there is such an opposition seems confirmed by the growing literature emphasizing the cultural difference between the "productive class" and the "new class" (Bell 1976).[11] On the other hand, increased corporate participation in the provision of public services may simply exacerbate the existing tensions, since it would threaten the established turfs of some members of the new class.

The main argument against pragmatism is that profit-maximizing private corporations that contract to provide public services will be tempted to cut corners and to neglect noneconomic values and policies. For example, a for-profit elementary school that is paid by a local government on the basis, say, of the number of students it graduates from each grade each year who can pass certain standardized tests, will be tempted to skimp on the acquisition of library books and the development of social skills, and it may try to keep out or discourage applicants who are likely to be poor learners—a group that may contain disproportionately more members of minority groups. These tendencies could be controlled by explicit rules, but (so the objection would go) the rule-making that would ultimately be needed would be extremely cumbersome and costly to enforce. How potent this objection is will obviously depend on the context. More about this problem follows.

A RECONCEPTUALIZATION

Most discussions of the business corporation's role in meeting social needs approach the problem with a focus on the corporation and its decisionmakers. Economists typically consider what corporations do, what their managers are legally required to do, and what the managers might be encouraged to do. That is the approach reviewed in the first part of this chapter. A more productive approach might be to focus on *activities* oriented to the general public interest and to ask whether we can develop a good theory of the proper *location* of such public-regarding activities. This approach suggests that we start by considering which activities are considered and which should be considered to "belong" in some sense to the "public sector"; then consider why a governmental unit sometimes internalizes its characteristic activities, and sometimes externalizes them; and finally consider why, when a governmental unit does externalize activities, it sometimes delegates only to private and nonprofit corporations, and sometimes delegates also to private for-profit corporations.

Distinguishing among "Public Sector" Activities

Social welfare theory as developed by economists (Baumol 1952, 1965) makes a coherent and reasonably clear distinction between activities that belong to the private sector and those that belong to the public sector. The public sector is supposed to produce "public goods" (Samuelson 1954, 1955), prevent and correct market failures, and redistribute wealth; the private sector is supposed to do everything else. This statement of the division does not isolate in adequately precise terms the essence of governmental institutions, however. A distinction should be made between essential governmental functions and appropriate types of governmentally mandated activities. At the core of government is coercive resolution of collective action problems, not public-regarding activities themselves.

Perhaps this point can be made clearer by a series of definitions. *The government* is defined as the set of organizations in society that carry out core governmental functions. *Core governmental functions* mean (1) the setting up of rules mandating the principal kinds of public-regarding activities and (2) the control and deployment of ultimate means of coercion for the purposes of enforcing such rules. *The principal kinds of public-regarding activities* are the redistribution of wealth (for example, through taxing and spending programs); the establishment and maintenance of basic institutions that form the matrix in which the nongovernmental activities take place (for example, such institutions as contract law, property law, and the antitrust laws in our political system); the production of public goods; and the correction of market failures. Under these definitions, it is logically possible that many or even all of the principal kinds of public-regarding activities will not be carried out by the government. Sometimes the very organizations comprised by government will internalize the conduct of those activities, but sometimes they will externalize them. Internalization is a process that usually corresponds to using employees of the governmental organizations, while externalization usually corresponds to some form of contracting out. Ideally, however, one should not equate externalization to contracting out, a technical legal concept that may lack clear meaning in some political systems and contexts; instead it should be understood in a more institutional sense as referring to activities not done within some actual, sociologically recognizable government organization.

History and contemporary practice give us many examples of both externalization and internalization of public-regarding activities. The collection of taxes is certainly a public-regarding activity in this sense, but it has sometimes been accomplished by independent tax collectors rather than by government organizations and employees. Similarly, redistributive spending and the provision of social services is often accomplished externally. Consider, for example, that the federal medicare program not only relies on private hospitals and private physicians to provide the services paid for by the program, but also contracts out the payment function itself to numerous "fiscal intermediaries"—principally the Blue Cross and Blue Shield Plans—that are private corporations. National defense is a prototypical public good, but many governments have hired mercenaries, even mercenary armies, and in our own system most of the design and production of weapons has been contracted out to private enterprises. Reducing the negative externalities of a market economy is also a classic public-regarding activity, but the degree to which its actual accomplishment is assigned to governmental versus nongovernmental organizations varies substantially over time and across jurisdictions. In particular, there are shifts in the balance between private versus public enforcement of rules about externalities. In an earlier phase of our industrial history, pollution generated by business tended to be attacked, if at all, by private plaintiffs in tort actions. In more modern times, government bureaucracies have been created to grant or deny licenses, to make inspections, and to bring enforcement actions.

Determining the Degree of "Vertical Integration" of Governmental Organizations

What factors determine the mix between internalization and externalization of public-regarding activities? There is no satisfying general theory to answer this question, but several apparently major influences can be mentioned. They can be divided into normatively appropriate factors and normatively irrelevant or objectionable factors.

First, a major form of justification for internalization is that it permits better coordination of governmental activities and better assurance of reliability and stability in their performance. Or, more abstractly and with somewhat different connotations, it permits a reduction in transaction costs, namely, the costs (defined very broadly) of contracting out. This kind of rationale is parallel to the reasons given by managers of business corporations and by historians of business (Chandler 1962) to explain why so many business corporations have resorted to vertical integration.

Second, a major form of argument for externalization is that nongovernmental organizations exist that can perform the public-regarding activities more efficiently and expertly. Whether this is true, and the nature of the public-regarding activities with respect to which it is true, obviously depend heavily on the actual nature and level of development of the particular governmental and nongovernmental organizations that exist in a society when the question is raised. Consequently, even as a purely normative matter, the optimal equilibrium between internalization and externalization will be extremely contingent upon the historical and cultural context. It may make sense for governmental organizations, as the society in which they operate becomes larger, more complex, and more technologically advanced, to become significantly more vertically integrated in some respects and much less so in others.

In addition to the two factors mentioned, there are undoubtedly others that are important but regrettable. One obvious possibility is that top-level bureaucrats in government have a natural tendency to expand their bureaus because doing so will often give them greater prestige and power and thus to internalize public-regarding (and other!) activities well beyond the optimal point. This tendency may be bolstered by an ideological framework that leads them to a systematic discounting of the value and potential value of nongovernmental organizations.

Allocating Activities to Nonprofit and For-Profit Organizations

An extremely important fact about government's externalization of public-regarding activities is that government is not equally ready to delegate to or to contract with private nonprofit and private for-profit corporations. The government is willing to contract for weapons manufacture and highway construction with for-profit corporations, for example, but seems willing to give tax subsidies for education only to nonprofit corporations. Many similar withholdings of governmental support to for-profits can be found in our medical care delivery system (Clark 1980). (To facilitate the present discussion, I am here assuming, as many people do, that education, or at least elementary education, and the provision of medical care contain significant public-regarding elements and are therefore appropriate arenas for substantial government intervention.) What determines when public-regarding activities may be contracted out or delegated to for-profit corporations?

The answer to this question should be sought in the emerging theory of the nonprofit corporation. The main legal distinction between the for-profit and the nonprofit corporation is the application to the latter of a rule that might be labeled "the nondistribution constraint." Ordinary business corporations have shareholders who are allowed to receive the residual earnings of the enterprise by means of distributions—that is, dividends, stock redemptions, and payouts on liquidation of the enterprise. By contrast, the members of a nonprofit corporation are expressly prohibited from receiving any part of the assets or property of the corporation for themselves. This means that all residual earnings must be rededicated to the corporation's activities, which are usually specified in the charter to be of a charitable, religious, scientific, educational, or similar nature. The leading current theory of nonprofit enterprises (Hansmann 1980, Clark 1980) claims that the rationale for use of the nonprofit form lies in the chief function of the nondistribution constraint, namely that it helps to overcome "contractual failure" in situations where such failure is quite likely to occur.

Contractual failure is characterized by the inability of a buyer of services to gain assurance that he is getting what he intends to be contracting for; in more general terms, it denotes high monitoring and enforcement costs. The nondistribution constraint is supposed to be helpful in such situations because it gives the buyer some reason to believe that those who appoint and control the actual providers of services and goods will not have an incentive to take advantage of his vulnerability as consumer. In a for-profit enterprise, by contrast, both the shareholders and the managers (who are accountable to shareholders and whose interests are usually made to coincide in part with those of the shareholders, by such means as stock option plans) have an incentive not only to be as efficient as possible and thus to outperform competitors, but also to take advantage of all market imperfections.

Some examples may illuminate this theory. First, consider privately initiated redistributive activities, that is, gifts. Nationwide flower-delivery services are operated by decidedly for-profit corporations, yet the donors who pay the corporations for helping to carry out their redistributive programs are not deterred by this fact. By contrast, an international food-delivery service is operated by CARE, a nonprofit corporation, and its nonprofit status seems very important in encouraging donors to contribute to it. Why the difference? One important distinction is that if the flower-delivery firm fails to perform, or performs badly, the donor is likely to find out about it, at least eventually, and to take remedial measures. He may demand a refund, complain to the Better Business Bureau, spread the bad word about the corporation among potential customers, and so forth. If an organization like CARE fails to perform adequately, however, the donor is unlikely to find out about it. This is because the donor and the intended donees are very unlikely to have a personal relationship to each other, so that reliable feedback on performance would naturally be sent along established lines of communication. In short, this donor faces a serious monitoring problem—a form of contractual failure afflicts him—and he may be comforted to know that CARE's sponsors are legally prohibited from getting a personal benefit out of its activities.

Consider, as a second example, basic scientific research, an activity that, if successful, leads to production of a public good. Many organizations for basic research are in nonprofit form, whereas firms that do applied research are often in for-profit form. Why? The problem facing government agencies and private donors who "purchase" basic research is that even the most diligent, competent, and well-conceived basic research may yield no clearly valuable output. If the research organization receives and spends a large sum of money and then comes up with nothing but an apologetic report, the situation may reflect the luck of the draw just as readily as a waste of resources. Unless the purchaser is willing to become an ever present policeman watching the researchers' processes and activities and has the technical and professional competence to second-guess the quality of their activities, he will be hard pressed to tell the difference. In short, he faces a serious monitoring problem, and therefore may seek protection against his vulnerability as a consumer by going to a nonprofit organization. The purchaser of applied research, for example, a marketing survey done for a particular business, is much less afflicted by such problems. He can go to a firm that is driven by competitive forces and a profit-making purpose to be as efficient as possible, yet still have reasonable protection against overreaching and poor performance.

Finally, consider complex personal services like education and medical care. Much more than with other essentially private goods and services, these services are often provided by nonprofit organizations. Why? One possible justification again relates to severe monitoring problems and the consumer vulnerability that they generate. For one thing, the recipients of such services lack the professional's esoteric knowledge and canons of judgment needed to evaluate the quality of services they are getting. Perhaps even more important, there is often profound disagreement among professionals and expert observers of their behavior as to what constitutes good education or good medical care, and these disagreements reflect, among other things, vast areas of ignorance about relevant empirical questions. For example, with respect to a very large percentage of practiced medical procedures, physicians have no solid evidence, such as the results of randomized clinical trials, of the procedures' effectiveness, let alone their rationality in cost-benefit terms. When general goals cannot be reduced to an agreed upon, operationally defined set of particular objectives and results, it is obviously difficult or impossible to monitor and assess performance of those who undertake to provide services aimed at achieving the general goals. Accordingly, consumers may have a preference for nonprofit service-delivery organizations. To be sure, the question whether, in a given context, nonprofit organizations actually do serve to mitigate the problem of consumer vulnerability is a difficult and separate inquiry; and there is a strong basis for answering the question in the negative in the case of nonprofit hospitals in the United States (Clark 1980). But the notions of contractural failure and consumer vulnerability may at least help to understand why many people have an intuitive bias in favor of nonprofit organizations in certain contexts.

The principal implication of this theory of nonprofit enterprise for our present purposes is that contracts by for-profit business corporations to provide services to governments are only likely to flourish where governmental goals have been clearly defined and the services are specified in terms of outputs and activities that are easily monitored yet meaningfully related to the goals. Since many unmet social needs seem to call for activities that involve complex personal services or other hard-to-monitor activities, resembling elementary education more than weapons manufacture, this implication is an extremely important one. What it suggests is that priority ought to be given to attempts to define public policies in operational, but sensible, terms. Business corporations may be able to help in these attempts, by offering and justifying such operational definitions of public policies, but the final determinations will undoubtedly have to be made by governmental organizations.

CONCLUSION

In trying to make the corporation's role with respect to social needs a more fruitful one, the most important task facing the legal system is not that of choosing among different conceptions of corporate purpose. Such an exercise is likely to be inconsequential or misguided. In addition, each of the main conceptions of purpose has serious drawbacks. The dualist viewpoint has great strengths but presupposes and depends on a just distribution of wealth and acceptable institutional arrangements in government. Monism tends to be uncritically conventional and merely palliative. Modest idealism is not likely to be widely practiced. High idealism, if it were ever adopted, would simply spread the basic failure of government—confusion of ends and absorption of energies in the endless squabbling of interest groups—while destroying the chief virtue of business corporations, their capacity to achieve definite goals efficiently. Pragmatism is a benevolent idea, but it will not be implemented on a truly significant scale unless government puts its house into better order.

A much more important task is to reform collective decisionmaking processes in ways that will facilitate sharper definitions of public policies. How to do this in a world where political consensus is often impossible to achieve is a difficult question, but the need to attempt answers cannot be avoided. At least it is not *inevitable* that lack of consensus will lead to statutes that express multiple, vaguely expressed, and unranked goals. Without clearer definitions of public goals, private sector involvement in meeting social needs is unlikely to increase significantly. Or, if it does, it is likely to have questionable consequences. When public policies are conceived of in more nearly operational terms, however, good governmental monitoring of corporate commitments to meet them will be feasible, and expanded corporate involvement in public-regarding activities will tend to follow naturally.

NOTES TO CHAPTER 9

1. 204 Michigan 459, 170 N.W. 668 (1919).
2. See, for example, ALI–ABA, Model Business Corporation Act Annotated, Section 35: "A director shall perform his duties as a director . . . in a manner he

reasonably believes to be in the best interests of the corporation, and with such care as an ordinarily prudent person in a like position would use under similar circumstances."

3. See, for example, *Selheimer v. Manganese Corporation of America*, 423 Pa. 563, 224 A.2d 634 (1966); *Barnes v. Andrews*, 298 F. 614 (S.D.N.Y. 1924); *Bates v. Dresser*, 251 U.S. 524 (1920).

4. See, for example, *A.P. Smith Manufacturing Co. v. Barlow*, 13 N.J. 145, 98 A.2d 581 (1953).

5. See, ALI–ABA, Model Business Corporation Act Annotated, Section 4(m).

6. U.S. Internal Revenue Code, Section 170(b) (2).

7. In the *A.P. Smith Manufacturing Co. v. Barlow* (note 4 supra), the court remarked that "modern conditions require that corporations acknowledge and discharge social as well as private responsibilities as members of the community within which they operate" 98 A.2d at 586. But this language seems unnecessary to the holding, given the court's espousal of the theory that the gift in question was for the corporation's indirect benefit, and it is unclear that the court intended anything more than to express a rationale for traditional corporate giving, which was sanctioned by statute in New Jersey, where the corporation was domiciled and the donee organization located. In *Medical Committee for Human Rights v. SEC*, 432 F.2d 659 (D.C. Cir. 1970), vacated for mootness, 404 U.S. 403 (1972), the circuit court expressed the view that Congress's concern for shareholder democracy meant that a proposed shareholder resolution to ask the directors to consider causing the company to cease making napalm was a fit subject for shareholder action within the meaning of the federal proxy rules, even though the proponents were motivated primarily by humanitarian rather than profit-making concerns. But the court nowhere declared explicitly that profit making was not the corporation's residual purpose; and in any event, such a pronouncement by a federal court about a state law question would not have been definitive.

Other lines of decision, such as those determining when a shareholder does or does not have a right to inspect corporate books and records, tend to confirm the realist viewpoint emphatically. See, for example, *State ex rel. Pillsbury v. Honeywell, Inc.*, 291 Minn. 322, 191 N.W. 2d 406 (1971) (purpose to persuade company to adopt certain social and political concerns, irrespective of economic benefit to company, was not proper purpose justifying inspection).

8. Consider reactions, in connection with the Pinto case, to Ford's use of a cost-benefit analysis.

9. See, for example, ALI–ABA Model Business Corporation Act Annotated, Section 35.

10. Pragmatism seems to me to describe the philosophy of corporate social responsibility worked out by William C. Norris, chairman and chief executive officer of Control Data Corporation. See his article, "Let's Let Business Help Run the Cities," *New York Times*, September 13, 1981.

11. Another prominent writer sounding this theme is Irving Kristol.

REFERENCES

Baumol, William. 1965. *Welfare Economics and the Theory of the State.* Rev. 2d ed. Cambridge, Mass.: Harvard University Press.

Bell, Daniel. 1976. *The Cultural Contradictions of Capitalism.* New York: Basic Books.

Chandler, Alfred, Jr. 1962. *Strategy and Structure.* Cambridge, Mass.: M.I.T. Press.

Clark, Robert C. 1980. "Does the Nonprofit Form Fit the Hospital Industry?" *Harvard Law Review* 93: 1416, 147376.

Easterbrook, Frank, and Daniel Fischel. 1981. "The Proper Role of a Target's Management in Responding to a Tender Offer," *Harvard Law Review* 94: 1161, 118288.

Engel, David. 1979. "An Approach to Corporate Social Responsibility." *Stanford Law Review* 32: 1.

Hansmann, Henry. 1980. "The Role of Nonprofit Enterprise." *Yale Law Journal* 89: 835.

Hirschman, Albert. 1970. *Exit, Voice and Loyalty.* Cambridge, Mass.: Harvard University Press.

McEachern, William. 1975. *Managerial Control and Performance*, pp. 25–30. Lexington, Mass.: Lexington Books.

Nader, Ralph; Mark Green; and Joel Seligman. 1976. *Taming the Giant Corporation.* New York: Norton.

New York Times Magazine, September 13, 1970, p. 33.

Olson, John F. " 'Constituency' Directorship: Serious Problems Ahead," *Legal Times of Washington*, November 19, 1979, p. 13.

Samuelson, Paul A. 1954. "The Pure Theory of Public Expenditures." *Review of Economics and Statistics* 36: 387.

_____. 1955. "Diagrammatic Exposition of a Theory of Public Expenditures." *Review of Economics and Statistics* 37: 350.

Schultze, Charles. 1977. *The Private Use of the Public Interest.* Washington, D.C.: Brookings Institution.

Steuer, Richard M. 1979. "Labor on the Board: Director's Seat for the UAW Stirs Antitrust Issue." *National Law Journal*, November 12.

Stone, Christopher. 1975. *Where the Law Ends: The Social Control of Corporate Behavior.* New York: Harper & Row.

U.S. Bureau of the Census. 1979. Department of Commerce, *Statistical Abstract of the United States.*

Vagts, Detlev. 1966. "Reforming the 'Modern' Corporation: Perspectives from the German." *Harvard Law Review* 80: 23.

Weiss, Elliott. 1981. "Social Regulation of Business Activity: Reforming the Corporate Governance System to Resolve an Institutional Impasse." *University of California, Los Angeles, Law Review* 28: 343.

"Who Gets the Most Pay." *Forbes*, June 7, 1982, p. 74.

Williamson, Oliver. 1964. *The Economics of Discretionary Behavior: Managerial Objectives in a Theory of the Firm.* Englewood Cliffs, N.J.: Prentice Hall.

Chapter 10

Managing the "Social Markets" Business

James C. Worthy

Beyond the philosophical and public policy issues raised by proposals to address social needs as business opportunities are a number of practical problems involved in managing this new kind of business. In a very fundamental and literal sense, *all* business activity is directed to serving social needs. The provision of food, clothing, and housing is clearly responsive to social needs. At bottom, all human needs are social, and serving unmet social needs is not only a legitimate business purpose but the only business purpose that has any social justification. Finding means to convert unmet social needs into profitable business opportunities is the businessman's prime responsibility.

However, it is not the purpose of this chapter to examine the management of activities traditionally recognized as the special province of business; on this there is already a considerable literature, backed by a formidable academic establishment. Rather, this chapter considers the managerial dimensions of efforts by business to address social needs that traditionally have been considered the primary responsibility of institutions other than business: governments, churches, private charities, and the like. Managerial literature is totally silent on this type of business activity, and academic attention to it has been nil. It will be useful, therefore, to consider some of the special problems likely to confront businesses that elect to engage in undertakings customarily regarded as the distinctive province of nonbusiness institutions.

I

Broadly speaking, there are four ways business can address unmet social needs that are beyond the traditional scope of profit-making enterprise: as outright charities with no purpose other than to relieve undesirable conditions; as means for improving the *general* environment within which the business system operates; as measures for correcting weaknesses in the economic structure that have a negative impact on a *particular* business; and as direct markets in themselves. The managerial characteristics of business activities in these four areas differ greatly from one another and from traditional fields of business enterprise.[1]

As to the first approach, two general categories of charitable giving may be identified: giving by individual businessmen and giving by corporations. As noted in the chapter by Peter Drucker, Andrew Carnegie was the prototype of the man who makes his fortune in business and upon retirement devotes a substantial part of it to "good works." Other than the fact that the resources used were derived from business, this type of charity is a personal and not a business activity. It expresses the donor's personal values, is exercised at his discretion, and does not necessarily reflect the concerns of his business. Depending on the size of the fortune he is distributing, he may have managerial problems, but they are his rather than those of his business.

Even when charitable donations are technically made from corporate rather than personal funds, they do not always differ materially in motivation and effect from personal donations. More frequently than many businessmen would be willing to admit, charitable contributions by corporations are in reality more a reflection of the personal interests of the chief executive than any genuine assessment of corporate interests, however commonly they may be classified for tax purposes as "ordinary and necessary business expenses."[2] While this type of charity draws on corporate rather than personal resources, it imposes little in the way of managerial requirements on the corporation that is the nominal donor. The chief executive officer still makes the decision primarily in terms of his (or her) own preferences, and few if any others in the company have much to say about it.

A new element is introduced when a deliberate effort is made to relate corporate giving to the long-term interests of the business: as, for example, to improve the environment in which business operates through efforts to strengthen education, advance racial harmony, or promote culture and the arts, to name only three broad categories of fairly common corporate philanthropy. Although the personal preferences (and prejudices) of senior officers continue to exert a marked influence on the choice of beneficiaries, the fact that an attempt is made to take the needs of the business into some reasonably realistic account requires at least some rudimentary means for identifying corporate interests, defining contributions policies, and processing the sizable volume of appeals for support that companies of more than moderate size are likely to receive in the course of a year. Typically these take the form of a contributions committee, which may or may not be assisted by a small staff. Increasingly in recent years, major companies—among which Dayton-Hudson Corporation under the leadership of Kenneth Dayton is a notable example—have established corporate foundations to provide a more systematic, business-oriented means for administering their corporate philanthropies.

The key point in the present context is that even with the introduction of corporate interest as a significant criterion in making philanthropic decisions, addressing unmet social needs as charities imposes no managerial problems of consequence on the corporation. While committees and foundations introduce a measure of rationality and deliberation into the process, only the highest levels of corporate management are involved, and only incidentally to their prime responsibilities; the corporate foundation, in fact, is usually administered as an entity wholly separate from the business. However important corporate charity may be to its recipients and however useful it may be in improving the general environment for business, it is essentially extraneous to the business itself.

A few corporations—not many—carry the concept of corporate interest in social problems a long step forward by recognizing that certain social ills are the result of basic structural weaknesses in the economy that not only impair the well-being of large numbers of people but hurt particular businesses as well. Corporate measures to correct such structural deficiencies may therefore be seen not only as good in themselves but also as sound corporate strategy.

In Peter Drucker's formulation, Julius Rosenwald of Sears, Roebuck was the prototype of this approach. He initiated what became the highly effective U.S. county agent system as a means of encouraging farmers to improve their farming practices. In doing so, he helped make them better farmers—and better customers. Rosenwald's successor, Robert E. Wood, launched a series of programs whose objective was to break the grip of one-crop agriculture on the American South. His strategy was to promote poultry, hog, and cattle raising on the sound premise that animals in the barnyard required crops other than cotton in the fields. The strategy worked. Southern agriculture prospered, and with it Sears. In a parallel effort, Wood encouraged the manufacturers from whom Sears bought to locate in southern cities some of the new plants they needed to meet Sears' constantly increasing merchandise requirements; this policy was not the only influence at work, but it contributed significantly to the industrialization of what had been a predominantly rural region. By promoting diversified agriculture and accelerating the pace of industrialization, Wood helped bring about major improvements in southern ways of life, and in the process strengthened materially the market for Sears merchandise. By helping make the South a better place to work and live, Wood made it a better place for Sears to do business.

While the outright charitable approach to the amelioration of social ills makes few demands on corporate management, moving purposively to correct structural economic weaknesses requires considerably more management ingenuity and attention. If management's purpose is not simply to deal with symptoms, as charities often do, but to strengthen its markets by correcting basic structural weaknesses, as Rosenwald and Wood sought to do, the corporation must play a proactive, initiatory role. In the typical charity-supported enterprise, leaders of the beneficiary entity conceive the need, design the program, and launch the cause; the corporation is the passive partner and its contribution is usually confined to financial support. Not so with the Rosenwald-Wood type approach. When correcting a structural deficiency is conceived as a means for serving an unmet social need and in the process strengthening a market, the corporation becomes an active partner in the undertaking. It is no longer enough simply to pay someone else to work on the problem; the corporation itself must become intimately involved in correcting the conditions that are causing the problem.

In these circumstances, the heart of the task lies in finding grounds of mutual interest, where serving the needs of disadvantaged groups can be made to serve the needs of the business as well. The Sears program, for example, was planned and carried out in close cooperation with county agents, the 4-H clubs, the National Grange, and other farm organizations. Areas of mutual interest both to the corporation and disadvantaged groups are not always self-evident, and means for serving them in mutually advantageous ways are not always easy to devise. High orders of creativity are required, and much, though by no means all, of this must be provided by management. A certain amount of top management attention is essential, and a small cadre of specialized staff is usually necessary for program design and administration; for example, a dozen or so people were required to implement General Wood's agricultural program.

Even so, this corporate approach to the amelioration of social ills affecting a particular business makes no great demands on its management. While a primary purpose of the approach is to help promote the business, it has little direct connection with the day-to-day conduct of the business; from a managerial standpoint, it presents few problems worth dwelling on.

II

The same most emphatically cannot be said of addressing unmet social needs as direct markets for business products and services, the fourth approach identified at the outset of this chapter. As previously noted, the types of unmet needs under discussion are those typically served by nonbusiness institutions, but which a few companies are coming to see as important business opportunities in their own right. The problems of managing enterprises embarking on this largely uncharted sea differ sharply from and are often far greater than those of managing enterprises serving traditional business markets.

As Andrew Carnegie and Kenneth Dayton, each in his own way, personified the outright charitable or philanthropic approach, and Julius Rosenwald (with Robert E. Wood) personified the market-strengthening approach, William Norris of Control Data Corporation personifies the needs-themselves-as-markets approach. The experiences of the company he founded will be drawn upon heavily in exploring the managerial aspects of this highly proactive concept for dealing with stubborn social ills.

It is beyond the scope of this chapter to describe in any detail Control Data's programs[3] in nontraditional areas, but briefly naming some of them will provide points of reference for the discussion that follows. In the area of education, for example, Control Data is using its PLATO computer-based system to correct deficiencies in basic reading and numerical skills that, if left unremedied, will blight the lives of thousands of young people. The company's Fair Break Program is designed to prepare culturally and educationally deprived young men and women to become employable and productive. The Homework Program provides an innovative means for restoring homebound, physically handicapped people to meaningful, satisfying, and remunerative employment. Two joint ventures, City Venture and Rural Ventures, deal with the persistent problems of the deterioration of urban communities and the morbidity of small-scale agriculture; Control Data is a leading partner in both. And a variety of corporate undertakings are directed toward the encouragement and support of job-creating small businesses.

The pursuit of these hardly traditional types of business activity absorbs a major part of the attention and concern of Control Data's management. Control Data has identified major unmet social needs, designed means for serving them within the framework of profit-oriented business enterprise, and brought the needs and the means for serving them together to create markets where none had existed before—at least, not in the *business market* sense. It should come as no surprise that Control Data has encountered managerial problems along the way that differ from those ordinarily experienced in serving traditional business markets.

Before examining such problems, the important fact should be noted that the approach Control Data has taken to dealing with social ills is inherently more stable than any of the other approaches previously identified in this chapter. Personal charities, whether using individual or corporate funds, are the least stable because they are subject to changes in personal preferences and turnover in executive suites. Considerably stabler are corporate charities guided by reasoned efforts to assess the interests of the business community in helping solve social problems; but such charities are costs, and while they may improve the business climate, they do not in themselves generate revenues. Corporate charity suffers from a fundamental instability because in hard times the contributions budget, having no direct impact on revenues, is the easiest budget to cut. A significant characteristic of the market-strengthening approach is that while it is a cost it is expected to contribute at least indirectly to revenues and for this reason is likely to be more stable than ordinary charitable giving and less likely to be cut in times of budgetary stringency.

When needs are approached as markets, however, we are dealing with an entirely different situation. Expenditures for the development of markets are *investments* that are intended to produce direct revenue in excess of costs. If made imaginatively and with good business judgment, they should be expected to generate a reasonable return on the amounts put at risk. In addition to making substantive contributions to the needs to which they are directed, they should broaden and strengthen the company's business base. In times of economic adversity, efforts to develop the new markets or to serve them better after they have been developed are more likely to be redoubled than reduced because the revenues and profits of the business depend on serving them well. When the needs themselves become the markets, social responsibility and business responsibility are no longer dichotomous. They have become one and the same.

III

First, of course, a need must be identified as a potential market. The task of identifying market opportunities—and, where necessary, restructuring the context in which particular needs are served to create opportunities for profit—is the classic role of the entrepreneur. Markets are artifacts. They do not arise sui generis. They must be created. The man who sees as a potential market the need to convert culturally deprived youth into employable workers—to transform human raw material into productive human capital—is no different from, and in fact may be the same, as the man who saw as a potential market the need for more powerful computers than anyone had ever built before.

Identifying unmet social needs as business opportunities differs in only one important respect from so identifying any other unmet need. It is likely to demand a higher than usual order of entrepreneurial creativity, the ability to see bona fide business opportunities in areas outside those businesses are accustomed to serving and outside the businessman's customary patterns of thinking.

Unmet social needs of the kind addressed by Control Data Corporation are typically far more complex than the needs for standard goods and services, which are the meat and potatoes of most business enterprises. The production and distribution of food, the building of houses, the manufacture of clothing, the repair and service of household and office equipment—even the design and fabrication of computers—are relatively straightforward matters in comparison with converting the chronically unemployed into productive workers, or arresting the process of urban deterioration, or revitalizing small-scale farming, or improving the climate for new business and new job creation. In addressing such needs, there are far more variables to be taken into account, many of which are much less susceptible to control than those entailed in serving needs within the traditional spheres of business endeavor. More interests are likely to be involved, and these are often divergent and conflicting.

In moving into what for want of a better term may be called "social markets," it is necessary not only to develop measures to deal effectively with the problems themselves but to do so in a manner consistent with the company's role as a profit-making institution. The needs themselves are easy to identify, at least in their symptomatic manifestations: idle youth on street corners, dilapidated houses, rural poverty. Measures for dealing effectively with root causes are somewhat harder to visualize, but even these can be conceived, at least in principle, without too much difficulty. It is harder still to tailor prospective measures to take proper account of all significant variables and potential conflicts of interest. But what is likely to be really hard and to require the highest orders of entrepreneurial creativity is finding means to accomplish all of this in ways that will be responsive to the needs while simultaneously generating revenues and producing a profit.

The opportunities with the most potential are likely to require considerable experimentation and long lead times to bring to profitability. These call for substantial financial resources as well as diverse managerial capabilities and hence are usually beyond the scope of small-scale, marginally financed enterprises. Successful entry into such markets is therefore generally restricted to larger, financially secure companies and may in fact be the principal area of new business opportunities for big business in the years ahead.

Addressing unmet social needs as business opportunities is subject to the same entrepreneurial and managerial rules as any other class of business activity. Companies are well advised to build on their own technologies and experience, which can give them special competence for certain tasks, rather than venture into entirely unfamiliar terrain. Control Data Corporation, for example, has elected to engage in a number of new businesses addressing certain unmet social needs that, however superficially dissimilar they may appear, share a common characteristic: They are all based on the management of information, primarily in the form of computer-based education. This is an area in which Control Data has a large body of technology and experience, which gives it special competence and important competitive advantages.

At the same time, Control Data has not allowed itself to be the prisoner of its technology. It has always been willing to bring in ancillary technologies (for example, from the fields of education and social work) to supplement those in which it is already expert to deal effectively with particular new classes of problems. It has not, in other words, tried to redefine problems to fit into technology. Instead, it has started from the base of its own technology, adapted the technology to fit the problems, and added new technologies as needed.

It goes without saying that not all companies can engage successfully in the nontraditional businesses Control Data has entered. But many possess other technologies and experience on which they can build to meet other social needs and in so doing create profitable new business opportunities. The essential requirements are, first, the entrepreneurial capacity to identify the need; second, a reservoir of know-how on which to draw; and, third, the managerial skill to adapt the know-how to serve the need.

In addition, the entrepreneurial function may well require the discovery or development of new forms of financial resources. The great transcontinental railway system could not have been built without new forms of federal aid. The vast electric utility industry was financed by the invention of the open-end mortgage bond. The birth of our modern industrial society itself had to await the establishment of orderly security markets.

Developing markets in many of the so-called social needs areas may present a special kind of financing problem. Often, the persons whose needs are to be served do not themselves have the resources to provide the revenues required. The pattern is already well established, however, that the provision of funds to address many of the more pressing of these needs is a responsibility of government as a general agent of society, and vast sums are already being appropriated for such purposes by every level of government. What is missing is not the funds but, rather, enough problem-solving approaches on the part of private industry to justify government funding.

There is, of course, a predisposition in many quarters—including business—to assume that when public funds are used to deal with social needs, the work should be performed by a governmental or nonprofit agency. There is no such predisposition concerning the use of public funds for a host of other public purposes. The U. S. Department of Defense does not manufacture its own aircraft, tanks, and ships, or NASA its own computers; state highway departments do not build their own roads; local police departments do not design and fabricate their own communication systems or detection devices. These are all public needs that are served by private, profit-making institutions and financed by public money. A very large sector of the national economy is engaged in providing goods and services on a for-profit basis to agencies of federal, state, and local governments; there is no reason in logic or practicality why governments should not contract in a similar manner for the local governments; there is no reason in logic or practicality why governments should not contract in a similar manner for the performance of useful services in the social needs areas.

A major reason why more of this is not done has already been cited: the dearth of creative, innovative ideas from industry itself. Many business leaders—in fact, the great majority—agree with the critics of business that social problems should remain the special preserve of social agencies and have confined their entrepreneurial interests to areas comfortably within the established business orbit.

If more businessmen recognized the magnitude of the opportunities awaiting discovery in the social needs markets and if more devoted thought and effort to devising new and effective means for dealing with them, they probably would find receptive listeners in influential positions who could effect significant changes in prevailing governmental practices. In a very real sense, what is most urgently needed is an imaginative broadening of the entrepreneurial function in the American business system.

IV

But more than a broadening of the entrepreneurial function per se is needed. Developments and refinements in managerial practices are likewise required, and it should be recognized at the outset that these must differ greatly from those needed for the management of charitable giving or efforts to remedy basic structural weaknesses in the interest of strengthening markets.

When needs themselves are the market, serving them *becomes* the business and the organization must be restructured accordingly, since a company's means for conducting its established operations are unlikely to be well-adapted to the special requirements of the new field of activity.

Just as the manufacture of computers requires an organization specifically designed for that purpose, the delivery of services to revitalize a badly run-down urban community requires an organization responsive to the unique needs of that particular task. Some of the essential activities of the undertaking may differ from those with which the organization is familiar, but even when the types of work involved are not in themselves strange—for example, the creation of computer-supported data bases—the work will be performed in an unfamiliar context and must be adapted accordingly. Certain activities, whether adaptations of customary procedures or wholly new ones, may be assigned to existing organizational units, but extensive modification may be necessary to facilitate their proper performance. It may be wise to place new ventures in a special niche within existing organizations to facilitate the closer attention they are likely to need and to avoid distorting the operating results of established units.

Companies diversifying into new kinds of business invariably encounter problems in learning how to organize activities with which they are not already familiar. If the experience of Control Data Corporation is indicative, a fair amount of trial and error is inevitable in the process of creating reasonably effective managerial arrangements, together with appropriate systems of reporting and control.

While it is always prudent to base new business ventures on a firm's established experience and technology, ventures into untried areas may, as previously noted, require the acquisition of ancillary technologies. This in turn may necessitate the addition of new kinds of staff with which the organization is unfamiliar, presenting problems of selection and integration. People accustomed to hiring engineers may be uncomfortable hiring social workers, and a high-technology staff may find it difficult to relate to new members skilled at working with community organizations in distressed areas; the reverse, of course, is also true.

Especially difficult from an organization and management standpoint are such problems as how to price the services offered, how to promote and sell them, how to direct and control their performance, and how to evaluate and reward the efforts of those involved.

The generation of revenues is likely to present special problems because, as mentioned earlier, many of those whose needs are served—the unemployed, the handicapped, the slum dweller—do not have the means to pay for the services they receive. Typically, the source of funding required to serve these needs is a government agency or a charitable foundation that does not itself benefit from the rendering of the service but finances its provision on grounds of public policy. For certain kinds of services, the contracting agency and source of funding may be another corporation interested in the well-being of its employees. To illustrate, a number of companies now purchase health maintenance services for their workers from Control Data.

Where the market is for a standard business product, whether a tube of toothpaste or a digital computer, customers extend or withhold their patronage on the basis of their own satisfaction with the product. But under conditions of third-party financing—such as the Comprehensive Employment and Training Act (CETA), for example, or another corporation—funds are appropriated or denied depending on the *funding agency's* assessment of the "product's" worth. Presumably, these judgments take into account the extent to which intended beneficiaries actually benefit, but it is someone else's judgment, not that of the beneficiary, which is controlling. Third-party financing thus not only complicates the marketing process but carries with it an inherent danger of misdirection of effort and misapplication of resources.[4] Under these circumstances, management must design products and services that respond to social needs and at the same time appear sufficiently attractive to funding agencies to elicit the required financial support. Where the criteria of satisfaction are not entirely coterminous, as is likely to be the case, management may be tempted to satisfy the funder at the expense of the presumed beneficiary. It is management's job to satisfy both, which is not always easy.

Beyond the problems inherent in third-party financing, many unforeseen difficulties are likely to be encountered, and these often can be overcome only through trial and error. Management must be prepared to learn by experience and to make tactical adjustments as it goes along, which will take time; the basic entrepreneurial concept must be sufficiently sound to warrant allocation of enough resources to provide the months or even years for the necessary learning to take place.

The uncertainties faced by management are greatly enhanced by the fact that potential revenues in many social markets are exceedingly difficult to estimate in advance. Such markets, by and large, are new to business and there are few base points from which forecasts can be made with confidence. Even the most sophisticated market analysis techniques are of little use in trying to quantify the potential *business* market in such areas as urban or rural revitalization, remediation of illiteracy, or preparation of the educationally and culturally deprived for productive employment. Gross estimates of the magnitude of the needs themselves can be made, but translating such magnitudes into business revenue potentials is another and far less certain matter. Fortunately, there is a measure of safety in the fact that these magnitudes are so great in most areas of unmet social needs that management's task lies not so much in trying to make firm business forecasts as in finding effective means for serving the needs. Nevertheless the inability to make reasonably reliable forecasts is apt to create problems for managements uncomfortable in the face of high uncertainty.

A prominent characteristic of efforts to develop social markets is the much longer than usual time periods likely to be needed to bring the undertaking to the levels of profitability required by the economic imperatives of the business. This not only calls for patience on the part of management; it also calls for large measures of understanding and confidence on the part of the corporate directors to whom management is responsible and who, in turn, are responsible to the company's shareholders. Managements that embark on the uncharted seas of converting unmet social needs into business opportunities cannot be held to the narrow confines of fiscal tolerance appropriate for those navigating well-traveled waters. Corporate directors must therefore be capable of thinking in broader and longer than usual business terms, and they must be aware of the complexities with which management is seeking to deal. Good business and financial judgment is always required on a corporate board, but boards of companies moving into areas such as those under discussion need to be competent in other ways as well.

These added competencies do not have to include expertise in the specific areas being addressed. To draw a parallel, it is not necessary for all directors of a computer company to have degrees in engineering or physics; there are many other means than service on the board by which management can assemble the array of talents needed for any particular purpose. But just as it is useful for a computer company to have at least a few people on the board who are engineers and physicists, there is value for a company seeking to establish a position in the educational system to have one or more directors with personal knowledge of the organization and processes of American education. In general, the competencies a board should have that are relevant to dealing with unmet social needs as markets include: a broad understanding of the origins, character, and dynamics of the general class of problems being addressed; a grasp of major social, economic, and political trends at work in the society; an appreciation of the importance of the role corporations can play in the resolution of troublesome problems; and a genuine concern for the human aspects of the social malfunctions management is seeking to correct.

These requirements are more attitudinal, moral, and philosophical than technical. But they deal with basic values of American society and are fundamentally important for companies that are not content with pursuing the more narrow traditional role of business and wish instead to move into fields of endeavor such as those under discussion here. If business is to render useful service in these new and broader areas, corporate boards must take a broader view of their functions and think through the implications of the added responsibilities they are assuming.

If a substantial part of a company's total business involves the *developmental* stages of work in social market areas, the downward pressure on corporate profits may be sufficient to exert a negative impact on the market performance of the company's securities. Market analysts are accustomed to viewing corporate performance in shorter time frames than are usually necessary to bring ventures of this kind to profitable maturity. Moreover, most financial analysts are not prepared by training or experience, or by the generally accepted canons of their trade, to evaluate such ventures with any degree of understanding or precision. They are likely to be uncomfortable contemplating undertakings that do not fit neatly into customary categories, and they may as a result underestimate the prospects for their eventual success. Control Data Corporation entered the social market areas in a serious way in 1967, and ever since then the stock market has consistently undervalued its stock. This is a risk companies must be prepared to accept until such time as the investment community develops a higher order of understanding and sophistication in judging business prospects in this still unfamiliar field. Meanwhile, company directors have a special responsibility for giving their managements the support they need to weather this period of trial and to do what they can to hasten the needed changes in the investment community's outlook.

V

More than ordinary entrepreneurial, managerial, and governance skills are required of companies that undertake to address unmet social needs as business opportunities. More than ordinary political skills are likewise essential. A business corporation of any size is a political as well as an economic institution. It comprises people of widely varying capabilities, interests, and personal goals whose energies must be mobilized and coordinated into coherent efforts to achieve corporate objectives that have only derivative values for the individuals themselves. This is a central task of management that becomes increasingly important at successively higher organizational levels and is a major component of top management responsibilities. The chief executive officer, in particular, must personify and articulate values with which diverse groups within the organization can identify, and foster the development of policies to provide a framework within which the pursuit of organizational goals can also serve personal goals. In this respect the role of the chief executive of a corporate enterprise does not differ materially from that of a head of state.

When a company heretofore engaged only in traditional types of business activity ventures into nontraditional fields, apprehensions can arise among key people as to top management's business judgment and possible adverse effects on the existing organization. This is likely to be especially true where executives are compensated on a performance basis and the new venture is seen as possibly undermining the performance elements on which executive work is evaluated. Even where compensation per se is not threatened, executives in established lines of work may resent the diversion of top management attention to matters they consider extraneous to the company's primary interests. "When are those guys in the front office going to forget these do-good ideas and get back to running our real business?" is a complaint apt to be heard in companies that elect to move into fields considered alien by traditional-minded business people.

Under these circumstances, appropriate steps, essentially political, must be taken to avoid or at least minimize possible adverse effects the new venture may have on the existing organization. It is incumbent upon top management to communicate clearly to all key people the rationale behind the course it is pursuing and the benefits that can be expected to accrue from it. And it is incumbent upon the key people in turn to communicate a similarly informing and reassuring message to successively lower levels of organization. Those at higher organizational levels (especially the top) must be willing to take whatever measures are necessary to mobilize the required support; this may require a greater than ordinary degree of educational effort, as well as some changes in existing compensation and budgetary arrangements. Easy acceptance of any significantly new policy line is not to be expected.

In addition, higher levels of management must work to maintain effective relationships with other organizations in the corporation's institutional environment, including other corporations in the same industry; the general business community; governmental regulatory and funding agencies; and various civic, trade, and other organizations dealing with matters of direct or indirect concern to the business—to name only a few. Where nontraditional types of business are involved, these relationships are likely to be more numerous and complex and occasionally more sensitive than those with which management is accustomed to deal. For example, Control Data finds it necessary to work closely with various agencies of federal, state, and local governments; churches, foundations, and professional societies; a wide variety of social service organizations and local civic, business, and neighborhood groups; and a host of other entities with which most businesses have little occasion to deal in ways other than as vehicles for eleemosynary endeavor.

The development of cooperative relationships so necessary to success is often seriously impeded by the marked suspicions aroused in certain quarters by the company's frank avowal of its profit-making intentions. There is a deep and abiding strand in the American tradition that is distrustful of business, particularly big business, and views profit-making as inherently evil. There are those who may see addressing social ills as business opportunities as tantamount to making money out of human misery. Others may see the ills themselves as by-products of the profit system and question the ability of profit-oriented endeavors to cure them. And questions may be raised as to what happens when the requirements for profit-making and the needs of the problem conflict: if the "best" solution is less profitable than a second or third best, which is the profit-seeking organization likely to pursue?[5]

Admittedly, the experience of many people in our society with business gives a measure of legitimacy to such concerns. Regardless of whether harsh judgments and antagonisms are justified, they are facts of life with which business must learn to live, if it is to have any hope of building the grass roots support essential for many of the kinds of activities it may undertake in seeking to deal with unmet social needs as business opportunities.

The history of American labor relations is replete with cases in which management responded inappropriately to criticism, whether outright or veiled. Many companies that in preunion days had tried most sincerely to be good employers became most bitterly antilabor when their employees organized. There is an analogous danger that companies that devote themselves to restoring the economic viability of small farms, or bringing jobs to urban ghettoes, or otherwise improving the human condition will overreact to what they perceive as unjust accusations and say, in effect, "To hell with it!" and withdraw to less exposed and more comfortable fields of endeavor.

Management's good intentions may in themselves make it more vulnerable. The very fact that management means well and wants to change social conditions for the better may make it overly sensitive to those who question its motives. Management must learn that meaning well neither excuses mistakes nor assures approbation. It must realize that its good works or efforts to perform good works will not shield it against attacks and may in fact invite and increase the fury of attacks. He who sets himself up as a white knight invites the skeptic to throw mud; if a flaw is detected in the knight's armor, the mud may be followed by a spear.

Just as the preacher who is suspected of doing wrong is run out of town more quickly than the town wastrel, from whom objectionable behavior is expected, corporate undertakings labeled as well-intentioned are apt to be subject to closer and less sympathetic scrutiny than more traditional business ventures.

Matters become particularly complicated and the going rougher when projects promoted by the company are perceived—rightly or wrongly—as competing with or otherwise adversary to plans to which other groups are committed. Under these circumstances, opposition to the company's plans is easily organized. Charges that the company is seeking to capitalize on human ills for selfish, profit-making motives can greatly inflame local passions and poison the atmosphere in which the company is trying to work.

Dealing with individuals and organizations with different values calls for political skills of a much higher order than those required for the conduct of traditional kinds of business. Essential to the development of such skills are large measures of understanding and patience. Management needs to understand that it is moving into areas in which the presence of business is unexpected and its purposes easily misapprehended. It also needs to recognize that opposition to its undertakings is not necessarily a reflection of narrow-minded bigotry; on the contrary, those opposing the company's efforts may be activated by what they consider the highest and purest motives. But if the area into which the company is proposing to move is one they have long considered their own private turf, they are likely to feel threatened and react with hostility.

Very often, groups initially opposed to a company's plans to address a given set of social ills are precisely those whose cooperation and support are urgently needed to ensure success. This is especially true with respect to locally based business, civic, and community organizations and certain more broadly based groups, including segments of the academic community, with professional interests in significant problem areas. It is greatly to the advantage of everyone concerned that management understand the role of such groups and the aspirations of their leadership.

If management undertakes to address social needs as business opportunities, it perforce assumes the role of entrepreneur, and that role carries with it the responsibility for identifying and mobilizing all the diverse elements—economic, civic, and otherwise—essential to the success of the undertaking. It also demands that management be prepared to hear criticism and respond to it calmly and professionally. In the end, the only way to deal with suspicion and antagonism—the only effective way, that is—is by *performing* well, not simply *meaning* well. People judge business not by what it says but by the experiences they have with it. If some people have had unfortunate experiences, it is doubly incumbent on businesses entering into sensitive areas to behave consistently in a manner that will build public confidence and trust.

VI

At this point the businessperson being urged to consider the possibility of serving unmet social needs as business opportunities may well ask why he or she should undertake anything so fraught with difficulty, so risky, so subject to attack, and so likely to require long lead times for satisfactory returns. There are two compelling reasons for doing so. First, many grave social ills will remain ineptly attended to unless means are found for converting them into business opportunities. Second, the long-run profit prospects are highly attractive. The first point has been addressed in some detail in other chapters of this book; a few further thoughts with respect to the second are pertinent at this point.

For one thing, business is already picking up most of the tab for social ills and doing the best it can in a sick society; prudent investments in addressing such ills are simply good business.

Management's first responsibility is to preserve the viability and serviceability of its enterprise. The thesis put forward here is simply that an effective means for dealing with many problem areas that have traditionally been dealt with as charities, or simply ignored, is to convert them into businesses.

More than any other level of management, top management must be concerned with the economic, social, and political environment in which the enterprise functions. Broadly speaking, there are two aspects of the environment that require special top management attention: those that constitute present or potential threats and those that are or may be fashioned into economic opportunities. In today's business environment, there are multiple threats and multiple opportunities, and many situations represent both threats and opportunities.

The long-range vitality of the enterprise is ultimately dependent on the vitality of the society of which it is a part. Anything that threatens the well-being of society threatens the well-being of the enterprise. Some of the more obvious threats in the last decades of the twentieth century include widespread poverty, unemployment, illiteracy, and inequality of opportunity. Given the high levels of expectation built into our culture (due in significant part to the achievements of business itself), the persistence of grave problems threatens the integrity of our institutional framework. We are, after all, a democracy, with political power broadly dispersed. The disadvantaged and the disenchanted, and those who would capitalize on their discontents, represent a potentially powerful political force. There is always the danger that the force will be used to seek remedies through political measures directed to symptoms rather than causes. Not only do such measures typically fail to provide effective solutions; they are also likely to impose burdens and constraints that, cumulatively or catastrophically, can gravely compromise the ability of business to perform its economic functions.

A prime task of management is to foresee dangers that lie ahead and to take steps to avoid them or deal with them. A threat is a threat, whether originating from economic factors or otherwise, and management's responsibility for the health and vitality of the enterprise requires that threats be identified far enough in advance for appropriate action to be taken. Speaking strictly in terms of *business* responsibility, management has an obligation to do what it can through its business policies and practices to correct or relieve conditions that are likely to be inimical to the long-term viability of the enterprise; protecting and improving the quality of its environment is simply a part of what management must do to keep its house in order.

The environment within which business operates is not entirely a given, and business is not merely a passive target of environmental influences. By the way it conceives its role and conducts its affairs, business helps create its own environment and profoundly influences its character and continuing development.

The task of identifying profit opportunities—and, where necessary, restructuring the context in which particular needs are served to create those opportunities—is the classic task of the entrepreneur. By and large, business leadership has been sadly deficient in applying its entrepreneurial skills in the area of social problems. In the broad spectrum of human needs, there are sectors representing tremendous markets that are poorly served under present arrangements. The greatest business opportunities always lie in markets where existing services fall most critically short of potential demand. By this measure, some of the unmet needs of contemporary society (for example, those of the decaying central cities) are among the most promising of today's untapped markets. The companies that move quickly and effectively to define and develop these markets will gain the kind of competitive lead captured by pioneer entrepreneurs in any new market. Just because a particular area has not typically been considered business is no reason to believe that it cannot be converted to business.

VII

But economic concerns are not by themselves adequate motivation. If management undertakes to convert unmet social needs into business opportunities it must have genuine concern for correcting ills, not merely making money. An entrepreneur may set out to manufacture widgets with no interest whatsoever in widgets other than as a source of revenue and profit. But the entrepreneur who moves into social problem areas as a business must have an interest in and concern for the problems themselves and make an honest commitment to finding solutions that will contribute significantly to improving the quality of human life. Only if the undertaking is embarked on in such a frame of mind and with such a commitment are the entrepreneur's efforts likely to survive the vicissitudes they will encounter. Those whose mental set is such that they can back away as easily as the manufacturer of widgets can drop a troublesome product line should stay with widgets.

The driving force that has brought most technological innovations to brilliant entrepreneurial success has been total commitment to an idea and a determination to overcome any and all obstacles that may arise. Typically, the successful entrepreneur is obsessed with the idea itself, not with the money to be made from it. Cyrus McCormick and Harvey Firestone come readily to mind. In this respect, the social entrepreneur and the technical entrepreneur share a common characteristic: an overpowering compulsion to make an idea work. It is of such stuff that human progress is made.

NOTES TO CHAPTER 10

1. Excluded from the present discussion is work performed under contract for government agencies (e.g., garbage collection, munitions manufacture, equipment supply). In terms of managerial characteristics, the only way such work differs from any other business activity is the identity of the customer.

2. Fortunately for many charities, the Internal Revenue Service is fairly relaxed in its interpretation of this criterion, an attitude encouraged—indeed, made possible—by the fact that "ordinary and necessary business expense" is something less than a precise term, and with a little ingenuity susceptible to considerable flexibility. Without unseemly casuistry, a rather wide range of charitable endeavors can be gathered together under a "business interest" umbrella. In any event the total volume of *all* corporate charitable contributions is only a small fraction of the amount allowable under IRS regulations and hardly enough for government to waste much time verifying in other than gross terms.

3. For a more complete description of Control Data programs, see Chapter 11, by William C. Norris.

4. For an insightful commentary on this point, see Peter F. Drucker, *Management Tasks, Responsibilities, Practices* (New York: Harper & Row, 1973), pp. 141-142.

5. Professor Harvey Brooks in a private communication has emphasized the importance of these points in the formation of public attitudes toward business. In any given situation, of course, there may be more than one definition of what is "best," and different participants or observers may apply different criteria in making their judgments. Also, a second- or third-best solution that is attainable may well be superior to a putative "best" that is beyond reach. Social issues by their very nature are likely to bring conflicting sets of values into play, and it is important that management be alert to and understanding of the conflicts that may ensue.

✳ *PART IV*

OPPORTUNITIES FOR THE 1980s

 *Chapter 11*

A New Role for Corporations

William C. Norris

For decades we have seen a relentless growth in many major unmet societal needs. They have been worsening, even in years when the economy performed well. They have defied government paternalism and private philanthropy and have reached ominous dimensions. Fortunately, their growth *can* be stemmed, indeed reversed, if corporate America will assume a new role. Corporations must use their vast resources more efficiently by taking the initiative, in cooperation with other sectors of society, to address major unmet needs as profitable business opportunities. The spectrum of needs I am talking about includes reduction in unemployment, especially for disadvantaged youth and the handicapped; more responsive education and training; revitalization of poverty-stricken urban and rural areas; a more viable small business sector; and lower cost, more efficient public services.

CONTROL DATA PROGRAMS

Control Data adopted such a strategy in 1967, and it has proven sound.

Poverty-Area Plants. We began by taking jobs to people by establishing manufacturing plants in blighted communities. The first plant was built on the north side of Minneapolis a few months after fires and rioting in that area in 1967. Since then we have built six additional plants and announced plans to build two more in depressed communities. Total employment in the seven plants now exceeds 2,000, with annual payrolls totaling nearly $40 million.

Education. Our most extensive program addresses the worldwide need for better, more available and less costly education and training. The only practical way to make significant progress in addressing this massive and urgent need is through the use of technology such as television, audiovideo tapes, and telephone and satellite transmission, all coordinated in a network learning system with computer-based education.

Control Data has been engaged in developing such a system, called PLATO computer-based education, for twenty years. The effort includes scores of cooperative projects with the government, universities, foundations, large companies, small companies, and individuals.

Most of the initial funding came from the National Science Foundation in support of a cooperative project between the University of Illinois and Control Data. After expenditures of approximately $25 million in government funding, feasibility of the approach had been verified; since then, most of the funding, in excess of $900 million, has been provided by Control Data. The project with the University of Illinois continues to be financed by Control Data and is now only one of forty projects with universities. In addition, there are many more cooperative projects with other organizations and individuals for the purpose of creating computer-based training and education courses.

To facilitate the delivery of PLATO courses, Control Data Learning Centers have been established as rapidly as feasible, and there are now more than 100 in the United States. We also operate 44 vocational training schools called Control Data Institutes, which offer courses in computer programming, operation and maintenance and a number of more specialized courses such as bank teller training. Soon to be added is robotics technician training.

Fair Break. PLATO is also central to a program called Fair Break, which prepares disadvantaged persons to find and keep jobs—and helps make jobs more available to them. Fair Break centers have operated in more than 200 locations throughout the country; each center delivers innovative training in basic skills, job readiness, life management, and job-seeking skills. Students also work part-time to provide a source of income and to help identify any problems that should be resolved before attempting full-time employment. The program is delivered in cooperation with public schools and with funding primarily from government programs. More than 10,000 students have enrolled at the centers since they started four years ago. Survey results indicate 83 percent have successfully completed training with a job placement rate of nearly 80 percent.

OUTREACH. A program called CAREER OUTREACH builds on the Fair Break experience. Its objective is to help disadvantaged youths get started in careers by linking education and work experience. It is financed entirely by Control Data.

Students begin working in grade 10 or 11, part-time during the school year and full-time in the summer. Their eligibility for the program is certified by a unit of city or county government. During high school, they are given counseling similar to that offered under Fair Break to help them overcome barriers to employment. After high school, their vocational training or college is financed by a combination of a Control Data loan and job income. OUTREACH began in St. Paul, Minneapolis, and Toledo in 1981. Twenty students were selected in each city.

Small Business. Having already launched major programs for taking jobs to people and getting people ready for jobs, we decided in 1975 to complete the employment spectrum with a program to create jobs by assisting small businesses to start-up and achieve profitable growth.

More than 80 percent of the new jobs created in the last 10 years have been provided by companies with 100 or fewer employees. Yet the environment for small business has been deteriorating because of increasing competition from large companies, increasing government regulation, and decreasing availability of technology and capital. At the same time, most of the technology, management, and professional expertise and capital resources are in big business and are underutilized.

Recognizing the need and opportunity, Control Data has developed a wide range of offerings for small enterprise, including financial assistance, data processing services, education and training, management and professional consulting, and technology transfer. Another very important service is our Business and Technology Centers (BTCs), which provide various combinations of consulting services; shared laboratory, manufacturing and office facilities; and other services to facilitate the start-up and growth of small businesses. Economies of scale make it possible to provide occupants of the centers and small companies located nearby with needed facilities and services of much higher quality and considerably lower cost than any would be capable of obtaining or providing for itself.

We also assist small business by fostering public-private cooperation over a broad front. More specifically, we are helping to launch and have been participating in the operation of community-based organizations with those objectives. I will describe two: the Minnesota Cooperation Office for Small Business and the Minnesota Seed Capital Fund.

MCO. The Minnesota Cooperation Office, or MCO, fosters the start-up and profitable growth of small businesses in the state of Minnesota. The MCO is a nonprofit corporation being financed during the early years by contributions and grants. It is planned that the organization will eventually become self-supporting from client fees and funds generated by investments in client companies. The MCO's board of directors consists of leaders from all major sectors of society. The approach is simple: An entrepreneur has an idea for a new product or service and wants to start a company; the MCO helps develop a business plan and obtain financing. The permanent staff is small, but the MCO draws on a volunteer advisory panel of engineers, scientists, and executives for the specific expertise required to evaluate and help prepare business plans. Because these plans are expertly conceived, the chances of receiving adequate financing and achieving economic viability are substantially increased.

Minnesota Seed Capital Fund. Capital from more conventional sources such as venture capital companies and banks is often not available for new companies during their initial formation and early development stages. Because of this, the Minnesota Seed Capital Fund has been formed, with an initial capitalization of $10 million. It is receiving growing support. Recently, two pension funds became investors and several more are considering investment.

Job Creation Network. The MCO, the Seed Fund, and the BTC constitute what is called the Minnesota Network for Job Creation, which provides the support needed by small enterprises to become successful. Unfortunately, in our present economic system, such assistance is left too much to chance, with an undue burden on the entrepreneur. As a consequence, a high percentage of new businesses fail. On the other hand, through expanded initiatives and cooperation among industry, government, and universities, the necessary support can be provided to vastly increase the success rate for new enterprises and help assure the profitable growth of existing enterprises. The Minnesota Network is being replicated in other communities.

Urban Revitalization. In the case of urban revitalization, Control Data has joined with other companies and two church organizations to form a for-profit consortium capitalized at $3 million, called City Venture Corporation. For the first time, adequate resources have been assembled in a unique and efficient pooling of the resources of individual organizations.

City Venture plans and manages comprehensive programs for the revitalization of urban centers. Its approach mandates that plans for restoring a community must be based primarily on meeting the needs of residents for high quality, accessible, and affordable education and training—and, even more important, their needs for decent jobs. Small enterprises are a major source of those jobs, as well as an important means for building, rebuilding, and maintaining housing and commercial centers. Small businesses also participate in providing health care, education, and other social services. City Venture is three years old. During that time, government-funded contracts have been obtained for projects in many cities, including Minneapolis; Toledo; Philadelphia; Baltimore; St. Paul; Charleston, S.C.; San Antonio, Texas; Miami; the South Bronx; and London Docklands in the United Kingdom.

The most advanced City Venture project is in its third year in the Warren-Sherman community in Toledo. Progress is evident in implementing a comprehensive plan that emphasizes job creation, and better, less costly education and training, linked with jobs and improved housing.

In the words of George Haigh, the chief executive of Toledo Trust and one of the leaders responsible for the effort to revitalize the Warren-Sherman area in Toledo:

> The project began with a neighborhood that suffered unemployment in excess of 32 percent; inadequate, run-down housing; low household incomes; inadequate shopping facilities; lack of small business; and lack of recreational facilities. Crime, arson and pride-sapping neighborhood decay were all too evident.
>
> Using City Venture as a catalyst and gaining the trust and active decision-making involvement of neighborhood people, neighborhood organizations, the City of Toledo, and several private businesses, a unique program began to rapidly take shape. Not a program featuring handouts, but one that would provide improved neighborhood housing, training and education for hundreds, over a thousand additional neighborhood jobs, a Business and Tech-

nology Center to help minority business, a new shopping center, new parks for recreational use—and the list goes on. Most importantly, however, is that these programs are all investments that are aimed to produce profit for the private sector, pride for the neighborhood, and real opportunities for people.

Rural Development. The need for rural development has been approached through another for-profit consortium called Rural Ventures Corporation. Like City Venture, it was capitalized at $3 million. Investors include businesses, church organizations, farm cooperatives, foundations, and individuals. Rural Ventures' main thrust is to increase the productivity and profitability of small farms and to assist in the start-up and profitable growth of small businesses in rural communities. With respect to small farms, it is evident that with proper selection and application of existing and emerging technologies, and with adequate ongoing research and development, small family farms can reduce the cost of food, make a significant contribution to food production, do it in more environmentally protective ways, and provide a decent living for the operators.

Computer technology is the centerpiece of the strategy. Data banks of agricultural technology are being assembled and computer-based education courseware is being written primarily through cooperative efforts between Control Data and a large number of universities and other organizations. Computer-optimized selection of crops, livestock, equipment, and other technologies are made for each small farm, and a full range of computer-based education and training programs are available to help individual farmers apply the technologies efficiently.

Many Rural Ventures contracts are underway. In New England, Rural Ventures is providing production and marketing assistance to small-scale sheep growers to assist them in rebuilding their region's once-flourishing sheep industry. In Alaska, Rural Ventures is managing two projects north of the Arctic Circle; the tundra is being cleared to grow food locally and thereby build a more self-sufficient society in these remote areas. In north central Minnesota, forty low-income farmers planted their first commercial vegetable crops under Rural Ventures guidance.

EVALUATION

By now, you must be wondering about results—about reactions by our many constituents, as well as profits and other benefits. High on the list of benefits to Control Data has been the favorable reaction by employees. Our programs provide the opportunity for employees to participate directly and visibly in serving society as part of their work responsibilities. As a result, they have a sense of pride and gain a special kind of enjoyment in being part of Control Data's broad-based effort to address unmet needs. Prospective employees, especially those just entering the work force, also view our strategy very favorably as demonstrated by a college recruiting success rate much higher than other companies.

Control Data has also enjoyed good support from its stockholders. We have always communicated the essence of our strategies, including the longer than average time required for most programs to achieve attractive profitability.

On the other hand, our strategy was subjected to more than twelve years of criticism by many financial analysts, fund managers, and other Wall Street people who judge corporate financial performance on a fiscal quarter-to-quarter basis and arrive at their long-range assessments primarily by projecting current earnings five years ahead. Some characterized Control Data's strategy with such expressions as "a passion for experimenting with business methods to solve social problems" or "good works that restrain profitability." More recently, however, rising profitability at Control Data and the debacle in Detroit is causing them to do some soul searching and have second thoughts about our strategy. Had the automobile manufacturers been cooperatively addressing the basic *need* for more energy efficient transportation instead of perceived *wants*, they could have avoided the crucial loss of market that resulted in staggering losses of billions of dollars and hundreds of thousands of jobs.

The following individual program evaluations illustrate the scope and benefits of our activities. By working closely with local community organizations and with partial government funding for training, Control Data has succeeded in making poverty-area plants as profitable as its conventional operations. At the same time, the interests of each community are being served and a path provided for disadvantaged persons to enter the mainstream of industry.

In addition, local communities have a highly positive perception of the plants. In the early days of the program, there was some skepticism of Control Data's motives and we were characterized as "fat cats" or "rip-off artists." There were those who predicted our plants would be vandalized. The criticism has long since disappeared, and there has never been any vandalism—not even grafitti on the walls.

Education and Training. In education, our total program is not profitable—and will not be, by design, until 1984—because of continuing investments in courseware and new learning centers. However, based on estimated revenue growth, the total program *will* turn profitable during that year and rise steadily thereafter to become the largest producer of profit in the company. Although the *total* education program is not profitable, the Control Data Institutes are nicely in the black, with an operating profit rate higher than any other unit in the corporation.

We never thought for a moment being successful in education would be easy. History shows that more than 200 years went by after the book was introduced before it was used by teachers. Our plan provided for a few carefully chosen fields of entry where resistance to change would be the least and for a gradually increasing commitment of resources for whatever length of time required to be successful. The initial fields chosen were proprietary vocational education, business and industry training, education and training for the disadvantaged and handicapped, and engineering education.

Significant progress is being made with PLATO in spite of continuing reservations by most of the educational establishment, and progress is accelerating as additional high-quality PLATO courseware becomes available and delivery costs continue to decrease. Using the small PLATO microcomputer as the delivery device, the hourly instructional cost averages about 75 cents. Also, PLATO courseware is gradually becoming available for delivery by some of the more commonly used microcomputers made by other companies for an average cost of 50 cents per hour.

The proliferation of personal microcomputers coupled with high-quality PLATO courseware will greatly enhance learning in the home. Parents will begin to put pressure on the public school system to speed up the introduction of computer technology into the educational process. In order to take full advantage of this technology, the *management* of schools should be contracted out to business, which has the expertise to use advanced technology efficiently. Control of education policy, of course, should remain in the hands of school boards and boards of trustees, and there is no need to abrogate the responsibility of teachers for diagnosing student needs, selecting curriculum materials, or any other teaching duty. Even more important, private management provides time for teachers to nurture.

Small Business. With respect to small business, many of Control Data's services are producing attractive profits; however, overall profitability is being held down by rapid expansion in the number of locations offering them. Our willingness to devote substantial resources to assist small business enhances our company's image not only among small companies but also with the general public, especially in Europe, where countries are taking stronger initiatives than the United States to accelerate the creation of jobs by assisting small businesses.

We started a program of equity investments in small companies, most of them newly formed in 1979. The program is not yet profitable, but there are enough obvious winners emerging to assure attractive profits. Even more important, many of the companies are developing products and services, especially computer-based education courseware, which will be marketed by Control Data in the years ahead. This type of program capitalizes on the strongest attributes of both large and small enterprise. The small company, inherently the more creative and flexible because of low overhead, can develop new products and services sooner and for less cost. The large company, with its vast resources, can excel in marketing. By the year 2000, we estimate that small companies will supply 30 percent of Control Data's products and services.

Urban Revitalization. By far the toughest field is urban revitalization. From the beginning we knew the problems City Venture was setting out to solve would not be easy or they would have been solved long ago.

The initial phase of an urban revitalization project can be an adventure in a hornets' nest. Communities are often divided because numerous neighborhood organizations have differing perceptions of what should be done or how. It is difficult, sometimes impossible, to obtain a consensus. There are always a number of angry people who are abusive during meetings with outside organizations. Some neighborhood groups are corrupt, and many of the more activist types resort to unconscionable tactics. At times it appears as if there is a conspiracy to undermine our private enterprise system.

On the other hand, the vast majority of neighborhood groups are dedicated to bettering their community; they are achieving results in spite of chronic deficiencies in resources and differing views. Lack of consensus also plagues business, government, and other parts of the community. This is most often manifested by the absence of a true commitment to a revitalization effort.

Even groups that are truly committed to developing their community may have very different goals and priorities. Mediating among many parties, each of whom has a valid goal, when there are not sufficient resources to satisfy all of them, requires special sensitivity, talent, and expertise. With experience, City Venture is developing keen mediation skills that add greatly to its ability to create new business opportunities.

One of the most important things to recognize about urban revitalization is that instant successes are not possible. Usually, at least two years are required to show tangible evidence of progress, much longer to reach job creation goals. This allows time for those in opposition to create doubts—and in two City Venture projects, in Minneapolis and Miami, to prevent them from progressing beyond the planning stage. However, in spite of the many difficulties, City Venture has proven it can effectively serve in the role of catalyst and coordinator in helping to obtain a consensus and in working with a community in planning and implementing a revitalization effort.

On the other side of the coin, City Venture is not yet profitable; however, profitability is projected to be achieved next year. Reaching an attractive level of profitability is important in proving the concept of City Venture, although the amount of profit relative to earnings of the corporate investors will not be significant for many years. Therefore, the main benefit to be derived from City Venture by corporate stockholders is the identification of new markets in their fields of interest. Unfortunately, this potential has yet to be perceived by many of the corporate stockholders, who, bless them, invested because "it was the right thing to do."

One consequence of that motivation has been the resignation of representatives of two corporations from the board of directors soon after adverse publicity when the City Venture project in East Minneapolis was not continued. Opponents, of course, claimed City Venture failed and the newspapers were only too eager to play up that aspect. In the light of this and other experiences with stockholders, City Venture is engaged in designing procedures to assist corporate stockholders in identifying business opportunities in their fields of interest.

Rural Development. In contrast to City Venture, the corporate shareholders of Rural Ventures have a much better perception of the potential for new business opportunities. Also, Rural Ventures has had only relatively minor problems with neighborhood and community groups, presumably because they are fewer in number and because there are fewer conflicting interests in the competition for resources. Rural Ventures is making excellent progress and is projected to achieve profitability this year. In the very near future, Rural Ventures will commence a project overseas in a developing country in the Caribbean.

Overall Profitability.   Control Data's profitability is rising. It will continue to rise, because major and worldwide unmet needs are being served by Control Data products and services, which are at the forefront of technology.

PROGRAMS BY OTHER ORGANIZATIONS

Control Data is not the only company actively involved in addressing social needs. A number of banks, insurance companies, and industrial companies have established minority enterprise small business investment companies (MESBIC). By far the largest is EQUICO, owned by the Equitable Life Assurance Company, with paid-in capital of $10.5 million.

In addition, banks and insurance companies have invested in commercial and housing construction and rehabilitation in poverty-stricken neighborhoods. One of the companies most aggressive in making such investments is Toledo Trust. Plants have been established in inner cities by Lockheed, IBM, Digital Equipment Company, Owens Illinois, and some other companies.

While these and other examples of investing could be cited and represent a considerable amount of activity, the aggregate is very small compared to the size of the needs. But it *is* a start.

PRIVATIZATION OF PUBLIC SERVICES

Further words need to be said about privatization of public services. Earlier, I mentioned that the management of schools should be contracted to business. With a fee structure based on performance, business could make attractive profits and the public would benefit from a more responsive and productive educational system.

Prisons are in critical need of better management, to reduce both the present staggering costs of operation and excessive recidivism. Given adequate incentives, business could provide the needed management and creativity. Control Data is offering prison management services based on extensive experience accumulated from PLATO education and training programs in prisons, manufacturing in a prison, leasing cars to ex-prisoners, and other programs.

State and local government should also spin off programs for business to manage in many other areas such as child care, assistance for senior citizens, recreation, rehabilitation for ex-prisoners and people discharged from state hospitals, and so on.

If public services were privatized, the role of government would change from one of providing services to one of establishing standards, licensing, and monitoring. The size of the public bureaucracy would be dramatically reduced. The quality of the services would be dramatically improved. As an additional benefit, many new opportunities would be available for small business.

Much more could be said about these and other programs. However, it is evident that jobs can be taken to poverty-stricken areas; education and training can be made responsive and affordable; disadvantaged and disabled people can be trained and placed in meaningful jobs; small businesses can be helped to start up and grow and create more new jobs; poverty-stricken urban and rural areas can be revitalized; and public services privatized. All of these actions can be accomplished efficiently and, in the long run, profitably through broad-based cooperation.

The question is occasionally raised about the appropriateness of an investment strategy for every company. It is true that it is easier to visualize how the existing products and services of some companies, such as Control Data, can be applied in meeting needs than it is for others. Still, it is clear to me that there are significant business opportunities for every company.

However, such opportunities may not, indeed normally will not be apparent without a dedicated effort to find them. The broad horizon of attractive opportunities for Control Data that we see today was not visible in 1967 when we took the first major step by establishing an inner city plant.

Skeptics ask how a steel company could possibly find an investment strategy meaningful. Considering just steelmaking and the dismal innovation record of most steel companies in recent years, it is clear that they could help themselves enormously by adopting an aggressive program of investing in small businesses. The proven creativity of small enterprise could point the way for badly needed innovation in many areas. Even small steel mills can be profitable.

Of course, many steel companies are vertically integrated and diversified, so there are opportunities beyond those just related directly to steelmaking. Again, cooperation with small companies can be profoundly beneficial not only for steel companies but for all large companies. In short, for any company, it is, "Seek and ye shall find."

President's Program. Given evidence that an investment strategy works, that it is appropriate for every company, and that the market is enormous, will it become widely adopted? There are a number of reasons for optimism:

1. One is the existence of a conducive environment created by increasing public concern about growing needs and the shrinking government resources available to address them.
2. Another is that corporate America is increasingly embracing the concept of corporate responsibility, which is resulting in increased philanthropy. In addition, substantial contributions are being made each year by foundations.
3. A third is the myriad of volunteer neighborhood and community-based organizations that have been spawned and are improving housing, creating jobs, and in other ways improving neighborhoods and helping the needy.

All of these are important, and much is being accomplished; however, the effort is fractionated and insufficient.

Furthermore, the status quo of nearly fifty years has been disrupted by President Reagan's cuts in federal budgets for many human and economic development programs, the shifting of greater responsibilities to states, and the President's call for the private sector to provide alternatives consisting mainly of increased volunteering and contributing.

Much has been written and said about how the private sector should respond. Initially the prevailing view was that corporations and individuals should increase their charitable contributions to bridge the gap. However, facts about giving make it clear that this is very unlikely to happen.

It is also not realistic to expect a substantial replacement of federal dollars with state funds because of strong negative reactions to tax increases. Even in the unlikely event that federal dollars could be replaced with state and private funds, the results at best would be to maintain the status quo—with no significant improvement in our social condition.

Mounting public concern, shrinking government budgets, expanded community-based efforts, increasing acceptance of the concept of corporate responsibility and the disruption of the status quo have set the stage for business to provide the initiative, the focus, and the additional resources through investment. What is lacking is a means of reducing both the risks and the longer than average period required to achieve adequate returns on investments.

The public-private partnerships that the president is advocating can provide these answers if expanded to include investing—along with volunteering and contributing and appropriate financial incentives. It is this possibility that caused me to accept President Reagan's invitation to be a member of his Private Sector Initiatives Task Force. Let me briefly describe what I envision can be accomplished to effectively address the objectives of the task force by devising a structured program, with incentives, to expand investing, volunteering, and contributing.

The objective of the President's Task Force on Private Sector Initiatives can be broadly stated as follows:

> Facilitate the replacement of government paternalism with public-private sector partnerships in every community for assisting needy persons and depressed areas.

At this point, I should make clear that public-private partnerships are equivalent to the broad-based cooperation I talked about earlier— just the words are different:

There are two ways of providing assistance to the needy:

1.   Treat the symptoms of social ills.
2.   Address the root causes.

At the present time the first approach is the most common. Unfortunately, in the face of unprecedented need for permanent solutions, it is also the least effective. For a program to have lasting impact, it must treat underlying causes: primarily unemployment. Given enough jobs, most people and most communities can solve many of their other problems.

The need for expanded employment is so great that the only practicable way to achieve an adequate response is a focused approach by corporations, foundations, churches, labor unions, and individuals in cooperative programs consisting of volunteering, contributing, and, most important as I stressed earlier, *investing.*

PROGRAM FOR EXPANDING EMPLOYMENT

Specifically, a program is being recommended for expanding employment that includes incentives for increasing:

1.   Job-creating capabilities in every community;
2.   Community development efforts;
3.   The employment of disadvantaged youth;
4.   The employment of the disabled;
5.   Corporate investing, contributing, and volunteering;
6.   Volunteering and contributing by individuals.

Figure 11-1. Public-Private Sector Partnerships.

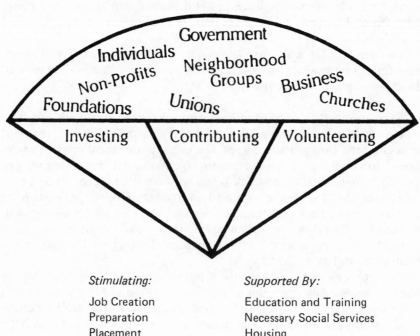

Stimulating:

Job Creation
Preparation
Placement

Supported By:

Education and Training
Necessary Social Services
Housing

The underlying concept of the program is shown by Figure 11-1. Implementation requires interaction among public-private partnerships focused on the greatest need in our society today: jobs. Only with this kind of focus will our always limited resources be applied in enough depth to make real progress toward permanent solutions. The concept is based on methodology proven sound by Control Data and many other organizations. Hence implementation is essentially a matter of replicating what has worked.

Each part of the total program relies on partnerships of various types. In addition to partnerships that primarily address specific issues, a broad-based partnership is needed with membership from different sectors of the community to assure that neighborhood goals are in consonance with those of the larger community—be it city, county, state, or region. There is also the matter of marshalling and allocating resources.

Many examples of successful broader based partnerships can be cited. One is the Greater Milwaukee Committee for Community Development, which has members drawn from labor, education, and business. The Greater Toledo Economic Planning Council is another, with members drawn from business and city government. A third example is Minnesota Wellspring, a statewide organization with members from state and city government, education, labor, business and foundations.

To help further articulate the essence of the program, I will elaborate briefly on major parts and identify incentives that will be needed to gain adoption nationwide.

Expansion of Job Creating Facilities.   Starting then with job creation, virtually every community needs a more effective means of creating jobs through the use of resources under local control as opposed to relying on large companies to expand existing operations or establish new ones. Since small businesses are the source of most new jobs, this can be best accomplished by establishing public-private partnerships in each community to assist in the start-up and growth of small enterprises. In urban areas, the focus would be on small businesses; in rural areas, attention should be given to both small businesses and small farms.

The core elements constitute a job creation network identical to the Minnesota Network described earlier (Figure 11-2). As noted, the Cooperation Office in Minnesota is currently financed by contributions and grants, and the point to be added here is that it has been

Figure 11-2.   Public-Private Initiatives in Job Creation.

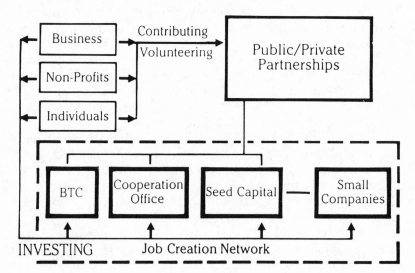

very difficult and time consuming to obtain the required level of support. Hence tax credits are needed both to stimulate contributions to efforts of this type and to induce corporations to volunteer the services of their professional and executive employees. Some states, such as Indiana, already provide tax credits for volunteer services. Tax credits are also needed to stimulate investments in Business and Technology Centers. The payout period for a BTC is typically eight years, and this is perceived as too long by most investors.

Community Development. Small business cannot flourish in an area where crime is rampant, housing is run down, streets are in disrepair, and so on. Conversely, a decent living environment can neither be established nor maintained where opportunities for employment are few and far between. Thus community development is essential to creating a supportive atmosphere for small business, and small business is essential to community development.

Different communities have different needs. There is no single model for community development that can be applied across the board. It is suggested that communities be divided into two broad categories, *more fortunate* and *less fortunate*, and that a distinct approach be taken to each type.

For more fortunate communities, where deterioration is not severe, the recommended approach is to replicate the Network for Job Creation. When employment is at a reasonable level, communities can usually cope with most other problems.

For less fortunate communities, where deterioration is severe and unemployment high, the recommended approach is that the replication of the Network for Job Creation be supported by a comprehensive revitalization program. The Toledo Warren-Sherman Community Revitalization Program described earlier is an example of such a program, which emphasizes expanded employment, more responsive education and training, and improved housing.

Financial Incentives. A comprehensive revitalization plan cannot be expected to succeed unless sufficient financial incentives are offered to both investors and lending institutions. Especially important is seed capital for small business. In addition to not being generally available, as noted earlier, there is the added deterrent of the small businesses being located in high-risk areas. In order to stimulate investors to provide the needed seed capital, I am recommending a 100 percent write-off for new equity investments in small businesses located in Enterprise Zone areas. Also, to attract the large-scale investment required for inner city commercial and residential projects, special tax incentives are being recommended.

EMPLOYMENT OF THE DISADVANTAGED

Getting the enormous numbers of disadvantaged persons in the United States job-ready and placed is a task of overwhelming dimensions. A more realistic approach is to concentrate on disadvantaged youth. Many adult members of the disadvantaged population have learned to cope somehow through welfare, assistance from neighbors, and other means; too many of the young are still at sea.

There is a growing public awareness that education and training must increasingly be linked with jobs. The OUTREACH program, described earlier, is an efficient way to get disadvantaged youth into meaningful jobs. Implementing OUTREACH requires an investment beyond the normal costs for employment and training. Therefore, the program will not be widely replicated unless participating businesses can both recover the extra costs incurred and realize a reasonable profit on the investment.

Tax credits would serve these purposes and at the same time represent a good investment for the government. Studies have shown that, on the average, a job is conservatively worth some $52,000 per year to the federal government. If 25 percent of that $52,000 value were shared each year with employers of disadvantaged youths in the form of tax credits extending over a ten year period, all parties would benefit handsomely. The employer would acquire an experienced employee and, in the process, make a reasonable profit, and the employee would be launched on a career. The program would be more than self-financing, resulting in a net gain to society as a whole.

EMPLOYMENT OF THE DISABLED

Current efforts aimed at providing employment for the disabled should be expanded. There are many fine organizations assisting disabled persons to gain employment, but they need more support in order to take advantage of recent technological advances. Computer-based education, work terminals, robotic controls, and a variety of new sensory devices have opened new doors for the disabled. Equipment of many types exists for helping disabled persons to be productive. Personalized adaptations and training are invariably required, however, and these are expensive. A tax credit could greatly expand employment for the disabled. It could be similar to the credit recommended earlier for disadvantaged youth. The amount would vary according to the type of disability and the corresponding costs of adapting equipment, education, and training to individual needs.

CONTRIBUTING AND VOLUNTEERING

Tax credits have been recommended to stimulate corporations and individuals to make contributions and volunteer time. Specifically, a tax credit should be made available to corporations and individuals contributing to community-based organizations supporting job creation activities, such as a cooperation office. In addition, a credit should be provided to corporations to offset the salaries of employees who volunteer their professional and management assistance to small businesses during working hours. For individuals volunteering services on their own time, increased credits could be given for car mileage and for some percentage of the value of the time donated.

GETTING FROM HERE TO THERE

The question is, will President Reagan's program be implemented? The answer is yes, although budget constraints may dictate that it occur in steps. There are several reasons for my optimism.

One is that it is responsive to the wishes of the president. In speeches, he has said, "We want an American partnership that can and should be replicated in every community." What has been described meets that desire.

A second is the momentum building for Enterprise Zone legislation which, if properly structured, could provide a meaningful start toward establishing job creating capabilities in poverty-stricken areas. Congressional leaders predict federal Enterprise Zone legislation will be passed. In addition, eight individual states have already passed zone legislation or are considering it. Discussions with governors have convinced me that state enterprise zone legislation will play a significant role in revitalization—perhaps, in the long run, more important than federal legislation.

Most important is the president's continuing promotion of his concept of less government welfare and more private sector voluntary actions, which is increasing awareness of the need for and advantages of cooperation. This will be further magnified by the private sector initiative task forces being established by individual states. But there is also a growing awareness that increased volunteering and contributing are not going to adequately address the root cause of social ills— lack of employment.

Therefore, with a nationwide perception of the need for cooperation established and a mechanism in place for sponsoring and coordinating cooperation—the stage is set, waiting for business to provide the initiative and make the investment.

One word summarizes what I have been saying: *cooperation.* Without a vast increase in cooperation, our nation will sink further in the mire of festering social problems. But with widespread cooperation to achieve more efficient use of existing intellectual, physical, and financial resources, the decline can be arrested, followed by gradual improvement.

I am speaking not only of cooperation between business organizations; I am speaking particularly of public-private cooperation. To be effective, public-private cooperation requires innovative strategies both in the area of public policy and in private corporate activity. Business leaders can contribute to more effective cooperation by helping develop new public policy approaches through the democratic process, as well as by expanding their own entrepreneurial roles.

When I first began to advocate widespread cooperation more than twenty years ago, even before the formal adoption of our corporate strategy, the words sounded somewhat esoteric to me; and I felt like a preacher without a congregation. Spoken and unspoken reactions from my audiences confirmed these feelings. It wasn't that I didn't have the conviction of its merits; rather, it was the realization of the difficulty, seemingly overwhelming at times, to achieve it.

However, the enormous benefits that Control Data has already enjoyed have long ago replaced that early uneasy feeling with one of determination to overcome whatever great difficulties stand in the way of establishing broad-based cooperative efforts. Those cooperative efforts *will* come—and they will provide the basis for a new, exciting, and more productive role for corporations.

✳ *Chapter 12*

Matching Public Policies
and Business Strategies:
The New Context

Robert B. Reich

Many of the social needs discussed in this book are attributable to the failure of our economic system to utilize fully the nation's human and capital resources. When, as now, almost 30 percent of our factories and equipment lie idle, and 10 percent of our employable workers have no job, an array of social problems are apt to arise; and these in turn are likely to frustrate further economic growth as they divert resources from productive investment into welfare, unemployment insurance, health expenditures associated with the strains of economic duress, and crime control. Thus a vicious circle sets in. As the national economy slows down, social costs begin to mount; and these costs render sustained economic recovery even more difficult.

The central theme of this essay is that government policies can forestall much of this vicious circle by easing the process of economic adjustment. Macroeconomic policies that merely manipulate public taxing and spending and the money supply are not fully adequate to deal with the new problems of adjustment stemming from global competition and oil supply shocks. We need a more detailed—although not necessarily larger or more intrusive—set of economic policies, which are matched to the competitive strategies of American businesses. This approach calls for the same sort of public-private partnership that is the subject of the rest of this book, but on a larger scale: converting social needs into business opportunities by altering the system of competitive incentives.

JAPAN'S PUBLIC-PRIVATE PARTNERSHIP

A comprehensive analysis of the relationship between public policies and business strategies would recognize that businesses change over time, as does the nature of competition within industries, among industries, and among national economies. The process of change and the speed of adjustment to change are critical to business strategy. The same factors also should be critical to public policy. The failure of public policy in the United States to understand and respond to them is becoming of larger consequence as the U.S. economy has become more integrated into the international economy.

Imports and exports now constitute 24 percent of our gross national product, up from 14 percent in 1970 (OECD 1980). Since the early 1970s nearly a million manufacturing jobs have been lost to foreign trade in the region stretching from the factories of Baltimore to the automobile plants of St. Louis and another million jobs have been lost in the rest of the country. Over that same period the share of the world market claimed by U.S. manufacturing goods has fallen by 23 percent (OECD 1980). Twenty-eight percent of our domestically sold automobiles are now made abroad, compared to 9 percent in 1970; over 50 percent of our consumer electronics products, compared to 10 percent in 1970. The list goes on, growing longer year by year: hand calculators, cameras, metal-forming machine tools, food processors, sporting equipment, motorcycles, stereo components, textile machinery, watches, tires, video components, pianos, footwear (OECD 1980). Much of this foreign invasion, but by no means all of it, is from Japan. At the same time nearly one job in six is dependent on exports. We fear to tamper with imports for the sake of protecting American jobs without considering the longer range effect on our exports.

After having lobbied for tax cuts and supported a tight monetary policy, many business leaders have found it awkward to place blame for their present troubles on the administration in Washington. The search for scapegoats therefore has come to focus, as it so often does in times of national crisis, on a foreign nation. The villain of the present piece is, of course, Japan. The "Japanese challenge," which began as the extraordinary cleverness and ability of Japanese managers, has gradually been transmogrified into the devious, high-handed, insensitive, and inscrutable policies of the Japanese government. And yet, the two cannot be separated. What appears to many Americans as the "art of Japanese management" is in fact a particular set of strategies at the level of the firm that are intimately tied to a particular set of industrial policies emanating from the Japanese government. These business strategies and public policies have evolved together, complementing one another as they have been adapted over time. They constitute a form of public-private partnership, writ large, on a national level.

Neither side of the equation can exist without the other. Any brave American manager who tried to guarantee his workers permanent employment and to invest for long-term growth instead of short-term profits would find his company bankrupt and himself without a job in short order. Such business strategies need the benefit of tax and credit policies that ease the burden on the firm during troughs in the business cycle, and of subsidies that ease the transition of capital out of industrial segments becoming less competitive in world markets and simultaneously promote the development of segments whose competitive future is more sanguine. By the same token, any inspired Washington bureaucrat who sought to pick industrial winners and losers, and to direct investment to the former and away from the latter—without the benefit of an intricate network of strategic market information such as Japan's, which links Japanese firms, industries, banks, and key government agencies—would be doomed to ignoble failure.

This match between business strategies and industrial policies in Japan is not due to Japanese character or culture. Many of the practices that are considered peculiarly Japanese today were not conspicuous until relatively recently. During the past twenty-five years, Japanese industrial policies have focused almost exclusively on the goal of transforming the Japanese economy toward ever higher valued industries. In 1959 Japanese exports were mainly in relatively low-skill, labor-intensive industries like clothing, shoes, and toys. In the 1960s, Japan pushed its economy into more capital-intensive industries, such as steel, motorcycles, and ships, and industries derived from petrochemicals. By the mid-1970s, Japan had repositioned itself to compete successfully in industries that incorporated complex machinery, such as home appliances, automobiles, and television receivers. By the end of the 1970s, Japan's export mix began shifting once again, toward high technologies like computers, robots, semiconductors, office equipment, and numerically controlled machine tools. Rather than try to preserve its industrial base at any given time, Japanese industrial policies have sought to propel it into the future, while at the same time casting off older industries in which Japan's competitive position was declining.

The Japanese government has accomplished this feat by astutely using industrial policies to reenforce market forces in the Japanese economy and thereby to push Japanese businesses into becoming more competitive internationally. Apart from its politically sensitive agricultural sector, Japan has employed tariff and nontariff barriers only to protect "infant industries" until they reach a scale at which they can compete internationally. By contrast, the United States has consistently used its tariffs, quotas, orderly marketing agreements, tax breaks, and bailouts of various kinds to protect older industries that have become uncompetitive in world markets. These policies have retarded structural change in the American economy.

The textile industry offers one example. Its competitiveness has declined in every industrialized nation as the industry has shifted its production to lower wage labor in less developed countries. Anticipating this change, Japanese firms in cotton, rayon, and synthetic fibers have actively diversified their production in Japan, and transferred their textile manufacturing to other East Asian countries, often in joint ventures with foreign nationals. But the United States has been engaged for over twenty years in a desperate attempt to protect its domestic textile industry against foreign imports. The cost to American consumers of tariffs on apparel alone is estimated to be $1.9 billion a year (Morkre and Tarr 1980).

Another example: in 1958 Japan made the critical decision to run down its high-cost coal industry and to base its industrial expansion on imported fuel, largely oil. The Japanese Ministry of International Trade and Industry's (MITI) subsequent policy of discouraging nonessential consumption by allowing oil prices to rise with world market prices prepared Japan to deal effectively with the oil shocks of the 1970s. By September 1980, only fifteen months after the second oil shock plunged its international payments into deficit, Japan was able to register a $38 million trade surplus. The United States, by contrast, imposed among the world's lowest excise taxes on petroleum products throughout the 1950s and 1960s. It instituted controls on the price of domestic oil after 1974. Simultaneously, through price controls on natural gas, which created physical shortages of energy supplies for industry, it stimulated a switch from gas to oil by industry, thus encouraging oil imports. Both these policies in effect subsidized dependence on oil imports and made America even more unprepared to deal with the 1979 oil shock than it had been to cope with the 1974 shock.

Shipbuilding had been a key industry for Japan in the 1960s. But changes in the world economy and worldwide overcapacity made that industry less competitive. Japan therefore created a cartel in shipbuilding under special depressed industries legislation passed in 1977. With the cooperation of industry over 40 percent of existing shipbuilding capacity was scrapped. The United States, however, continues to spend over $500 million per year and provide over $6.3 billion in loans and loan guarantees, in order to prop up its ailing shipbuilding industry (Magaziner and Reich 1982).

In high-technology industries, Japan has been careful to preserve domestic competition by giving firms equal access to key government-business research projects, such as the recent effort to build state-of-the-art very-large-scale-integrated (VLSI) circuitry. Five major Japanese firms were involved in that project, and MITI provided all with information and support. Competition in Japanese government projects extends even to foreign firms.

Long-term financing provided to Japanese firms by city banks, in cooperation with the Bank of Japan, Ministry of Finance, and MITI, has enabled the firms to drop their prices when faced with declining demand or temporary overcapacity. Rather than match these low prices, American firms have charged Japanese firms with unfair dumping and have sought countervailing duties and other forms of import barriers against them. America's steel industry, for example, was for decades habituated to lock-step price increases set by its industry leader, U.S. Steel. When Japanese steelmakers reduced their prices in response to the steel glut of the late 1960s, the U.S. steelmaking oligopoly was unable to respond in kind. Instead, U.S. steelmakers lobbied for protection. Their lobbying paid off. The first round of voluntary restrictions on steel imports from Japan went into effect in 1968. It was renewed in 1971 and then in 1977 was replaced by the Trigger Price Mechanism. Meanwhile, between 1966 and 1972, the Japanese steel industry invested heavily in more efficient production facilities, increasing its assets by more than 23 percent a year, in an attempt to become the world's most efficient steel producer of the 1970s. Once the U.S. steel industry gained protection against Japanese imports, its capital expenditures slowed to an average growth of 4 percent per year. This, despite the fact that between 1966 and 1972 the eight largest U.S. steel producers had a 3.8 percent average return on assets, as opposed to a 1.8 percent return for the five largest Japanese steel companies. The secret of Japan's success was not dumping. It was long-term financing (U.S. Comptroller General 1980). A similar story can be told about American automobiles and consumer electronics, both of which are now protected behind tariff walls or "voluntary" export agreements.

As developing nations have become capable of taking on progressively more complex manufacturing processes, and as the costs of worldwide transportation and communication have continually decreased, the speed of industrial evolution has quickened. Japan has anticipated this evolution and accelerated the process of structural change in its own economy in order to meet it. With each step in Japan's evolution from textiles and toys, to steel and ships, to appliances and automobiles, and finally to high technologies, the other nations of the region—South Korea, the Philippines, Taiwan, Hong Kong, and Singapore—have been one or two steps behind. By accelerating its own industrial evolution, Japan has helped to accelerate theirs. Within each nation, central banks have provided long-term financing for future growth sectors; highly skilled bureaucrats in economic ministries have devised tax incentives, export financing, and subsidized research programs for the same sectors; and powerful industrial groups, business associations, and general trading companies have gathered detailed intelligence on trends in world markets, which they share with the central banks and economic ministries. These vast networks of interlocking public and private bureaucracies are continually involved in strategic planning of their economies—a process that is focused on the dynamics of international competition. Is the United States capable of designing and implementing public policies that match business strategies this well?

TOWARD A NATIONAL ECONOMIC STRATEGY

American business cannot achieve competitive leadership in today's international environment without the cooperation of government. This does not mean that government should supplant or second guess the strategic decisions of business. It simply means that the strength of the economy as a whole, as a reflection of the collective competitive strength of individual firms, requires public policies that reenforce and complement the international competitive strategies of the individual firms.

To achieve and maintain competitive leadership in the international arena, firms must adapt to changing conditions in the world economy. Cost advantages and investment barriers change as technology, customer requirements, tastes, and factor costs all undergo change. At any given time there will be opportunities that can be exploited for competitive success but also disadvantageous positions in which firms are unlikely to maintain competitiveness over the long term. Such effective adaptation requires more than successful strategy, of course. Firms that seek to exploit new opportunities or move out of disadvantageous positions must also have the resources to adapt, in the form of appropriate capital and labor.

Government can reduce the cost of adaptation by working with the private sector to ensure the availability both of capital and of labor with the skills necessary to exploit new competitive opportunities, and by simultaneously easing the movement of capital and labor out of declining positions. It can thereby accelerate the adjustments that capital and labor markets otherwise would achieve more slowly on their own, by reducing the side-effects of such adjustments—unemployment; regional and community decline; an absence of infrastructure, like roads and ports; and a lack of the necessary skilled workers, basic research, and experience in foreign trade.

Arguably there was less need in the 1960s for government to help accelerate these adjustments of capital and labor markets. Full employment, relative affluence, and rapid economic growth all made it comparatively easy for the economy both to adapt through market forces alone to changing competitive conditions and to endure whatever costs were associated with failing to adapt. There were an abundance of capital for new projects and adequate job opportunities in most areas of the country for workers who found themselves suddenly unemployed. But since the early 1970s—with a sudden increase in the cost of imported oil and the slowing of our economic growth, coupled with the easier flow of capital and technology to developing countries and the improvements in transportation and communication upon which flow is based—adaptation within the national economy has become much more difficult. Capital is now in relatively short supply. Unemployed workers now find it more difficult to locate new jobs. Moreover, we have become irrevocably dependent on international trade, so that sudden shocks or even gradual changes in world market conditions now have profound effects on our domestic economy.

Simultaneously, and for all these reasons, the cost of *failing* to adapt to changes in world market conditions has grown significantly. Tariffs, quotas, voluntary restrictions, bail-outs and other means of maintaining business whose underlying competitive position is declining in world markets have vast multiplier effects for the rest of the economy, increasing the price of the inputs upon which many of our industries are dependent for their competitive survival. And because many of the world's emerging industries permit substantial reductions in unit costs with higher volume and experience, the penalty for not entering these industries early enough is never being able to catch up.

Thus every advanced industrial country must now deal with two key issues of economic adjustment. First, each country must cope with its businesses that face long-term competitive declines due to the increasing cost of raw materials, the cost advantages of low-wage countries, and the easy migration of capital and technology abroad. Second, each country must concern itself with its businesses that are capable of gaining long-term competitive leadership in world markets. These two sets of concerns do not require that national governments engage in picking winners and losers, if this is taken to mean actively intervening in the market to promote certain industries and gradually throttle others. The fact is that governments inevitably will be called upon by the private sector for assistance; in deciding to grant or deny these requests, governments must at least understand that declining and advancing businesses present different problems and opportunities, and that government assistance to business can either retard or accelerate the process of economic change and adjustment.

Declining Businesses. A nation has two practical choices it can make with regard to declining businesses. It can ease the adjustment of capital and labor out of these businesses by assisting workers with retraining and relocating, by subsidizing the development of new businesses within the same region or community, and by salvaging those subsectors of declining businesses that are capable of becoming competitive on their own. *Or* it can broadly protect declining businesses from foreign competition by erecting tariffs, quotas, or voluntary export agreements, and thus compelling either consumers, taxpayers, or both to subsidize the cost of maintaining these businesses in the face of more competitive imports. A third alternative— doing nothing and thereby allowing the market to work on its own, with resulting bankruptcies, unemployment, and community or regional decline—is often politically unacceptable in a democracy, and therefore not a realistic option.

The United States has inadvertently chosen to rely primarily on the second alternative, while its major trading partners—particularly Japan and West Germany—have actively sought to depend more on the first. As a result, America has maintained businesses whose overall competitive position is declining. We have thereby increased the cost to other domestic businesses of obtaining goods and services that are protected from international competition and thus jeopardized the international competitiveness of these other businesses as well. In short, rather than accelerate the adjustment of capital and labor to changing conditions and world markets, we have retarded these adjustments.

By contrast, other advanced industrial countries have devised a variety of public and private measures for accelerating the movement of capital and labor out of declining businesses. While they have also on occasion resorted to various forms of protection, in recent years Japan, West Germany, and to a lesser extent France, have grown more sophisticated in their policies for retraining and relocating workers, for developing new industry in depressed regions, and for restructuring declining industries in ways that boost their most competitive firms. To be sure, all industrialized countries continue to face substantial adjustment problems stemming in part from the oil shock of 1979, and all have suffered in recent years from sluggish growth and mounting unemployment. But several other industrial nations—including Japan and West Germany—have managed to achieve higher growth and lower unemployment than the United States, at least in part because they have explicitly promoted positive adjustment rather than protection or preservation.

Growing Businesses. A nation also has two practical choices with regard to businesses capable of gaining long-term competitive leadership in world markets. It can explicitly hasten their development by reducing the short-term cost to them of obtaining the capital and labor they need. It can reduce the cost of capital in the short-term by helping the businesses to fund research, by subsidizing certain high-risk investments, by helping to finance export sales, and by sharing the cost of developing foreign markets. It can reduce the cost of labor in the short term by subsidizing education and training. *Or* a nation can allow its promotional policies to be shaped by politically influential businesses and geographic regions and by the necessities of its defense programs. This second alternative results in a variable hodgepodge of subsidies, loan guarantees, tax expenditures, and procurement contracts, some of which inadvertently promote businesses capable of gaining long-term competitiveness but many of which do not.

While U.S. defense procurement and defense-related research and development programs have spawned some highly competitive industries, these programs have been undertaken without specific regard for their impact on the commercial development of civilian markets. Accordingly, these positive effects have been accidental. Other subsidies, meanwhile, have been dictated more by the political pressures of influential business groups than by competitive strategy. By contrast, other advanced industrial nations have developed explicit measures to encourage their potentially most competitive businesses—

measures that seek to complement the strategies employed by the businesses themselves. To be sure, these explicit measures have not always been successful, as exemplified by France's "Plan Calcul" and Concorde, and Britain's failed attempts to enter the computer industry. But our trading partners are becoming increasingly sophisticated in nurturing their emerging industries—consider the West German, French, and British Airbus, or Japan's semiconductor industry. At the very least, this sophistication has helped them to distinguish between industry requests for protection and requests for aid in restructuring to become competitive.

For reasons of ideology or politics, or both, we have clung tenaciously to the notion that government can and should be "neutral" with regard to market adjustments. Our vast array of tariffs, quotas, voluntary export agreements, and bail-outs for declining businesses are viewed as isolated exceptions to this rule of neutrality, while our defense-related expenditures, tax breaks, and assorted subsidies for other industries are not viewed from the standpoint of international competitive strategy. As a result, we have neither neutrality nor a rational policy of nonneutrality. Meanwhile our leading trading partners are becoming ever more adept at designing and administering intervention strategies, which reenforce the competitive strategies of individual firms.

The explicitness of the competitive strategies of our trading partners has made it much easier politically for them to forge a consensus in support of these strategies. In consequence organized labor and the financial and business communities are in closer agreement regarding the appropriate directions for economic development, and each is thus better able to accept the sacrifices necessary to attain their shared goals. In the United States the failure to acknowledge any need for a national strategy to maintain or regain competitiveness in the world market invites a fragmented and disjointed response to political manipulation by narrow interests. Overall competitiveness has low visibility in the political agenda, and this makes it more difficult for government to mobilize a wide consensus for an internally consistent approach rather than treating problems of each industry as an isolated problem unrelated to the others. It is only very recently that even such generalized policies as tax benefits for investment or research or relaxation of environmental regulations have been seriously debated. There are serious questions, however, as to whether such shot gun approaches can produce benefits in specific problem areas that justify their overall costs to society.

A coherent national economic strategy that involves the cooperation of public and private sectors is necessary for the following reasons:

1. *Government already shapes industrial development through its military procurement and research and development programs.* Although these programs are intended to accomplish goals other than improve our international competitiveness, they have a substantial effect on the growth of specific industries, some of which constitute a large part of our export trade. (See Table 12-1.) Indeed, government procurement as a percentage of GNP is twice as high in the United States as in Japan, which has a far more explicit industrial policy. Equally important, the federal government currently funds over 35 percent of all U.S. industrial research and development and employs (directly or indirectly) over 30 percent of our nation's scientists and engineers (National Science Board 1980). These effects will be larger in the years ahead, as the defense budget increases as a percent of GNP. Procurement and research and development programs have the effect of channeling billions of dollars of private capital to particular industries.

These programs therefore should be undertaken with due regard for their effects upon the future competitiveness of civilian markets. Policymakers should consider whether a large procurement program for a particular product or technology will allow domestic manufacturers to exploit economies of scale and gain substantial experience that can be used in commercial production, or whether the military's needs are so different from the commercial market for that product or technology that the procurement program has the opposite effect—draining off skilled engineers, research, and productive capacity from commercial development, and thereby enabling foreign manufacturers to gain a competitive edge.

2. *Government inevitably affects the pattern of commercial investment through a host of related programs that respond to special interests.* The federal government in effect promotes specific industries through a host of unrelated programs: tariffs, quotas, and

Table 12-1. Federal Procurement as a Percentage of U.S. Industry Sales, 1979.

Procurement Category	(percent)
Aircraft	56
Radio and TV communications equipment	57
Engineering and scientific instruments	23
Electron tubes	33
Nonferrous forgings	36
Optical instruments and lenses	12

Sources: U.S. Department of Defense, Military Prime Contract Awards (1979); Electronic Industries Association Data Book (1980).

orderly marketing agreements; tax laws and rulings; loan guarantees and subsidies; public lands management; and publicly financed insurance. Selective industry promotion has been growing at a rapid rate. As Table 12-2 shows, targeted promotional programs in 1920 totaled $6.2 billion (in 1978 dollars) and represented 3.4 percent of GNP. By 1950 the total had reached $77.1 billion, representing 9.2 percent of GNP. In 1980 the total was $303.7 billion, representing 13.9 percent of GNP. Between 1950 and 1980, both procurement and tax exemptions almost tripled as a percentage of GNP.

None of these programs has been viewed through the lens of international competitiveness. None has been seen as an aspect of a coherent industrial policy. Instead, each has been formulated by agencies and congressional subcommittees closest to well-established industries and therefore most susceptible to special pleading. The result has been a political hodgepodge of subsidies, which have not served to improve our international competitive position. They have channeled capital toward industries that are sheltered from international trade, such as housing; industries whose cost structures depend to a large extent upon low-wage labor, such as footwear and apparel; and industries in which we no longer have a competitive advantage over developing countries, such as shipbuilding. They have channeled capital away from emerging industries or growing segments of established industries, such as semiconductors and new materials technologies, in which we could obtain a competitive advantage in world markets.

This perverse effect is attributable in large part to politics. Old or established industries gain political influence to the extent that communities and regions become dependent on them for jobs, tax support, and the purchase of a vast array of locally produced goods and services. This political influence often translates directly into special government subsidies, advocated by mayors, governors, congressional representatives, or White House political "operatives"—all of whom have a stake in the continued viability of such industries. Larger industries also tend to have more direct political influence, in terms of easier access to the political process. By contrast, emerging industries and newly growing segments of established industries lack such political influence because the present economy is far less dependent on them, notwithstanding that the *future* economy may depend on them for its very survival.

So long as these subsidies are hidden from public view there can be no public debate about their wisdom or long-term consequences. The only alternative to an *explicit* strategy designed to improve competitive performance of our economy in world markets is an implicit one, in which the government cedes the formation of policy to the politically strongest or most active elements within each industry.

Table 12-2. Industrial Development Programs.

	1920		1950		1980 (est.)	
	1978 (in billions)	*Percentage of GNP*	*1978 (in billions)*	*Percentage of GNP*	*1978 (in billions)*	*Percentage of GNP*
State and federal expenditures on infrastructure	5.2	2.8	47.7	5.9	162.0	5.9
Federal government procurement	1.0	0.6	10.2	1.3	94.4	3.8
Federal government expenditures on research and promotion	—	—	8.2	1.0	25.1	1.1
Tax expenditures	—	—	7.9	1.0	62.4	2.9
Cost of outstanding loans and loan guarantees	—	—	0.3	—	3.6	0.2
Total	6.2	3.4	77.1	9.2	303.7	13.9

Sources: Bureau of the Census, U.S. Department of Commerce (1975); budget of the U.S. Government (1920) (1950) (1980); Congressional hearings on select tax expenditures and loan guarantees.

3. *Government is needed to remedy the problems of labor adjust-ment.* When large, labor-intensive industries begin to lose competitive advantage in world markets, many thousands of workers may lose their jobs. In order to obtain other jobs they may have to relocate or gain new skills both of which are costly, particularly for the newly unemployed. Because the movement of capital is relatively swift while the movement of workers is often slow and painful, such unem-ployment can have lasting effects, particularly as its economic impact is multiplied through a local or regional economy.

Government must be more active in promoting the adjustment of labor to structural changes in the world economy in *advance* of industry decline. Failure to do so will result not only in substantial unemployment in impacted areas, but also in the consolidation of political coalitions opposed to economic change. Workers threatened with losing their jobs through the decline of a major regional indus-try can be readily mobilized to support tariffs, quotas, loan guaran-tees, or other forms of public subsidy designed to maintain the industry. Indeed, notwithstanding an overall trend toward reduced tariff levels, in recent years a wide variety of products—notably tex-tiles, apparel, footwear, television, and steel—have been subject to import quotas that have been "voluntarily" negotiated between the United States and particular foreign governments. These restrictions have been voluntary of course only in the sense that foreign coun-tries have acceded to the request of the U.S. government to limit their exports under possible threat of a unilateral tariff, the with-drawal of military aid, or some other more objectionable alternative.

These voluntary restrictions have been politically convenient be-cause they have allowed the president to avoid the necessity of ask-ing Congress to enact unilateral tariffs or quotas or to rescind any aspect of our multilateral tariff agreements. They also have permitted administrations to maintain a theoretical commitment to free trade while avoiding the high visibility of a formal tariff or quota. Finally, these voluntary restrictions have enabled the United States to avoid the negative effects upon foreign policy associated with an across-the-board tariff or quota.

But these restrictions have shared many of the disadvantages of unilateral tariffs and quotas. In addition, they have at most merely postponed the competitive decline of the U.S. industries they have sought to protect because they have not conditioned protection on an industry's willingness to restructure itself to improve its long-term competitive position. The U.S. steel industry failed to take advantage of the breathing space it enjoyed in the wake of the first round of voluntary restrictions that went into effect in 1969. Indeed, the industry's capital expenditures for each of the six subsequent years during which the restraints were in effect were below its 1968 level. Nor even after the trigger-price system was initiated in 1977 did the industry undertake any major restructuring. The same failure to engage in restructuring has characterized the textile, apparel, and color television industries.

Another part of the problem—perhaps more serious—is that the government has not assisted industries in raising the capital necessary for restructuring. Banks or investors are understandably reluctant to sink money into enterprises that show little promise of profitability in the short run. While the Trade Act of 1974 authorized the government to provide loans and loan guarantees for the purpose of industry restructuring, it limited eligibility to companies that had already experienced an absolute decrease in sales or production. As a result, funds for restructuring often have come too late, after serious decline has already set in. Moreover, only the weakest companies have been eligible for funding, rather than those within the industry that have had the best chance of regaining market share. Worse still, the funding has been too small. In the apparel industry, for example, the average grant has been approximately $1 million—far too little to permit major retooling.

Moreover, U.S. government programs designed to retrain workers have focused primarily on the chronically disadvantaged (under the Comprehensive Employment and Training Act) rather than semiskilled, skilled, or technical workers. Special job relocation and training assistance has also been provided to workers who can demonstrate that they have suffered directly from an increase in imports; but this program (under the Trade Act of 1974) has not been extended to workers in industries that supply firms that have been injured by imports. Meanwhile, the Commerce Department's Economic Development Administration has provided very little aid to declining communities and regions. Indeed, program funds have been spread so widely and thinly that the program has been relatively ineffective.

4. *Government is needed to respond to the competitive strategies of other advanced industrial nations.* In many industries, international competition among advanced industrial countries has become a race in which the first manufacturer to achieve high volume and gain experience can underprice all potential international rivals. Government can provide a head start in this race by subsidizing the growth of such industries. New technologies often require massive and accelerated infusions of capital in order to achieve the scale of production and know-how necessary for competitive development—larger and quicker than capital markets often can provide. Our present competi-

tive advantage in aircraft and semiconductors is due in no small measure to government initiative: U.S. military procurement accounted for 92 percent of all our aircraft sales in the 1950s; a whole generation of commercial aircraft were spun off from these defense-related prototypes. Similarly, military procurement of transistors accounted for close to 40 percent of all transistor sales in the 1950s, providing a guaranteed market and attracting private investment with loan programs and write-offs; our present competitive position in semiconductors can be traced to this origin. See Table 12-3. A similar story can be told about computers (see Table 12-4), rayon, synthetic rubber, antibiotics, communication, and satellite technology—all major international competitors.

Foreign governments have promoted industries through subsidies, loans, and tax advantages, and are providing generous incentives for

Table 12-3. Federal Semiconductor Purchases as a Percentage of All Sales.

Year	(percent)
1955	38
1957	36
1959	45
1961	39
1963	35
1965	22
1967	28
1969	17
1971	13
1973	6
1975	8
1977	12

Sources: 1955–1961: Ginzberg et al. (1976: 12–21); 1963–1973: U.S. Federal Trade Commission (1977); 1975–1977: Charles River Associates (1980).

Table 12-4. U.S. Computer Sales to Space/Defense as a Percentage of All Sales.

Year	(percent)
1954	100
1955	79
1956	62
1957	60
1958	71
1959	72
1960	60
1961	55
1962	48
1963	47

Source: Ginzberg et al. (1976: 12–21).

semiconductors, biotechnology, and laser technology. For example, the Japanese semiconductor industry is favored by special tax privileges, a protectionist policy that virtually bars imports, easy access to capital, and direct government subsidies of approximately $400 million per year (Charles River Associates 1980; U.S. Federal Trade Commission 1977). The Japanese government spends an additional $250 million annually on research in very large-scale integrated circuits. Similarly, the French government provides its semiconductor industry with $140 million in subsidies each year; Great Britain, $110 million; and West Germany, $150 million. By contrast, the only direct subsidy provided by the U.S. government to the American semiconductor industry is $55 million in research funds, as part of the Defense Department's VHSIC (Very High Speed Integrated Circuit) program (the industry also benefits, of course, from $4.6 billion in government procurement).

Unless the U.S. government explicitly promotes its emerging high-technology industries, the United States is in danger of losing the "experience curve" race to foreign competitors. A coherent economic strategy therefore is a practical necessity. This does not, however, imply a neomercantilist insensitivity to the welfare of the rest of the globe. A strategy to build our national wealth is entirely consistent with the growing wealth of developing economies, because it anticipates and accelerates structural changes in the world economy. As developing economies become capable of producing internationally traded goods more cheaply than we can produce them, we should allow them to do so rather than seek to protect our industries behind a network of tariffs and subsidies.

What would a coherent economic strategy look like? At its most basic level it would seek to anticipate structural changes in world markets. National governments are effective in designing industrial policy only insofar as they become agents of the world economy—recognizing its structural trends and shaping their own domestic economies to conform. This implies that government policymakers would employ a method of analysis that is at once microeconomic and macroeconomic, and explicitly dynamic. Within each key industrial sector an analysis would consider risk, uncertainty, technological change, likely changes in markets and business conditions, comparative advantage, and potential cost reductions made possible through scale and experience. The central question would be similar to those faced by a single firm: given limited resources and a dynamic and uncertain environment, what investment strategy is likely to yield the most competitive overall position in the future, and thereby generate the highest national income?

This method of analysis would have important implications for every facet of government policy. *Military procurement*, for example, would be undertaken with due regard for its effects upon the future competitiveness of civilian markets.

Similar questions would be raised with regard to government *management of credit markets*. For example, do federal loan guarantees and credit subsidies targeted to homeowners, farmers, and certain endangered corporations result in an undesirable increase in the cost of credit for small, high-technology businesses or other emerging industries?

Tax policy would comprise another subset of national competitive strategy. Many seemingly neutral tax rules affect the pattern of investment, allocating investment to industries with particular life cycles or to older firms that are in the best position to use tax credits and depreciation allowances. Should newer businesses in emerging industries, with no prospect of profits for many years to come, be permitted to offset their losses against the personal incomes of their shareholders, or be freed from the host of levies (franchise taxes, gross receipts taxes, Social Security taxes) that now apply in full force whether or not a business has any profits out of which to pay them? Should interest deductions be targeted to apply only to fresh investments like new construction, rather than to the trading of current assets like existing real estate? Should tax depreciation rules be changed, so that the useful life of an asset is measured in terms of how long before competitive pressures require that the next generation of machinery be purchased, rather than the time until the old machine wears out?

Antitrust and trade policy would constitute a fourth subset. Seemingly neutral antitrust rules actually may penalize firms that otherwise could compete effectively in international competition. Are some U.S. industries potentially so affected by import competition that reducing tariff and nontariff barriers is a more sensible national competitive strategy than restructuring the industry or restricting horizontal merger? Are there some industries in which cost reductions associated with experience and scale are so significant that pricing below marginal cost should not constitute evidence of predation? Are there some firms that show so much promise of becoming strong international competitors that government should allow them—even encourage them—to engage in horizontal or vertical mergers and to expand capacity rapidly, notwithstanding that these strategies may lessen competition in domestic markets in the short run? Should government antitrust officials relax restrictions on merger for failing firms on condition that the merging companies maintain local employment or provide retraining and relocation assistance? Should antitrust law and its administration recognize a "failing work force" and "failing community" as justification for mergers that could speed the pace of worker and community adjustment but might otherwise be deemed illegal?

INSTITUTIONAL STRUCTURE

While other national goals that underlie these discrete policies should not necessarily be subordinated to that of international competitiveness, we should at least address these sorts of questions in a coherent manner and understand the tradeoffs they imply. This is no mean task. At present we lack even an institutional structure in which these questions can be raised and explored. Government agencies responsible for separate aspects of public policy as it affects business strategy—procurement, credit, tax, antitrust, tariff and trade policy— jealously guard their respective bureaucratic territories, and are unwilling or unable to consider a wider range of issues. The federal courts—divided among ninety-five districts and eleven circuits, and bringing to bear no particular knowledge about world market trends and conditions—are singularly ill-suited to function as forums in which these questions can be debated. Unless or until there is established within government an institutional mechanism for analyzing these issues we will remain incapable of recognizing them.

Even if we had an institution within the U.S. government established to manage industrial policy, such an institution would seem to rest uneasily amid our vastly decentralized system of government authority—balanced as it is between Congress and the president, the federal government and the states, and shared with an array of commissions, agencies, boards, administrations, congressional committees and subcommittees, and departments. The genius of our democratic system is that it requires a wide consensus among many centers of power, any one of which can veto a proposed action, in order to get anything accomplished. Bargaining, log-rolling, wheeling and dealing in promises, favors, and subtle threats—these are the channels through which power flows. Arbitrary decisions are rare since power is so widely diffused.

The disadvantage of this system is that it is necessarily ad hoc and reactive. Coalitions are fleeting. Attention-spans are short. Issues arise with a rapidity that renders comprehensive policymaking all but impossible. Indeed, there is so much noise in the system—in the form of immediate problems to be remedied and deals to be struck—that issues must be at or near a point of crisis and already distilled into relatively clear choices, before a large enough coalition can be mustered to get action.

By contrast, a more coherent national competitive strategy requires coordination among government programs and decisionmaking in anticipation of future events. It also depends upon careful analysis of world market trends and of competitive advantages and disadvantages likely to be experienced by U.S. firms. How can such a holistic, predictive, and analytic process coexist with the hurly-burly of our democratic system? More specifically, how can industrial policymakers be sufficiently above politics that they can avoid the special pleadings of declining industries and businesses and yet at the same time be politically accountable for their decisions?

Every U.S. administration since that of Calvin Coolidge has sought to overcome this seeming incompatibility by establishing tribunals composed of functional representatives from government, business, and (occasionally) labor, which would have responsibility for economic development within particular industries. None of these experiments with functional representation has worked very well. This is because all of them have rested on the false premise that industries are essentially monolithic blocs of businesses with identical interests, instead of recognizing that they are composed of segments with different and often conflicting competitive positions. All too often, well-established businesses have been overrepresented, and consumers (for whom productivity improvements may result in lower prices) and innovative businesses that seek to enter the industry have been underrepresented. As a result, business-government tribunals typically have enabled the least competitive but most entrenched segments of an industry to consolidate their political bases and form powerful coalitions against structural change in the economy.

Industrial policymaking is incompatible with our democratic institutions only to the extent that it avoids forging a broad public consensus for its programs. But, as we have experienced in wartime, such a consensus can be achieved. Coalitions of emerging industries and growing segments must be able to join in support of structural change, and no group should be forced to bear a disproportionate part of the burden of such change. Thus the coordination, planning, and analysis upon which a national competitive strategy depends must rest in the first instance upon public knowledge and support.

Industrial policymaking therefore must be explicit and public. It must seek to achieve a broad agreement about how American industry can improve its competitive performance in world markets. It must involve consumers, small businesses, emerging industries, and nonunion workers, as well as organized labor and big business. It must also summon the best minds from the private sector—business executives, academics, financial analysts. In short, industrial development must be part of the public agenda, an ongoing process of debate and analysis, reflected in newspapers, journals, public affairs programs, and classrooms. That is its greatest challenge.

For too long we have treated various aspects of public policy as self-contained units, without acknowledging or exploring the close interrelationships among government procurement, banking and credit, tax, patent, antitrust, trade regulation, and international trade. Nor have we made adequate use of models of business strategy for analyzing and evaluating public policy. Nor have we fully acknowledged the critical importance of public policy in shaping business strategy, both nationally and internationally, and the potential tensions existing between multinational business strategy and national public policy. Nor finally, have we begun to explore systematically the effects of government policies upon industrial development within advanced economies or set about the task of devising analytic tools for measuring and evaluating such effects.

At this point the design of a coherent economic strategy raises more questions than it answers. How can policymakers avoid the special pleadings of declining industries and sectors and yet be politically accountable? To what extent should the government actively seek to channel private investment into internationally competitive segments, over and above the inevitable channeling effects of government procurement, credit, tax, and trade policies? Precisely how can government use business strategy models to identify competitive segments, and more difficult still, to determine the appropriate level of investment in such segments? And what are the implications of a national industrial policy for *global* welfare?

Our current problem of international competitiveness is not yet a crisis but will become one unless we better understand the possibilities and limitations of government policy for industrial growth. The lenses through which we have come to view economic policy—microeconomic and macroeconomic—are either too small or improperly focused. We need a new lens that focuses our attention on national income over the long term, given the realities of international competition and the interaction of business strategies and public policies in shaping a nation's international competitive strategy. In the long run, this may be the ultimate example of public-private cooperation in meeting social needs by creating business opportunities.

REFERENCES

Bureau of the Census, U.S. Department of Commerce. 1975. *Historical Statistics of the United States.* Washington, D.C.: U.S. Government Printing Office.

Charles River Associates. 1980. "Innovation, Competition, and Government Policy in the Semiconductor Industry." Unpublished paper.

Ginzberg, E., et al. 1976. *The Economic Impact of Large Public Programs.* Salt Lake City, Utah: Olympus.

Magaziner, I., and Robert Reich. 1982. *Minding America's Business.* New York: Harcourt, Brace, Jovanovich.

Morkre, Morris E., and David G. Tarr. 1980. *Effects of Restrictions on U.S. Imports.* U.S. Federal Trade Commission. Washington, D.C.: U.S. Government Printing Office.

National Science Board. 1980. *Science Indicators 1979.* Washington, D.C.: National Science Foundation and U.S. Government Printing Office.

Organization for Economic Cooperation and Development. 1980. National Accounts Series.

U.S. Federal Trade Commission. 1977. *Staff Report on the Semiconductor Industry.* Washington, D.C.: U.S. Government Printing Office.

Chapter 13

Doing Good to Do Well:
The New Opportunities
for Business Enterprise

Peter F. Drucker

I

In the early years of this century, two Americans, independently and, in all probability, without knowing of each other, were among the first businessmen[1] to initiate major community reforms. Andrew Carnegie preached and financed the free public library. Julius Rosenwald fathered the county farm agent system and adopted the infant 4-H Clubs. Carnegie was already retired from business as one of the world's richest men. Rosenwald, who had recently bought a near-bankrupt mail-order firm called Sears, Roebuck and Company, was only beginning to build both his business and his fortune. Both men were radical innovators.

The monuments that earlier businessmen had erected for themselves were cultural: museums, opera houses, universities. In Carnegie's and Rosenwald's own time the leading businessmen, A. Leland Stanford, Henry E. Huntington, J.P. Morgan, Henry C. Frick, and a little later, Andrew Mellon, still followed this tradition. Carnegie and Rosenwald instead built communities and citizens—their performance, competence, and their productivity.

But there the similarity ends. The two held basically different philosophies. Carnegie (Hendrick 1932) shouted his from the housetops: The sole purpose of being rich is to give away money. God, Carnegie asserted, wants us to do well so that we can do good. Rosenwald, modest, publicity shy, unassuming, never preached; but his deeds spoke louder than his words. "You have to be able to do good to do well," was Julius Rosenwald's credo, a far more radical one than that of the anarchist steelmaster from Pittsburgh. Carnegie believed in the social responsibility of wealth. Rosenwald believed in the social responsibility of business.

Rosenwald (Emmet and Jeuck 1950) saw the need to develop the competence, productivity, and income of the still desperately poor and backward American farmer. To accomplish this it was necessary to make available the enormous fund of scientific farming knowledge and farming skills amassed in decades of systematic study of agronomy and farm marketing, but which, in 1900 or 1910, were still largely theoretical and inaccessible to all but a tiny minority of more affluent agriculturalists (Arndt, Dalrymple, and Ruttan 1977: 63, 66, 70). Although his motives were partially philanthropic, he also saw that Sears, Roebuck's prosperity was linked to the prosperity of its main customer, the farmer, which in turn depended on his productivity. The county farm agent—and Sears, Roebuck for almost a decade single-handedly supported this innovation of Rosenwald's until the U.S. government finally took it over—and the 4-H Club were clearly philanthropy. But they were also Sears, Roebuck's corporate advertising, public relations, and above all market and customer development. Their success partially explains how the near-bankrupt Sears, Roebuck became within ten years the country's first truly national retailer and one of its most profitable and fastest growing enterprises.

After World War II, another American businessman developed yet another approach to social responsibility. William C. Norris, the founder (in 1957) and chairman of Control Data Corporation, sees the solution of social problems and the satisfaction of social needs as opportunities for profitable business. He too is a philanthropist motivated by concern for his fellow man. He picks his projects (skill training and employment in the inner city ghetto; rehabilitation and training of prisoners; teaching problem-learners) by social need rather than by market demand. But he directs his investment and his corporation's human resources where information-handling and data-processing, his company's expertise, can create a business that, while solving a problem, will become self-sustaining and profitable.

Like Carnegie's philanthropy and Rosenwald's community development, Norris's investments in social needs aim at creating human capital in the form of individuals capable of performance and of a healthy community able to help itself. But Norris's social enterprises also aim at creating economic capital. Carnegie's public libraries were strictly philanthropies, though they did create opportunities for individual self-development. Rosenwald's community projects were not business ventures. However much they benefited Sears, Roebuck, they did so indirectly. They were good business, far-sighted investments in market development, but not themselves business. Norris's good works or excursions into social problem-solving are capital investments in new profit-making businesses, in a stricter sense. He is an entrepreneur.

In its view of social responsibility much of American business and the American public still follow Carnegie. They accept as he did that wealth and economic power entail responsibility for the community. The rich man as social reformer, Carnegie's innovation, established a uniquely American institution: the foundation. One after the other of the superrich, from Rockefeller to Ford, followed Carnegie's example. And Carnegie also set the tone for what is now known as the social responsibility of business, a phrase that has become exceedingly popular.

Julius Rosenwald has had far fewer followers. The best known is probably Rosenwald's own successor as head of Sears, Roebuck, General Robert E. Wood (Worthy 1984). Even greater perhaps was the impact of James Couzens (Barnard 1958), cofounder of the Ford Motor Company, for ten years Henry Ford's partner as the company's financial and administrative head, then Mayor of Detroit and finally, from 1922 to 1936, U.S. senator from Michigan and, though nominally a Republican, one of the intellectual fathers of the New Deal. Couzens introduced skill training into American industry as a social responsibility of business.[2] A few years later, in 1913, he established, over Henry Ford's strenuous objections, the famous five-dollar-a-day wage—both out of deep compassion for the suffering of an exploited work force and as a highly successful and indeed immediately profitable cure for high rates of absenteeism and turnover that threatened Ford's competitive position.

In our own time J. Irwin Miller of the Cummins Engine Company in Columbus, Indiana has systematically used corporate funds to create a healthy community that, at the same time, is a direct though intangible investment in a healthy environment for his company. Miller specifically aimed at endowing his small industrial town with the quality of life that would attract to it the managerial and technical people on whom a big high-technology business depends.

The thesis of this chapter is that in the years to come the most needed and effective approach to corporate social responsibilities will be that exemplified by William Norris and Control Data Corporation. Only if business learns how to convert the major social challenges facing developed societies today into novel and profitable business opportunities can we hope to surmount these challenges in the future.

Government, the agency looked to in recent decades to solve these problems, cannot be depended upon alone, because the demands on government are increasingly outrunning the resources that it is politically realistic for it to tap from the private sector. Social needs can be solved only if their solution in itself creates new capital, profits, that can then be tapped to initiate the solution for new social needs.

II

Fundamental changes in technology and society have changed the nature of social needs. Today we are very conscious of *technological change*. Few people realize that what actually is changing are not technologies but the very concept of technology. For 300 years technology has had for its ultimate model the mechanical phenomena inside a star such as the sun. This development reached its climax with a technology that replicates the mechanical processes inside the sun, that is, with nuclear fission and fusion. Now the dynamics of technology are switching to what might be called an organic model, organized around information rather than around mechanical energy.

Fossil-fuel energy has been a mature, if not declining, industry since 1950, well *before* OPEC and the energy crisis. In all developed countries the ratio of energy usage to gross domestic product has been falling steadily and rapidly since then. Even in sectors that until then still showed an incremental energy growth—private automobiles, aviation, both civilian and military, and residential lighting, heating and air conditioning—energy consumption per unit of output has been declining since well before 1973 and is almost certain to continue to do so, almost irrespective of cost.[3]

Biological processes progress in terms of information content. The specific energy of biological systems is information. Mechanical systems are organized by the law of physics; they express forces. Biological systems obey the laws of physics, of course. But they are not organized by forces but by information (e.g., the genetic code).

As a consequence, the shift from the mechanical to the biological model calls for a shift in the human quality that constitutes capital. Before the mechanical age, animal energy, that is physical exertion, constituted human capital. Skill was of course highly prized. But there was so little market for it that it had to be organized as a monopoly, with access strictly controlled through apprenticeship programs and guild regulations. Skill beyond a minimum was simply not employable; there was no market for it. And knowledge was pure luxury.

In the age of the mechanical model, in the last 300 years, human skill increasingly became the productive human resource—one of the greatest advances in human history. This development reached its culmination in this century when mass production converted the laborer into the semiskilled worker. But in an age in which information is becoming the organizing energy the human resource is knowledge.

This shift in the meaning of technology that is now well underway represents a far more important change than any technological change, no matter how rapid or how spectacular, and deserves even more attention than it gets.

Demographic changes may be even more important. Fortunately the educational explosion of the last fifty years in all developed countries coincided with the shift in technology. In the developed countries now about half of all young people undergo formal schooling beyond secondary school, developing the human resources needed to make the new technology operational, productive, and beneficial (Drucker 1981a). In turn the new technology creates the employment opportunities for the new work force of the developed countries. Which is chicken and which is egg no one, I dare say, could determine.

These changes create major discontinuities and problems. First, in the developed countries there is the transition problem for a labor force trained to operate in the age of the mechanical model and left stranded in the shift to the technology of the biological model. And the remnants of what today we would call preindustrial society—for example, those in the inner city ghettos or Chicano immigrants fleeing the destitution of overpopulated Mexico, who are prepared only to use physical strength as the resource they are getting paid for— are problems in today's developed countries.

Second, between the developed and the poorest countries there is a new and dangerous discontinuity. Up to 300 years ago there were no "poor countries." There were rich people in every country—not very many; and there were vast hordes of poor people in every country. One hundred years later—that is, by 1700—when the new technology of the mechanical model first began to make a difference, the world began to split into rich countries and poor countries. By 1900 average per capita income in the then developed countries was as much as three times as high as per capita income in the developing countries. By now the gap has widened to an unprecedented and probably unsustainable 10 to 1, or worse. Today the poorest proletarian in developed countries has a higher standard of living than all but a minute minority of the rich in the poorest countries. The class conflict of earlier times has become a North–South cleavage, if not a source of racial conflict. There is another discrepancy between developed countries, that is, countries with a high standard of formal learning, and thus with access to the opportunities of the biological model, and countries that at best can begin to form human skill capital. One-third of humanity, in the developed countries, is ready to exploit the opportunities of the biological model, while two-thirds, in the developing countries, are just entering the stage in which their human resources are prepared for the opportunities of the mechanical model.

Just as the technology of the mechanical model requires a skill base, which is slowly and painfully being built in some of the developing countries, so does the technology of the biological model require a broad knowledge base. This, we now know, cannot be improvised but requires a long period of hard work and above all a capital investment far beyond the means of any but already highly developed countries. Thus for the foreseeable future the world will remain divided into societies with the knowledge base to convert the new technology into major economic and social opportunities and those without the broad base of schooled people on which the technology of the biological model rests and with a surplus of people equipped only for the technologies of the mechanical model.

It is the conjunction of the shift in technology and demographics that creates the social needs business will have to learn to transform into opportunities.

III

Developed countries are facing a situation for which there is no parallel in recent economic history. We will have growing labor shortages and at the same time growing unemployment. A large and growing share of the new entrants into the labor force will have sat in school too long to be interested in traditional manual, blue collar work. By 1982 the proportion of Americans who enter the civilian labor force with only an elementary school education was down to about 3 percent. The proportion entering with only a high school education was down to 50 percent. And the trend is most unlikely to be reversed.

This means that the basic employment problem of the United States and of every other developed country is to create challenging, satisfying, and well-paid jobs for people with so much schooling that they are qualified only for putting knowledge to work. It also means that demand for capital formation in the developed countries will go up rapidly. In particular, jobs for which capital requirements were traditionally lowest, that is in clerical and service areas, will be transformed. Whatever the office of the future will look like, it will be capital intensive, with capital investment per worker going from a meager $3,000 at present to something like $20,000 or $30,000 within ten years or so. Knowledge jobs, on the average, require a multiple of the capital that manual jobs, skilled or unskilled, require. For—a point that all the OECD studies on the subject overlook—they require a high and growing investment in schooling before the individual can begin to contribute, and, increasingly, substantial investment in continuing or refresher education. In other words they require an investment in human resources at least matching that in physical capital.

At the same time there will be redundancies of workers in traditional blue collar employment. In developed countries traditional blue collar manual labor will simply not be economical. This is in part because work based on information, whether this be called automation or data processing, will have so much greater value added per unit of effort. Whatever processes can be automated—that is, shifted to an information base—must be automated. Otherwise industry cannot compete, especially with the very large and abundant low-cost labor resources of the Third World. It is almost certain that by the year 2010, that is within twenty-five years, the proportion of the labor force in the developed countries that is engaged in traditional blue collar work in manufacturing will be down to what it is now in our most highly scientific and most capital-intensive industry, modern agriculture. Manufacturing blue collar labor accounts for almost one-fifth of the labor force in all developed countries. But the proportion employed in modern agriculture is about one of every twenty or less.

For the transition period, the next twenty-five years, there will be highly visible and highly concentrated populations of traditional blue collar workers who are being made redundant and who have nothing to offer except skill or, more often, semiskills. That there will at the same time be shortages in certain places of manual, blue collar workers, because so many entrants into the labor force will have too much education to be interested in blue collar jobs, will not help these redundant workers. They will not be where the shortages are and will, usually, not have the skills the available jobs demand.

The blue collar workers who are being made redundant by the shift of manufacturing from work requiring brawn and skill to knowledge-intensive work are typically found in high-wage jobs in the mass production industries. For the last fifty years these groups have been among the favored groups in industrial society, the groups that have gained the most in economic and social position with the least increase in their actual capacity to perform. They are likely to be older people; younger people move before an industry decays. They are highly concentrated in a very small number of metropolitan areas and thus both visible and politically potent. Eight hundred thousand automobile workers, for instance, are concentrated mostly in twenty counties in the Midwest, from Milwaukee to Dayton and Cleveland, and in only four states. And they tend to be unionized and to act collectively rather than as individuals.

Paradoxically, the labor shortages will be as real as the redundancies. What is needed to bring the two together? Is it training? Is it organized placement? Is it moving industries in need of traditional labor into the areas where the redundancies will occur? Above all, there is need to anticipate redundancies and to organize the systematic placement of individuals in new jobs (Drucker 1981a).

Unless we succeed in bridging the gap between labor shortages in manufacturing and unemployment in manufacturing, which may coexist even within the same geographic area, but will be particularly sharp between different sections of the country, different industries and different wage levels, we will be in grave danger. Instead of promoting the new information-based industries and their employment, which fit the needs and qualifications of the young population, economic policy will focus on maintaining yesterday's employment. We will, in other words, be sorely tempted to follow the example of Great Britain and sacrifice tomorrow on the altar of yesterday—to no avail, of course.

IV

Government cannot tackle this problem, let alone solve it. It is a problem for the entrepreneur who sees in the available labor surplus an opportunity. Government can provide money; the best examples are probably the retraining grants of West Germany, which now amount to 2 percent of West German GNP but, according to some German estimates (for example, those of the West German *Arbeitsministerium*), save as much as four times the amount in unemployment and welfare benefits. But the actual training, to be effective, has to be focused on a specific job the individual can be assured of getting once he reaches the required skill level. It has to be individual rather than general; and it has to be integrated with placement. Government, we have learned in sixty years of work on "distressed industries" and "distressed areas," going back to Lloyd George's first post-World War I cabinet in Great Britain, cannot do either. By its very nature government focuses on large groups rather than on *this* person with *his* or *her* specific skills, background, and needs.

Also the new jobs are likely to be in small and local rather than in big, national business. Since about 1960, unprecedented growth in the American labor force and employment has occurred. The great majority of all new jobs (between two-thirds and three-quarters) have been created in the private sector, not in large, let alone giant, companies, but in businesses employing twenty employees or less. During this period employment in the Fortune 500 companies actually declined by 5 percent. And since 1970 the former rapid increase in government employment, federal, state, and local, has leveled off.

Finding workers about to become redundant, identifying their strengths, finding new jobs for them, and retraining them as needed (and often the new skills needed are social rather than technical) are tasks to be done locally and for this reason are business opportunities.[4] But unless redundancy is seen systematically as an opportunity, and above all by existing businesses with the knowledge and capital to act, we will suffer an ever-worsening problem that threatens the future of any developed economy and especially of the American economy.

Several other severe social problem areas, which offer business opportunities, are of particular interest. Within every developed country, and particularly in the United States, there is the problem of the preindustrial population, which in an American context means primarily racial minorities and, above all, the blacks. Only a minority of blacks by now have not been able to acquire the competence needed to become productive in an economy in which brawn is not adequate to provide the kind of living developed societies consider standard. Yet few of the many attempts to educate these groups have lived up to expectations. Part of this failure is due to the fact that training and education succeed only where there is a vision of the future. It is the lack of vision, grounded in decades, if not centuries, of frustration, failure, and discrimination, which prevents education and training from being converted into confidence and motivation.

But we also know that these people work well if the opportunity is provided for them. Until the job is there, there is no motivation for training, no belief that it will lead to a permanent change, and a conviction that this effort too will fail.[5] There is thus a major task of putting human resources to work and developing their competence. Opportunities exist in all kinds of services, if only because the supply of people willing and able to do this work will fall far below the demand, whether in hospitals, in maintenance, or in repair and services of all kinds.

One company that has turned this social problem into an opportunity is based in Denmark. It operates in some fifty countries of the world, mostly developed ones. It systematically finds, trains, and employs preindustrial people for maintenance of office buildings and plants, at good income, with a minimum of turnover, and with only one problem: It cannot find enough people to satisfy the demand. It does not train people. It employs them, making high demands on performance that then create self-respect and workmanship. It provides career opportunities for advancement within the competence of the individual. This company, which now has sales well in excess of a half billion dollars, started with one small crew less than twenty years ago. The opportunities are there—but is the vision?

Then there is the unprecedented problem of the earthquake fault between the developed countries, with their large supply of highly educated people and shortages of people qualified and prepared for traditional manual work, and the Third World countries in which, in the next fifteen years, unprecedentedly large numbers of young people will reach adulthood prepared and qualified only for traditional blue collar manual work. These young blue collar workers will find employment opportunities only if labor-intensive stages of production are moved to where the labor supply is, that is, to the developing countries. Production sharing is the economic integration ahead of us. If it cannot be developed as a successful business opportunity, we face both fast-decreasing standards of living in the developed countries, where traditional manufacturing work cannot be performed both because there is an absolute shortage of labor and because the price of manual labor will become totally noncompetitive, and social catastrophe on a massive scale in the Third World. No society, no matter what its political or social system, whether capitalist or communist, can hope to survive the strains of 40 or 50 percent unemployment among young, able-bodied people prepared for work and willing to do work and familiar, if only through television and radio, with the way the rich countries of the world live.

V

Why shouldn't government do these tasks and tackle these problems? Governments have had to concern themselves with social problems since time immemorial. There were the reforms of the Gracchi in Republican Rome in the second century A.D. and the Poor Laws of Elizabethan England. But as part of a systematic theory of government the idea that the solution of social problems is permanently a task of government and one for which no other social institution is fitted dates back only 200 years. It is a child of the Enlightenment of the eighteenth century; it pre-supposes a modern civil service and a modern fiscal system. It was first expressed and practiced in the most enlightened of the enlightened despotisms and, so to speak, their development lab, the Habsburg Grandduchy of Florence where, between 1760 and 1770 the first countrywide hospital system, the first countrywide public health planning and—first in Europe—a countrywide system of free compulsory schooling were established.

The nineteenth century saw the blossoming of this new idea. From the British Factory Acts of 1844 to Bismarck's Social Security legislation in the 1880s, one social problem after the other was tackled by governments—and solved triumphantly.

The twentieth century and especially the last fifty years saw this idea elevated to an article of the faith, to the point where a great many people consider it practically immoral and certainly futile for a social need to be tackled any way other than by a government program, and where a substantial majority, only a few years ago, in the heady Kennedy and Johnson years, was convinced that *any* social problem would almost immediately yield to attack by a government program. But the years since then have brought increasing disenchantment. There is now no developed country, whether free enterprise or communist, in which people still expect government programs to succeed.[6]

One reason is surely that government is doing far too many things (Drucker 1969: ch. 10). By itself a social program accomplishes nothing except the expenditure of money. To have any impact at all such a program requires above all the hard work and dedication of a small number of first-rate people. First-rate people are always in short supply. There may be enough for a very few social programs at any one time, though the two most successful entrepreneurs of social programs with whom I have discussed this, the late Arthur Altmeyer, the father of America's Social Security program, and the late David Lilienthal, the builder of Tennessee Valley Authority (TVA), both said—and independently—that in their experience there were *at most* enough first-rate people available at any one time in any one country to launch *one* major social program. But under the Johnson administration the United States in four short years tried to launch a half dozen—in addition to fighting a major overseas war!

One might also say that government is congenitally unsuited to the time dimensions of social programs. Government needs immediate results, especially in a democracy where every other year is an election year. The growth curve of social programs is the hyperbola; very small, almost imperceptible results for long hard years, followed, if the program is successful, by years of exponential growth. It took eighty years before America's program of agricultural education and research began to revolutionize American farming and farm productivity (Arndt, Dalrymple, and Ruttan 1977). It took twenty years before every American at work was covered by Social Security.

Would the American electorate have waited twenty, let alone eighty, years before seeing major results from President Johnson's War on Poverty? And yet we know that learning has a long lead time before it shows massive results. Individuals, not classes, learn; and there has to be built up, one by one, a large stock of individuals who have learned, who serve as examples, as leaders, who give encouragement.

Paradoxically, government that finds it hard to start small and to be patient finds it even harder to abandon. Every program immediately creates its own constituency, if only the people who are employed by it. It is easy, all too easy, for modern government to give. It is all but impossible for it to take away. The rule for failures is therefore not to bury them but to redouble the budget and to divert to them the able people who might, if employed on more promising opportunities, produce results.

Furthermore, it is all but impossible for government to experiment. Everything it now does has to be nationwide from the start; and everything has to be finite. But that, in anything new, is a guarantee of failure (Drucker 1981b). It is no coincidence that practically all successful New Deal programs had been pilot tested as small-scale experiments in states and cities over the preceding twenty years—in Wisconsin, New York State, New York City, or by one of the Chicago reform administrations. The two total New Deal failures, the National Recovery Administration (NRA) and the Works Progress Administration (WPA), were also the only genuine inventions without prior experiment at the state or local level.[7]

Surely William Norris is right when he speaks, as he does in this book, of his company's social business enterprises as research and development. Long lead times, willingness to experiment and to abandon in case of nonresults are precisely the characteristics of research and development work. But R&D is, we now know, not done well by government, for a variety of well-studied reasons. It is done best in autonomous institutions, whether university laboratory, individual hospital, or business laboratory, although the provider or source of the funds might well be government.

Equally important as an explanation for the inability of government to tackle successfully the kind of social problems we face is that they are hard problems, as Bendick points out in this book (see also Drucker 1981b). A hard problem is one in which there are so many constituencies that it is difficult, if not impossible, to set specific goals and targets. It is perhaps here that the social problems of the midtwentieth century differ most fundamentally from those of the eighteenth and nineteenth centuries. But the problems we face in the decades ahead will be even harder than those we now handle so poorly. Each of them has powerful constituencies with radically different, indeed mutually exclusive, goals and values, which practically guarantee that government could not succeed in solving them.

Reindustrializing America, for instance, means to the labor union preserving traditional blue collar jobs in traditional industries in central cities or at least slowing the shrinkage of traditional jobs. However, if reindustrializing America means restoring the country's capacity to increase the output of manufactured goods and to compete internationally, it unambiguously means the fastest possible automation of traditional processes and in all probability a shift to new and decentralized locations. It means liquidating Big Steel in Pittsburgh and Chicago and shifting to mini-mills near customers. The first definition is politically acceptable for a short time. But it can only lead to failure, as the British or the Polish examples show. But can any *government* program embrace the second definition? Even the Japanese who reportedly invest in winners and starve losers (at least according to a currently popular American myth) are finding that it cannot be done politically. Indeed the Japanese have found that they cannot give up support of a retail distribution system that everyone in Japan knows to be obsolete and frightfully expensive but the only social security for a fairly small group of older people.

Nongovernmental institutions, whether business or institutions of the rapidly growing nonprofit third sector, can, however, direct themselves to a single objective. They can break down hard problems into several easy problems, each capable of solution or, at least, of alleviation. And because nongovernmental institutions can and do compete with each other, they can develop alternate approaches. They can experiment.

The increasing inability of government to tackle effectively the social needs of contemporary society creates a major opportunity for nongovernmental institutions and especially for the most flexible and most diverse of nongovernmental institutions, business. Increasingly, even countries organized on what are proclaimed to be socialist principles will have to reprivatize.[8] It will be necessary, in other words, to create conditions under which a task is outlined by government and the means to perform the task are provided for either by government (as for instance in the case of the rapidly growing private health care insurance in Britain, which is reimbursed by the National Health Service) or by third-party payers, but in which the actual performance of a task is done by nongovernmental institutions, especially business, locally and on a competitive basis.[9]

A good example is the American communication system, in which increasingly the tasks exclusively done fifty years ago by the post office are now carried out by a host of agencies competing with one another and with the Postal Service. Quite clearly, garbage removal, health care, and many other services will become reprivatized in such a way that the service itself is grounded in public policy and law (if only through tax advantages), while the performance is the task of competitive private business enterprises.

The true mixed economy of the future will consist of three parts. There will be a private sector in which government limits itself to protection against fraud, extreme exploitation, collusion, unsafe working conditions, and deprivation of civil rights. There will be a true public sector, for defense (excluding procurement) or justice, in which government will both specify the job and do it. And there will be a mixed sector, the best example being the American hospital system, which is primarily a private system. Nonprofit community hospitals, church-affiliated hospitals, and proprietary-for-profit hospitals are increasingly organized in large and growing chains. All then compete for patients, yet most of their income is public money, whether it comes directly from the government via the tax system or through compulsory private health insurance plans. Another well-known example is defense procurement.

VI

In most of the present discussion of the social responsibility of business it is assumed that making a profit is fundamentally incompatible with social responsibility or is at least irrelevant to it. Business is seen as the rich man who should, if only for the good of his soul, give alms to the less fortunate.

Most people who discuss social responsibility, including its opponents, would be exceedingly suspicious of any business that asserts, as does for instance William Norris, that it is the purpose of business to do well by doing good. To those hostile to business, who believe that profit is a "rip-off," this would appear the grossest hypocrisy. But even to those who are probusiness and who then, as did Andrew Carnegie, demand that business, the rich man, give alms and become a philanthropist, doing good in order to do well would not be acceptable. It would convert what is seen as virtue into self-interest. And for those who counsel business to stick to its last and to leave social problems and issues to the proper authorities, which in fact means to government (this is where Milton Friedman stands), the self-interest of business and the public good are seen as two quite separate spheres. But in the next decade it will become increasingly important to stress that business can discharge its social responsibilities only if it converts them into self-interest—that is, into business opportunities.

The *first* social responsibility of business in the next decade will be one not mentioned in the discussion of the social responsibilities of business today. It is the increasingly important responsibility for creating the capital that alone can finance tomorrow's jobs. The shift from the mechanical model of technology to the organic model will require a substantial increase in capital formation. In fact, the oldest and perhaps the only truly valid definition of economic progress is the shift to jobs requiring more capital investment per worker. The demand for capital formation will be as great as the demand was a hundred years ago when today's modern industries emerged, and there will be equal need for a surplus to pay for the R&D needed when technology, as well as the world economy and society, is rapidly changing.

It is becoming clear that we are entering, indeed have entered, the first phase of what one might call a new Kondratieff cycle. We have been in a phase in which existing technologies were extended and modified with fairly low marginal costs, as a result of which there was a fairly low need for capital formation. Now we are well past that stage. To be sure, old industries are still declining or are being restructured, but more important, new industries are exploding—information, communication, biochemistry, bioengineering, and genetic medicine, for example. And with them emerge other new industries, such as the continuing education of already well-educated adults, which may well be the major growth industry of the next ten years and which increasingly is in the hands of entrepreneurs.

The early stages of a Kondratieff cycle make the greatest demands on capital formation. But what does "capital formation" actually mean, especially in a modern society in which the traditional incentives to personal savings have largely been eliminated? Different countries have different savings habits—with America traditionally fairly low in its savings rates. Savings rates in all countries tend to go down with two factors: one, an increase in the proportion of the population past retirement age, who as a rule do not tend to save but who primarily consume; and two, the degree to which Social Security takes care of the risks and contingencies for which individuals traditionally save. One example is the United States, where savings rates have gone down in direct proportion to both the aging of the population and the extension of social services to cover such risks as retirement, illness, and unemployment. Another is Japan. In the last ten years the savings rate in Japan has been going down steadily, although it is still high.

Furthermore we now have conclusive proof that rising income levels for wage-earning families do not materially increase the savings rate. We know that new consumer needs, rather than investment, take over. As a result, in a modern economy the main source of capital formation is *business profits*. Indeed we now know that the term "profit" is a misunderstanding. There are only costs—costs of the past and costs of the future, the costs of economic, social, and technical change and the costs of tomorrow's jobs. Present revenues must cover both, and both costs are likely to go up sharply in the next twenty years.

The first social responsibility of business is then to make enough profit to cover the costs of the future. If this social responsibility is not met, no other social responsibility can be met. Decaying businesses in a decaying economy are unlikely to be good neighbors, good employers, or socially responsible in any way. When the demand for capital grows rapidly, surplus business revenues available for noneconomic purposes, especially for philanthropy, cannot possibly go up. They are almost certain to shrink.

This argument will not satisfy those who believe that today's businessman should become the successor to yesterday's prince, a delusion to which businessmen unfortunately are themselves only too susceptible. But princes were able to be benefactors because they first took it away, and, of course, mostly from the poor.

There are also those, again especially among businessmen, who feel that to convert problems into business opportunities is prosaic and not particularly romantic. They see business as the dragon slayer and themselves as St. Georges on white chargers.

But the proper social responsibility of business is to tame the dragon—that is, to turn a social problem into economic opportunity and economic benefit, into productive capacity, into human competence, into well-paid jobs, and into wealth.

NOTES TO CHAPTER 13

1. Only five others preceded them, to my knowledge: Robert Owen (1771-1858), utopian socialist and successful manufacturer, with his model mills in Lanarkshire in Scotland, in the 1820s; the two Brothers Pereire, who as the closest disciples of another utopian socialist, Saint-Simon, invented development banking with their ultimately unsuccessful *Credit Mobilier* (1850); their far more successful follower, George Siemens (1830-1910), founder, in 1870, of the *Deutsche Bank* and of modern banking altogether; Shibusawa Eichii (1840-1931), the banker-industrialist-educator who, in melding European development banking and Confucian ethics, laid the conceptual, moral, and financial foundations for modern Japan. On all five see my *Management: Tasks, Responsibilities, Practices* (New York: Harper & Row, 1973).

2. In Germany skill training by the employer at the place of employment was invented in the 1840s by August Borsig, the Berlin locomotive builder, against strenuous resistance by civil servants, teachers, and craft guilds; it was perfected a generation later by Ernst Abbé, the physicist-businessman, the driving force behind the Zeiss Works and the father of the German optical and photographic industries. Couzens was deeply influenced by Abbé's ideas.

3. This paragraph—and indeed this entire chapter—is heavily indebted to suggestions and criticism by Professor Harvey Brooks.

4. Control Data Corporation's program for providing business services to small business may be a move in this direction. There are three precedents. The earliest was the training and placement program for redundant workers in the Mitsui *Zaibatsu* in Japan, after the Russo-Japanese War, the program out of which "lifetime employment" evolved. After World War II a group of industrialists in Toledo, Ohio developed a similar program when the city, within a few months, lost its then largest employers, a number of independent automobile companies. Finally, from about 1955 till 1975 Sweden had the "Rehn Plan" for speeding up redundancies and moving workers from old to new industries; the plan was nationally financed but locally managed by employers and union representatives. The three plans differed in details but were very similar in concept and purpose. All three cost next to nothing and yet were eminently successful. For further discussion see my book: *Managing in Turbulent Times* (New York, Harper & Row, 1980), esp. pp. 143-150.

5. This too is borne out by Control Data Corporation's experience in its business ventures in the inner city.

6. Japan was an exception until a few years ago. But there too widespread cynicism now exists about the wisdom, competence, and effectiveness of government and especially about the likelihood that programs addressed to social problems will result in anything except a huge bureaucracy and uncontrollable expenditures.

7. The best discussion of the government as a doer and of its role, its competence, and its limits in social needs—and altogether a pioneering analysis in public policy and public administration—is "Many Providers, Many Producers," by Ted Kolderie (1982).

8. I coined this term (in my 1969 book *The Age of Discontinuity*) and have regretted it ever since, for almost everyone misunderstood it to mean turning activities over to profit-making business. But nongovernmental, nonprofit institutions, whether Harvard University, the Boy Scouts, or Blue Cross are private too, and were meant to be included in my term.

9. Again Ted Kolderie's 1982 paper is a profound and brilliant discussion of reprivatization—by far the best I have seen.

REFERENCES

Arndt, T.M.; D.J. Dalrymple; and V.W. Ruttan, eds. 1977. *Resource Allocation and Productivity in National and International Agricultural Research.* Minneapolis: University of Minnesota Press.

Barnard, Harry. 1958. *Independent Man: The Life of Senator James Couzens.* New York: Charles Scribner's Sons.

Drucker, Peter. 1969. "The Sickness of Government." In *The Age of Discontinuity.* New York: Harper & Row.

———. 1973. *Management: Tasks, Responsibilities, Practices.* New York: Harper & Row.

———. 1980. *Managing in Turbulent Times.* New York: Harper & Row.

———. 1981a. "Demographics and American Economic Policy." In *Towards a New U.S. Industrial Policy,* edited by Michael L. Wachter and Susan M. Wachter. Philadelphia, PA.: University of Pennsylvania Press, pp. 237–256.

———. 1981b. "How to Guarantee Non-Performance." In *Toward the Next Economics and Other Essays,* edited by Peter Drucker. New York: Harper & Row.

Emmet, Boris, and John E. Jeuck. 1950. *Catalogues and Counters: A History of Sears, Roebuck & Co.* Chicago: The University of Chicago Press.

Hendrick, Burton J. 1932. *The Life of Andrew Carnegie.* (2 vols.) New York: Harper & Brothers.

Kolderie, Ted. 1982. "Many Providers, Many Producers." Hubert H. Humphrey Institute of Public Affairs, University of Minnesota.

Worthy, James C. 1984. *Shaping a Great American Institution: General Wood and Sears, Roebuck.* Champaign: University of Illinois Press.

Chapter 14

Privatization: No Panacea
for What Ails Government

James L. Sundquist

When Ronald Reagan ran for president crying "Get government off the backs of the people" and "Government is not the solution, it is the problem," he touched a responsive chord in the electorate. The American people have not been enamored, of late, with government at any level. Vietnam and Watergate and inflation have robbed the national government of much of the respect and confidence it enjoyed as late as the Great Society days of the middle 1960s. As for state and local government, Proposition 13 at one end of the country and Proposition 2½ at the other, and various imitative propositions in between, reflect the pervasive popular feeling that government costs too much and delivers too little for the tax money it receives.

This, then, is a good time to push for the "privatization" of public services. Such proposals take advantage of twin articles of the American political-economic faith—not only the conviction that government is inherently wasteful, lacking the incentive of the profit motive, but also the certitude that private enterprise is inherently efficient, because inefficiency is penalized, immediately and harshly, in the marketplace. Neither belief is, to be sure, fully accurate: on the one hand, government managers in most places, in these times, are under relentless cost-cutting pressure from chief executives and legislatures, which are always drawing the budget cinch one notch tighter, and that is at least a partial substitute for the profit motive. On the other hand, the efficiency that competition in the marketplace is supposed to bring to private enterprise depends on the existence, in fact, of competition, and the private sector has always devoted some significant share of its entrepreneurial ingenuity to devising ways of restricting competition, both through legalized natural monopolies and tariff protections and through usually illegal but sometimes sanctioned cartel arrangements.

That governmental inefficiency and private efficiency are both exaggerated in the popular perception is in large part because public agencies are required to operate much more openly, in the proverbial goldfish bowl. Waste and inefficiency in government become the stuff of investigative reporting because public officials are denied (and properly so) most of the rights of privacy that in the private world are taken for granted. Freedom of information acts and government-in-the-sunshine laws are deliberately written to guarantee public, and media, access to whatever is done by the officials who act in the public's name, but their reach stops at the public-private boundary; they do not extend even to monopoly industries that enjoy a public franchise and conduct their affairs under public regulation or to industries, such as weapon manufacturers, that exist wholly or largely on public funds.

Perhaps, if the affairs of private corporations were equally accessible to public view, the media would expose private inefficiency with the same vigor they now devote to public waste. But there is reason to be skeptical, for the media do employ something of a double standard. Even when government officials and private corporations are charged with colluding on criminal misconduct or nonfeasance, the media spotlight is focused more intensely on the government than on the corporate malefactors; an Anne Burford and a Rita Lavelle can be toppled from their posts in the Environmental Protection Agency while their private executive counterparts are not only left unscathed, for the most part, but are not even identified. As for simple inefficiency, editors and reporters assume, like everybody else, that waste in the private sector can be left to the invisible hand of the marketplace to rectify, while only they, the media, can assure that the same faults are rectified in public bodies. Moreover, the media are themselves part of the fraternity of private enterprises, so while prominent media spokesmen have repeatedly and explicitly declared it their responsibility to take an adversary posture toward agencies and officials of government, none has expressed a comparable sense of obligation to expose the shortcomings of private enterprises. A compound of media opportunities and media attitudes, then, has helped to build the public view that the public and private sectors represent opposite poles on the scale of efficiency and inefficiency.

Nevertheless, while the supposed antithesis is substantially a myth, it is not wholly so. Everyone has read the horror stories about New York City's open-handed pension systems for municipal employees and the extraordinarily generous retirement provisions for federal employees, neither of which have counterparts in private enterprise below the top executive level. Public managers are more likely than their private counterparts to be chosen for reasons having no relation to managerial ability. Their driving interest may not lie in cutting costs, but, even when it does, they may find that both political patronage and civil service systems protect malingerers and incompetents in government to an extent not often tolerated in the private sector. For all these reasons, when public services are turned over to competitive private enterprises, costs can sometimes be cut and service delivery improved.

Yet, while privatization has something to offer both the taxpayer and the recipient of public services, it is being dreadfully oversold these days as the solution to what ails government. And the whole concept is being tarnished by the indiscriminate jumbling of a false concept of privatization with the genuine one.

PRIVATIZATION TRUE AND FALSE

One could ignore the conceptual confusion and talk only of privatization in its true sense were it not that the politics of the early 1980s has given such currency to, and won so much acceptance of, the bogus version. Virtually every day's news wires since Inauguration Day of 1981 have carried stories about how the Reagan administration, or the Congress, has succeeded in "turning back" some function of government to private industry, or voluntary organizations, or local communities, or families, or individuals, or is proposing to do so. The federal government has, allegedly, usurped responsibilities that were being exercised by someone else, the taxpayer is therefore being bilked, and right-thinking citizens should unite in a crusade to restore the division of functions that prevailed before the federal empire-builders had their way.

On the day this is being written, for instance, a news story relates the efforts of President Reagan and his White House aides to abolish the federal Legal Services Corporation on the ground that legal services for the poor, insofar as they are necessary at all, have been and can be provided by voluntary legal aid societies and charitably inclined law firms. The same argument has been used for eliminating, or drastically reducing, many other federal welfare activities and programs in aid of education, the arts, community development, and so on. But if the administration succeeds in eliminating the federal legal services program, or other comparable activities, it will not have privatized anything, for what goes on in the private sector will not by those actions have been changed at all. If legal aid societies had been able to meet the needs of poor people for legal counsel, the federal program would not have been established—with the support of the organized legal profession—in the first place, And abandonment of federal responsibility will not enhance the capacities of those organizations significantly, for taxpayer gratitude is hardly likely to express itself noticeably and directly in increased contributions.

It may be observed, parenthetically, that if private contributions did rise to offset the cut in public spending, that would defeat the purpose of the tax and budget cuts, which were put forward as the key to stimulating savings and investment. If the money saved by abolishing a federal program is to be spent for the same purpose anyway (and presumably with no increase in efficiency, for voluntary organizations do not benefit from the profit motive either), the activity might as well, from the standpoint of economic effects, have continued as a federal responsibility. The declared purposes of Reaganomics will not be served unless the total volume of spending for services, public and private combined, is reduced. But it will be reduced, of course, for private giving will not rise to fill the gap created by drastic federal budget cuts in this or any other field (Salamon 1981; Salamon and Abramson 1982; Smith and Rosenbaum 1981). And the same applies to functions "turned back" to state and local governments; the National League of Cities reports that cities, like voluntary organizations, are giving up on trying to find local funds to replace the grants the federal government is withdrawing (*New York Times*, January 3, 1983).

In instances where the intent is for the abandoned federal responsibility to be assumed by private enterprise—as in the president's abortive suggestion that each private firm hire one additional worker to solve the unemployment problem—that purpose runs counter to the central argument in favor of privatization: the private sector is more efficient precisely because the profit motive forbids it to spend money in significant amounts for purposes that do not contribute to producing income. Only the government and voluntary groups, because they lack the profit motive, can indulge in make-work or distribute welfare.

A case can be made, of course, that legal services, or employment of the jobless, or any other federal program that one cares to name should be abandoned, but it would elevate the public debate to argue the case on those terms, not on the pretext that the function will be privatized. The national government is entitled to decide that it does not care what happens to the poor or the jobless or any other disadvantaged group, not to mention the advantaged who are the beneficiaries of national programs. Candidates who propose to cut social programs have every right to run on platforms of not caring. None, however, do. They claim, instead, to care intensely, and it is the very depth of their concern that impels them to seek the someone else who will meet the people's needs more efficiently, more sensitively, and more equitably. So privatization is advanced as the solution. But in the false sense, for to abandon a program is not to privatize it—unless something happens on the private side.

If the national government does care, it has to satisfy itself that the balls it drops are in fact picked up. There is but one way to ensure that end: as Peter Drucker suggests in his chapter, the government must pay. Instead of doing the job itself, it can contract and may get the job done better. Rather than operating its own shipyards and own ordnance manufacturing plants, as it once did, it can procure. The responsibility is not shifted, only the actual performance of the work. That is true privatization.

In true privatization, the government's role is only reduced; it does not disappear. And what is relinquished may be the easiest part of the whole job—the doing. The conceiving, planning, goal-setting, standard-setting, performance-monitoring, evaluating, and correcting all remain with the government. If these are done badly, the public interest suffers, and so, usually, does the private contractor. That is why privatization is no panacea for governmental incompetence. And it is why the most ardent advocates of privatization should be among the most vociferous in demanding the improvement of governmental capacity. For it takes able and effective governmental organs to make privatization work in the manner that is desired and intended.

THE IRREDUCIBLE ROLE OF GOVERNMENT

If we list the elements of the role that still remains for government when activities are privatized, we indicate the range of possibilities for error that incompetent government can make. First of all, it is government that *must decide whether and what to privatize.* And that requires a capacity to gather and analyze pertinent data and make correct judgments. There are no rules that provide automatic answers. Even garbage collection, which appears to be everybody's favorite candidate for contracting out, may be handled quite satisfactorily by public employees in some jurisdictions, at no greater cost, and with perhaps greater responsiveness to citizen opinion. Do private janitorial companies do a better job of cleaning public buildings, at less cost, than do janitors who are on the public payroll? Perhaps, but if the decision is to be based on better grounds than ideology, prejudice, and campaign contributions, it must be based on analysis—by government. A mistake on garbage collection or janitorial services is, of course, of no great moment, and is readily corrected. But other functions carry greater risk. Would private companies provide pure water at less cost than city water departments, or would the profit motive in that case provide a perverse incentive, impelling private managers to trim essential safeguards in the course of cutting costs? If the national forests were turned over to Weyerhaeuser and Potlatch, and the national parks to Disney and Marriott, would those companies yield to the pressure for quick profits at the expense of the concern for future generations that the Forest Service and the National Park Service claim to have? To choose wisely the functions that are best privatized calls for the greatest of skill on the part of public officials in both the legislative and executive branches. Where new technology permits privatization of subfunctions or tasks—electronic teaching processes within a school, for instance— the public officer has the exacting duty of separating out the privatized activity so that it can be performed effectively while still integrating it into the whole pattern of operations.

Once the decision is made to privatize, it is government that *must choose the private agent and define the terms of the relationship.* Some functions, such as garbage removal, may lend themselves to competitive bidding under contracts that define simply the service to be rendered and the required standard of performance. But in other fields, the activity to be performed and the standards to be met are not so readily described. In privatizing education, for instance, a public authority that tried to define the whole curriculum to be taught would only defeat itself. Sometimes a public function is privatized for no better reason than the public body does not quite know what should be done or what is the best way to do it, and desires to enlist private imagination in the task of finding out. Research and experimentation benefit from a diversity of approaches, and advance definition of what is to be done can only stultify. But if the task to be undertaken cannot be defined precisely, then how can private organizations bid competitively? The public authority must retain discretion to select the contracting firm on the basis of its reputation and the preliminary ideas it puts forth. Which schemes for synthetic fuels development hold promise enough to justify a public subsidy?

Which company's fighter plane still on the drawing boards should be chosen for prototype development? Whose plan for downtown redevelopment should be selected to receive the benefits of public land assembly? These are subjective judgments, and they will be no better than the competence of the public officials who make them, and of the staff men and women who develop the criteria, communicate with prospective bidders, and analyze their proposals.

And along with the identity of the contractor, the terms of the compensation must be determined. Here the interests of the public depend on the ability of the government to drive a proper bargain. So much of the urge to privatize having arisen from the conviction that the government is wasteful, how is waste, including collusion and favoritism, to be eliminated from the contracting process? Unless genuine competitive bidding can be used as a control, privatization merely adds a new set of opportunities and incentives for waste. Economy still depends on the ability of the governmental agency, not to perform a service efficiently but to procure it efficiently, and the latter may be as difficult as the former. Jordan Baruch aptly observes that in the interest of the taxpayers as well as of private contractors, the public sector must have "creative negotiators" who become effective customers for the private sector.

Finally, the government *must monitor the performance of the contractor and enforce the standards set forth in the contract.* If a parks department's swimming pool is operated by a private concessionaire, the superintendent of parks must still satisfy himself and the taxpayers whose money is being spent, that the pool is open when it should be, that lifeguards are properly trained and on duty, that the water is drained and filtered in accordance with the contract, and order is maintained. Yet there are pressures on public officials to be lax in setting standards in the first place and to be timid and superficial in enforcement. To properly supervise a privatized function usually requires that the public agency have staff with as much expertise as the employees of the contractor, but this requirement is difficult to meet. Contractors can pay more—which is sometimes the fundamental reason for privatizing a public function—and so they can drain away the ablest personnel from the supervising agency. Strict enforcement always creates tension between the government agency and its contractor, which may lead to subtle or overt pressure upon political officials to tell their subordinates to take things easy. In times of budget stringency, officials looking for ways to save money without reducing services may see inspection and enforcement as a ready target; inspectors produce no service, fewer of them will mean less conflict, and maybe everything will turn out all right if the contractor is simply trusted to do his job. That would all be in the spirit of getting government off the backs of the people anyway.

Privatization calls for special talents on the part of the public administrators responsible for functions contracted out, because their authority is not commensurate with their responsibility. They must guarantee the quality of the service rendered without being able to exert direct control over the people who perform the service. To keep informed on what is going on, they must determine their information needs with precision, perhaps prescribe the records system that will produce it, and require regular and accurate reports—and do all this without getting themselves condemned for imposing bureaucratic red tape on the private sector. In short, they must inspect without irritating, enforce without provoking undue resistance, keep fully informed while maintaining an arms-length relationship. And, in all likelihood, they will not be able to rest their supervision on the power to discipline, for the authority to penalize a contractor (including the ultimate penalty of terminating the contract) will inevitably become a matter to be decided by political officials, and for a score of practical reasons the administrator may find it virtually impossible to recommend effective sanctions.

The public seems to understand these difficulties and the risks of poor performance that they involve, for it tends to resist the privatization of public functions where life or property, as distinct from mere tax money, is involved, or where mistakes are irreversible. In such cases it wants its elected officials to take undivided responsibility and exercise full control, through their own employees whom they can select, direct, and discipline. Despite the low repute of government, the cynical public still prefers to have its water supply, its fire protection, its police protection, its food and drug inspection, its air traffic control, its military defense, and so on, performed by public bodies—even, in the case of municipal functions, in cities that are notoriously corrupt and wasteful. Cost effectiveness is only one concern of citizens and taxpayers, and on activities of high risk they prefer to maintain unambiguous lines of responsibility and avoid any possible public-private conflict of interest, even at the loss of whatever increased efficiency and innovativeness might be attained through privatization.

Yet, to say that the government has an irreducible role—both to supervise and control functions that have been privatized and to directly operate those that cannot be—is to cast the government-business relationship in terms too negative. For beyond the minimum role lies an enormous range of constructive opportunities for the use of governmental powers and resources in support of business, in relationships that range from simple subsidy to outright partnership. Many activities in aid of business are well-established and by now outside the realm of controversy, except for marginal disputes over the size of budgets. They include most of the core functions of the U.S. Departments of Commerce and Agriculture and many of those of Interior, Transportation, and Energy—patent and copyright protection, collection and dissemination of statistical data, mapping and charting, aid for airports, agricultural extension, and research in agricultural production, marketing, and utilization, and in minerals and energy, to name a few—as well as corresponding functions of state and local governments. It is hardly too much to say that, from the beginning, the central objective of the government in its domestic activities and in its diplomacy as well has been to support business, and organized private interests have played a leading role in promoting the growth of government. It was no accident that Herbert Hoover rose to the presidency, as a conservative Republican, on the basis of his success in finding new ways for the Department of Commerce he headed for eight years to come to the aid of business.

In the last couple of decades, a wide variety of innovative efforts have been undertaken by the federal government, in cooperation with states and local governments, to encourage economic development in particular places, including urban renewal, area redevelopment, Appalachian regional development, new community development, and urban development. These newer programs have been controversial; urban renewal and new community development have been abandoned, the Appalachian program is scheduled for termination, and Republican presidents have tried to curtail and eliminate most of the others. But even the Reagan administration has advanced its own scheme for Urban Enterprise Zones, which suggests some degree of bipartisan consensus on the notion of government-business partnership in economic development. And when President Reagan set up his Task Force on Private Sector Initiatives, he echoed his campaign rhetoric with a call for an end to "government paternalism" but nevertheless left a large, if undefined, role for government. He declared the objective to be "public/private sector partnerships in every community for assisting needy persons and depressed areas." William Norris, a member of the Task Force, puts meaning into the partnership concept in his chapter in this book.

It is not too great a leap of imagination, perhaps, to carry the partnership principle to the national level and call, as does Robert Reich in his chapter, for national planning and action to stimulate and influence the development of particular U.S. industries to enhance the competitiveness of this country's exports in the world. Unless the lagging productivity and weakened competitive position of American industry revive miraculously on their own, and quickly, one can expect political candidates in the future to vie with one another in advocating one form or another of "national industrial policy," on the models of the Western European countries and Japan.

THE DEVELOPMENT OF GOVERNMENTAL COMPETENCE

Given the vast array of present governmental activities that are indispensable or merely useful, and the certainty that more will become useful or even necessary, privatization can offer at the most only a minor contribution to the solution of what ails government. But, worse than that, it can lure attention away from the compelling need—which is to make governmental institutions work as they ought to work. It can be a way of giving up on government when the country cannot afford to give up.

Robert Reich and Peter Drucker, in their chapters, provide a provocative framework for a discussion of those problems. For while Reich calls on government to undertake new and challenging ventures, Drucker dismisses governmental efforts as condemned to failure at the outset. If Drucker is right, then Reich's ideas become hopelessly visionary.

Fortunately for the Reich argument, Drucker's bill of particulars in condemning government falls short of being wholly convincing. He does not explain, for instance, why, if government cannot succeed in "doing" things itself, because of a shortage of first-rate people, it can succeed in "outlining the tasks" and "providing the means," which calls for first-rate administrative organizations, or how private contractors can find the first-rate people that the government cannot. If enough such people exist to justify Drucker's unlimited faith in the capacity of private enterprise, the question becomes simply one of how government gets its necessary share. And while he finds government "congenitally unsuited" to undertake programs that require long lead times to show results, he cites as an example of a successful long-lead-time program Social Security, which as it happens was a governmental program too.

Yet Drucker is certainly correct in his central points. Government, specifically the federal government, is less than competent in these days to undertake great challenges. Assuredly, the government lacks the people's confidence; Reich's proposals for new forms of extensive governmental intervention in the economic system are bound now and for some time ahead to die aborning, in the absence of some crisis of unprecedented scale, because of the prevailing public view that the government, if it launched any such ambitious venture, would only mess it up. And Drucker has also identified accurately the prime cause. The government—the national government, at least— is not getting, keeping, and using its share of first-rate people. Here is where the imperative job of improving governmental competence must begin.

In its institutional arrangements for the management of governmental programs, the United States stands in stark contrast to the other developed countries with which it must compete. Western European countries and Japan entrust the operations of government to professional civil servants, highly trained and highly respected, while the U.S. government relies heavily on politically selected amateurs, who may or may not have relevant experience when they assume their posts and do not usually remain long enough to learn much on the job. The comparative competence of government bureaucracies defies precise measurement, but it is easy to make a prima facie case that other governments have capacities far exceeding ours. The case rests on a few truisms:

- Government administrators, like private managers, improve their capability as they gain experience, which makes professionals usually more competent than short-term amateurs.

- Persons who rise to the top in a professional civil service, like those who become corporate executives, have passed a series of stiff competence tests and demonstrated a superior level of ability throughout their careers.

- Administrators chosen for their managerial capacity are more likely to succeed in directing the operation of government programs than are administrators placed in their jobs for ideological reasons or as rewards for service to a political candidate or party.

- Amateurs who are simply taking a fling at government service are not likely to engage in the long-run tasks of developing top-to-bottom competence and responsiveness in the organizations temporarily under their direction, while professionals who intend to stay awhile have an incentive to build for the future.

- A government service that enjoys high prestige will attract a larger share of first-rate people than one that is constantly derided.

The high status of the European and Japanese civil services has origins deep in history. Before there were parliaments and democratic politicians in those countries, there were civil servants, the agents and retainers of kings and emperors. Clothed with the royal power, they commanded respect, and for the best of them the pay and perquisites were generous. So their jobs were prized; leading families had no higher ambition for their sons than to place them in government office, and as universities developed, the public service drew a large share of the educated elite. By the time the executive agencies passed from monarchical to parliamentary control, the character and standing of the men who staffed them were well established. Top civil servants so clearly outranked their democratically elected political superiors in educational attainments and in the mastery of governmental matters that the politicians automatically deferred to them—and, since the attainment and the mastery have not markedly diminished, they still do.

The United States, in contrast, came into being as a democracy. The common citizen was king, and his agents could only be common citizens like himself, elected and appointed by their peers to serve in public office. Elitism lingered for a while after the Revolution, but there was really no proper place for it, and with the election of Andrew Jackson in 1828 the remnants of the old ethic were swept out by the victorious, egalitarian frontier democrats. In its place was planted the antithetical democratic doctrine, that any citizen could perform any public duty. In partisan politics, this democratic concept translated into the spoils system: if any citizen could fill any office, then why should not the government be staffed by citizens of the party the voters had endowed with responsibility for public functions? On such a concept, strong political party organizations could be built, and they were. Party leaders cemented their power by distributing public jobs, and the spoils system flourished. Both as a practical success and as a logical element of democratic government, it became deeply embedded in American tradition.

But the spoils system had obvious weaknesses, and in the second half of the nineteenth century elitist concepts began a comeback. It became plain, particularly as governmental functions became more technical, that the democratic doctrine when carried to the extreme became fallacious. Many jobs did require special skills, and citizens were disgusted by the visible waste as experienced and able public servants were replaced by new appointees who at best were inexperienced and at worst might be incompetent. Politicians themselves sought relief from the sheer burden of deciding which of their followers deserved which reward. So, after President Garfield was shot by a rejected office-seeker, the first civil service act was passed.

The Pendleton Act of 1883, however, marked not the end, but the beginning of a struggle between the opposing doctrines that has proceeded ever since. Its coverage was by no means universal, and many later laws and presidential orders were required to extend the merit system in the federal government upward, outward, and downward (in the phrase of President Franklin Roosevelt's Committee on Administrative Management in 1937). And decades of steady pressure by reformers were necessary to supplant state and local spoils systems with merit systems, a process not yet complete. But at the national level, progress came to a halt three decades ago, and since then the concept of a professional civil service has been losing ground to a revived version of the old Jacksonian idea that any citizen can perform any public job.

The beginning of the Jacksonian revival can be dated with precision: 1953, when the inauguration of President Eisenhower marked the first change in party control of the government in twenty years. During the preceding two decades of Democratic dominance, a career service of considerable capacity had developed, formed first from a generation of young people attracted to the federal service during the Depression by the leadership and ideals of Franklin Roosevelt and second from an influx of able, patriotically minded people just before and during the early years of World War II. By the late Truman years, career civil servants had advanced to top managerial posts throughout the government, including the Executive Office of the President and the White House itself. The president or a department head charged with organizing a new program or reorienting an old one had a corps of experienced people on whom he could call with confidence. To a very large extent, the permanent government was under their control. But to the incoming Republicans of 1953, the career officials who administered domestic programs were highly suspect—and with good reason, for they did not constitute a politically neutral service in the European sense. They had been recruited by Democratic administrations, had served only Democratic administrations, and for the most part were Democratic by temperament and philosophy. Many left voluntarily, including virtually all of those in the White House and other posts filled by presidential appointment. Some made their peace with the new Republican leaders. But others were assigned to lesser duties, encouraged to retire, or in a few cases dismissed, their places filled by Republican political appointees. By later standards, the attack on the career service was not virulent, but careerists clearly suffered in status, responsibility, and morale. The effects were most sweeping, of course, in those areas of the government responsible for administering programs caught up in partisan controversy; technical and scientific agencies were generally spared, though not always. And in some agencies, in those years, the de-moralization was compounded by the impact of McCarthyism.

After 1953 control of the executive branch alternated between the parties at eight-year intervals, until 1980, when the interval was cut in half. And each shift in control saw a repetition of the events of 1953, but with broadening scope and accelerating intensity. Each incoming cadre of political appointees tended to suspect any hold-overs in whom the previous administration had placed its trust, even those who had survived from earlier administrations. New batches of careerists were forced out, to be replaced by new groups of political appointees, who in turn were discarded at the next change of party control. The Nixon administration even produced the how-to-do-it "Malek Manual" instructing its officials on how to gut the civil ser-vice.[1] In 1976 Jimmy Carter campaigned as an opponent of the Washington establishment, and on taking office pushed a Civil Ser-vice Reform Act of 1978 through the Congress as the means—as he presented it to the legislators and the public—of expediting the re-moval of malingering and incompetent careerists (Sundquist 1979). Ronald Reagan went Carter one better by campaigning against gov-ernment itself, and he brought into office with him a host of ideo-logues determined to dismantle everything they could on the domes-tic side of government and cut back unmercifully on what remained. Civil servants, as the symbol of governmental regulation and the wel-fare state, were treated as targets and as enemies. The current morale of the government's top career officials is measured by the Reagan administration's own poll in 1981, which found that 46 percent of the members of the Senior Executive Service were considering leav-ing government service within two years, though most of them would still be in their peak productive years. Of 800 alumni of the Federal Executive Institute responding to a 1982 survey, 70 percent said they would advise bright, competent young people to seek their careers in the private sector rather than in government. A majority of 58 percent reported themselves "generally pessimistic" about the prospects for rewarding government work during the next ten to fifteen years; only 12 percent were "generally optimistic" (Federal Executive Institute Alumni Association 1983).

The depletion of the government's career service through the severe and continuing brain drain—or, to put it in different terms, the failure of the U.S. government ever to develop a civil service that could attract to the government its share of first-rate people and hold them there—is at the heart of the problem of governmental competence. It is a truism that the performance of an organization can be no better than the people who make up the organization. Yet, whether blinded by ideology or merely inattentive, the most vociferous critics of governmental competence these days have overlooked the obvious.

Those who, like Reich, would have the United States emulate the business-government relations of Japan and Western Europe must find the way first to emulate the public administration of those countries. The models are clear enough. The administrative structures can be readily designed, and within a generation after the decision to do so is made, the government can be staffed with its share of first-rate people. But first of all, a change must somehow be brought about in the attitude of the American public toward government, and toward the people who serve in governmental posts.

This is not to argue that, given its share of first-rate people working under competent managers in a professionalized career service, governmental organizations will be as efficient and effective as private ones, or more or less so. Advocates of privatization will contend that government bureaucracies are bound to be less vigorously motivated, less flexible, less enterprising, more realistic, more compelled and inclined to do it by the book. An inverse set of governmental virtues can be induced from this list, of course, and examples can be found of public agencies that seem not to suffer—or suffer unduly, at any rate—from the common weaknesses. By definition, government bureaucracies operate in a political environment, which means that they must satisfy political constituencies, even if that sometimes must be done at cost to efficiency. One may argue, perhaps, that if a function that is deeply embedded in a political context is privatized, the context will go with it and the private operation will suffer a loss of efficiency as well. But this whole controversy is beside the point. The issue is not the relevance that comparison of public and private bureaucracy in the abstract may have for privatization decisions; those decisions must rest in any event on case-by-case, not general, comparisons. Government must be made as competent as possible as an end in itself, whatever level of privatization that may be desirable or attainable, simply because government will remain an indispensable institution.

The blunderbuss attacks on government-as-the-problem and bureaucrats-as-the-enemy have been aimed most directly at the national government, but they have also impaired governmental capacity in the states and communities, where most governmental services are delivered. The public service has been derogated and depreciated at every level (California's Proposition 13 and like campaigns are the counterpart of the Reagan crusade against the national government), and the respect and status of public employees everywhere have suffered, leading bright and able young people to look for careers elsewhere. Superior material rewards can compensate for a moderate volume of abuse in any career, but the budget cuts forced by federal aid cutbacks, economic recession, and tax limitation initiatives have removed or severely reduced any advantages that public agencies once offered. Salary freezes and real wage losses have been widely visited on public employees, and even the supposed lifetime security of civil service jobs—an important competitive advantage for public bodies in recruiting staff, though not necessarily the most desirable advantage—has lost dependability.

Over the years, it is the political conservatives who have led the assault on government and disparaged those who work for it. So it is they who must come to recognize that they have as much stake as liberals in governmental competence. After all the dismantling possible has been accomplished, after every governmental function that can be privatized has been let out to contract, whoever is in power will still find that government is an instrument that must be used for an extensive and irreducible range of purposes and that to permit government to fail through sheer administrative incompetence is to imperil this country's unity and progress at home and its position in the world.

NOTE TO CHAPTER 14

1. The manual was popularly named for Frederic V. Malek of the Office of Management and Budget, although not properly so, he contends, because he was not involved in its preparation or approval.

REFERENCES

Federal Executive Institute Alumni Association. 1983. *FEIAA Newsletter*, January 1983.

Salamon, Lester. 1981. *The Federal Government and the Voluntary Sector: Implications of the Reagan Administration Budget Proposals.*

Salamon, Lester M., and Alan J. Abramson. 1982. "The Nonprofit Sector." In *The Reagan Experiment*, edited by John L. Palmer and Isabel V. Sawhill. Washington, D.C.: Urban Institute, pp. 219-243.

Smith, Bruce L.R., and Nelson M. Rosenbaum. 1981. "The Fiscal Capacity of the Voluntary Sector." Unpublished paper, Brookings Institution National Issues Seminar, Washington, D.C., December.

Sundquist, James. 1979. "Jimmy Carter as Public Administrator: An Appraisal at Mid-Term." *Public Administration Review* 39 (January-February): 3-11.

✳ *Chapter 15*

Potential Contributions of Western Business to the Service Sector of LDCs

Franklin A. Long

Service activities constitute a large and rapidly growing component of the efforts of most of the less developed countries (LDCs) just as they do for developed countries. The services of primary importance to the two groups are much the same: health, education, research and development (R&D), and information and planning. (This list excludes some activities that are often called services, but that relate closely to industry and agriculture, such as trade, transportation, communications, and national defense.) The enterprises that provide these various services are usually a mixture of public-sector and private-sector organizations. Some service activities are reserved almost exclusively for the public sector: national defense, airlines, railroads, and many educational programs. In others the private sector plays a large role.

Business firms of the Western nations, notably the transnational enterprises (TNEs), are extensively involved in the less developed nations, but their commercial involvement in the service programs of the LDCs has so far not been extensive. Yet modern technology of the kind developed in the West makes considerable contribution to service programs, and Western based TNEs can bring to them two important contributions: technical knowledge and management capability. Given the rapid growth of private-sector participation in service programs of the developed nations, one can expect increased participation of the TNEs in service programs of the LDCs as well.

Already TNEs that operate in LDCs often find it desirable to supply some services to their own employees and sometimes to an entire local community. Technician training is an example of the first, and local hospitals and medical services are examples of the second.[1] Often because of low labor turnover the benefits from these programs do not extend significantly beyond the local employees and their families, but where there is high labor turnover the impact can be widespread. A spectacular example of this is the training activities of international construction companies like Fluor and Bechtel. A large construction project for a refinery or a gas processing plant in one of the poorer LDCs may require the training of several thousand local employees in such skills as carpentry, plumbing, and welding. Once the project is completed, typically after three or four years, these trained employees return to the local labor force with obvious benefits to the local economy (Fund for Multinational Management Education 1981).

Because large private-sector companies, in particular the TNEs, usually develop effective programs of training for technicians and management, and programs of research and development, LDCs frequently offer incentives to encourage wider participation of private enterprises in education and R&D. A recent study gives examples of some of the service-oriented contributions of TNEs in developing countries and discusses ways in which specific host countries have attempted to increase these contributions (Long 1980). However, the most substantial and lasting reason for the private sector to increase its activities in service programs of LDCs is the opportunity to develop profitable businesses.

In analyzing private sector participation in service activities of LDCs, it is convenient to discuss the situation in LDCs in terms of the functional categories of major services that are important to them. Table 15-1 lists these.

The sections that follow examine several of the service activities that are important to LDCs and consider the kinds of contributions that TNEs from the developed world might make. Two important caveats must be noted. One is that a generalized analysis of the situation for a particular service activity like education will unavoidably underemphasize the very great diversity in philosophies, capabilities, and organizations that characterize the diverse LDCs of the world. The second caveat is that the service activities that are linked to the physical infrastructure of the nations—transportation, communication, and provision of such utilities as electricity and water—will not receive much emphasis even though service functions that support these major infrastructure activities will be discussed.

Table 15-1. Service Activities by Function.

Education
  Formal (primary, secondary, university)
  Technician training
  Continuing education in, e.g.:
    Technical skills
    Management
    Planning
    Data handling (computers)
    Paramedic skills
Health
  Medical care
  Hospital management
  Public health programs
Research and development
  Agriculture
  Industry
  Health
Information retrieval and dissemination
Planning and data management
Extension service programs
  Agriculture
  Small business
  Public health
Maintenance and repair of scientific and
  technical instruments

EDUCATION

Table 15-1 subdivides education into three components: formal education, technician training, and continuing education. In virtually all LDCs chief responsibility for formal education is assumed by the government—sometimes the central government, in other cases those of the states. Privately operated universities, often run by religious groups, operate in several LDCs, but usually as a supplement to the state-operated systems. The LDC universities vary greatly in quality. Most have difficulty in obtaining and maintaining modern equipment. It is also difficult for faculty to keep up to date in recent developments in science and engineering; information about recent Western developments is a continuing problem, and libraries often are inadequate. When instruction is not in English, French, or German, the task of translating Western books and journals can be onerous. Continued academic exchanges between the LDC and Western universities can alleviate some, but not all, of the problems. The information problem is part of a more general one and is considered later.

Technician training is an important task for LDCs, especially those that are trying to industrialize rapidly. Two principal training modes exist in the typical LDC. Large industries, especially the TNEs, have training programs for their own employees. Governments operate schools for technician training, usually at two or three levels. One level is the "vocational secondary high school" as an alternate to the academic secondary school. Another is a one- or two-year post-secondary school that gives a higher level of training, usually reaching into more specialized areas. The mission of these latter schools over-laps that of the occasional technical college, which gives a broader education, but one that is still oriented toward practical skills. Very commonly the technician training given by the large TNEs is con-sidered superior (for example, a certificate of completion of the tech-nician training course of Volkswagen of Nigeria is apparently more prestigious in that country than is a certificate from any one of the state schools). A consequence is that several LDCs have established incentives or laws to enhance technician training by private compa-nies. The compulsory apprentice program of SENA in Colombia, under which larger Colombian industries are required to have 5 per-cent of their employees be two-year apprentices, is a particularly suc-cessful program of this sort.

As LDCs become increasingly industrialized, there is a rapidly expanding market for programs of continuing education in which new skills and new procedures are taught to industrial employees and civil servants. Examples of subjects are: technical skills, management techniques of various sorts, computer use, computer programming, accounting, quality control, and utilization and maintenance of ad-vanced instrumentation. Local branches of TNEs commonly teach various of these subjects to groups of their employees, sometimes by sending more senior employees to a company-operated international training center. Fewer opportunities exist for continuing education for employees of small business and for civil servants.

Specialized education in LDCs offers many opportunities for the private sector, particularly for TNEs from developed nations, since they can offer instruction on the newer information processes and procedures, and can also utilize in their instruction some of the newer educational techniques, such as computer-based instruction. Also, the TNE linkages with their home operations permits them to be continuously up to date in their information and instructional methods, not an easy task for a local LDC firm.

RESEARCH AND DEVELOPMENT

As in developed nations, the principal institutions in LDCs for carry-ing on R&D are government research laboratories, industrial labora-tories, and universities. Universities in all but the more advanced

LDCs are poorly funded for research facilities and for technical assistants, so that their research output is low. Industries in most LDCs perform little research, and their development programs are usually focused on adaptation and modification of imported technologies. This is true even of the large TNEs, which stress the use of modern technology, but whose R&D is mostly done in their facilities in developed nations. Many LDCs wish to see private enterprises perform more R&D locally, and the governments often offer tax or other incentives. Partly as a result of this, industrially supported R&D is growing rapidly in most LDCs, although the total amount remains small.

This leaves government-supported laboratories and field stations as the chief practitioners of R&D in the developing nations. In most LDCs applied agricultural research is a substantial part of the total effort. Because of the clear relevance of this research to farmers' needs, R&D in agriculture is often the best-managed and most important component of overall government efforts in R&D. Private industries also contribute considerably to agricultural R&D, particularly in studies on utilization of hybrid seeds, fertilizers, and pesticides. Fortunately the private and governmental efforts for agriculture usually seem to be fairly well integrated.

Other R&D laboratories in LDCs involve standards, chemical analyses, instrumentation, forestry, and oceanography. LDCs may also have laboratories for nutrition, important local products (e.g., rubber), and industrial development. Even in countries with many public sector industries, the separate industrial development laboratories turn out not to be very effective, primarily because industrial innovation, which is the main goal of R&D for industry, is rarely accomplished without active and continuing participation of the manufacturing units.

All too often the R&D laboratories in LDCs are not productive. They have difficulty staying abreast of world developments; their facilities and libraries are often inadequate, and, most important, their linkages, either upward to government decisionmakers or downward to potential users of their findings, tend to be poor. Part of the problem is isolation; few such laboratories are located adjacent to a university or to other laboratories.

It is not evident what role the private sector might play in enhancing the capabilities of these R&D laboratories. It is tempting to describe their problem simply as inadequate management and to suggest that seminars on management and on information would be helpful. However, the more fundamental problems are probably those of the basic charters for the laboratories and of their interactions with the various governmental organizations that sponsor them and that they are presumed to serve. An appropriate private-sector group might evaluate the role of the public laboratories to see what the private sector could contribute. It is probably not possible to suggest a way for the private sector to participate in these laboratories until the functions and orientations of the laboratories themselves have been clarified.

HEALTH CARE SERVICES

For virtually all developing nations, health care services rank second only to education in costs and effort. Health care is decidedly more complicated to provide effectively than is education. The field of action is more dispersed geographically, the need for detailed social interaction with the populace is more extensive, and the knowledge base on which the service must be provided is enormously larger. A complex hierarchy of people is required, including ministers of health, district officers, medical doctors, hospital administrators, nurses, paramedics, and social workers. To complicate the situation, services that are provided by nonhealth agencies such as the provision of pure drinking water, also have strong implications for health care.

Consequently it is virtually mandatory that health care be treated as a complicated *system*. The system must be *appropriate* in terms of the mixture of facilities and people, but also in terms of relative costs of its possible components. Furthermore a developing nation will usually require not one, but several, health care programs, depending on whether the region is urban or rural, and on the education and financial status of the population. It is therefore not surprising that the two words that occur most frequently in discussing health care systems are *planning* and *management*. For an analysis by the World Bank of problems in improving health conditions in LDCs, see Appendix A.

Governments of the developing nations will have a central role in planning, management, and resource allocation for health care programs. The medical profession, regional administrators, and paramedics will also be involved. Will there be a role for private sector groups? The answer is almost certainly yes. Active participation of the private sector in medical services has become common and appears to be rapidly increasing in many developed nations. In the U.S. the management and construction of hospitals has become a major industry involving such large and growing companies as American Hospital Corporation and National Medical Enterprises. The major role of the private sector in nursing homes in the United States is also well known. U.S. companies have been extending their activities to some of the wealthier developing nations. A good example is the Whittaker Corporation, which is now providing hospital management and other health services in Saudi Arabia, Abu Dhabi, and North Yemen. However, Middle East countries are somewhat special, in that they are underdeveloped but also rich, so they can afford Whittaker's relatively expensive services. The more interesting question is, are there opportunities for U.S. and other developed-nation corporations in the poorer of the developing countries?

The answer to this question must be yes for all but the very smallest and poorest of nations. Information systems, efficient management, and training of paramedics and others, might plausibly be best supplied by private-sector groups. Central responsibility for health care will reside with the governments, but the problem is formidable, and effective collaboration from other groups, private sector or otherwise, can be very helpful.

Private-sector groups can supply many specialized services and play an integrative role in providing health care in many developing nations. A concrete illustration is the program that the Control Data Corporation has operated at the Rosebud Indian Reservation in South Dakota. Appendix B gives a description that illustrates that it is very much the kind of service that a rural region in a developing nation could well wish to have available.

INFORMATION RETRIEVAL AND DISSEMINATION SYSTEMS

Continuing provision of adequate information is one of the most serious problems that developing nations face. The need for information retrieval, particularly from the developed world, is obvious enough. Most of the science and technology of interest to a developing nation comes from the outside. New information dealing, for example, with agricultural and economic growth must be continuously updated. Information must also be available to universities, health care programs, research and development centers, and business enterprises. Furthermore, information must often be translated into a language other than the three international languages of science and technology—French, German, and English.

Information systems tend to be sophisticated and costly, so care is needed in selecting one that is not unduly large or complex, and in continuously updating it. Important new technologies such as computers and modern storage devices will be needed (Kernen and Harmon 1980). Only in a few of the developing nations will there be an adequate number of trained people to devise and operate an effective information system.

Two kinds of information systems are of interest to developing nations. They can be developed together or separately. One might be called a socioeconomic information system, useful to planners, government economists, and university groups. The other is a science and technology information system that will be of interest to industry, government offices, universities, and research institutes within the country. A good example of the second kind of information system is the South Korean system for science and technology called KORSTIC. This government-supported service has been in existence since 1969, but attained its modern organization and equipment only in 1976. Appendix C, which comes from a 1980 Korean bulletin on KORSTIC, gives a detailed flow sheet for the KORSTIC information system, a description of its activities, and a list of the publication services that are supplied. Some idea of the capabilities of the system can be gained by noting that since December 1978 the central computer for the system has been an IBM 370/138. Informal discussions with users indicate that KORSTIC has been competently operated and its services have been widely used, especially by industries in Korea. It has been somewhat less successful with universities and R&D laboratories, due apparently to the fact that the capabilities of the system have not always been adequately explained. Finally, it appears that South Korea may be moving toward an integrated information system by combining KORSTIC with a somewhat similar system for socioeconomic information.

There is clearly a useful function for knowledgeable private-sector enterprises, including regional offices of TNEs, in planning and designing appropriate information systems, supplying equipment for them, and training managers and operators. Another role for the private sector of LDCs is developing and supplying specialized information services to particular groups of users and developing and updating the needed software. It is not common for enterprises from the developed nations to be involved in the day-to-day operation of the information systems in developing nations. However, there is a good case for this if their linkages with the appropriate agencies and enterprises in the developed world can put them in a position to bring about the modifications and increases in efficiency that more modern equipment and improved software will permit.

SERVICES FOR PLANNING
AND MANAGEMENT

The needs for planning and management permeate almost all government activities in LDCs. Many of the local private-sector industries have similar needs. Information systems represent important support for planning and management in both public and private sectors. Specialized services, such as engineering and architectural design and consultation, can contribute to planning and management, as can training courses in management, accounting, and computer programming.

Private industry fairly commonly plays a role in supplying specialized services in developing countries. As an example, there are close to a score of private engineering consulting firms in Kuala Lumpur, the capital city of Malaysia, with professional engineers trained in Malaysia, the United Kingdom, and the United States. Specialized services are also frequently supplied in LDCs by transnational enterprises. The chemical companies, for example, that supply fertilizers, herbicides and pesticides, typically work closely with farmers and agricultural experiment stations in LDCs to determine the most effective formulations, application rates, and optimal time schedules for local use. However, these activities must be seen as a part of the sales effort for the companies, not as a profit-making service in and of itself.

A different question is whether there is a role for TNEs and other large private-sector enterprises in the broader planning and management activities of developing nations. In agriculture, as is well known, large corporations frequently operate plantation-type farms in developing nations. Large-scale rubber and oil palm plantations in Malaysia are one example; pineapple plantations in the Philippines and the Dominican Republic are another. Even more interesting is whether such companies can participate profitably in supplying planning and management services to groups of individual farmers. A recent workshop on this concluded that the large corporations could be useful but that their utility was greatly enhanced if it was accompanied by a phenomenon that they named intermediation (Truitt 1981). The workshop examined twelve case studies of large corporations that are working with small farm groups in about a dozen different developing nations. In many cases the interaction was successful and worked to mutual benefit, but not in all. It was clear that the large enterprises offered important resources to the farm groups in management, technology, capital, and very commonly, in marketing. However, the general problem was one of a mismatch between the ways of doing business of corporations and those of the small farmers. It was to minimize the problems of mismatch, or perhaps better, to help achieve a match, that made an intermediator important.

The definition of intermediation between a corporation and a group of smaller farmers is "the provision of additional services which are not customarily needed in the operation of a [large] business or a farm of limited resources, but which are necessary to make the linkage between the two economically productive, financially less burdensome, and socially constructive." The case studies showed that often such services are provided by a discrete autonomous organization such as a voluntary agency, a government institution, or a separate business entity.

This study group did not pretend that intermediation (or any other single tactic) could provide the magic ingredient whereby corporations could work harmoniously and successfully with small farm groups or even small business groups, but pointed out the difficulties and possible solutions. The hope is that with time and experience this kind of mutually beneficial cooperation could be increasingly successful. The collaboration involved between a corporation and a diverse group of small farmers or small businessmen is a good deal more hazardous than the specialized collaboration that involves contribution of modern Western technology to receptive professional users. However, the problem of greater efficiency on the small farm is of very great consequence, and even limited success in discovering improved ways of planning and management could be of considerable importance.

One management area in which there has been much recent interest is that of farmer and small business cooperatives in developing nations. These are usually referred to by the abbreviations PC for producer cooperatives and IPC for industrial producer cooperatives. A 1982 book on participatory management devotes two study chapters to PCs and IPCs in developing nations. The first study (Abell and Mahoney 1982) is concerned with the fact that, despite much encouragement, the rates of establishment and of success of IPCs in developing nations have been comparatively low. The economic performances of eight cooperatives in India and Peru were compared to performances of local capitalist enterprises of similar size. The conclusions were "that the problem that small IPCs face is not so much one of investing sufficient capital but managing it effectively," and "that a support organization will be necessary to propagate a viable cooperative sector," a suggestion that has much in common with the notion of intermediation recommended by Truitt (1981). This support organization might well be, and in some fields might preferably be, a private-sector enterprise. A second, more optimistic study of Jamaican sugar cooperatives (Richards and Williams 1982) also concludes that adequate organization and management are key factors to success.

It is not uncommon for TNEs to collaborate with small farm groups in LDCs in assisting them to manage their business more effectively. The usual driving force is that the TNE is interested in an assured supply of a major farm product (milk for Nestlés, vegetables for Hanover Brands, etc.). However, the provision of planning and management services to cooperative and other small business groups is in itself a potentially interesting business activity for a TNE or other private sector concern.

THE ROLE OF INTERNATIONAL ORGANIZATIONS FOR ASSISTANCE

A wide variety of international organizations that assist in the development process are prepared to supply information and help in improving the service sectors of LDCs, including assistance in understanding the potential role of private industries. The organizations include UN organizations such as UNESCO, UNIDO, WHO, and ILO; other international organizations such as Pan American Health Organization; nationally based development assistance programs such as AID of the United States, IDRC of Canada, and SAREC of Sweden; nongovernmental organizations such as the Ford and Rockefeller Foundations of the United States, and several international religious groups.*

Direct hands-on assistance to the service programs of developing nations is supplied by nonprofit private volunteer organizations (PVOs) of many nations. Some have headquarters in developed nations and operate in a number of LDCs; others are local, with a local focus. Many are affiliated with religious organizations. Most of them operate through direct involvement of volunteer teams in small, often rural programs of a cooperative or self-help nature. Volunteer religious groups especially have played a large role in rural development in many areas of the world, notably in the poorer areas of

---

*UNESCO—United Nations Educational, Social, and Cultural Organization; UNIDO—United Nations Industrial Development Organization; WHO—World Health Organization; ILO—International Labor Organization; AID—Agency for International Development; IDRC—International Development Research Centre; SAREC—Swedish Agency for Research Cooperation with Developing Countries.

Latin America. The most substantial programs of these volunteer groups appear to concern education, food production and agriculture, and medicine and health.

A PVO of a different nature is VITA, Volunteers in Technical Assistance. This is a U.S.-based PVO whose volunteers are mostly retired professionals from the U.S. business community. VITA operates from a central office in New York City. It has an answering service for responding to technical inquiries and a consultancy service to supply volunteer consultants to programs in developing nations and distributes publications. VITA volunteers often operate in an intermediator role, similar to those discussed earlier. The essential difference is that VITA volunteers participate at a higher level of technology and management.

There are three main reasons for broader participation of TNEs in the service programs of developing countries. One is to obtain new markets by extending into LDCs service businesses that have already been developed in the West. Examples are hospital management and data processing. A second is to stabilize or enlarge an ongoing business in the LDC by providing related service efforts (e.g., provision of information and extension services by an agribusiness TNE to enhance sales of its principal products). A third is to respond to a new business opportunity (e.g., a construction company like Bechtel deciding to establish a subsidiary for adult education in particular skills, building on its already established capabilities in such education). In all these cases profitability of the service activity would be one goal. But others will often enter, e.g., protection of a principal business by being a "good citizen" or by acceding to government pressure.

There will, of course, often be cogent arguments *against* entering into service-oriented businesses in LDCs. Even TNEs whose principal business is in services may be reluctant to extend their activities into certain developing nations because of government attitudes or general instability. Other TNEs will be reluctant because they recognize that government agencies already are involved in these service functions and a private sector company may be seen as a competitor, or at least as subject to extensive regulation. Above all, however, there will be doubts that the contemplated service activity will be a sufficiently good business to justify entering into it.

Access of TNEs and other private enterprise groups to markets for service activities in developing nations is by no means always easy or assured. As noted earlier, in most LDCs there are several sorts of service activities in which only government agencies may participate. But even in fields not reserved for governments, the TNEs may sometimes find entrance difficult or impossible. Nations with socialist governments are usually unwilling to give market access to private foreign-based enterprises, except in areas where foreign know-how appears essential. Also, certain service activities may sometimes be seen as inappropriate for foreign participation, even if the local private sector is encouraged. Nonetheless market opportunities will exist in many LDCs; but even in receptive nations sensitivity to local traditions and mores will probably be a criterion for success in most service fields.

Broader entry of TNEs into service programs will often lead to establishing local subsidiary companies for such service activities. In this case it may be wise to establish a joint venture enterprise with a local group to obtain better access to local opportunities as well as to local customs and constraints. Furthermore, joint ventures are generally more favored by LDC governments, which may be frequent clients. Finally, both government pressures and business judgement will dictate minimal use of expatriate employees, and this is consistent with a joint venture. There is, however, one important linkage that may be harder to maintain for a joint venture. This is the close connection with the "home office" and other Western-based activities of the enterprise, which is important to maintain a continuing flow of new technology and new knowledge into the LDC subsidiary.

Expansion into service programs will not be desirable for all transnational enterprises, nor will all service ventures be successful. However, the service needs of LDCs will expand, as will opportunities for private sector participation. TNEs that respond successfully will have the twin satisfaction of developing profitable businesses and responding to important needs of their host country.

APPENDIX A
FROM "HEALTH SECTOR POLICY PAPER," WORLD BANK, WASHINGTON, D.C., FEBRUARY, 1980

Improving Health Conditions in the Developing Countries

Despite the large expenditures on health, and the technical feasibility of dealing with many of the most common health problems, efforts to improve health have had modest impact on the health of the vast majority of the population in most developing countries. This is commonly attributed to two main reasons. First, health activities have typically overemphasized sophisticated, hospital-based care, while neglecting preventive public health programs and simple primary care provided at conveniently located facilities. Second, even where health facilities have been geographically and economically accessible to the poor, deficiencies in logistics, inadequate training of staff, poor supervision, inappropriate services, and lack of social acceptability have often compromised the quality of the care they offer and limited their usefulness.

Though not present in all developing countries, the following problems are frequently encountered:

- Health facilities are geographically inaccessible to the majority of people. Women with children are most likely to experience difficulties in reaching a source of care.

- Economic barriers exclude many people. Even where users are not charged for service, the costs of transportation and time away from work can be prohibitive for the poor, particularly those who live in urban areas.

- Curative care is emphasized while prevention and early treatment are neglected.

- Hospital facilities built are excessive relative to primary health care facilities.

- Education of physicians is often not geared to the conditions in the country; it neglects common local health problems and appropriate technologies, while emphasizing rare diseases and the use of costly equipment.

- Health workers, particularly those in rural health positions, frequently are not sufficiently trained, supported, or supervised.

- The availability of services is erratic, particularly in more remote areas, because of unreliable delivery of drugs, pesticides, and other essential supplies.

- The services provided are sometimes not socially acceptable or not perceived to be efficacious by their intended beneficiaries.

- Community participation and integration with other sectors is underdeveloped.

It is now evident that the most persistent problems in improving health do not result from the complexity of medical technology, and only partially from the scarcity of financial resources; rather, they derive principally from problems in the design and implementation of policy, management, and logistics.* The obstacles most frequently encountered by the Bank in its lending for health components are:

- Lack of sound, long-term planning, particularly for the financing of recurrent costs, and for the coordination of program elements.

- Limited capacity for implementing new programs.

- Inconsistencies between new health programs (especially for training paramedical workers) and existing laws and regulations.

- Inadequate methods of procurement, distribution, and control of drugs and pesticides.

- Insufficient and poorly managed transport.

- Inadequate technical supervision and personnel administration.

- Poorly designed curricula for training health manpower and insufficiently prepared procedures for clinical care.

*Declarations at the Alma-Ata Conference on Primary Health Care in September 1978, organized by WHO and the United Nations Children's Fund (UNICEF), confirmed that this perception is held by the health authorities in most developing countries. Delegates to this conference, representing the entire membership of WHO, unanimously endorsed the idea that low-cost, accessible, relevant health care, supported through community participation, should be pursued and integrated with broader efforts toward economic and social development.

APPENDIX B

HEALTH PROGRAM OF CONTROL DATA CORPORATION AT ROSEBUD INDIAN RESERVATION, FROM "THE PATHWAY TO BETTER HEALTH," W.C. NORRIS, CHAIRMAN, CONTROL DATA CORPORATION, JUNE 1979

Another resource [for health care programs of Control Data] comes from the experience gained in a project delivering primary health care to the isolated Rosebud Reservation of the Sioux Indians in South Dakota. In order to be most effective in improving health care, one should have the experience of tackling the very worst problems and, as noted earlier, those kinds of problems certainly exist on Indian reservations.

On the Rosebud Reservation, Control Data has worked with Indian health providers to dramatically improve the health of that tribe through technology and managerial resources. Previously, one small hospital was the only source of health care for 8,500 Indian people. Those who required that care had to travel up to 130 miles to get it, and the number of professional staff was woefully inadequate to the task. Significant improvements are evident since Control Data's health van began traveling the Reservation, providing care to 900 residents per month. In addition, Indian community health workers have been trained and now, as a further improvement, four small clinics will be established.

APPENDIX C
PARTIAL DETAILS ON SOUTH KOREAN INFORMATION SYSTEM FOR SCIENCE AND TECHNOLOGY. FROM A 1980 BULLETIN ON KORSTIC

◇ **KORSTIC** 情報流通体制 ◇

KORSTIC INFORMATION SYSTEM

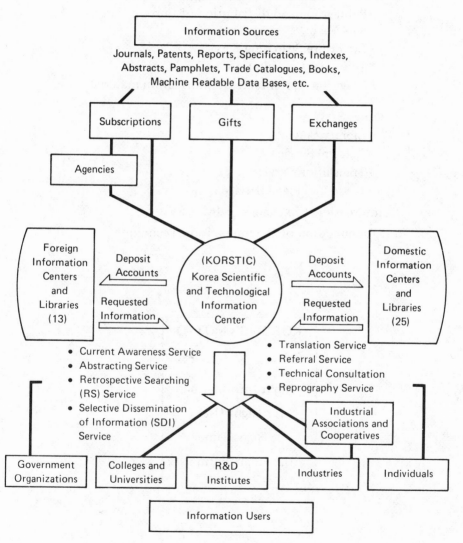

DESCRIPTION
OF ACTIVITIES

1. Acquiring and Organizing of Information Materials
2. Information Processing
3. Information Dissemination
     * Publication and distribution of Current Awareness Media
     * Literature Searching Service
     * Technical Consultation
     * Provision of full texts of information material

   Other Services
     * Library Service
     * Referral Service
     * Translation Service
     * Trade Catalogue Service
4. International Exchange of Information
5. Dissemination of Documentation Technique

KORSTIC's MOTTO

Right Information

for Right User

at Right Time

in Right Form

NOTE TO CHAPTER 15

1. The Jersey Standard Oil Company, now Exxon, was deeply involved in the 1930s and 1940s in medical services and in schools for their local employees and their families in remote locations in Venezuela, Peru, and other LDCs. Comparable involvement often occurs currently, for example, in remote areas of Indonesia.

REFERENCES

Abell, P., and N. Mahoney. 1982. "The Performance of Small-Scale Producer Cooperatives in Developing Countries: Capital Starvation and Capital Management." In *Participatory and Self-Managed Firms*, edited by D.C. Jones and J. Svejnar. Lexington, Mass.: Lexington Books.

Fund for Multinational Management Education. 1981. "Technology Transfer by the Bechtel Organization." New York.

Kernen, C., and L. Harmon. 1980. "Information Service Issues in Less Developed Countries." In *Annual Review of Information Science and Technology*, vol. 15, edited by M.E. Williams. White Plains, N.Y.: Knowledge Industry Publications, pp. 289–324.

Long, F.A. 1980. "Contributions of Transnational Enterprises to Scientific and Technological Capabilities of Colombia, Indonesia, Kenya and Nigeria." Program on Science, Technology and Society, Cornell University.

Richards, V., and A.N. Williams. 1982. "Institutional and Economic Aspects of the Jamaican Sugar Cooperatives." In *Participatory and Self-Managed Firms*, edited by D.C. Jones and J. Svejnar. Lexington, Mass.: Lexington Books.

Truitt, G.A, ed. 1981. "Multinationals: New Approaches to Agricultural and Rural Development." Fund for Multinational Management Education, New York.

PART V

ACHIEVING DEMOCRATIC LEGITIMACY

✳ *Chapter 16*

Political and Economic Markets: The Public, Private and Not-for-Profit Sectors

Lance Liebman

For the United States, the decade after 1964 was a period of challenge to established institutions. Questions were raised about government, the corporation, the university, and the church. Novel arguments were made for participation, openness, and the redistribution of power and reward. New definitions of integrity were propounded. Many institutional changes occurred, as attempts were made to restore legitimacy through rules, and to assure integrity through procedural checks and balances. Some new mechanisms did not survive. Others failed to achieve all the ends that their proponents promised. Still others had unintended negative consequences.

A different intellectual climate now prevails. In the 1980s arguments for business—for investment, deregulation, and the profit motive—are strong. Government is hard to defend. Even those who work in the public sector argue that it is an inefficient world, and that it should play a smaller role in social affairs. The argument is not only that tasks of government should be transferred to profit-seeking enterprises. It is also that the third sector should be strengthened: the voluntary sector, the nonprofit but nonpublic sector, the sector of mediatory structures. By definition this is an argument for collective activity, unregulated by the profit motive in its conventional form, that is not directly governed by majority rule but is, however, influenced and to a significant degree determined by policies and decisions of government and business.

Something else happened in the 1970s: we became pessimistic about human control of social life. In some ways, this is surprising, given the remarkable achievements in developed countries since the Second World War, and given too the wide sense that we are on the verge of technological changes that will permit major economic and social changes in the near future. Yet "finite" seems to have become a crucial word. Oil and other resource shortages have been an important cause. But there is much more to the sense that great ventures were tried in the sixties, and that many of them failed because they were beyond our capacity. It is not that we made mistakes and can learn from them and will choose differently the next time. Rather it is that the tasks themselves—full employment, school integration, abolition of poverty—are not appropriate, at least as aims of government intervention, because the means that are available do not correspond to the ends.

An additional factor affects the current intellectual climate. The American economy and those of other advanced societies appear to be entering a period of intense change. The wide use of new information technologies, just beginning to be predictable, may be about to change the nature of work, the value of productive resources, indeed the very ways that people live, to a degree that can be compared to the industrial revolution, the movement from farms to cities, and the coming of the automobile. It is far too early to think with clarity about the economic significance of the computer, much less its social implications. But certain categories of issues can at least be broadly foreseen and are of major significance.

In the past, periods of economic change driven by new technologies have sometimes caused painful social dislocations. Old ways have changed. Expectations have been defeated. Generations have contested. The development of appropriate political mechanisms has lagged or has been accompanied by violence. This time, the social environment in which the changes will occur is very different. We are in a period of social self-consciousness, a period of keeping track and identifying trends, a period of planning. It is not that we are doing a good job of seeing social consequences, attempting to control them, and achieving our social goals. But it is inconceivable that organized society will refrain from seeking to understand and influence the direction, pace, and consequences of economic rearrangements. This is especially so because the core of the change is information technology—the dramatic increase in the capacity to understand and to influence people and their relationships.

Some economic situations seem to require autocracy. Think of the Incas and the Egyptians, for whom (in different ways) facts about water called for unchallenged central authority. Science fiction can describe wired societies in which the computer is an instrument inconsistent with equality, democracy, and participation. Pollyannaish or not, this chapter proceeds from the assumption that the age of law—of shared and limited power, of wide participation, and of authority ultimately grounded in consent—is not over, and that at least in the near future the claims of what we regard as social liberty will guide and dominate technological change. Thus issues of delegated authority and legitimate expectation and fair process will be as central as they have been in the recent past.

BUSINESS

The most heated of the legitimacy challenges of the last decade have been those directed at the business corporation. Yet the corporation as a social form has weathered those challenges with less apparent structural response than has occurred in such institutions as government, the universities, and foundations. Nevertheless business power continues to pose fundamental intellectual issues, essentially summarizable as the corporation's place in our sort of democracy.

Robert Clark has given us ways to think about the corporation and its place that are a step beyond the standard categories. As a matter of political economy, the central issue is influence upon the society's processes of capital allocation. Profit is an ambiguous and clumsy tool for disciplining investment, although so far the best we have. What is profit? What is the appropriate interest rate for a firm allocating its retained earnings? In a period of uncertainty, as this period of technological and international change will continue to be, how can managers make estimates of future return that are more reliable than studying the innards of a sheep?

In the past, societies that could not tolerate unchecked managerial discretion invented three kinds of limiting mechanisms. First, attempts were made to increase the leverage of some of the factors that business must coordinate in performing its task. This really means labor, a factor different in important ways from physical capital. Statutes, enacted by legislative processes responsive to working-class votes, sought to permit labor to obtain a larger share of output and, in addition, a voice in decisions about workplace practices and conditions. As well, efforts were sometimes made to increase the leverage of local communities, of raw materials providers (agriculture, for example), and of customers (antitrust, consumer protection).

Second, there were attempts to limit managers on behalf of owners—shareholders. Today, of course, a substantial ownership role is in the hands of managers of other people's interests—pension funds, for example. Soon, we will seek additional mechanisms to make sure that those who manage these assets are adequately responsive to the concerns of the beneficiaries of the funds; and new mechanisms for making difficult choices (whether to invest in risky stocks; whether to sell stock in antiunion companies or in companies doing business in South Africa) on which individual beneficiaries disagree. Meanwhile, legal scholars are engaged in debating the duty of high-priced executives when an outsider offers shareholders a higher price for their stock and a consequence of the takeover could be unemployment for the executives. What should shareholders be able to do if management invests in projects that have a small chance of profit but advance social or political objectives in which management believes?

Third, government has imposed substantive limits on the actions that can be taken by firms. For antitrust reasons, government bars predatory pricing. For environmental reasons, it bars certain kinds of pollution. For foreign policy reasons, it bars sales of advanced computers to the Soviet Union. These situations are straightforward because the democratic state, in areas accepted as appropriate, lays down relatively clear rules: produce only with safe equipment, do not force retirement before age 70, pay your taxes.

But government's influence is exerted in so many less straightforward ways. Government purchases, making itself a customer with unusual market power. It makes law for relations among private enterprises. For example, government decides whether it is a tortious offense to emit fumes that damage a nearby orchard; or whether a company that filled Navy specifications for asbestos must now pay workers who contracted cancer while working in the naval shipyard. Government subsidizes, changing the firm's calculations of risk and profit. It plans, influencing corporate calculations of future economic activity. It cajoles, the president urging every firm to hire an unemployed person.

We do not really believe that today's corporation acts solely on a calculation of discounted future profits, constrained only by legally binding norms. The firm is an ongoing entity, inevitably affected by its history, its local communities, its workforce, its customers, its culture. To a degree, capital markets discipline. If decisions that do not maximize profit let domestic or foreign competition prevail, the enterprise will find itself consuming its capital. But those constraints appear to leave a significant area for satisfying constituencies and concerns other than profit. Also, the calculations of future return are often so subjective that managers have substantial discretion to follow their hunches, their preferences, their values. Indeed, their diversity in doing so is exactly the economic and political argument for ꞌelegated authority to invest. But once we recognize the discretion, how can we explain and justify shareholder delegation to managers of the decision to choose directions; or exactly the current degree of effective worker, community, and direct and indirect governmental constraint on managerial choices? That is the social problem presented by corporate theory. It is much less of a problem when the economy is growing and our choices are about the division of increasing affluence. When growth is slow, when changes are taking place, and when some outcomes are catastrophic for entire regions and entire labor categories, arguments for further constraints on markets—for limits to the power to close or move a factory, for tariffs, for job protection for current workers—become very strong.

Now comes the final problem with the theory (if the word is appropriate for doctrines so ambiguous in their application). It is obvious nonsense to think of an autonomous government deciding the limits to place on independent firms. In every way government makes business firms what they are. In even more ways firms tell government what to ask of them. Business influence in Washington and the state capitals is well understood. Then how can we explain the legitimacy of the procedures or the outcomes of the mixed economy if by expertise, intensity of involvement, and corporate contributions to candidates, business constrains the choices of government at least as much as government constrains the actions of business? What we have is not just an arbitrary set of democratically determined limits on the ability of business to impose costs on society; but a structure of intertwined business-corporate authority, in which the system functions to maintain the power of those already holding it. From time to time, developments of culture and technology bring changes in the structure of power. External events—Soviet grain purchases or Japanese productivity—may be beyond the reach of the U.S. business "system." But certainly business plays a large role in defining the demands that society places upon it and the rewards that society offers to it.

What can be said with certainty is that under proper conditions, Western business is a marvelously successful social instrument. The conditions seem to include genuine competition, appropriateness of the profit measure, and effective outside limits to the imposition of external costs. When there is no competition, a business soon becomes tired, inefficient, and without innovation. When profit cannot be measured or can be measured only by leaving out important non-quantifiable ingredients, managers have too much discretion, and others begin to question whether the managers' values, inevitably the bases for their exercises of discretion, are any better than anyone else's. And when neither government nor countervailing (and legally authorized) private interests can constrain externalities, business— even competitive, profit-seeking business, witness the robber barons— invites social intervention.

A question raised in this volume is whether those conditions— the necessary requirements for business activity that is socially acceptable—exist or can be created so that business can take over collective tasks now carried on by government, and do so more effectively than government now performs them.

It is hard to generalize about public services, hard even to speak of instances broader than the lunch program in a particular school system or trash collection in a certain village. Notice, however, that most public services are *either* or *both* natural monopolies or activities in which a quantitative bottom line is difficult to specify and measure. Where monopoly is the problem, imaginative solutions may be available. It is possible to divide areas; to require regular rebids; to encourage the survival of competing suppliers; to monitor by comparing neighboring geographic units. Government is an inefficient sole supplier of direct services, because like other monopolists it becomes lazy; because it is not institutionally organized to innovate; and because one production factor, labor, has both a strong moral claim and political power that is of great impact on a system responsive to intense minority interests. This analysis suggests that contracting out to a private monopoly provider will, over time, be liable to exactly the same dangers. The business enterprise will become lazy and uninnovative if not imaginatively watched and pushed. Government, not structured to monitor and push itself, is not currently good at stimulating efficiency from its suppliers and contractors. Employees of private firms who sell their service to public authorities may be strongly placed to influence decisions about staffing and compensation. The business itself, whether a bus line or a waste disposal plant or a job training center, may have political incentives and opportunities to influence its customer. In other words, for government to achieve efficiency as a consumer by contracting out may require that government develop oversight and monitoring resources that it does not now have. Perhaps it would be easier for government to become efficient at this task than to become an efficient deliverer. James Sundquist and Ted Kolderie offer interesting insights about this question. But it is not obvious that what it takes to be an effective consumer is easier to achieve than what is needed to be a competent producer. Certainly Marc Bendick's chapter in this book suggests that some governments that have tried contracting out have not reaped immediately the fiscal benefits they sought.

The second situation, where the bottom line is hard to specify and measure, presents even greater challenges. Schools and hospitals and prisons and police departments serve various social needs. Emphases among those goals, and even the definitions given to the goals, change from time to time and vary among geographic regions. Satisfaction is not readily measured or described. Do we want the police to deter crime, to apprehend perpetrators, to honor constitutional rights? Do we want prisons that punish, deter, or rehabilitate? What do we mean by rehabilitation? What are appropriate means for achieving it? What risks are we prepared to take with the safety of employees? With the safety of nearby residents? As to public education, many such questions about goals are regularly asked.

No modern society would think it appropriate to give a private enterprise the authority to make choices among public goals. (It is interesting that we do let such enterprises decide what sort of automobiles to build; and how much new capacity to make steel should be built; and how many trees to harvest from their forests. But these are situations where there is competition, profit has at least an ambiguity-filled relevance, and major external effects can be limited by public bodies. Public services are public in part because these three conditions cannot be met.) Democratic government, for all its limitations and weaknesses, is a fluid, responsive, participatory instrument that we find our most satisfactory agency for resolving conflicts among goals. That does not mean there are not roles for business in delivering public services that have conflicting and ambiguous ends. But it probably means that for private involvement to be appropriate, legitimate public processes must achieve a degree of specification of ends and a degree of clarity about measurement.

To speculate about specific examples, it is easy to imagine a contract with a private firm to provide food in a prison or to give specified hours of computer instruction to inmates. But think about providing perimeter security (when to shoot); or deciding on placements (who should be in what institution or in what part of an institution); or disciplining those who commit offenses within the prison; or deciding what to do with a prisoner whose life has been threatened by other inmates. The distance from the ultimate expression of democratic validity—the ballot box—to these refined assertions of life-or-death public power is very great. There is no way to claim that the electorate has made the decision, or monitors it, or elects the person who decides. But the causal chain from election to decision is nonetheless valid, because the matter can be the subject of public discussion when some event makes it salient. An elected governor chooses the corrections commissioner who chooses the warden who appoints the disciplinary board. Angry relatives (whether of inmates or of officers) have places to go to complain and assert. And all public decisionmakers are barred from profiting privately from their actions.

Thus the major limit to for-profit participation of private companies in provision of public services is the degree to which it seems wrong to pursue value-laden and unquantifiable public goals through profit-maximizing entities. Where it is possible to separate choice of goal from efficiency-seeking implementation, then a public-private contract can be used; or even the sort of public-private joint venture about which Charles Haar writes. Where it is not possible, it is hard to imagine society approving delegation of vital power to an entity whose only ultimate legitimacy is its relationship with investors.

Perhaps it is the political theory of U.S. society that for-profit enterprise should be asked to perform tasks only when the parameters can be set—when the appropriate external constraints can be imposed, so that the business can be assumed to be seeking profit within those limits. When the essential goal and the limits are intertwined (again, think of schools and prisons, as well as hospitals), we do not feel comfortable in assigning the task to an enterprise whose charter and legitimacy arise from the pursuit of profit; and which, even if real-world corporations do in fact seek alternative and public-spirited ends, we authorize just because of its efficiency in seeking profit. That may be why, for complex public tasks, our effort to find alternatives to public management leads us to not-for-profit enterprises whose underlying legitimacy is found elsewhere than in profit maximization. It may also be why we should continue the search for new institutional techniques that might allow the capacities of private enterprise a larger role in public tasks. Again, Charles Haar is relevant, in his discussion of various forms of shared participation and responsibility. New schemes for designing incentives might work, especially if information technology improves the sophistication with which output can be defined and measured.

GOVERNMENT

It is not necessary to write at length about the demonstrated inadequacies of modern government. The past two decades have provided very little evidence of the success of official collective efforts, and repeated examples of failure, inefficiency, and scandal. If the history of American business in this period will also show failures (automobiles) and scandals (overseas bribery; illegal campaign contributions), there remain good bases for confidence in the capacity of private capital to adjust, to deliver, and even to innovate, when given the right incentives and when spared the wrong constraints. As to government, a much more fundamental conclusion of weakness has taken hold, reasons for which can be summarized as follows.

Government Cannot Decide

Government announces many goals, establishes bureaus to pursue many of them, but is not organized to choose among goals when they conflict, to allocate limited resources, or to state and observe priorities. The institutional structure of government is an important part of this problem. Elected officials have every incentive to promise and then to posture. Voters apparently will not see through this behavior and will not regard their alternative choices as any better. An example of what happens is passing tough laws and then not funding the enforcement mechanisms. Legislators in particular seem to be able to describe themselves as having personal goals desired by constituents even though their actions have been dominated by support of conflicting policies.

But there is a larger problem. The complexity of modern society and of government's place in it requires a vast diversity of points of public decision and action. Each comes to be the locus for a collection of concerned competing interests. Often neither strong presidential leadership nor agreement on a single comprehensive compromise consensus has created coherent reconciliation of these varied processes. When that is the case the sum of government's activities will not look like policy. Witness recent experience with energy policy, retirement income policy, health policy, and trade policy.

Government Cannot Deliver

As to some services, government's product is comparable to private-sector alternatives. Often, government delivers less service for more money. With other public services, there is no private alternative, and indeed the absence of imaginable private vendors is a strong argument for public activity. Even where government has no rivals, there is a broad perception that only unusually effective and lucky leadership can get quality service at a reasonable cost from a public agency. Civil service rules constrict. Public employee unions have great power over their employers. Proper tradeoffs between capital investment and operations do not take place because elected officials do not take a long view. It is hard to recruit, train, and reward good public managers.

It is fair to add that this issue is sometimes merely a reflection of the issue discussed previously. Government has many goals. The

charge of inefficiency is unfounded if the true goal is high employment or responsiveness to politically influential consumers with different agendas; or if competing goals have never been reconciled, as
is the case with prisons, public schools, and farm price supports.
Nevertheless, there are institutional facts about public services that
make efficiency losses a predictable characteristic.

Government is the exercise of official authority. In addition, however, *government is about power.* Public life is constantly recreating
the terms of future politics: changing the rules, assigning new bargaining chips, ratifying the fairness of certain sorts of claims. There is
a logical problem here. How can a system remake itself? In particular, how can we expect it to advance itself toward equality, or fairness, or progress, or efficiency, or toward all of these at the same
time? In gross, the point is that there is a limited extent to which a
legislature of steelmakers will commit the country to a shift from
steel to computers. On the other hand we have seen in recent decades
major shifts of power and culture mediated through democratic institutions. It is wrong, however, to think such transitions can be accomplished on straight-line paths.

If modern government has by its nature these characteristics, what
reform strategies seem sensible? After all, the society plainly has
needs and goals that cannot be achieved without major governmental
involvement; and demands for official intervention have hardly
diminished. Indeed, many of the contributors to this book argue that
the United States needs competent, effective government to get the
best results from business.

First, it seems desirable to force on government new institutional
mechanisms requiring that goals be stated and progress recorded and
reported to a greater degree than now occurs. Business is required to
speak honestly, so that capital markets can function efficiently. If
government had to do the same, democracy—the political marketplace—would have a better chance. Take only one example, but one
with large dollar amounts at issue. Companies must report their pension fund liabilities, and under federal law must fund their plans over
forty years. Government is famous for making pension promises to
current workers, appropriating insufficient money, and in effect
saddling future generations. Reporting, and full funding as well, seem
clearly desirable.

Government is not business: a social mechanism living with various constituencies and goals, but held together by a myth—and not
an entirely false one—of commitment to a concept called profit.
But government could be more like that concept of business. It could

be a set of relationships, at least partially guided and driven by a commitment to *social welfare*. To be sure, social welfare is a concept filled with ambiguity. For example, we cannot agree whether it is anything more than the sum of the welfares or utilities of individuals, or whether distributional considerations—"fairness" or "justice"—should take precedence over the aggregation of individual utilities. But we could give more content to the idea of social welfare than we now do. We could do a better job of quantifying aspects of it. We could limit more than we now do the most egregious deviations from it.

To change the public sector in these directions, we would need more process, a recommendation one makes with hesitation in the current intellectual environment. Process can certainly be costly and counterproductive. But there is a larger problem. When business needed discipline (mechanisms that constrain managers by requiring a degree of openness and subjecting at least some of their numbers and their decisions to professional evaluation), government was the obvious institution to provide it. The Securities and Exchange Commission, the Environmental Protection Agency, and other such institutional responses were the proper mechanism. But *quis custodiet ipsos custodes?* Who can regulate government? We have moved toward ethics commissions, budget bureaus, campaign finance regulations, and the like, with at best limited achievement. There are incentives for securities analysts who excel at parsing corporate balance sheets. Who would gain by analyzing the relative success of different job training programs? And who would have an incentive to act on the information even if it were available?

When government delivers public service, the citizenry pays two kinds of costs. First, we pay whatever is the efficiency price of public delivery. All intuition and some evidence suggest that the price is substantial. Second, public institutions are not forced to do their most serious job, making official choices that are legitimate and fair. Government as service provider diminishes government as purchaser and allocater.

There are risks in the use by government of private contractors to perform public functions. They can be tagged the Dotheboys Hall risk and the military-industrial complex risk. A for-profit contractor can take public money and serve warm water to the clients, as the Yorkshire boarding schools described by Dickens stole the funds paid them to feed and educate their pupils. Or, probably more likely in this era, the public-private collaboration can result in self-dealing, monopoly power, and political influence, as is sometimes the case with U.S. weapons procurement from private companies. The summary answer is that effective use of private providers by government requires a public sector able to identify, rank, and monitor its goals. But expanded use of private for-profit providers might nonetheless be an important step toward development of those capacities within the public sector.

America's most significant adventure with rational government is the story of the Administrative Procedure Act (APA), the general statutory attempt to impose a system of rational choice on federal agencies. Crucial to the APA model is the distinction between rule-making and adjudication: between policy decisions delegated by the legislature and quasi-judicial determinations applying these rules to particular circumstances. The system of administrative process is our institutional adaptation to the fact of the mixed economy, and to the goal of sharing economic authority between public-sector regulation and guidance and private-sector enterprise and innovation. It does not have to work perfectly to be necessary to the current social and economic regime.

Some of the contributors to this book are asking that the government-business relationship be restructured institutionally in ways as far-reaching as the changes symbolized by the Administrative Procedure Act. Robert Reich in particular calls for a more coherent and ambitious sort of economic planning. Can the society invent processes that would for example control inflation without restricting output, target investment, increase intergenerational harmony, and compensate transitional losers? What is interesting about goals of this sort is that they are complicated, involve many different interests, are hard to achieve by some single pronouncement by central authority, and indeed seem to require widespread consensual participation. No single policy generalization can be uttered that is obviously correct, and against which plausible opposing arguments, made to be sure by those specially concerned but nonetheless echoing accepted languages of fairness and appropriateness, cannot be put. Investment is good, but where and on what? At a reduction in whose consumption? Reducing demand for what current output? And so forth. During wars, this country has granted central government the authority to make basic allocative choices of this sort. In peacetime, attempts to limit inflation or to coordinate energy policy have not fared well. It seems that complicated and (for many) sacrificial changes can occur only when the sense of necessity, of morality, of fairness is very great. Any national economic planning effort undertaken outside grave crisis, even if sponsored in the good faith belief that it is necessary to avoid crisis, would not have necessity or morality. Could it have enough process to be legitimate solely because of the way the compromises had come about?

There are two ways to obtain legitimacy through process. One is by agreement of appropriate parties. The problem with this route to economic policy, the equivalent of social contracts in (smaller) European nations, is that it is impossible in a society of the size and complexity of the United States to build a satisfactory representation machine. What entities get what weight? Only the combination of the U.S. Congress and the presidency can stand as appropriate for that purpose. And their multiple interests have recently prevented coherence on choices that extend across policy areas and beyond short-term accommodations.

The second way to make valid policy is by technical or scientific consensus that is perceived as correct and therefore necessary. As to U.S. economic and social policy, there is no prospect of any coherence of that sort, and indeed recent experience probably makes it less likely.

Quite different considerations are involved as to less grand undertakings of government: to deliver the mail and pick up garbage and teach six-year-olds to read. Here, the goal might be procedural changes that would encourage explicitness, openness, candor, and comparability. In an age of dramatic efficiency gains at storing and processing information, and with a population likely to improve at quantitative literacy, it may be possible to imagine procedures that will increase significantly the extent to which government can purchase social welfare with a $1 expenditure. One key will be formulation of reasonable goals. Another will be new ways of describing future impacts in current terms. Federalism offers the possibility of particular agencies of government assuming the task of monitoring the information and the performance of institutions at other levels. The New York City Financial Control Board, born in the City's fiscal crisis, may be a model; certainly the Control Board, which must pass on the numbers used by the city in its budget process, has increased the possibilities for democratic participation, not ended them as its critics predicted. What would have to occur is public demand for improved mechanisms of accountability and control. The likelihood of such demand will increase if the society generally becomes more accustomed to thinking and working with numbers. If we become more precise in evaluating the costs and benefits of government services, an increase in "contracting out" may occur, but that will not be a necessary result. Government as internal service deliverer could become more able to deliver quantitatively satisfactory outputs. There is no reason in principle why the procedural innovations devised to bar public-sector fraud (independent comptrollers, for example) should not be extended to impose standards of efficient service, with competing goals stated and explained, with the citizenry coming to feel that meeting such demands is an obligation of legitimate government. But much of what government does would inevitably remain so ambiguously focused as to be unaffected by any such procedural alterations.

NOT-FOR-PROFIT ORGANIZATIONS

The United States has long been noted for the number, variety, and economic and social significance of private nonprofit organizations. Recently social scientists have tried to perform measurements of what some of them call "the voluntary sector." Although the counting is difficult and imperfect, it is clear that in this country it is large, important, and stable.

Nonprofit vitality is not only a consequence of the well-known characteristic of Americans to be joiners. In a diverse and pluralistic society, individuals seek attachments that allow them to express their ethnic, professional, political, religious, and even athletic interests.

But it is just as important and interesting that much of the growth of public-sector spending in the past twenty years has not been on services delivered by government but has been an increased use of tax-generated funds to obtain for individuals services actually provided by non-governmental but non-profit entities. There are for-profit hospitals, nursing homes, and day care centers. But a vastly larger part of publicly financed but nonpublicly delivered service is provided by nonprofit hospitals, universities, child-care facilities, adoption agencies, and so forth.

It is easy to see the advantages that the private nonprofit institution has over government provision of service. When government delivers, it either uses an existing bureaucratic structure—which may have inflexible routines and high wages—or, if it makes its staff larger, it may well find itself committed to the new activity into the indefinite future. The private agency may have no employee union. It may draw on significant volunteer effort. And a contract can be carefully drawn to apply only for a stated period. Second, the private organization may be decentralized and specialized in its clientele and concerns. Government could not itself place Catholic babies with Catholic families. Third, the recent Supreme Court decisions holding that Fourteenth Amendment due process limits do not apply to schools and nursing homes receiving most of their income from government or to a heavily regulated "private" utility give such entities efficiency advantages that are sometimes significant. Government, in short, is clumsy and homogeneous. Using private delivery mechanisms can add to flexibility, diversity, and impermanence. This is in part a way of saying that private agencies mitigage some of the problems of government as monopolist.

But if that explains the use of private deliverers, it does not say why for-profit entities do not dominate the field. There is economic literature about profit-seeking versus nonprofit hospitals. In that area and in some others, nonprofit organizations have been given significant financial advantages (tax benefits, public-subsidized capital funds, protection through statutory bars to assigning tasks to for-profit entities) that explain some of their dominance. But the fact requiring explanation is not that nonprofit organizations have achieved a large share of the market for publicly paid services, but that we seem so committed to using them that we make sure they hold their place.

The explanation seems to be that for certain services, the profit motive is a troubling ingredient in the mix of considerations that govern institutional behavior. If government could make its desires objective and measurable, it would satisfy them from the lowest bidder as it buys pencils. But government cannot describe in bid documents a day care center that has tender loving care along with the peanut butter sandwiches at lunch. It has trouble specifying good work at placing children for adoption or at supervising foster homes. It has tremendous difficulty establishing the contours of appropriate medical care.

It is something of a solution to this problem if the providing institution has no or little incentive to take the government's money and do as little service as will meet the government's enforceable minimum requirements. It is more of a solution if the institution has a tradition and an ethic of service. These characteristics do not assure that the government's money will buy exactly what the government most wants or what the client or consumer wants. But they make it likely that the sorts of considerations that the government cares about will have priority in shaping the details of the services for which public money is being spent.

But seeing that purpose for public use of nonprofit intermediaries poses anew the issue of democratic legitimacy. If the publicly responsible purchaser could specify its goals, any contractor—for profit or not-for-profit—could merely be supplying what government was ordering. But if nonprofit contractors are used because their choices among alternative values are respected, then we must have reason to be confident that they are structured to make these choices in acceptable ways.

What nonprofit organizations really reflect is another aspect of a society with diverse institutions for responding to intense commitments held by those with resources. Just as those who want something from government and have time and money to invest have a good chance of achieving their purpose, so those who will focus their energies on a "voluntary" organization can use that vehicle to influence social outcomes. "Voluntaries" allow like-minded individuals to combine in behalf of the interest they share. Cultural organizations are a good example, as are medical research charities, hospitals, veterans organizations, neighborhood day care centers, and all sorts of ethnic and professional groups. Sometimes these organizations begin with substantial cash endowments, which of course add to their ability to obtain public backing for their exercise of discretionary choices.

It is interesting that there seems to be so little discussion about the public support regularly given to nonprofit institutions. These organizations represent stability, elitism, diversity, decentralization, charity, and social commitment. They often act out of concern for perpetuation of their own mission and their own institutional interests, and in order to maintain a secure place for their staff and leaders. The fact that they are not committed to economic profit hardly prevents them from being self-serving or from failing to reconsider what may be tired definitions of the public welfare. Of course except for those forms of public support, such as tax exemptions, that apply to all nonprofit organizations and thus give them an advantage over for-profit entities, government remains free to pick and choose among organizations and purposes. On the other hand the public seems to have exactly the right attitude: an awareness that these organizations are a device that avoids some of the problems with publicly provided service without turning complex public tasks over to enterprises primarily focused on economic return; and a sense that the dangers of unequal status and of power unvalidated through public institutions are offset, in ways important to a country so worried about centralized power, by the advantages of diversity.

CONCLUSION

Our goals are high and our means are overcommitted. In particular, it is extremely difficult for the U.S. public/private/not-for-profit system to engage in subtle, discreet, and focused policy interventions. If the attempt is to create jobs in inner cities or for minority youths, immediately there are questions of how the categories are defined, how only those meant to be aided can be on the list, and how consistently public policy will remain committed to particular ends that may require many years to accomplish. In theory Charles Haar's concept of negotiated partnerships is just right. In practice, each one may require so much of a resource in extremely short supply—dedicated, effective public sector leadership—that it is wrong to expect the whole idea, the various partnerships taken together, to have macro effects. Indeed the story may be a cold-weather version of Orlando Patterson's account of his efforts in Jamaica. In any case, whatever discreet attempts are tried may be overwhelmed by other developments in the economy, or other public policies, so that the individual partnerships are weakly powered boats on a very strong sea. For example if the purpose of a particular project is to create jobs, any achievement may be overtaken by other decisions motivated by concerns for inflation, budget deficits, the desire to impose costs in behavior-affecting ways (workers' compensation, unemployment insurance), and the readings of politicians about the short-term reaction to various means of raising public funds. It is obviously appropriate for government to change incentives to facilitate job retention and creation; but also to compensate injured workers with funds raised by a charge to the employer; and to encourage the shift to technologically advanced production modes; and to make specially generous payments to those whose unemployment results from foreign competition; and to slow the decline of geographic areas specially affected by technological change; and to give special job training to deserving and identifiable sufferers from change; and to undertake certain quite defensible infrastructure projects, especially when jobs will thereby be created. What is difficult is to see how these activities, taken together, can reflect *either* a coherent and efficient economic strategy *or* an overarching conception of fairness. If not one or the other, they must be episodic ventures, each the result of the status of political influence in some particular institutional subsetting on a particular day. Arguments of appropriate claim are relevant, of course, but they are available—especially given the modern surplus of persons able to spin words around claims—to far more claimants than can conceivably be satisfied.

Thus our dilemma is not that we do not recognize that the actions of business can meet social needs and that some of the most important actions of government are those that invite (or avoid deterring) business behavior that is socially valuable. Our problem is that although we see these possibilities, and indeed often set out to pursue them, the list of such opportunities is longer than our resources and individual items are often at odds with other legitimate public endeavors. The outcome is neither fairness nor efficiency, because we are not institutionally set up to know, to measure, to rank, and to choose.

The problem with a larger role for business, urged in this volume by Peter Drucker, is that government will not, and in truth should not, avoid attempts to guide and restrain and encourage specific exercises of delegated power by managers that have consequences extending beyond the individual firm. The problem with a more coherent and focused public role, urged in this volume by Robert Reich, is that so far the size and diversity of this country have not allowed the most difficult and important choices to be clearly posed and responsibly answered; and institutional changes that would permit more central direction have been thought to be a threat to traditional liberties and to the wide distribution of power and influence. There is every reason to expect that the tensions reflected in this debate will be at the center of our politics in the period ahead.

Index

Abatements, 80

Abu Dhabi, 325

Administrative Procedure Act (APA), 352

Agency for International Development (AID), 143

Agriculture, 291, 295

Aid for Dependent Children (AFDC), 4

Alaska, 248

Altcare, 108-09

Altmeyer, Arthur, 295

Alum Rock, CA, 162

American Hospital Corporation, 324

American Tobacco Company, 41

American Transit Enterprises (ATE), 100

Amherst H. Wilder Foundation, 108-09

Antitrust/antitrust laws, 44, 176, 203, 280-81, 343-44

Asia, 37

Automobile industry, 8, 249

Bank of Japan, 267

Basic human/social needs. *See* Social needs/problems/programs

Basic research, 191-92, 216

Beard, Charles A., 40

Bell, Alexander Graham, 25

Bellamy, Carol, 79-80

Beneficial externalities, 189-90

Biddle, Nicholas, 40

Big business sector/corporations, 40, 45, 52; automation in, 291; charitable donations by, 200, 222-24; control/regulation of, 44, 199, 201; cooperative relationships, 235, 237; decisionmaking in, 206-10, 218, 344-45; economic improvement programs, 222-25; and economic, social and political environment, 238-39; employment in, 290-92; goals, 196-99; and government, 57, 207-09, 210-11, 268-69, 277, 282; interest group accomodation by, 205-10; international competitive strategy, 268-72, 282-83; investment strategy, 254-56; legitimacy of, 47, 56, 353, 355; and less developed countries, 319-29; mergers, 280-81; and national economic policy, 268-81; political skills/strategy for social programs, 234-37; and politics, 56, 274; private goals/interests, 200-201; profits/profit maximization, 25, 104, 196-201, 203, 205, 211, 227-28, 233-36, 238, 300, 344-45, 348; public goals/interests/ policy, 199-200, 205-11, 218; and public schools, 128; public subsidies to, 276; residual earnings, 215; rise of, 41-42, 45-46, 56; role of, 195-96; social needs markets developed by, 232-33, 239; social needs

About the Editors

Harvey Brooks is Benjamin Peirce Professor of Technology and Public Policy, Harvard Division of Applied Sciences and Kennedy School of Government, and former president of the American Academy of Arts and Sciences (1971-1976). He served as a member of the President's Science Advisory Committee from 1959 to 1964 and of the National Science Board from 1962 to 1974. From 1967 to 1972 he was chairman of the Committee on Science and Public Policy, National Academy of Sciences. He has also served on boards of various educational and scholarly organizations. In addition to numerous publications in nuclear engineering, physics of solids, underwater acoustics, and science and public policy, his writings include *The Government of Science.*

Lance Liebman is associate dean and professor of law, Harvard Law School. His main fields of interest are urban law and social welfare law. He has served as law clerk to U.S. Supreme Court Justice Byron White and as assistant to Mayor John Lindsay of New York City, and he was a successor trustee of the Yale University Corporation from 1971 to 1983. Among his publications are books on city government, race and ethnic relations in America, and the moral obligations of government officials.

Corinne S. Schelling is associate executive officer of the American Academy of Arts and Sciences. She is co-editor of *When Values Conflict* (with Laurence Tribe and John Voss), of *Corners of a Foreign Field* (with Robert McC. Adams), and of *Race and Schooling in the*

369

City (with Adam Yarmolinsky and Lance Liebman). Trained as an economist, she has participated in a wide range of Academy studies on public policy issues.

About the Contributors

Jordan J. Baruch, an engineering and management consultant, served as assistant secretary for science and technology, Department of Commerce, from 1977 to 1981. He has taught at Massachusetts Institute of Technology, Harvard Graduate School of Business Administration, and the Amos Tuck School of Business Administration and the Thayer School of Engineering at Dartmouth College. He is a frequent contributor to books and professional journals and holds several patents.

William J. Baumol has a joint appointment as a professor of economics at Princeton University and at New York University. He is a past president of several professional societies, including the American Economic Association, has been on the editorial boards of numerous scholarly journals, and has served as a consultant for government agencies and private industry. His publications include *Performing Arts: The Economic Dilemma* (with W.G. Bowen), *The Theory of Environmental Policy* (with W.E. Oates), and *Contestable Markets and the Theory of Industry Structure* (with R.D. Willig and J.S. Panzer). Most recently he was project director and author of *Productivity Policy: Key to the Nation's Economic Future,* a statement by the Research and Policy Committee of the Committee for Economic Development, 1983.

Marc Bendick, Jr. is a senior research associate at the Urban Institute. His research has been on employment, human resources and economic development, and efficiency in the delivery of public assistance and human services programs. He has forthcoming publications on reemploying midcareer workers dislocated by economic change and on corporate social responsibility. His recent publications include *Housing Vouchers for the Poor* and many articles in professional journals.

Robert C. Clark is a professor at Harvard Law School. His teaching and research are in the fields of corporations, financial institutions, and health care regulations. Among his publications are numerous law journal articles, including "The Four Stages of Capitalism," *Harvard Law Review*; "The Interdisciplinary Study of Legal Evolution," *Yale Law Journal*; and "A New Look at Corporate Opportunities" (with V. Brudney), *Harvard Law Review*. Before becoming a law professor, he was in private legal practice.

Peter F. Drucker is Clarke Professor of social science, Claremont (California) Graduate School. He has been a newspaper correspondent, an adviser to banks and major business corporations and governments in several countries, and has written extensively on various aspects of management. Among his recent books are *Managing in Turbulent Times*, *The Changing World of the Executive*, and a work of fiction, *The Last of All Possible Worlds*.

Charles M. Haar is the Louis D. Brandeis Professor of Law at Harvard Law School. He served as the first assistant secretary for metropolitan development, U.S. Department of Housing and Urban Development, from 1966 to 1969, and has been a member of numerous federal and state government task forces. He has also been appointed Special Master to the Superior Court to hear cases concerning Boston public school financing and the cleaning up of Boston Harbor. A frequent contributor to legal and planning journals, he has published several books on property, planning, and law.

Ted Kolderie, a senior fellow at the Hubert H. Humphrey Institute of Public Affairs, University of Minnesota, has been working on the problem of public service redesign. As a reporter and editorial writer in Minneapolis and later as executive director of the Citizens League, he was involved in the reorganization of government and finance in the Twin Cities metropolitan area during the 1960s and 1970s.

Franklin A. Long, professor emeritus of chemistry and of science and society at Cornell, is involved in research on the contributions of science and technology to developing countries. He has done extensive work relating to Korea and India. His other major field of interest is arms control, military technology, and U.S. national security policy. He is author of *The Genesis of New Weapons: Decision Making for Military R&D* and co-editor of *Appropriate Technology and Social Values: A Critical Appraisal* (with Alexandra Oleson).

Thomas K. McCraw, a historian by training, is a professor of business administration at Harvard University. A specialist in business-government relations, he is the author of numerous articles and of four books: *Morgan versus Lilienthal: The Feud within the TVA, TVA and the Power Fight, 1933–1939, Regulation in Perspective* (editor), and *Architects of Regulation.*

William C. Norris is founder and chairman of Control Data Corporation. He has served as an adviser to the White House Conference on Balanced National Growth and Economic Development and recently as a member of the President's Task Force on Private Sector Initiatives. He is the author of *New Frontiers for Business Leadership.*

Orlando Patterson, professor of sociology, Harvard University, has served as special adviser to the Prime Minister of Jamaica. His major areas of research have been urbanization and urban policy in Jamaica, ethnicity and migration, and slavery. His most recent book is *Slavery and Social Death: A Comparative Study.* In addition to scholarly articles and books, he has published several works of fiction.

Robert B. Reich, a lawyer and economist, teaches at the John F. Kennedy School of Government, Harvard University. He has been director of policy planning, Federal Trade Commission. A consultant to corporations and government agencies, he is the author of *The Next American Frontier, Minding America's Business* (with I. Magaziner), and numerous articles on regulation, economic policy, and business strategy.

James L. Sundquist, a senior fellow at the Brookings Institution, is the author, most recently, of *The Decline and Resurgence of Congress* and *Dynamics of the Party System* (2nd edition). He is a former deputy under secretary of agriculture and member of the Bureau of the Budget and White House staffs.

James C. Worthy, professor at the J. L. Kellogg Graduate School of Management, Northwestern University, served as assistant secretary of commerce from 1953 to 1955, and in several capacities, including vice president for public relations, at Sears, Roebuck & Company, 1956–1961. He has been a member of governmental commissions and an officer or on the boards of educational, political, and business organizations. His most recent publication is *Shaping a Great American Institution: General Wood and Sears, Roebuck.*